DR. ROGER J. WILLIAMS is perhaps responsible for more original work in the field of vitamin research than any living scientist. He was the first man to identify, isolate and synthesize pantothenic acid, one of the most important B vitamins. He also did pioneer work on folic acid, and gave it its name. From 1941 to 1963, he was Director of the Clayton Foundation Biochemical Institute, where more vitamins and their variants have been discovered than in any laboratory in the world. He was the first biochemist to be elected president of the American Chemical Society, is a member of the National Academy of Sciences, and is the recipient of many awards and honorary degrees. Dr. Williams is the author of several important books on organic chemistry and biochemistry and numerous books for lay readers, including the famous bestseller, **Nutrition in a Nutshell.**

Nutrition Against Disease

Environmental Prevention

Dr. Roger J. Williams

NUTRITION AGAINST DISEASE: ENVIRONMENTAL PREVENTION

*A Bantam Book / published by arrangement with
Pitman Publishing Corporation*

PRINTING HISTORY
Pitman edition published 1971
Bantam edition published March 1973
2nd printing
3rd printing
4th printing

PRINTED IN THE UNITED STATES OF AMERICA

Contents

Preface

This book is written primarily to bring new information and hope to the millions of people who are groping for a better understanding of how our bodies work and how health may be maintained. It is important for the public to have this new information because it points the way toward a vastly improved approach to health, both from the personal and the public standpoints.

The fundamental premise on which this book is based —that the microenvironment of our body cells is crucially important to our health—is, I think, by now unassailable on any responsible scientific grounds. But the conclusions that I have derived from this premise, although powerfully supported by laboratory evidence, are in some cases so unorthodox that they will doubtless give rise to objections.

Most of these objections, alas, will probably come from members of the medical profession. Laymen tend to be more open-minded about unorthodox medical theories than those who have had to undergo long years of formal training and have had, perhaps, all too little leisure to reexamine the fundamental assumptions on which all their early indoctrination and most of their subsequent practice have been based. No doubt men outside the medical profession are prone to similar afflictions.

I should emphasize here that I make a careful distinction in my own mind between what individual physicians think and what the medical establishment teaches them. I am personally and professionally well acquainted with many admirable, able, and dedicated doctors, some of whom are either actively or potentially interested in the subject of how disease may be prevented through improved nutrition. But it is only fair to add that those physicians who do recognize the importance of nutrition in the medical scheme of things have done so as the result of individual research and extra training, and *not* as the result of anything they were taught in the course of their formal medical education.

I do not mean to be quarrelsome about this, but I do regard our present-day medical education as seriously— I might almost say willfully—deficient in certain matters of extreme importance, matters that intimately affect the health and well-being of every person on the surface of this planet. I think I should be remiss in my obligations both as a scientist and a citizen if I were to fail to speak my mind on matters about which I have such deep convictions.

It is only natural that physicians should experience a kind of "psychic wrench" when assumptions they long have taken for granted are challenged. And no doubt my strictures on the content of contemporary medical education will give unintended offense in some quarters. I can only say that the conclusions I present here are very far from being light-minded; they are the result of a lifetime of scientific inquiry, of extensive laboratory research, and long hours of contemplation. I hope that my scientific and medical colleagues will accept that I advance these conclusions with no desire to shock or provoke, but solely because I believe they are true and that they are important.

Of course I do not expect physicians—or, for that matter, laymen—to accept unsupported assertions. For that reason I have included an appendix composed of notes, comments, and approximately 1100 medical and scientific citations. The length of this appendix is in itself suggestive of the large quantity of research data that has yet to be assimilated into conventional medical thinking.

A final word: The analyses, conclusions, and speculations that I have advanced in this book are very definitely not the last word on the subject of the relationship between nutrition and disease. I should be more than content if they were to be only a modest positive beginning. There is a desperate need for massive and painstaking research in the matter of the multiple origins of disease, just as there is a desperate need for the medical profession in general to devote far more attention than it ever has to the prevention, and not simply the cure, of disease. It is upon health, not upon ill-health, that our sights should be fixed.

Acknowledgments

My primary acknowledgment must go to S. Rodman Thompson without whose intelligent help in searching out and collecting scientific material, this book could not have been written. His initiative, his keen interest and the many hundreds of hours he spent in scientific and medical libraries played an indispensable role which entitles him to a substantial share of the credit for this book. I acknowledge with gratitude his invaluable help.

I owe much to many colleagues at The University of Texas at Austin and to a large group of prominent scientists and leading physicians who have made suggestions and offered encouragement. These will not be named individually lest the unwarranted conclusion be drawn that they may be held accountable for the contents of this volume.

For more detailed help and cooperation, I acknowledge my thanks to my immediate associates Drs. James D. Heffley and Man-Li Yew, and to Messrs. Charles W. Bode, James Moon, and Reuben Wolk.

I own signal gratitude to Mr. Benjamin Clayton for his consistent and highly intelligent material and moral support of this as well as all my scientific endeavors.

To Mr. John Kirk I owe sincere thanks for his expert and imaginative editorial help.

My lasting thanks also goes to my secretary, Mrs. Margaret Johnson, who has devotedly and expertly participated in preparing the manuscript.

My wife, Phyllis, has contributed much sound sense and has held my hand during the writing process, and to her as well as the other members of our immediate family I express heartfelt gratitude.

1 The Flaw in Medical Education

No physician in his right mind would claim that he had healed a broken bone simply because he had set it. The careful alignment of the fractured bone ends, the splinting, bandaging, plaster casting, and all the rest are important, but, after all, secondary. The real job of healing is done by something else, something that we do not fully understand and cannot reproduce, something that, for want of a better term, we vaguely call "nature."

The situation is much the same when we treat infection. The physician uses whatever medicines are appropriate to help the body beat off the invading viruses or bacteria. Sometimes (although perhaps less often than is claimed) the intervention of the physician is decisive; sometimes it is secondary. But the fact remains that the battle against infection is never less than a collaboration. Unless the forces of the patient's own system are deployed in fighting the disease, all the physician's medicines will be useless.

1

That the art of the physician is grounded on cooperation with nature is so well known, so intrinsically obvious, one would suppose that the point does not bear repetition. Alas, I think it does. In this book I shall argue, among other things, that orthodox medical training has already drifted dangerously far from this fundamental perception of the physician's role. The undesirable effects of this drift, I shall contend, are several and serious. For one thing, it has distorted the physician's choice of the most appropriate weapons to use in fighting disease. For another, it has tended to deemphasize what I shall call the "human element" in the disease-fighting equation: the individual patient's contribution to the struggle. And perhaps most baneful, it has tended to make doctors think almost exclusively in terms of combating the manifestations of illness rather than in terms of maintaining good health.

It may seem presumptuous for a biologist to be so critical of contemporary medical education, but I persist in the old-fashioned view that medicine ought, properly speaking, to be thought of as a subdivision of biological science; and I am of the opinion that modern medical training has not adequately kept abreast of certain important advances in biological research. I believe, in fact, that medical training today does not prepare the physician to recognize either the leading cause of noninfective disease or the related conditions for effective resistance to infections.

The central thesis on which these ideas are based— and which this book will explore in some detail—is really very simple. In essence it is not a new thesis, and in a restricted sense it is generally accepted as fact. The thesis is that *the nutritional microenvironment of our body cells is crucially important to our health and that deficiencies in this environment constitute a major cause of disease*.

In cases of scurvy, pellagra, beriberi, or kwashiorkor, no physician would be inclined to question that the cause of the respective disease lies in the deficient microenvironment of the cells involved; but in orthodox medicine physicians are taught to think of this as a restrictive principle and to assume that the majority of illnesses with which they deal have virtually no connection with nutrition at all.

Is this restrictive attitude really warranted? There is little evidence to support such restrictions and much evidence in favor of a wide extension of the nutritional approach to medicine. It is my opinion that medical theory, medical education, and medical practice have taken a wrong turn, and that all of us are the worse for it.

Why was this wrong turn taken? I suspect the reasons are largely historical. At the very time when the relationship between nutrition and disease might have come to the fore, medical science experienced a revolution and became intoxicated with the success of treatments that derived from Louis Pasteur's dramatic discovery that microbes cause disease.

When Pasteur—a chemist, not a physician—first promulgated the novel doctrine that microbes may cause disease, he met with great resistance and the medical men of his day would have none of his theory. It was not that they had a better idea; it was simply that they found new ideas distasteful. To the next generation of doctors, however, the theory of the microbial origin of disease was not new. Spurred by what they could see through microscopes and by the spectacular demonstrations of Pasteur, Koch, and others, the medical men accepted Pasteur's doctrine wholeheartedly—carried it farther, in fact, then he probably would have. Pasteur had never said that *all* diseases are microbial in origin; yet that was the assumption the profession now seemed to make.

Accordingly, when at about the time of the death of Pasteur experiments began to suggest that the occurrence of beriberi among rice-eating people might be due to a nutritional lack, this new idea was in its turn immediately rejected. When Eijkman, a physician, was sent from Holland to Java in 1886 to study beriberi, the microbial origin of disease was so firmly established as *the* orthodox position that he was given specific instructions to find the organism responsible for the disease.[1]

Eijkman himself resisted the nutrition idea, and in

spite of his own extremely suggestive experiments, in which he produced beriberi in chickens and cured them nutritionally, he is quoted as saying as late as 1898 that infection was still the most probable cause of the disease. During the next eight years he changed his mind; thirty-one years later he received a Nobel prize for the discovery of vitamin B.

Casimir Funk, a young Polish-born biochemist, certainly did not become a medical hero when in 1911 he set forth the "vitamin hypothesis" to the effect that not only beriberi but rickets, scurvy, and pellagra were caused by the nutritional lack of certain unknowns. Rejected at first, this strange new idea gained acceptance only grudgingly, inch by inch, as conclusive evidence piled up. And this evidence was generated largely outside the medical profession. This series of historical facts has tended to turn medical thinking *away from* rather than *toward* nutrition.

From the standpoint of Western medicine, the discovery that some diseases were of nutritional origin had little impact, and did not carry the same sense of universality as did Pasteur's discovery. Beriberi was rare in the Occident; scurvy occurred largely on long sailing voyages (which were already nearly a thing of the past); pellagra was regional; and in the case of rickets, sunlight could take the place of vitamin D. These diseases were regarded as rare and, from the standpoint of Western medicine, minor.

The evidence adduced by Eijkman, Funk, and others about the existence of deficiency diseases was not easy to come by, but it was clear-cut enough when developed. Yet in view of the professional resistance it encountered, one can easily imagine the kind of reception the medical profession would give to the corollary, but less easily demonstrable thesis, that good nutrition might help to prevent the occurrence of diseases normally associated with infection by microbes. In a straightforward deficiency disease the relationship between diet and symptom is direct and easily shown. Remove ascorbic acid from the diet and scurvy will eventually result; restore the ascorbic acid and the scurvy will eventually clear up. Such relationships are not so obvious in the case of infectious diseases. That is not, however, to say that they do not exist.

As an example, let us take the case of pulmonary tuberculosis. We know a good deal about this disease. Considerable and valuable efforts have been made in isolating the guilty bacillus, studying its habits, and trying to find chemicals that will kill or disarm it without at the same time injuring the person it has infected. Yet for all that, our knowledge of tuberculosis is curiously lopsided. We do not know why some people seem far more resistant to tubercular infection than others, and we certainly do not know how this resistance works. We are aware that persons with inadequate diets are statistically more vulnerable to the infection than others, and we know that adequate diet is an essential part of the treatment for tuberculosis. Regarding the scientific interpretation of all this, we remain ignorant, for medical research has never seriously bothered to explore the matter. To do so would, after all, not be in accord with our microbe-oriented orthodoxy.

Of course, tuberculosis is only one example of a disease that has not been explored from the standpoint of how heredity affects cellular environment. We can ask the same questions about almost any infective or noninfective disease: What do some individuals possess that makes them resistant? What can be done by way of altering the nutritional environment to prevent or cure? The answers are not forthcoming, and the ideology fostered by current medical education simply does not prompt us to find them. Our study of diseases is thus pitifully incomplete. Ignorance is pardonable, but I am not so sure about neglect.

Some twenty years ago my colleagues and I presented in *Lancet*,[2] a British medical journal, a generalized concept about the origin of many diseases. This article included the two questions I have just mentioned. About six years later in a full-length book, *Biochemical Individuality*,[3] I published extensive documented evidence in support of this "genetotrophic" (i.e., hereditary-nutritional) concept. But because of the preoccupation with traditional and conventional approaches, plus the high degree of specialization in discrete areas related to medicine, this broad, unorthodox thesis has *never been tested with respect to any major disease*. Yet its soundness has been demonstrated in the case of some minor diseases, and the all-pervading biological observations on which it is based have never been questioned.

As applied to the disease tuberculosis, one might put the hypothesis thus: Those individuals who are susceptible to the disease have, because of their biochemical individuality, distinctive patterns of nutritional needs that are not adequately met when they eat in their accustomed manner. Such deficiencies make these individuals easy prey for tubercle bacilli; they furnish a peculiar environment to which these organisms can readily adapt, and the susceptible individual's own tissues lack the wherewithal to combat the specific enemy attack.

If one were to test the validity of this hypothesis it would probably involve exploring the nutritional quirks in susceptible and resistant individuals—the "human element" in the disease—and should result in finding ways and means whereby susceptible individuals can be made resistant. I do not for a moment suggest that this would be easy, but in view of the potential value of the results, I should say that it is important.

Both the role of cellular malnutrition in the etiology of disease and the human element in disease might have received very different consideration if the medical profession had not become so well organized into one unified comprehensive group. There was a time when medicine was fragmented, and medical schools in different cities cultivated different points of view. Not all schools had the same objectives or requirements, and they did not award the M.D. degree on the basis of the same training.

All this has been changed. Medical schools in this country are now standardized (if not homogenized), and no matter what medical school one attends, one gets essentially the same instruction. Of course, there is no overt demand that compels individual medical educators to think alike, but no one can deny that a strong orthodoxy has developed, and that this has put a damper on the generation of challenging ideas. Research is strongly encouraged, to be sure, but only within the framework of the accepted ideology.

Advanced students generally work with their professors on problems in which the professors are interested. Editors of medical and related journals have been brought up to think along similar lines, and this, of course, influences their thinking when they accept, reject, or modify submitted manuscripts. There is nothing intentional or mean-minded about this, but it leaves little room for the basic truth enunciated many years ago by Orville Wright: "If we all worked on the assumption that what is accepted as true is really true, there would be little hope of advance."

It is easy to see that if in America we had only one church, all religious schools and seminaries and all weekly and monthly religious periodicals would echo essentially the same teaching. The parallel with the medical profession is a close one. Since we have one kind of medicine—established medicine—all medical schools teach essentially the same things; the curricula are so full of supposedly necessary things that there is too little time or inclination to explore new approaches. It becomes so easy to drift into the conviction that what is accepted is really and unalterably true.

When science becomes orthodoxy, it ceases to be science. It also becomes liable to error. Early in my career I received a benevolent letter from the well-known editor of a leading biochemical journal in which I had experienced difficulty in publishing some of my material on yeast nutrition. He advised me, in effect: "Stop playing around with yeast; the way to find out more about vitamins is to work with animals." He was presenting the orthodox position. Fortunately, I paid no attention to his advice. Anyone familiar with the field knows that what has since been discovered about vitamins through using yeast and other microorganisms is incomparably more than from all the animal experiments put together.

Similarly, about thirty years ago, one of my col-

leagues began to find evidence that cancer viruses exist.
This was contrary to the orthodox view. The evidence
had already been weighed, and it had been solemnly
and finally decided by the opinion-makers of that day
that viruses were *not* involved in cancer etiology. I can
remember assailing this orthodox position twenty-five
years ago at a meeting in Atlantic City—to little avail.
Yet within a decade, it became evident to all serious
students of cancer that cancer viruses do exist. The
orthodox position had been completely wrong.

Such examples could be multiplied, and we shall
probably touch on some others in later discussions. But
the point is plain. Conventional wisdom is never sacred.
Many of the things that modern medicine routinely
believes have, as yet, little or no basis in fact. And
some of the things modern medicine believes are flatly
contradicted by facts we do now possess.

In this connection I should like to say something
about modern fashions in medication. The use of a
large number of chemical substances now applied to
combat disease, or the symptoms of disease, could only
be construed as collaborating with nature in the most
Pickwickian way. I am referring to those drugs which
are wholly unlike nature's weapons but which, for unknown reasons, appear to bring relief from specific
symptoms. In principle, one would assume that top
priority in the treatment of disease should always be
given to those medications which are most similar to
nature's own biological weapons, and that one should be
cautious about introducing alien chemicals into any
patient's system. But this principle hardly describes the
practice of modern medicine or the policy espoused by
medical education.

The fact is that medicine has become addicted to the
administration of vast quantities of nonbiological medications which I should categorize as dubious or even
essentially "bad." I am not merely talking about such
obvious villains as thalidomide; there are any number
of common nonprescription drugs about which I have
severe reservations. The basic fault of all these weapons
is that they have no known connection with the disease

process itself. They tend to mask the difficulty, not eliminate it. They contaminate the internal environment, create dependence on the part of the patient, and often complicate the physician's job by erasing valuable clues as to the real source of trouble.

If this sounds extreme, let me put the case as simply and bluntly as I can: Do you really believe you have headaches as a result of your system's lack of aspirin?

Aspirin (acetylsalicylic acid) is a most remarkable chemical from the standpoint of its physiological effects and is the best known and most widely used nonbiological weapon. People buy it along with their groceries, and it is consumed in the United States at the rate of about fifteen tons a day. To damn aspirin is almost like damning motherhood, but in spite of its palliative effects it must be classed as an essentially "bad" weapon when it is used consistently to cover up trouble which needs more fundamental attention.

Aspirin is, for example, used extensively and continuously in the treatment of arthritis. Arthritis is obviously not caused by a lack of aspirin in the body, since aspirin probably never existed on this planet before it was made in the laboratory of the German chemist Gerhardt in 1852. By the same token, people who are free from arthritis do not stay this way because they have a self-generated supply of aspirin. Aspirin is a pain-killer, but it is not clear that it is either a remedial or a preventive medicine. It does not produce cures, but by disguising symptoms it may interfere with the task of finding cures.

Nor is that quite the whole story. We have long known that some people show symptoms of indigestion after taking small doses of aspirin. Others exhibit other untoward side effects. The technical journal *Science* recently (October 9, 1970) reported that aspirin produced ulcers in the intestines of laboratory rats. When we describe aspirin as a "safe" nonbiological medication, we had better add mentally the reservation, "comparatively."

But there are hundreds of other commonly used chemicals that are far less effective and less safe than aspirin. They are, moreover, usually applied at the wrong time—*after* disease attacks. Their use is not in line with the policy of collaborating intelligently with nature.

An example of such a chemical is nitroglycerin which, in minute doses, stops angina (heart) pains within a minute or two. No one understands how it works, and no one imagines that it strikes at the fundamental difficulty. It acts as a stimulus in some obscure way and temporarily eases pain and distress. It is not even distantly related, so far as we know, to any of nature's weapons. While its temporary use may be justified, it should not be used as a substitute for weapons that help eliminate the *cause* of angina pain. (Just what these weapons may be, we shall discuss in a later chapter.)

Many other nonbiological weapons are widely used. Among these are headache remedies which do not get at the cause of the headaches; barbiturates or other sleep-inducing drugs which do not get at the real reason for sleeplessness; and laxatives which, when taken chronically relieve but do not cure. Reducing pills may bring some weight reduction but are often dangerous because again, they do not strike at the real difficulty. Though "pep pills" may be off limits to many physicians, their use is nevertheless fully in line with a wrong-headed philosophy that says if one has a tired feeling, why not reach for something that will cover up the symptom?

Nor is the situation different in the case of the chemicals that affect our minds, such as tranquilizers and related drugs that are commonly prescribed when people have major or minor mental troubles. These drugs are chosen largely on an empirical basis; they are not designed to get at the root of the mental trouble, and while they might be regarded as "good" because they bring a kind of relief and get people out of mental hospitals, they may be thought of as essentially "bad" not only because they can make patients more vegetable-like, but because they stand in the way of cooperating with nature to prevent and cure mental ills instead of merely palliating them.

It is worth noting here that the treatment of the symptoms of mental disease, and the avoidance of nature's weapons to prevent mental trouble, promises to be one of the blackest pages in medical history. Current medical education gives to psychiatrists no adequate basis for understanding current advances in brain biochemistry. In a later chapter of this book, we shall examine the reasons for thinking that a fundamental trouble in mental disease—to which only emancipated psychiatrists pay attention—is, again, deranged metabolism and malnutrition of the brain cells.

Not all drugs are nonbiological weapons. Antibiotics, the wonder drugs of today, are different; they *do* strike at the cause of infectious diseases by incapacitating the foreign organisms while simultaneously giving the natural resistance of the host a chance to eliminate the invaders. Antibiotics are not native to our systems, but they are chemically similar to the weapons our systems use. Penicillin, for example, is a weapon originally produced in nature by a mold to keep its enemies in check. It is entirely probable that the resistance that some individuals have toward specific infections may be due to their ability to produce "antibiotic-like" substances.

Similarly, the use of hormone preparations or preparations of enzymes, coenzymes, antibodies, and other biologicals involve attempts to collaborate with nature. We know too little about how to make the best use of these substances, but fundamentally they are remedies of the right kind.

But the most basic weapons in the fight against disease are those most ignored by modern medicine: *the numerous nutrients that the cells of our bodies need.* If our body cells are ailing—as they must be in disease —the chances are excellent that it is because they are being inadequately provisioned. The list of the things that these cells may need includes not only all the amino acids and all the minerals, plus trace elements, but about fifteen vitamins and probably many other coenzymes, nutrilites, and metabolites. Ideally, the project of seeing that the various cells of our bodies get proper amounts of all the nutrients they need ought not to be left to amateurs. Physicians, with their background of knowledge as to how our bodies are built and how they function, are precisely the ones who should qualify to develop expertness in this area. Yet because medical education has developed a strong orthodoxy that excludes cellular nutrition, the research necessary for developing this expertness has never been undertaken.

I do not mean to suggest that medical education has no reasons for being skeptical about nutrition. It is often pointed out, for example, that some people who follow wretched nutritional habits nevertheless contrive to lead long and relatively healthy lives. But this hardly amounts to a convincing argument against good nutrition. Such people—and there are few enough of them —are to be congratulated on having had the good luck to inherit particularly disease-resistant constitutions. Improved nutrition probably would have made them even more disease-resistant. But these facts are not of much help to the rest of us.

I shall say more about individual hereditary differences in the next chapter, for it is extremely important; but for the moment I should like to return to the subject of how modern medicine deals with nutrition.

The job of the practicing physician is far from easy. He is constantly being faced with situations in which he must make immediate decisions on the basis of too little evidence. He has neither the leisure nor the facilities to base his diagnoses and prescriptions on his own research. To be effective at all, he must rely on those standard precepts and procedures that he has been so carefully taught. And if what he has been taught excludes consideration of the nutrition–heredity factor, he can hardly be blamed for inadequately applying it in practice.

Indeed, it is a wonder that there are any physicians who apply it at all. "Clinical nutrition is not even taught in most medical schools," N. S. Scrimshaw, M.D., of M.I.T. reminds us, "and not really adequately done in any of them."[4] It is only to be expected that this "woefully weak clinical nutrition education" (W. H. Sebrell, M.D., of Columbia)[5] should produce, in the words of Frederick Stare, M.D., of Harvard, "physicians [who] are not well trained to identify malnutrition except for gross under- and overweight, and this anyone can do."[6]

Of course the matter goes deeper than a mere question of deficiencies in medical school curricula. It is involved with the way the medical profession approaches the whole subject of preventing disease. Physicians, by and large, are humane and dedicated people who serve mankind in a most exemplary way. But they are also businessmen. Like the rest of us, they have children to raise and educate, debts to pay off, investments and savings accounts to be nurtured. Naturally they are not indifferent to whether they get paid.

Under present conditions they are paid for bringing their patients *back* to health; they are not paid when the patients stay healthy. If people do not become ill, under the present system physicians suffer financial loss. Physicians are humanistic; they certainly do not wish their patients to be ill; but the enhancement of their financial status depends upon *frequent illnesses*.

This is a real problem which the medical profession will somehow have to solve. We need able physicians, and they need to be paid well; but we must find some way to avoid this "breakdown-patchup" philosophy. In his book *University at the Crossroads* the medical profession's distinguished historian, H. E. Sigerist, points up the problem with a quotation from Sir George Newman: " 'The ideal of medicine is the prevention of disease, and the necessity for curative treatment is a tacit admission of its failure.' "[7] The answer, Dr. Sigerist points out, is not to be gained by adding a few more courses to the present curriculum. The real solution consists in cultivating an entirely new attitude in the medical profession. "The student," he says, "must be interested in health, not only in disease."

Other eminent medical men have raised their voices in protest to the "breakdown-patchup" philosophy. In *Time* magazine, Edward J. Steiglitz, M.D., is quoted: "The trouble is that doctors think entirely in terms of disease, and are ignoring their opportunities for making people healthier."[8] In his book *Changing Disciplines,* John A. Ryle reflects: "We are still a profession, thinking more about curing than preventing by attacking the basic causes of the disease."[9]

It is tempting to play with the question of just what institutional alterations would be needed in order to change the attitude of the medical profession. Suppose, for example, we only paid doctors when we were well, and immediately withheld payment whenever we got sick. I suspect that under such circumstances, prevention of disease would flourish. But the suggestion is frivolous; the problem is more complicated. And anyway, one doesn't alter attitudes by changing institutions. It is the other way around.

The problem is made more difficult by the fact that others besides doctors have a stake in the curative approach. The pharmaceutical industry derives enormous revenues from the sale of drugs and medications that are primarily remedial in application. While the world would be a healthier place if this consumption decreased, the drug manufacturers will not readily accept such an idea. That they are not exactly in the vanguard of the struggle for prevention of disease should come as no surprise.

The prospects for the development of disease prevention are bright only because this is clearly the direction in which the public interest lies. We live in rapidly changing times. Inside and outside the medical profession there is a rising awareness of the vital role played by the nutrition-heredity factor in the prevention and treatment of disease. When the accumulation of hard scientific evidence supporting this concept finally reaches overwhelming proportions, and when enough people become sufficiently aroused about the absolute desirability of a prevention-oriented medicine, the indicated changes will come. Not quickly, alas, and not without many difficulties and dislocations. But these may be less than some people fear. Competent physicians will always be needed, and the reduction or even elimination of many of the illnesses to which they now minister will leave them with plenty to do. We have conquered a great many diseases already through the use of vaccinations, antibiotics, and so on, but the shortage of doctors is still acute if not alarming. By the same token, the advent of prevention-oriented medicine need not spell ruin for the pharmaceutical industry. As we have seen, there are many essentially sound biological weapons now in medicine's pharmacopoeia, and probably many more yet to be discovered. They will continue to be needed, and money can be made by manufacturing them and selling them.

So, once again, we come back to the fundamental problem: attitudes. The relationship of the Food and Drug Administration at Washington to this problem is an interesting one. There can be no serious doubt that there exists in this organization a sincere desire to protect the public. There is also no doubt that the thinking of those who determine policies has been dominated by the traditional and circumscribed medical education of today. Thus Food and Drug Administration officials have consistently tended to leave out of their thinking both the *human element* in disease and the idea that *cellular malnutrition* is a prominent cause of disease.

The Food and Drug Administration is, in one sense, an enemy of bad weapons, because it scrutinizes new medicines to determine if they are judged safe. If not, the FDA prohibits their use. Unfortunately, in its zeal to restrict the use of what we have called "essentially bad weapons," the FDA has not always differentiated between nonbiological drugs and the natural nutrients that are needed by the cells of our bodies. Doubtless some exploitation is taking place in the sale of vitamins, amino acids, and minerals; and abuses obviously need to be corrected. But there is a world of difference between potentially harmful nonbiological drugs and innocent—if sometimes misapplied—nutrients. A few nutrients taken in grossly inappropriate amounts, can be toxic; but when taken in reasonable quantities, they are solely constructive. This cannot be said of drugs that are foreign to our bodies. Alien chemicals and natural nutrients should *not* be treated alike, and if medical education were on the ball, they never would be.

The Food and Drug Administration, and the medical

profession generally, has been particularly anxious about nutritional charlatans and food faddism. No doubt they are right to be concerned; much silliness and some quackery have flourished, all to the detriment of progress in an important field. But before the FDA and the AMA permit themselves to become too self-righteous, they ought to consider whether they may not be indirectly responsible for the misuses of nutrition to which they object.

Many laymen have become interested in nutrition because they have felt intuitively that nutrition is more important than is commonly supposed. Some have lapsed into faddism and others have been gulled by quacks, but it is difficult to blame them on this account. The very people who should have been able to give expert guidance to the layman's intuitions about nutrition have, in fact, virtually abandoned the field. If more doctors really were experts with respect to nutrition and heredity, they would be able to give their patients sufficiently intelligent advice so that quackery and faddism could have very little scope. A depressing aspect of the situation is that the layman's intuitions, uninformed as they may be, are more often justified than the physician's neglect.

Having created an intellectual vacuum regarding the subject of nutrition, medical education nonetheless deplores the fact that charlatans and ignoramuses have contrived to give it a bad name. Deplorable it certainly is. There are probably thousands of practicing physicians who would like to escape from the net of orthodoxy but who have felt that to show too much interest in nutrition would be infra dig, if not downright damaging to their reputations.

Yet in spite of obstacles, matters really are improving. The vast accretion of folly, ignorance, and neglect that has so long beset the nutritional approach to medicine is gradually being washed away by an irresistible stream of facts. One might wish that the stream were bigger, that more time, effort, and money were being allocated to the vital research that remains to be done; but one should be thankful for some

progress. It gives hope that some day medical education will be induced to move again in the direction of
the time-tested policy of collaborating effectively with
nature.

I have several times alluded to the compelling nature
of the evidence that has been adduced in favor of the
genetotrophic approach to the prevention of disease. I
intend to examine this evidence in detail with respect to
a number of specific illnesses; but first I should like to
clarify the twin concepts of heredity and cell nutrition
and provide the intellectual framework for understanding this evidence.

2 The Nutrition-Heredity Factor

It is ordained by nature that human beings may attain a certain size and may develop certain characteristics and capabilities. Their biochemical makeup is such that they have some weaknesses; they are subject to the diseases that characteristically attack human beings. It is also ordained by heredity that certain human beings are vulnerable to specific diseases while others are not.

Even in ancient times, Hippocrates recognized that "different sorts of people have different maladies." An early English physician, Parry of Bath, stressed (and perhaps exaggerated) the importance of this fact when he stated that it is "more important to know what sort of patient has a disease than to know the sort of disease a patient has." Apart from giving lip service to this fundamental perception, orthodox medical education has made few serious attempts to explore it. One might almost judge on the basis of orthodox medical curricula that the concern of medicine is not for the real men and women who exist in the natural world but, instead, for some sort of depersonalized statistical man who does not exist.

On several occasions in the previous chapter I made use of the word "genetotrophic." I shall use it often again for it is very important. It is composed of two Greek roots: *genesis* means "birth"; *trophikos* means "nursing" or "feeding." In medicine, when one refers to a "genetotrophic condition," one means a condition that is predisposed by heredity and precipitated by nutritional factors. As you may imagine, "genetotrophic" is not exactly a fashionable word in medicine these days.

Fashionable or not, there are a growing number of diseases that medicine is now compelled to recognize as genetotrophic. One such is the form of mental retardation known as phenylketonuria. We know that this malady is brought about in babies who have the biochemical peculiarity of being highly sensitive to phenylalanine—one of the nutritionally essential amino acids. If too much phenylalanine is in the diet, and thus in the environment of the body cells, the biochemical machinery of the susceptible child produces poisonous amounts of a chemical which damages brain cells and makes healthy development impossible. If the phenylalanine is suitably limited in the child's diet, the affliction disappears. Clearly the difficulty arises because of peculiarities in the child's inherited metabolic machinery.

Medical orthodoxy finds reasons for not regarding phenylketonuria as particularly significant: It is relatively rare; it is "manifestly the result of an abnormality" in inheritance; most other diseases, it is inferred, are quite different. Those who accept this position are unaware of, or not willing to face the facts of, biochemical individuality. The evidence is clear that a multitude of peculiarities of inheritance exist in the general population, and that drawing the line between what is normal and what is abnormal is virtually impossible. There is every reason to think that susceptibilities and resistances to *all* types of diseases are the result of peculiarities of inheritance and that in this sense phenylketonuria is a typical disease, not an outlandish one.

In order to apply knowledge of nutrition to our modern society, it is absolutely essential that the hereditary factor in disease be taken fully into account. Nutrition cannot be applied in a vacuum. It seems clear to me that if a man is ill, it is probable that his environment—which includes, preeminently, his nutrition—is at fault. And to improve this environment we must take into account his specific hereditary needs and potentialities. The alternative—to assume that disease is simply "in the air" and that we are born devoid of any particular susceptibilities or resistances—is not only unsound biology, but makes the intelligent prevention of disease nearly impossible. That is why I say that the genetotrophic concept is so vitally important.

Several years ago I became much involved as a consultant with the American Cancer Society. At that time it was unacceptable for any literature to be disseminated to the public that suggested that cancer has a hereditary origin. This, despite the fact, which every investigator knows, that susceptibility to cancer *is* inherited. We have long known, for example, that certain strains of mice become cancerous with almost complete regularity, while other strains may be only partially susceptible, and still others are almost totally immune. No one knows *why* (in biochemical or other definitive terms) and comparatively little effort has been put forth to find the answer.

To conclude that heredity is unimportant in the etiology of disease is to entertain a false assumption of how inheritance works. It is not by any means a simple like-begets-like phenomenon. It functions in mammals in an exceedingly intricate fashion, the details of which are largely unknown. But the crucial questions are these: When babies are born, are they biologically all alike? And if they are given the same environmental treatment, will they all turn out alike? If the answer in both cases is yes, then heredity is, indeed, unimportant.

But if the answer is no, then heredity is important regardless of the mechanisms which substantiate the negative answer. And the answer *is* no.

How different, in fact, are newborn babies one from another? It is only in recent years that there have been any substantial studies devised to answer this question. To summarize these studies: We now know that babies differ remarkably in the sizes of their internal organs. Their circulatory and muscle systems are various; their nerve patterns are unique, and their brain structures are highly distinctive in cellular makeup. The finger- and footprint differences which everybody knows about are inconsequential in comparison with these other aspects of hereditary difference.

Functionally, newborn babies have been found to be distinctive from the very start: the functioning of their special senses, their neuromuscular operations, their responses to various stimuli, their breathing, and their heartbeats. Yet scores of books have been written on how to deal with "the Baby," as though babies were produced by the same cookie cutter.

In understanding why we as a society have drifted away from thinking in terms of heredity, we must consider that out of human decency we tend to reject any idea that assigns "poor heredity" to certain members of the human race, thus sentencing them to a perpetual status of inequality. Galton, the "father of eugenics" (the science of being "well born") was largely responsible for bringing this unfortunate oversimplification into view. He considered himself well born and looked forward to the day when others would have the inherent advantages he had. Aside from introducing the repugnant idea of directed, controlled human breeding, his concept was unsound because it was founded on the idea that there are just two kinds of heredity, "good" and "bad." Actually there are a million kinds of heredity, and "good" and "bad" features are intermingled in all of them. What is "good" and what is "bad" is, in any case, a relative matter. To some, being able to solve mathematical problems is "good." To others, being able to paint pictures is "good."

It is not possible now, nor will it probably ever be, to enumerate all the specific characteristics that we human beings may inherit. The anatomical items alone would run into the hundreds, and the different combinations of these would run into the millions. More obscure items like the output of each individual's hormones or the varying ability to make certain biochemical transformations (which are probably basic to innate disease resistance) would swell further the number of combinations. As for our characterological differences, and the differences in our aptitudes and tastes, the range of variation is enormous, and the problem of sorting out how much is attributable to heredity and how much to environmental influence, is nothing short of staggering. Fortunately, our concern here is not with the most complex and subtle aspects of the problem, but with the relatively more manageable (though still very difficult) matter of purely physical inheritance.

I became interested in the practical aspects of heredity in connection with animal experiments. Ideally, if one does an experiment on a series of animals, the results should be the same (or about the same) for all the animals in the group. In order to approach this ideal, it is common practice to use inbred animals which are supposed to have a very similar heredity.

Early in our experience, especially after we became interested in biochemical individuality, my coworkers and I observed many disparities among those supposedly uniform animals.[1] Some inbred rats on identical diets excreted eleven times as much urinary phosphate as others; some, when given a chance to exercise at will, ran consistently twenty times as far as others; some voluntarily consumed consistently sixteen times as much sugar as others; some drank twenty times as much alcohol; some appeared to need about forty times as much vitamin A as others.[2] Some inbred baby chicks required seven times as much alcohol to bring about intoxication as others; some young guinea pigs required for good growth at least twenty times as much vitamin C as others.[3]

Such findings were made so often in very young

animals that we began to suspect that even the inbred animals differed widely from each other in *inheritance,* despite the fact that their breeding demanded that they have very similar genes.

In order to test this idea, we took advantage of the fact that female armadillos commonly give birth to a set of so-called identical quadruplets, all males or all females. These four all arise from one fertilized egg cell, and hence from identical nuclear genes.

By studying sixteen sets of these quadruplets at birth, we found the individual armadillos within the sets were not identical at all.[4] The weights of the hearts within one set varied in some cases nearly two-fold, as did their adrenal weights; their brains, kidneys, and livers sometimes varied 50 percent or more. Biochemical measurements of hormone levels and of amino acids in the brain often showed variations within a set of three-fold or more. The adrenaline content of the adrenal glands varied within one set thirty-two-fold! We concluded that since the genes are the same within a quadruplet set, the large inherited differences we observed must come about through the interplay of mechanisms *outside* the chromosomal genes.

It appears probable that the genes in the nucleus of the original egg cell determine *what kinds of cells* will be produced during differentiation, but that something outside the nucleus (in the cytoplasm) helps determine *how many cells of each kind* are going to be produced. Since each one of a quadruplet set gets a different sample of the original cytoplasm, the numbers of the different kinds of cells in the liver, adrenals, kidneys, brain, of each animal may be very different. This can give rise to vast differences in the total animals.

This type of inheritance is, of course, not limited to armadillos, but must take place in all mammals. Inheritance in single cell organisms, where no differentiation takes place, is much simpler, and it is in this area that so much progress has been made with respect to DNA and the genetic code. Yet even here, recent laboratory findings with respect to ribosomes and mitochondria[5] (small bodies that exist in the cytoplasm of cells and are responsible for the synthesis of needed proteins) suggest that our armadillo experiments were on the right track. There do, indeed, appear to be patterns of inheritance that are independent of nuclear DNA.

Such findings are extremely suggestive with respect to human inheritance. It is now known that the cellular makeup of various human brains may differ greatly. Many different types of nerve cells inhabit our skulls. The total population is said to vary from about five billion to ten billion. No one knows what the range is with respect to the different cell types, but over twenty years ago Lashley found "enormous" variations.[6] Each of us has a unique brain structure. We may all have about the same kind of cells, but by no means similar numbers of each.[7] This surely has something to do with the fact that we think differently.

We do not necessarily have "good" brains and "bad" brains. The total population of cells is probably not so important. Anatole France had a very small brain but not a "bad" brain. Most of us have brains that are good in some respects and not so good in others.

If we could only overcome our prejudice for viewing life in exclusively environmental terms, we might learn many interesting things about heredity which could be applied with great advantage. Inherited differences in brain structures, which we now know to be very striking, must have a profound bearing on the problem of mental disease; yet orthodox psychiatric training tends to treat considerations of heredity with the same largeness of mind as fundamentalists treat evolution. Medical education adopted as part of its "orthodoxy" the later teachings of Freud and his followers. These dwelt upon limited aspects of the environment and closed the door to considering heredity as a contributing factor in mental disease. The acceptance of this limited view has been particularly unwarranted because in his earlier days, Freud recognized the role of heredity.[8]

When inheritance is considered in the light of the facts we have been presenting, the production of geniuses by parents of modest mental stature becomes more comprehensible. To simplify matters, let us imagine that there are twenty-six inheritable qualities (one for each letter of the alphabet), and that each of these can be inherited *to different degrees* (associated in some way perhaps with disparities in the different cell populations). To make a genius of a particular sort, it might only be necessary that each of eight particular qualities (b, d, e, g, l, o, t, w, for example) be inherited to a high degree. This combination might be a very rare one, and yet be a pattern that could arise from almost any set of parents.

This picture is a crude one, but it suggests a concept that I believe is sound: Genius is not a unitary trait; it can arise from almost any set of parents; every child may possess some genius-like characteristics and if given the proper environment may become an exceptionally effective individual. Intelligence is not a unitary trait; it is made up of many elements, and an individual with seemingly modest intellectual endowments may have far more practical sense than one who is a mathematical or musical genius.

This concept of inherited brain patterns is in line with what we know about learning. A child's brain, regardless of its exact cellular makeup, needs to develop, and to do this the child needs a favorable total environment. This total environment includes good brain nutrition as well as learning opportunities. But without good nutrition and learning opportunities, development is impossible.

So far, we have talked about heredity in fairly general terms. Now we must look at the second part of the genetotrophic equation and consider specifically how inheritance relates to nutrition. In order to do so, we shall have to leave behind, for the time being, such fascinating and elusive topics as what constitutes genius and how children learn. Instead, we shall have to descend again into the realm of the biochemist—to the individual cells and to those manifold chemical transformations that, together, constitute life.

The fundamental activity of living cells is generally described as metabolism. By this is meant that ongoing process whereby the cell converts the nutrients it receives into the energy and the special materials it needs to perform its assigned functions. Those functions, as well as the efficiency with which a cell or a group of cells carries them out, are determined primarily both by the cell's inheritance and by the amount and quality of available nourishment. Although the upper limits of how well a given cell may perform its functions—multiplication, the manufacture of specific proteins and amino acids, and what not—may be established by hereditary and other factors, those limits are seldom even approached in nature.

My earliest studies involved watching individual yeast cells under a microscope while they were being nourished by solutions containing known and unknown chemicals. One of the first lessons I learned was that yeast cells can be nourished at all levels of excellence. They can be nourished so poorly that they barely keep alive; they can be fed solutions that will make them grow and ferment barely perceptibly; their feeding can be improved bit by bit almost indefinitely by the adjustment of the mineral, amino acid, and vitamin content of the environmental medium which bathes them. Their metabolic activity and reproductive capacity may vary from zero to a very high level, depending on their environment—particularly on what they receive nutritionally.

If a single yeast cell is given a highly favorable environment—plenty of air, water, a good assortment of nutrients, and a suitable temperature—it can easily produce a colony of 100 yeast cells in twenty-four hours. This means that a single small cake of compressed yeast, starting on a Monday morning with all the air, water, and nutrients it needed would, by the next Monday morning, weigh more than a billion tons!

From this simple example it follows that *in nature* yeast cells are always hampered by inadequate environment and imperfect nutrition. Otherwise, they would have engulfed the earth long ago. A fruit juice, for example, is a medium in which yeast cells can grow and multiply, but it is far from an ideal medium. By carefully supplementing it with minerals, amino acids, and vitamins, it can be vastly improved. Even in a commercial yeast factory, it is not practical to put into the fermenters the best possible nutritional medium. Passable nutrition is furnished, and many tons of yeast a day may be produced, but growth is always far below the optimum.

Brief reflection gives rise to the conclusion that imperfect nutrition must have been the universal rule for single-celled creatures ever since life began on earth. Many kinds of cells can generate even more rapidly than yeast cells if they get everything they need in reasonably balanced proportions. None of these has engulfed the earth. Why? Because, among other things, they have had to put up with imperfect nutrition. This is the only kind of nutrition that has ever been available in nature to single-celled organisms.

Organisms certainly did not escape from imperfect nutrition by becoming many-celled. On a picnic recently I was casually observing some lichens growing on the surface of rocks, and it occurred to me to think about their nutrition. In lichens, two kinds of organisms, algae and fungi, have taken up housekeeping together (symbiosis); because of inherited metabolic differences they have found they can live together and feed each other. Do they derive from this arrangement fully adequate well-balanced nutrition? Manifestly not. The lichens live a precarious existence, and the likelihood of their engulfing the earth is nil. They have to etch and scratch the rock on which they live for the minerals they need, and the rocks usually furnish a poor, ill-balanced assortment. Particularly difficult must be the acquisition of such needed trace elements as zinc, copper, molybdenum, and manganese.

Once the alga has built up its manufacturing plant, it can carry on photosynthesis; but in order to build this metabolic machinery, it must have water (from rain falling on the rock), essential minerals from the rock, and amino acids and vitamins that the fungus and associated microorganisms must synthesize, using traces of ammonia or other nitrogen compounds from the air.

Since the metabolic machinery of both fungi and algae must be maintained from these extremely uncertain sources of supply, it is clear that poor nutrition, both in quality and quantity, is all that lichens ever experience.

The situation does not change fundamentally when we consider other plants. Do they commonly grow in a soil that is perfectly balanced with respect to all the necessary nutrients—a soil that could not be improved by fertilization of any kind? The carbon dioxide content of air is low, and green plants would grow much more luxuriously if this raw material were furnished to them in fully adequate amounts. In general, plants always receive more-or-less unbalanced nutrition. If plenty of water is available, then something else—limited minerals, nitrogen sources, carbon dioxide, or available sunlight—checks their growth.

In all of nature—in the animal kingdom as well as among plants—living creatures are limited not only by the amount of food they get, but also by its quality and balance. In the laboratory we are able to give experimental animals something approaching balanced, good nutrition. When rat growth was first studied, the animals were fed the grain mixtures on which they normally lived and reproduced. Their growth was considered good if the weanlings gained a gram or so a day. Step by step over a period of thirty years the situation changed. By improving the quality of the proteins, by adjusting the minerals and supplying more adequate amounts of numerous vitamins, we can now make the diet so good that young rats can easily grow and develop five times as rapidly as those fed regular grain mixtures. This, incidentally, is healthy growth and maturation; the rats do not become fat.

How about human beings? Are they apart from all the rest of nature in this respect? When we choose food at a supermarket or restaurant, is this food of *optimal* quality? Do all the cells in our bodies always get an *optimal* assortment of all the nutrients—minerals, amino acids, and vitamins—that they need?

In the development of multicellular organisms such

as mammals, the original egg cell multiplies into many different *kinds* of cells—enormously different in size, shape, chemical composition, and in their biochemical functioning. Some of these cells lose the power of multiplication, and most of them generate new cells, if at all, at a relatively low rate, often only under special circumstances.

The process of producing multitudes of cells that are quite unlike the original egg cell (differentiation), is one of the grand mysteries of biology. It is also a mystery why and how the various types of cells live together in our bodies as an organized whole, in friendly competition. But there is no mystery or uncertainty about one fact: Every cell in our bodies needs to be furnished during its entire life with water, oxygen, a suitable ambient temperature, and food. All of these are needed merely to keep the cells alive and metabolically active. If the cells are of a type that, like those in the skin, need to proliferate and to produce new cells to replace those that are sloughed off, then these cells need extra food for building the new cells.

Some of the cells in our bodies can be cultured in a test tube, and it is known that they are not uniform in their nutritional requirements. In general, their nutritional needs are complicated—to say the least—but the needs of a particular type of cell are different from those of its neighbors. Sometimes—probably rather often—specific cells must derive part of their nourishment from substances that are produced elsewhere in the body by other types of cells.

It is a highly illuminating fact that all living cells existing on earth possess a similar kind of metabolic machinery, whether these cells constitute single-celled creatures such as yeast, bacteria, or protozoa, or whether the cells are among the billions that may enter into the makeup of multicellular organisms such as trees, insects, or human beings. How these billions of cells build their metabolic machinery differs enormously, but when this machinery is analyzed, we find in it the *very same* "nuts, bolts, spindles, and gears," in the form of certain universal amino acids, minerals, vitamins, lipids, nucleotides, etc. These universal parts of the cell machinery *do not* vary from cell to cell or from organism to organism.

How this metabolic machinery gets to be what it is, and exactly what the metabolic machinery is able to do, *does* vary greatly from cell to cell and from organism to organism. But every cell must build its own metabolic machinery, and it must get from somewhere, somehow, every necessary "nut, bolt, spindle, and gear." Minerals, for example, can never be produced by living cells; they always have to be furnished by nutrition from the outside. Amino acids and vitamins, on the other hand, are organic substances that can, in some instances, be built up from simpler substances by living cells. How effective cells are in building the amino acids or vitamins determines to a large extent what their nutritional needs will be. If certain cells, such as yeast, are able to build specific amino acids such as leucine and phenylalanine, or specific vitamins such as thiamine and riboflavin, then these parts of the metabolic machinery need not be supplied ready-made by nutrition.

The cells in our human bodies have, in general, limited synthetic abilities. There are a number of amino acids they can never build; these must be supplied in food. And all the vitamins must come from food. By definition, a vitamin is some needed thing that our body cells cannot produce. If a substance can readily be produced in the body (like a hormone or enzyme) it is not a vitamin, regardless of how important it may be for bodily functioning.

It is common knowledge that the cells in our bodies get their supply of raw materials largely from the circulating blood. It is not so generally known that each of us has a circulatory pattern of his own and that the dispensing of suitable amounts of oxygen and about forty nutrients to billions of diverse cells all over the body is a huge logistic undertaking. It can never be done with absolute perfection, giving every cell at all times exactly what it needs to be most active. No cell in any tissue would be likely to get, even if it were available, really optimal nutrition. Like other living cells in nature, the cells in our bodies have to put up with the kind of nutrition they can get.

There has been, since life began on earth, a furious scramble among all living cells for suitable food and other necessities. In our bodies it may appear to be a dignified scramble, but even here it is not always as orderly as might seem desirable. For example, the cells in hair follicles produce hair when they are furnished with everything they need. But in the scalp of a balding man, they do not get everything they need (probably because his circulatory pattern does not furnish his scalp with good circulation) and as a result, the hair-producing cells gradually die off. Here we have an example of a mild "disease" which is caused by cellular malnutrition.

How the metabolic activity of the various types of cells in our bodies is controlled is not fully known. Epithelial cells and fibroblasts, for example, are capable of multiplying at a substantial rate. If they were continuously furnished an optimal environment, including completely adequate nutrition, they might well produce tons of new cells within a few weeks. This doesn't happen of course; the cells are held in check by barriers (perhaps crowding or other, unknown devices). Limited and inadequate nutrition may well be one important means for regulating these cells.

Malnutrition of brain cells is a typical and, as it happens, important example of how cellular malnutrition works. These cells do not have the power of reproduction—this has been lost in the process of differentiation—but they are tremendously active metabolically. Brain cells use up about 25 percent of the total energy of the body even though they weigh only about 2 percent of the total. For this tremendous activity, the brain cells require ample nutrition.

While we are endowed at birth with many billions of brain cells (these develop but do not multiply), it has been estimated that in an adult they "normally" die off at the rate of about one thousand per hour. This means that a forty-year-old adult may have about ninety million fewer brain cells than he had ten years before.

This is nothing to be alarmed about, but does give one pause.

Why all this carnage? What happens to the cells to make them die off? Body cells in general die for two reasons: First, because they do not get everything they need; second, because they get poisoned by something that they decidedly do not need. No one knows precisely why nerve cells in the brain die off (peripheral nerves probably die off progressively also), but what more reasonable explanation can be offered than that they die of malnutrition?

The estimate of "one thousand brain cells lost per hour" is, of course, a statistical one. It would be interesting to know whether in some individuals the loss averages a paltry one hundred cells per hour and in others perhaps ten thousand per hour. It would also be interesting to know if those who lose brain cells slowly use more care and judgment in their eating than those whose brain cells die rapidly.

When people become elderly, malnutrition of the brain cells is accentuated by the fact that the blood vessels become encrusted inside with cholesterol deposits, and blood flow to the brain region is retarded. This means that there is less food and oxygen to go around. The activities of the cells are impaired, they die off, and the aging individual may suffer from loss of memory and confusion.

Cholesterol deposits in blood vessels is itself probably caused by unbalanced nutrition, and poor nutrition lowers the *quality* of the limited amount of blood which flows. It seems reasonable to suppose the quality of the blood of an aging person can be improved by better nutrition (even if the cholesterol deposits cannot be completely eliminated) and that furnishing the brain cells with a better quality of nutrition would prolong their life and usefulness.

In line with this suggestion, it has recently been found that giving an abundant supply of oxygen to the brains of senile individuals allows their brain cells to recover sufficiently from past deprivations, so that the individuals' memories and general mental conditions not only improve markedly but stay improved long after the extra oxygen is withdrawn.[9]

That brain cells need oxygen and glucose (the principal fuel of the brain), is well established, but they have many additional needs. Every living cell needs minerals, amino acids, and vitamins for the maintenance of its metabolic machinery. Brain cells are no exception, and there is every reason to suppose that elderly people's brains will respond favorably to improved nutrition.

At this point, it might be well to remind ourselves that this discussion of cellular malnutrition has led us by insensible degrees into a discussion of disease—for how else should we describe such conditions as senile dementia or cholesterol buildup in the circulatory system? From the viewpoint of orthodox medicine, we have been discussing two relatively unrelated subjects: nutrition and disease. From my viewpoint—and by now, I hope, yours—we have simply been discussing facets of a single subject.

Admittedly, my perspectives may in part be the product of my own particular training and experience. So far as I know, I am the only scientist of my own generation who was initiated into research by studying the nutrition of single-celled organisms. No doubt this predisposes me to think in terms of cellular nutrition and to apply the genetotrophic concept upwards, through groups of cells and multicelled organisms, all the way to that complex congeries of cells we call man.

But predispositions apart, at every stage I have found this concept to be wholly applicable and verified by laboratory experiment. That malnutrition—unbalanced or inadequate nutrition—at the cellular level should be thought of as a major cause of human disease seems crystal clear to me. It is the inevitable conclusion to be drawn from the facts produced by decades of biochemical research.

What do these facts suggest in terms of practical applications? To begin with, they tell us that we still have much to learn, but they do indicate where and how we should look for answers. More specifically, they tell us, first, that we need to develop techniques for identifying far more accurately than is now possible the inherited pattern of susceptibilities and resistances that is unique to each individual. Call it a "metabolic profile" or any other name you wish, but plainly it represents a necessary precondition for making rational programs of nutrition tailored to fit each individual's special requirements. The second thing that we need—and this is really only the other side of the coin—is to establish accurate correlations between specific nutrients and the prevention of specific diseases. A great portion of this book will be devoted to what we already know about this subject.

What are we doing to find these answers? As Chapter 1 made lamentably clear, not enough—hardly anything, in fact.

Can we rely individually on supposed "minimum daily requirements" when these may denote minimum daily health? Do the cells in our bodies, unlike all others in nature, automatically receive optimal nutrition? Can the general level of nutrition for our whole population be improved?

I think these are urgent questions. There is far more to good nutrition than we may imagine. We individually tend to be undernourished with respect to our special inherited requirements; collectively, we tend to be undernourished with respect to the basic things—"the nutritional chain of life"—which everyone needs.

In the next chapter we shall discuss why this is so.

3 A New Hope for Better Health

Adequate and health-building nourishment is a worldwide problem. Hundreds of millions of people struggle to get enough food merely to keep themselves alive. The fact that they do keep alive and propagate does not mean that their nutrition approaches the point of being conducive to good health. Throughout the entire biological kingdom, as we have pointed out, animals and plants consistently live and reproduce under conditions that are far below optimal; it would be most surprising if human beings were exempt from such problems.

Hence, for every person in the world—black, white, red, or yellow; rich, poor, or with medium income—fully adequate nutrition is a question mark. In our own country the problem is, of course, most severe in ghettos where poverty abounds and food supply and distribution is inadequate. Under these conditions people tend to consume far more of the starchy and sugary foods which are cheap, and less of the more adequate foods —meats, dairy products, and eggs—which are more expensive. Even the vegetables that are available are liable to be wilted and anemic.

It is, parenthetically, interesting and distressing for those who are concerned with food as a world problem to realize that we Americans have exported to other countries one of our most serious nutritional bad habits —excess sugar consumption. As a result, the sugar consumption of nine low-income countries during the postwar period increased 105 percent.[1] Greater sugar consumption spells poorer nutrition, because sugar provides calories that have been stripped of all the minerals, amino acids, and vitamins.

It is a serious mistake to assume that the problem of nutrition does not exist for Americans who are financially comfortable. True, they are able to buy supermarket food which if chosen with discrimination will provide them reasonably well-rounded nutrition. But because education about nutrition has not been provided, Americans usually do not know which foods furnish the best nourishment. Thus, for example, some people tend to dine on costly cuts of meat supplemented merely with bread and potatoes and perhaps a meager helping of salad. Such individuals probably have their amino acid needs fairly well taken care of; but many of the other items—minerals and vitamins—may be in distressingly short supply. Because they can afford it, Americans who have a weakness for sweets may consume large amounts of candy. If they like liquor, they tend to consume it in relatively large quantities. Even when these practices do not lead to obesity or diabetes or alcoholism, they always lead to poorer and poorer nutrition.

Even those of us who pay some attention to our eating (beyond simply getting what we like and can afford) too often adopt the policy of eating little dabs of "protective foods"—green vegetables, dairy products, fruits, and juices—on the supposition that this will give us what we need. It is true that by this means we do get some of every needed nutrient, but the quantities and balance may be very far from ideal. Food must supply fuel. Not only this, it must also supply continuously *fully adequate amounts* of all the nutrients in the "nutritional chain of life." These are needed to build and maintain one's metabolic machinery.

In a bulletin of the United States Department of Agriculture, 1965,[2] it is estimated that an average daily diet for Americans contains 10½ ounces of meat, fish, or poultry, about 1 egg, nearly 2½ cups of milk, about 4 ounces of potatoes, a little over a pound of vegetables, fruits, and juices, 6 ounces of bread and bakery goods, about 3 ounces of flour and cereal products, 2½ ounces of sugar and 2 ounces of fat. This listing does not include beverages, such as soft drinks, coffee, tea, beer, whiskey, and wine. The sugar and alcohol contributed by these beverage items furnish extra "naked" calories. These are substituted for the calories that might otherwise be furnished by such nourishing foods as meat, eggs, and milk.

This diet, taken at its face value, cannot be regarded as flagrantly deficient, but it is far from excellent, or even good. About one-half of the calories it furnishes are "naked" or poorly clothed. By this we mean that the sources of these calories contribute little to the well-balanced assortment of amino acids, minerals, and vitamins needed to keep our tissues healthy.

When a similar "average diet" was fed to young rats, they developed less than half as rapidly as they would have on an excellent diet.[3] The same "average diet" used on the rats conformed, in most respects, to the Recommended Dietary Allowances of the Food and Nutrition Board at Washington.

Diets such as these, when used as a guide to indicate the general population's eating habits, are relatively meaningless. While a substantial number of people may eat diets of roughly the same quality as represented by the "average," many millions will consume diets that are inferior.

If we think in terms of "average" diets we might infer that everyone gets more than the minimum daily requirement of every known nutrient. Aside from the fact that many individuals obviously eat diets poorer than the average, we must also face the fact that heredity is involved, and as stated in the authoritative *Heinz Handbook of Nutrition,* "the typical individual is more likely to be one who has average needs with respect to many essential nutrients, but who also exhibits some nutritional requirements for a few essential nutrients which are far from average."[4]

In this sense, the typical individual is quite different from the hypothetical average individual (who is not really an individual at all). Diets for the general population that would make even meager allowances for the varying requirements of typical individuals must provide amino acids, minerals, and vitamins in far more abundant amounts than minimum average daily requirements suggest. On the basis of this criterion "average American diets," as we find them described, are far from satisfactory.

The Food and Nutrient Board at Washington has, in fact, recognized that the well-known "minimum daily requirements" of the Food and Drug Administration may be inadequate, and has formulated a table of "Recommended Daily Allowances" which provides for larger amounts of many crucial nutrients. But no member of the Board would contend that it really has an adequate basis for judging how far to move in this direction. Too little is known about the variation in human needs for specific nutrients. The information that is available with respect to needs for calcium and several amino acids, for example, points clearly to the conclusion that five-fold variations are by no means uncommon.[5] Some of the experiments carried out in our laboratories show that even among inbred animals, the needs of individual animals for vitamin A and vitamin C vary at least twenty-fold. In Linus Pauling's recent book *Vitamin C and the Common Cold,* he makes a case for use of vitamin C in amounts as much as 100 times the minimum daily requirement "for the prevention and cure of the common cold."[6]

When we speak of average diets or minimum daily requirements, we are using broad terms which are unrealistic with respect to anyone's individual eating problems. We need to recognize that each individual's problem is based upon his or her own requirements which are not set by any committee. To understand these requirements, we must think in terms of what the various nutrients do when they enter our bodies and of the organs and tissues they affect. A few examples will make this clearer.

It is estimated that over a thousand different functioning enzymes are produced in our livers. Without these enzymes the blood cannot be purified and replenished, and life cannot continue. What do our liver cells need in order to produce these enzymes? They require a good supply of amino acids, minerals, and vitamins, all of which enter *directly* into the composition of the enzymes. What happens if the liver is given too little of these essentials? It does the best it can with what it is given, but its workings are impaired, and the blood may not be cleared of poisonous metabolites as well as it should be.

As a result of the presence of these mild poisons in the system during periods of poor nutrition, an individual may be afflicted with all sorts of undramatic disorders. Since no organs or tissues in the body are immune to the action of these poisons, the individual may lack vigor, feel as though he has "tired blood," or be subject to headaches, depression, indigestion, constipation, circulatory disturbances, infections, minor aches and pains—all because the liver has not been well nourished. And this can happen long before the liver cells are actually killed off (cirrhosis) or show overt damage.

Some people probably consume food so unwisely that their liver cells *never* get a "square meal." These liver cells may lead a perpetually deprived existence, like corn growing in an unfertilized field. Just as the corn might live and even reproduce at the rate of a few bushels per acre, the undernourished liver cells may also do enough of their necessary work to keep the individual alive, but not well. Ultimately, they may not even keep him alive.

Similarly, other organs in the body, like the heart, as may be inferred, have vital jobs to do. They also need good nutrition: fuel to burn and other nutrients to keep their metabolic systems in good working order. And they need each other. The heart, as we have seen, needs to be protected from metabolic poisons by the liver and by the kidneys. The latter, in turn, both depend on the heart for the distribution of nutrients. The brain needs a continuous supply of glucose—most of it derived from the liver. And so on and on.

Or consider the case of the endocrine glands. The endocrines have the job of producing specific hormones. The raw material for the hormones comes from food. Insulin, for example, is rich in sulfur-containing amino acids and contains other amino acids that cannot be synthesized by the body and can only come from food. It is quite possible that poor protein nutrition may be conducive to a diabetic condition simply because the individual (whose insulin-building machinery may be marginal in effectiveness) does not have an *abundant* supply of the indispensable raw materials. But not only must the raw materials for hormone production be furnished by food (e.g., sulfur-containing amino acids for insulin, iodine for the thyroid hormone, and phenyl-containing amino acids for the hormones of the adrenal medulla), all of the cells in the endocrine glands need good nutrition to keep them alive and healthy so that they are capable of manufacturing the hormones when the raw materials *are* supplied.

The defenses of the body against foreign organisms and viruses rest upon the ability of its tissues to produce antibodies, interferons, and related substances— possibly even antibiotic-like substances. Where does the body get the building materials? From food. How do these effective agents get built? Through the agency of healthy cells which must be well supplied with nutrients so that their manufacturing machinery will be kept in working order. Although physicians and others have been loath to say that any specific vitamin or other nutrient is specifically an "antiinfective," the fact remains that without adequate general nutrition, cells can only limp along as they try to do their assigned work of producing the natural agents that protect against infection. Thus good nutrition helps defend against all infective agents.

Liver cells, endocrine gland cells, antibody-producing cells—these are only a few examples of what is true for all body cells and tissues. All the cells of our body have functions to perform—some humble and some more spectacular—and all require nourishment in order to do their jobs. Whether we are talking about heart trouble or falling hair, about interferon production or brittle fingernails, we cannot escape the fact that the matter of cell nutrition lies close to the heart of the problem.

We know so much about this, and yet we still have so much to learn. There are whole areas in which we have only the vaguest clues as to how cellular malfunction due to poor nutrition may produce observable symptoms. Yet these clues are nevertheless very suggestive. We know, for example, that whole personalities can be changed by good nutrition.

According to a London study, seventeen delinquent girls (eleven to fifteen years of age) had been on a diet made up largely of white bread and margarine, cheap jam, lots of sweet tea, canned and processed meats.[7] When their diet was changed to one that was far more nutritious and diversified, not only did their complexions and physical well-being improve "almost beyond recognition," but they quickly became less aggressive and quarrelsome. Bad habits seemed to disappear; the "problem children" became less of a problem, and the bored ones began to take an interest in life.

A somewhat parallel experiment was carried out, also in England, with experimental rats.[8] Because rats are rats, experiments with them can be carried out with far more precision than human experiments, when psychological factors are difficult to control. When a group of twenty animals were housed together in a large cage and were fed a good diet, they grew, thrived, and lived happily together without complications. When

another group of twenty were similarly housed and fed
a diet similar to that which the delinquent girls had
initially consumed, the appearance of the rats soon suffered. Their hair lacked gloss and stood on end, they
were nervous and bit each other and the attendants.
After a few weeks "murder" became commonplace—
three animals among the twenty were killed and eaten
by their companions. In contrast to the well fed animals
that lived together without conflict, these poorly fed
animals had to be put in separate cages in order that
they might survive the experiment.

Well fed animals always groom themselves and maintain the counterpart of what we humans call self-respect.
Poorly nourished animals, on the other hand, appear
"not to give a damn" and become shaggy, disheveled,
and unclean. Is the same true of humans? Apparently.
What is the specific mechanism? We do not know. Is it
possible that poor nutrition, abetted by drug use, may
be an important factor in contributing to the sad state
of the "unkempt generation" of our present time? It
seems probable.

To summarize our biological argument, then, we
know that all the billions of cells in our bodies need a
continuous supply of nutritious food from which they
extract the different nutrients they need in order to live
and perform their various functions. None of these cells
ever gets an optimum supply of food, and thus no cell
ever performs at peak capacity. There are nevertheless
significant gradations in the quantity and quality of this
suboptimal supply. One may describe these gradations
loosely as "poor," "fair," "good," or "excellent." Too
often we are satisfied if this cellular nutrition is "fair."

Many of our cells have highly specialized functions
which are clearly absolutely vital. These cells—in the
skin, the muscles, the lungs, the liver, the intestines, the
kidneys, the blood vessels, the glands, the heart and,
crucially, the nerves and brain—*must* be well nourished
if we are to lead long and healthy lives. Contrarily, if
these cells are undernourished, disabilities and diseases
of every description can ensue.

The problem of insuring our body cells adequate

nourishment is most generally solved by what may be likened to a "shotgun" approach. We consume the cells of other living creatures—animal and vegetable. Since these cells always contain the essential "nuts, bolts, spindles, and gears" common to all metabolic machinery, we can be certain, if we follow this practice, that we will get *some* of everything we need. Departures from this practice of consuming the tissues of other organisms involve consuming the energy-yielding carbohydrates and fats which we extract from the *energy storehouses* of plants and animals. These include starches of great variety, sugar from beets, cane, or other plants, lard and other animal fats, and the oils derived from many plant seeds. When we consume these largely "naked" calories, we must watch our step, because these processed foods do not contain an assortment of the essential nutrients which are necessary for cellular well-being.

Scientific advances in the future will make it possible to detect with increasing ease specific deficiencies which may plague ailing individuals. This more sophisticated approach may be likened to a "rifle" rather than a "shotgun" approach. The two approaches are, of course, not alternative, but complementary. How well we apply both spells the difference, quite simply, between whether we will be well or ill.

Ray Lyman Wilbur, a physician who was president of Stanford University for twenty-five years, said, "Most people have but little idea how to care for their bodies, or how to use their brains, or be well and happy. . . . From childhood they never play fair with the finest machine on earth. The doctors themselves are not always good examples, and many of them care for their automobiles better than they do for themselves." More ominously, another famous physician said, "We dig our graves with our teeth."

When we "feed" an automobile, we give it fuel to furnish energy, lubricants to reduce friction and wear, put water in the radiator to keep it cool, and air in the tires to make them resilient to shock. The car cannot repair or rebuild itself when it becomes worn or broken down.

THE NUTRITIONAL CHAIN OF LIFE

THE NUTRITIONAL CHAIN OF LIFE

The food carton in the background may be imagined to contain the water, fuel, and roughage that an adult needs each day. In the foreground, depicted in actual proportion to one another in the form of a chain, are the other essential things that a person needs to get in his or her diet each day so that the body cells can be furnished a healthy environment. This environment permits the cells to burn the fuel, get the energy out of it, and do their work. The chain representation is used to emphasize the fact that all links are needed; if even one link is missing or weak, the whole chain is weak and the favorable environment disappears. The proportions depicted do not apply literally to any one individual's need. Everyone needs every link, but not necessarily in the exact proportions indicated.

The items depicted in the chain, listed in order in a clockwise direction are: iodide, cobalt, selenium, molybdenum, fluoride, copper, chromium, manganese, zinc, iron, magnesium oxide, calcium hydrogen phosphate, potassium chloride, sodium chloride, linoleic acid, choline, lysine, methionine, phenylalanine, leucine, valine, isoleucine, threonine, tryptophan, ascorbic acid, niacinamide, vitamin E, pantothenate, vitamin A, pyridoxine, riboflavin, thiamine, folic acid, vitamin K, biotin, vitamin D, and cobalamine.

This may not represent the *complete* chain. There may be additional unknown or incompletely recognized items. It may also be noted that the picture does not represent the entire chain of life. Every living cell has in it many other substances such as a multitude of organized enzymes, DNA, RNA, etc. These, however, are all regularly produced within the cells of our bodies if the nutritional chain of life is furnished in the food.

In our bodies the situation is different. A child's building material constructs his body and increases his size; it must be furnished in the food he eats. In an adult, there is not only some growth—skin, hair, and nails— but also a continuous complex process of tearing down, burning up, and building going on all at the same time. The proteins of the body are being torn down to amino acids and built back into proteins every instant of our lives. During this process, there is a continual loss; amino acids get burned up and they have to be replaced in the diet.

When and if all the cells of our bodies are well and happily coordinated—with no cells being seriously deprived or ailing—our bodies are well. This axiom will be accepted as true until someone comes up with contrary evidence. If our bodies are ill, there must be cells and tissues somewhere that are out of order.

In some medical circles, it has been accepted that there are two kinds of diseases: organic and functional. In an "organic" disease, there is something detectably wrong somewhere in the organs of the body. In a "functional" disease, seemingly nothing is wrong with the body structures, but nevertheless disease exists.

This classification of diseases is based on biological ignorance. If some important part of our makeup is not functioning well, something is wrong with the complex machinery. We admit that many sufferers from mental disease, for example, appear outwardly to have no organic trouble; but superficial appearances cannot be trusted. If we had some way to scrutinize the billions of brain cells of a mentally ill person, we would be sure to find serious chemical imbalances. Disease results only when cells are not well and hence are not functioning as they should. We agree with the famous Boston neuropsychiatrist Stanley Cobb, "All diseases are both organic and functional."

The cells of our bodies can become unwell and malfunctioning for two general reasons: First, they may be poisoned; second, they may lack a good supply of nourishing food. This nourishing food must be a complex mixture of chemicals (water is one of these "chemicals") in about the right proportions. Included in this food must be about ten or more amino acids, about fifteen vitamins, and a similar number of minerals, all in addition to the fuel—carbohydrate and fat—that our bodies need to run on in the sense that an automobile needs gasoline.

All of the food elements enter our body by way of

the open mouth, and the health of all the cells of our bodies depends upon whether or not we place within our open mouths the proper kind of food.

Nature is on our side. If it were not, we would not be here. First, we have the desire to eat; second, we are surrounded by plants and animals which furnish us food. We are not likely to get a good assortment of the essentials from any single source such as rice, corn, or beefsteak; but if we choose widely and wisely, we can thrive on what is available.

Nature is also on our side in that healthy cells and tissues have ways of crying out for what they need; health begets health. There are regulatory nerve cells that make us breathe—so we get oxygen; others generate thirst when we need water; others keep our hearts pumping, so that all our tissues get food and oxygen; others keep our temperatures steady so our chemical processes will not all go awry. Of special interest in connection with food consumption are the nerve cells (the "appestat") that generate hunger when our tissues need to "eat." *All* of these regulatory cells and tissues need fully adequate nutrition at all times. Otherwise they will resemble corn growing in an unfertilized field and will have to limp along doing a partial job.

If the nerve cells that make up the appestat are well and functioning, we eat when we need to and quit eating when the need no longer exists. Millions of people —as well as wild animals generally—have enough internal body wisdom so that with no special conscious effort on their part, they eat the right amount of food and maintain a relatively constant and healthy weight. It is only when the regulatory cells and tissues are malfunctioning—out of order—that people eat too much and become obese or eat too little and become emaciated.

Nature is on our side also in that when our bodies and all the cells in it are well nourished, we choose food with considerable wisdom. We know that if, for bizarre or capricious reasons, we set out deliberately to eat large quantities of sugar, or butter or salt, for example, our bodies detect that gross imbalance is impending.

They rebel, and ultimately the sugar or butter or salt becomes nauseating. If we persist, our bodies may reject what we have eaten by vomiting. There is no question that our regulatory mechanisms, if healthy, include means by which food is selected with at least some wisdom and with some regard for balance. The fact that we tire of eating the same food meal after meal and day after day is a part of body wisdom, and guides us in the direction of diversity.

From the practical standpoint we cannot neglect the facts of biochemical individuality. Of necessity, for reasons involving inheritance, every individual has nutritional needs which differ *quantitatively,* with respect to each separate nutrient, from his neighbors. The list of nutrients in the nutritional chain of life is presumably the same for every individual. If we were to indicate the quantities of each nutrient needed daily, however (e.g., calcium, vitamin B_1, leucine, and about thirty-five others), these amounts would be distinctively different for each of us. Some individuals, in the case of specific nutrients, may need from two to ten times as much as others. Each individual has a pattern of needs all his own.

If human beings were carbon copies of each other, life might appear to be simpler; the fact that each human being is unique makes possible the building of a reasonable hope for future health. If we can apply what is known and find out more about the amounts of known and unknown nutrients that individuals need, we have in our hands marvelous tools for ushering in better health and preventing disease. While individual laymen can often, by taking an intelligent interest, do a great deal to improve their own nutrition and health, physicians and scientists must become seriously involved before expertise is developed. What has been done up to now is basic but far from conclusive. What *will* be found will be of far more general application to humanity than anything we can hope to find on the moon or on Mars.

Having outlined in general terms the basic principles which underlie good health, we are now ready to launch into a discussion of specific diseases. In the next nine chapters, I propose to summarize what is known and what may reasonably be inferred about the relationship between many important diseases and the poor nutritional environments we often furnish to our body cells and tissues. Laymen and physicians alike will be surprised at the amount of evidence assembled linking disease with poor cellular microenvironments. Although I have studied in this general area for years, I have been astounded by how impressive the collected evidence is.

I predict that in the near future there will be a vastly increased interest in *internal environments* paralleling the surge of national and worldwide interest in *external environments* (e.g., pure air and water) which we have seen in recent years. I sincerely hope that the readers of these pages will help bring about the realization of this prediction, and will aid in bringing into being large-scale, well-financed, and scientifically responsible research devoted to increasing our ability to prevent and cure diseases by the expert use of the many environmental nutrients.

4 Stillborn, Deformed and Mentally Retarded Babies

If all prospective human mothers could be fed as expertly as prospective animal mothers in the laboratory, most sterility, spontaneous abortions, stillbirths, and premature births would disappear; the birth of deformed and mentally retarded babies would be largely a thing of the past.

It has been amply demonstrated throughout the entire animal kingdom that during the period of pregnancy nutrition must be at a particularly high level. It has been found repeatedly that specific diets that will support the adult life of rats, mice, dogs, cats, chickens, turkeys, fish, foxes, or monkeys will not be adequate to support anything approaching the nutritional requirements for normal reproduction.[1]

Even as far down on the biological scale as insects, the same principle holds. If bee larvae are given merely passable nutrition, healthy "worker" bees will be produced, but they cannot reproduce. If the nutrition of *the same* bee larvae is improved by the inclusion of generous amounts of "royal jelly" the larvae develop into "queens" which, when fertilized, lay enormous numbers of fertile eggs.

It seems to be universally true that nutrition that is merely good enough to keep adults alive may fail to support reproduction. If there is any doubt at all about the quality of the nutrition of human adults under ordinary circumstances, that doubt will be magnified many times when one thinks of the needs during reproduction.

Reproductive failures among human beings take the form of sterility, spontaneous abortions (miscarriages), premature births, and, most distressing of all, the production of mentally retarded or otherwise malformed infants. The number of miscarriages in the United States is estimated to be 400,000 annually.[2] The number of severely mentally retarded is at least 126,000 yearly.[3] Some estimates state that one child in eight is mentally retarded.[4] Besides these, there are large numbers of babies who are malformed in other ways. It is estimated that about 50 percent of the children in hospital beds in the United States are there because of various types of birth deformities, many of which are hidden from view.[5] Many people carry minor anatomical defects with them throughout life—defects revealed only by autopsies.

While we cannot, with certainty, blame all these troubles on the poor nutrition given to prospective mothers (genetic defects and interfering infections play a significant role), we have evidence that the *prime* factor involved in reproductive failure is the inadequate nutritional environment furnished the cells in the developing embryos.

We know that customary human diets are poor enough to cause reproductive failures in rats. When various "average American diets" have been fed to these animals, they remain alive, but there have always been serious reproductive failures when the experiments have been continued through the reproductive cycle.[6]

We know from experimental studies that animals can subsist and reproduce even when their nutrition would be rated *poor*. Poor nutrition can be improved successively to *fair, good,* or *excellent* in many ways: by adding more protein, by improving the quality of the protein, by improving the mineral balance, and by introducing a better assortment of vitamins in ample amounts. All gradations are possible, and as the quality of the diet advances from *poor* to *fair* or from *fair* to *good,* the animals fare better. As nutrition improves, a larger and larger proportion of the animals are able to produce healthy young. If the nutrition is good, most of the animals will be vigorous, healthy, and prolific;[7] if it is excellent, they all probably will reproduce healthy offspring.

The nutritional status of pregnant women in our country varies greatly because no two women eat alike. Some food may be good for one and only fair for another; what is excellent for one may be only good for another. Except in special extreme cases, it is almost impossible, because of the lack of information, to determine whether an individual's nutritional status is poor, fair, good, or excellent. We have previously quoted Frederick J. Stare of Harvard, as saying that most physicians know almost nothing about determining the nutritional status of individuals.

It seems likely that the large majority of people in the United States live their lives on a scale of nutrition no better than fair. Consequently, when they reproduce, there are many failures. The nutrition available to millions of humans is no better, relatively speaking, than that which was furnished laboratory rats many decades ago—long before modern nutritional knowledge began to accumulate.

What excuse can there be to justify the fact that nutrition for animals is far superior to that for humans? The truth is that the nutrition available to household pets and farm animals would very often rate good to excellent. But when the controlled microenvironment of the growing embryonic cells of animals is inadequate, all kinds of reproductive failures take place. Even if this were not readily demonstrable, we can be certain beyond question that well-formed babies cannot develop unless the embryonic cells are furnished an adequate assortment of every element these cells need for propagation.

It is unthinkable that anyone would experiment by giving pregnant women deficient diets in order to see how badly their babies might develop; but experiments of this sort have been done with animals and the results are clear-cut. In France, for example, a group of young female rats were fed a diet containing everything that rats need, except a limited supply of pantothenic acid, the vitamin that I discovered.[8] This vitamin is not well known to the general public, but it is an essential constituent of every kind of living cell.

When a group of female rats were given very little of this vitamin and then were bred, there were no continuing pregnancies at all. Without exception the fetuses that began to develop were subsequently resorbed and then disappeared. When the amount of this vitamin was increased slightly (in another group), the situation improved; still, over half the fetuses were resorbed, and only about 40 percent of the baby rats were born. Of those that were born, however, about half were seriously deformed. When a group of animals were given a still larger amount of the vitamin (about half enough), the reproductive record improved considerably. About 95 percent of the baby rats were born, a few fetuses were resorbed, and a very few were deformed. None of the animals in this experiment received more than half as much of the pantothenic acid as is probably needed for maximum reproduction in rats.[9] If they had received enough, there would have been no failures and no deformities.

We human beings start our lives as fertilized egg cells which appear as little round blobs approximately the diameter of the shank of a pin. About four weeks later we look like big-headed worms approximately the size of a pea. At this stage we are already made up of millions of cells of many different sizes, shapes, and chemical makeup.

During the entire period of development, when many different types of cells are being produced, the growing human being needs to be kept warm and supplied with plenty of water, oxygen, and available energy. But these are of no avail unless the cells in the developing embryo are supplied with an environment containing every link in the nutritional chain of life—all the amino acids, minerals, and vitamins that are needed for cell nourishment and for the building of billions of brand new cells.

The rat experiments just cited demonstrate that a single omission from the environmental supply is enough to prevent reproduction completely. Furthermore, it is clear that furnishing too little of a necessary element can also cause havoc. Prospective mothers need a plentiful supply of every essential nutrient.

Every woman, regardless of the state of her nutrition and health, has in her own body some of every amino acid, mineral, and vitamin that a developing baby needs. Whether she has a good, balanced supply and is able to maintain the supply to support a healthy baby is not so certain. Her own individual nutritional status may be so poor that she cannot become pregnant at all. If her status is a little better, she may become pregnant temporarily, but a miscarriage may result because her system is not able to support the infant's full term development. Or perhaps, most unfortunate of all, she may be able to produce only a malformed or mentally deficient baby.

Nature is so intent upon the continuance of the race, however, that people propagate even when nutritional conditions are bad. In impoverished countries, where the birthrate is high, many babies are defective and are unable to survive in the environment available to them once they are born.

There are reasons for thinking that a substantial number of human reproductive failures—stillbirths, premature births, malformed babies, and mentally retarded babies—are due to the lack, during pregnancy, of enough of the very same vitamin, pantothenic acid, that the French investigators showed was so crucially important for rats.

In the first place, this particular vitamin plays an unusually vital role in reproduction. For years the richest known natural source of it was "royal jelly," the mixture that, when fed to bee larvae, transforms them almost magically into queen bees able to lay eggs and reproduce. Subsequently, an even richer natural source of pantothenic acid has been found: codfish ovaries— again a source closely linked with reproduction. Rats are said to need ten times as much pantothenic acid for reproduction as they need at other times.[10]

An additional reason for suspecting that human beings would benefit from an increased supply of this vitamin during reproduction is the fact, which has been pointed out before, that it is probably an inherent characteristic of the human system to require relatively large amounts of this vitamin,[11] just as it is inherently characteristic of hogs to require relatively large amounts of thiamine (vitamin B_1). Human muscle, the most abundant tissue in our bodies, contains about twice as much pantothenic acid as the muscle of other animals, and it must all be acquired through nutrition. Human milk, which nature provides for human babies, is relatively rich in the vitamin.

Although pantothenic acid has been available for nearly thirty years, it has received almost no attention. Most physicians have been taught its name, but they have never been introduced to the idea that the *quantity* present in the diet may be crucial. While it can safely be asserted that no one in any country of the world ever ate a meal or snack without getting *some* pantothenic acid in it, it is wishful thinking to suppose that people always get enough. Anyone who questions that a deficiency of pantothenic acid (or any other nutrient) is likely to cause reproductive failures in human beings, may do so only by giving the lame excuse that "the whole idea is untried." It is all too true that the usefulness of an ample supply of pantothenic acid in preventing reproductive failures in human beings has not been investigated. The next question is: *Why* has it not been investigated?

I would be willing to give ten-to-one odds, that providing prospective human mothers with 50 milligrams of this vitamin per day would substantially decrease the number and severity of reproductive failures. In doses of this size, it is a perfectly harmless substance.[12] People have been given, on occasion, daily doses 250 times this high. Those receiving it were not only unharmed, they seemed better able to withstand emotional stress.[13]

It would be a gross mistake, however, to concentrate attention on only one nutrient and to suppose that the biological world revolves about it. Every link in the nutritional chain of life must be amply supplied to provide human beings with the healthiest possible way of developing.

Vitamin A was one of the first nutrients found to be necessary in the process of healthy development. Many years ago high grade breeding sows were fed a diet deficient in vitamin A during early pregnancy.[14,15] In one litter of eleven pigs, every animal was born without eyeballs. On the same diet, other abnormalities were also observed—cleft palate, cleft lip, accessory ears, arrested ascension of the kidneys. That the lack of vitamin A alone was responsible for the abnormalities was shown by feeding the same animals exactly the same diet with vitamin A added. There were no abnormalities in the litters to which plenty of vitamin A was supplied. Similarly, rats require about twenty times as much vitamin A for maximum reproduction as they need merely to maintain passable health and normal vision.[16]

Amino acids form another class of nutrients that is absolutely essential for healthy development of fetuses. They must be furnished *during pregnancy*. In one experiment, seventeen healthy, well-fed female rats were bred and placed on special diets.[17] Nine of them were given a diet during pregnancy that was good in every respect—except for the lack of one of the essential amino acids, tryptophan. Eight were given the same diet with tryptophan added. Not one of the nine animals on the tryptophan-deficient diet produced a litter of young; all eight of the animals receiving tryptophan did. No result could be more clear-cut. What actually happened, as subsequent investigations showed, was that the animals on the deficient diet did become pregnant. For a few days the fetuses developed normally, drawing on the mother rat's basic supply of tryptophan. Within a week, however, all the fetuses were being resorbed and had almost disappeared. This was nature's way of giving up; there was not enough tryptophan available to do the job.

There are many human studies that strongly indicate that inadequate protein (amino acid) nutrition, both prenatally and postnatally, often prevents the bringing into being of healthy, well-developed babies.[18] The nutritional failures that are observed in human populations do not usually involve single deficiencies such as that just cited in the rat experiment. It is more likely to involve several amino acids that are being furnished in inadequate amounts. In the Reference Notes I have cited at least fifty experimental reports concerning many such deficiencies: mineral, amino acid, vitamin A, vitamin E, vitamin C, thiamine, riboflavin, nicotinic acid, pyridoxine (B_6), pantothenic acid, folic acid, vitamin B_{12}, iodine, biotin, and so on. These deficiencies can play havoc with the reproductive process in experimental animals, often causing abnormal development.[19]

Zinc deficiency in pregnant rats, for example, caused many fetuses to be resorbed and 90 percent of the full term fetuses to show gross malformations.[20] Zinc is an element that has received little attention with regard to its role in nutrition. Only a few years ago the Food and Drug Administration required labels of supplements containing zinc to state that the need for it in human nutrition has not been established. This in spite of the fact that it has been known for many years that zinc is an essential constituent of an indispensable enzyme, carbonic anhydrase, and that zinc can *only* come from the diet. The deficiency of zinc is of special interest because in rats, even though the mother's skeleton may contain zinc in sufficient quantity, it is not passed on to the fetuses. Thus when there is a zinc deficiency in the diet during pregnancy, the mother may not suffer from the deficiency, but the offspring will.

Manganese deficiency causes, in addition to many other congenital abnormalities,[21] malformation in the labyrinth of the inner ears of rats, mice, guinea pigs, chickens, and hogs.[22] This results in abnormal balance and body-righting reflexes. A very interesting feature in connection with this particular abnormality is that while some rats have this malformation for genetic reasons, the genetic defect can be fully overcome by giving them a high level of manganese in their diets. It is entirely reasonable to suppose that although individual human beings may have very high inherited requirements for specific nutrients, when these needs are met, the individuals can prosper just as though the inherited weakness did not exist. This is parallel to the situation of someone who has astigmatism but is able to correct it completely by the slightly inconvenient expedient of wearing spectacles or contact lenses. The fact that hereditary factors are involved in faulty development does not preclude the possibility that such faults can be corrected by appropriate nutritional adjustments.

Also of particular interest are the observed results of folic acid deficiency in animals, for there is evidence that deficiencies of this vitamin during human pregnancies may be common. If this vitamin is omitted from the diet of female rats as early as the ninth day after conception, the fetuses cease to develop and are resorbed.[23] If its omission is delayed until the eleventh day, young are produced, but 95 percent of the baby rats have abnormalities.[24] A follow-up of these observations has shown that extremely diverse deformities can result from folic acid deficiencies. Fourteen kinds of skeletal deformities were counted.[25] Also, kidneys, lungs, and other internal organs were undeveloped; malformations in the heart and blood vessels were plentiful, as were cataracts in the eyes. Brain deformities were often extreme. Some animals were actually born without heads; some had the brains outside the skull, some had the brain cavity distended with fluid. Hormone-producing glands were in some cases underdeveloped or missing; sex development was abnormal. In addition to all these abnormalities, there was anemia, extensive edema, and many other biochemical abnormalities.

This experiment rather luridly demonstrates that a single nutritional deficiency can strike anywhere and everywhere in the body. The old idea that certain nutrients are valuable for certain parts of the body— calcium for bones, iron for blood, B vitamins for nerves—is quite misleading. Folic acid is one of the B vitamins, but it is evidently needed for the development of every part of the body.

Pregnant women are said to need four times as much folic acid as women who are not pregnant. In applying a rapid urine test to determine the existence of folic acid deficiency it was found, in one study, that 55 out of 250 pregnant women were deficient in this vitamin.[26] Such a deficiency, when mild, may not result in gross deformations like missing limbs, but nevertheless may cause obscure internal malformations which may not give serious trouble until later in life.

Animals do not need to consume flagrantly bad diets in order to produce malformed young. In an experiment in which healthy pregnant rats were fed a diet made up of a mixture of yellow corn meal, wheat protein, calcium, salt, and vitamin D, one third of the rats born had multiple gross abnormalities.[27] This, as a rat diet, compares favorably in quality with the diet of many people. Whole yellow corn provides energy, minerals, B vitamins, and vitamin A; wheat protein improves the amino acid supply. The diet as a whole contains something of everything that a rat needs. Evidently it did not contain *enough* of everything—it was poorly balanced—otherwise healthy young would have been born.

In one experiment using this diet it was found that two female rats produced five successive normal litters each, whereas all the other fifty-seven females included in the experiment produced deformed young.[28] Even among inbred animals, there is wide biological variability, and some animals can reproduce on diets that are inadequate for others. In other words, the diet as described was relatively good for two animals, and at the same time was poor for fifty-seven others. This observation illustrates how biological variability may help preserve a species. Such exceptional animals as the two female rats just mentioned would help the species to survive even when the nutritional conditions for many of the animals were poor.

As we have indicated, the period of reproduction is an exacting time. People and animals can often subsist at other times on diets that are only fair. In order to be safe during pregnancy, the diet needs to be vastly better. Some nutrients are needed during pregnancy in considerably augmented amounts. It is a striking fact that in the laboratory we can produce defective baby animals at will by giving the mothers poor or mediocre diets. We can also regularly produce well-formed baby animals by providing the mothers with superior diets.

If medical education were not deficient, the public would be more nutrition-minded and every prospective bride would be required to pass, before marriage, tests demonstrating that she had substantial knowledge about nutrition.[29]

Experiments which involve giving human beings deficient diets during pregnancy are out of the question, but numerous observations have been made showing how important nutrition is during this period. In a study at Harvard School of Public Health, the diets of middle-class mothers during pregnancy were rated as *poor, fair,* or *good,* and 216 babies born to them were also individually rated.[30] There were thirty-three babies which were rated poor; all of these were stillborn, deformed, premature, died a few days after birth, or had poor physical development. Of these failures, twenty-six came from mothers with poor diets, six from mothers with fair diets, and only one from a mother whose diet was rated as good. It is worth noting that none of the diets observed in this study were rated excellent.

The records of this study also showed that when their diets were superior, the mothers had fewer complications during pregnancy. Only 32 percent of the mothers on good diets had complications during pregnancy compared with 58 percent of those on poor diets. Not a single mother on a good diet had preeclampsia, while about 50 percent of the mothers on the poor diets suffered from this condition. Preeclampsia is often thought of as a normal symptom of pregnancy; it involves high blood pressure, edema (puffiness), and the excretion of some protein in the urine.

The greatest effect of poor diets, however, was on the infants. There were mothers on poor diets who came through relatively well, while their babies suffered. Babies are parasitic on a mother only to a degree; nature protects the mother, and she may have a false sense of security with respect to her baby, simply because she herself appears to be faring reasonably well.

Nutrition may be connected with the birth of malformed or retarded babies even in cases where there appears to be another explanation. Early in this decade, in West Germany, many hundreds of babies were born deformed—often minus hands—as a result of the mothers taking the drug thalidomide as a sedative or to overcome the nausea accompanying pregnancy.[31] There are excellent reasons for believing that this drug interfered with the nutrition of the growing fetus in early pregnancy. Every drug influences in some way the enzyme catalysts which govern chemical changes in the body. In the case of thalidomide there is some evidence that the enzymes that contain riboflavin, niacinamide, and/or pantothenic acid are involved.[32] To build the new cells that constitute the arms or legs, every item in the nutritional chain must be involved. A drug that interferes with any step in the building process obviously may cause abnormalities.

Recent studies have shown that a mild riboflavin deficiency greatly enhances the abnormality-producing effect of sodium salicylate when it is administered to pregnant rats. On the other hand, when there is an abundant supply of riboflavin, the growing fetus is protected. This observation may have far-reaching significance. It should suggest to us that women who are well nourished in every respect are likely to be protected against drugs that are foreign to their bodies. This makes sense, because enzyme systems are made strong by full nutrition, and it is reasonable to think that such systems will be more durable and resistant to outside influences when they are well nourished. Foreign chemicals which appear to bring superficial relief may actually play havoc, especially during the reproductive process. Good wholesome food, on the other hand, may protect against these drugs.

No part of the body is exempt from poor development if the individual has been supplied with deficient nutrition. In a later chapter we shall see that defective teeth often arise because of cellular malnutrition during pregnancy.[33]

Because of the crucial importance of the brain, I want to touch briefly on how cellular malnutrition is related to its development. We have already noted some of the extreme brain abnormalities observed in animals when their mothers were fed diets deficient in folic acid. Malformations in the brain can range from the extremely mild to the extremely severe. No one knows how many of us may be afflicted in a minor way. If any essential nutrient is in short supply, this can cause trouble in brain development.

Minor aberrations in brain development have not been studied in experimental animals. Nutritionists do not often put animals through maze tests to determine how well their brains function. When rats are reproducing on partially deficient diets, it is much easier to look for gross changes in the young than to go into the subtleties of brain structure or maze-learning abilities. Yet we do know that after rats are born and weaned, their intelligence (maze running ability) can be decreased when they are given poor diets and increased when the diets are good.[34]

In one experiment it was found that giving young rats less than 3 micrograms of thiamine (vitamin B_1) per day diminished their maze learning ability to below normal; whereas, if they got 100 micrograms per day, they performed supernormally.[35] (Rats are supposed to need about 12½ micrograms of thiamine per day.) Thiamine is, of course, only one of the links in the nutritional chain.

One extensive study emanating from Columbia University involved giving a nutritional supplement to expectant human mothers to see if it would affect the intelligence of their offspring at ages three and four.[36] Two groups of women were involved: one an urban group in Norfolk, Virginia, the other a rural group in Leslie County, Kentucky. The supplement used contained thiamine, riboflavin, niacinamide, and iron (these are the nutrients used in the enrichment of flour and bread) and was given to the women as soon as they registered at the free maternity clinics. Although the object of this experiment was worthy, its method was weak in at least three ways: (1) the inadequacy of the supplement, (2) the fact that supplementation was not started during the earliest stage of pregnancy, and (3) the possibility that the supplement may not have been taken faithfully by all who were supposed to receive it.

In spite of these uncertainties, the results showed a statistically significant increase in the intelligence quotients of the urban children whose mothers' diets were supplemented. The children of the rural mothers did not benefit from taking the particular supplement supplied (judged on a statistical basis), presumably because the rural diets were more nearly satisfactory. Far better experiments than this one could have been performed many times, as a matter of course. If the supplement had also contained suitably abundant amounts of vitamin B_6, vitamin B_{12}, folic acid, pantothenic acid, and vitamin A, for example, the chances of obtaining outstanding benefits would have been increased enormously.[37]

It is commonly stated that when a child is born, the quota of nerve cells is complete, since after that time no new cells are produced by multiplication. By no means, however, does this mean that brain development stops at birth. The brain greatly increases in size, myelination of nerve cells takes place, and enzymes and many other biochemically indispensable substances are produced. It is most interesting that when rats are given learning opportunities (playthings in their cages), their brain development—as judged by physical and chemical examinations—is more rapid and extensive than when they are merely left with nothing to do but eat and sleep.[38] Young infants learn at a terrific pace during their early years if they have learning opportunities, and their physical brains, like those of the rats, show corresponding developmental changes. During these early years, all the learning opportunities in the world will be of no avail, however, unless the infants are, at the same time, furnished with everything needed to build up their brain structures. Adequate postnatal nutrition is just as indispensable as adequate prenatal nutrition, insofar as brain structure development is concerned.

In a recent psychological study, young undernourished children were compared with children whose nutrition had been superior.[39] It was found that there were 22.6 IQ points difference in favor of the better nourished group. Every effort was made to eliminate other factors, such as differences in the intelligence of parents. It was concluded that not only were the undernourished children retarded in intellectual development because of poor nutrition, but intellectual development was indefinitely, and presumably permanently, impaired. Some of the undernourished were tested over a period of seven years. There was no improvement.

It is the duty of parents to provide their children with good wholesome food and to avoid loading them down with foods that are largely sugars and starches. Such foods do furnish energy, but it is unaccompanied by adequate proteins, minerals, and vitamins. Foods that contribute energy *only* are sometimes said to contribute "naked" calories; there are a good many other foods that could, at best, be called "underclad." After children cease to get their mother's milk, they still need to receive fully adequate nutrition, not a stripped-down substitute.

I have emphasized the importance of brain development not only because without it little else matters, but also because the brain encompasses nutritional regulating mechanisms. One of the reasons for good nutrition during youth is to provide the right raw materials for the building of the regulating mechanisms that tell us when to eat and when not to and also, to an unknown degree, what to eat. A Michigan study years ago showed that poorly-nourished children ate, when it was provided, more candy (sugar) than did well-nourished children.[40]

The whole subject of birth defects is an exceptionally painful one. Such defects can subtly affect or utterly ruin the lives of those who are afflicted. It can bring both despair and guilt to the parents. But if the evidence that we have been considering in this chapter means anything at all, it suggests that many of these tragedies can be avoided.

When the development of an embryo starts there are two fundamental factors at work. One is the complicated inheritance machinery; the other is the microenvironment in which the development takes place. If either the inheritance mechanism or the microenvironment is faulty, development goes awry.

When a healthy couple produces a malformed or mentally retarded infant, it is presumably *not* because of their own mental or physical deficiencies, *not* a case of passing bad inheritance onto their offspring. In most cases the fault lies in the poor nutritional environment furnished the developing embryo. Either the embryo is not getting everything it needs—the entire nutritional chain of life—or else it is being poisoned by some foreign drug.

Those who doubt that faulty microenvironments often distort the early embryonic development of human beings have no logical or scientific way to turn to justify their doubt. If human mates who are sound and capable of producing healthy offspring fail by producing malformed young, what more likely place shall we look for the fault than in the developmental environment?

If we cannot yet control nature, we do nevertheless have the means to control nurture. It is potentially within our grasp to eliminate vast numbers of defective births. We already know a great deal about the techniques for doing this. We *must* learn more.

5 Protecting the Hearts We Have

Of the more than a million people who die in this country yearly from heart and circulatory diseases, many succumb prematurely and needlessly simply because they have not provided a suitable internal environment for the tissues which perform vital work. Many of these victims are breadwinners—relatively young men who should still enjoy many years of usefulness. They often go quite unexpectedly, but there is nothing inevitable about these deaths; they can be prevented.

The key to prevention is a most thrilling and important one and, compared with it, all schemes for heart transplants and installing mechanical hearts pale into insignificance because of the small numbers of people involved in such last-resort measures.

All hearts (200 million of them in this country) require vastly better protection and maintenance than they are getting. The expedient is simple in principle and somewhat more complicated in execution. Since we cannot alter the heredity of cells and tissues already formed, our only recourse is to improve the environment in which these cells live. Nothing is so important in the microenvironment of the living cells in heart and blood vessels and elsewhere as the assortment of nutrient substances in which these cells are continually bathed.

If medical education could be induced to delve into the intricacies of these crucial environmental factors as they relate to cellular activity and well-being, we would be well on our way toward giving our hearts the protection they need.

Heart transplants and mechanical hearts have some appeal because human hearts are often defective and the thought of having something "brand new" to replace them may become attractive. Another way of overcoming heart defects is to have heart surgery. This is often very effective and is being performed on increasingly large numbers of people.

These questions arise: How do hearts become defective? Can imperfections be prevented? The answers are not absolute, but there are compelling indications that hearts become defective during fetal development because the embryos are not furnished with a fully adequate nutritional environment.

In the previous chapter we have noted that all kinds of deformities—a vast multitude of them—can arise when the environments of the growing embryos are inadequate. It has been found, for example, that up to 75 percent of the offspring of vitamin A-deficient rats had several types of malformations of the heart and the blood vessels.[1] In the folic acid studies referred to in the previous chapter it was found that a deficiency of this vitamin in experimental animals can give rise to exactly the same kinds of malformations in hearts and blood vessels found in human beings. What more likely source of heart malformations can be cited? Deficiency in the microenvironments of the developing embryos is probably a prime cause.

Protecting hearts should begin prenatally and should

be continued throughout our entire lives. Those of us who have gained maturity must usually put up with whatever imperfections and defects our hearts carry. If our hearts have a slight limp (many do), it means that they may require extra protection. Because nature is resourceful in mending and adapting, many people live to old age with hearts that are far from perfect specimens.

No one can say that the medical profession has not been concerned with the problem of heart disease and related circulatory diseases; these diseases account for more than half the total deaths in our country. Many studies have been made with the hope of discovering the causes.

These studies have been far too circumscribed, however, in that they have been based on the orthodox ideology of current medical education. Investigations have tended to be within this orthodox framework and have left out two most crucial factors: biological variability and the nutritional environment of the affected cells and tissues.

There has been far too much emphasis on "normal man," how he gets heart disease, and how he might be protected. The concern should be for the individuals who are vulnerable for diverse reasons based on inborn peculiarities—biochemical, physiological, and anatomical. Expertness in classifying people with respect to these innate vulnerabilities is practically nonexistent.[2]

Nutrition has come to be of medical concern in connection with heart disease, but it is too often thought of in terms of "carrots, lettuce, beefsteak, and beans" or in the slightly more refined terms of fats, carbohydrates, proteins and, as a special concession, cholesterol.

Actually, it is *cellular* nutrition that needs attention. Cells are dependent on the individual nutrients that come their way. The circulating blood continuously carries to the cells and tissues about forty or more of these essential nutrients, each of which fits into the metabolic machinery and has a special purpose. Faultless optimal nutrition at the cellular level is not something that can be taken for granted; whether or not it prevails is a big question, not only for every cell in our bodies, but also for every cell and tissue existing on earth.

The orthodox position advanced in medical education today appears to be this: "The blood routinely carries full nourishment to all the cells and tissues." This is preposterous biologically; it overlooks the crucial, undeniable fact that whether the blood carries adequate nutrition or not *depends upon what we eat*.

All arrows point toward the importance of nutrition in controlling heart disease. Dr. Frederick Stare says: "There is increasing scientific evidence of the importance of diet in heart disease."[3] This is an understatement, especially when the problem is viewed from the standpoint of cellular nutrition.

A vast amount of investigation and study by agencies of the medical profession support the idea that heart disease can be prevented by better nutrition. On the basis of present information, the best abbreviated advice for preventing heart disease is this: Concentrate on the *quality* of the food consumed. Wholesome foods like milk, eggs, fish, meat, and vegetables which are generously endowed with essential nutrients should take precedence over those processed foods that crowd out the good foods, contribute mostly calories, and provide very little in the way of amino acids, minerals, and vitamins. "Naked" calories or "seminude" calories may not be immoral, but they demoralize the tissues in the heart and blood vessels when the cells involved are forced to limp along on limited fare. In order to insure against serious gaps in the nutritional chain of life (needed by all cells), nutritional supplements, wisely compounded and intelligently used, can be a highly valuable protective measure against heart disease.

In the remainder of this chapter we will review the salient features of the vast scientific literature which touches on the role of good nutrition in the prevention of heart disease. The work on heart disease is so voluminous that even to keep up with it is virtually a full-time job. It has been our purpose to winnow out for discussion some of the more compelling reports.

(Additional technical material and discussion is provided for the professional reader in the Reference Notes for this chapter.)

First, we must be sure that we do not lose sight of the fact that each heart is anatomically distinctive, and this individuality in structure is accompanied by biochemical and physiological individuality.[4] Every investigation needs to be considered with the human factor kept in mind. It should be taken for granted that hearts may fail for different reasons and that there is no single "textbook picture" of a heart failure. Also, when we speak of cellular nutrition, we must realize that certain hearts and blood vessels may have nutritional needs that differ quantitatively from those of other hearts and blood vessels. Nutrition that is adequate for one individual may be inadequate for another.

I might say at this point that although I have tended to dwell on the importance of biochemical individuality as it relates to nutrition, it is no mere bias on my part. The phenomenon is generally recognized, even though too seldom applied. Here, for example, is an excerpt from *The Heinz Handbook of Nutrition,* a remarkably sound publication which has on its editorial staff leading experts in the field, including three physicians.

"Individual organisms differ in their genetic makeup and differ also in morphologic and physiologic aspects, including their endocrine activity, metabolic efficiency, and nutritional requirements. . . . It is often taken for granted that the human population is made up of individuals who exhibit average physiologic requirements and that a minor proportion of this population is composed of those whose requirements may be considered to deviate excessively. Actually there is little justification in nutritional thinking for the concept that a representative prototype of *Homo sapiens* is one who has average requirements with respect to all essential nutrients and thus exhibits no unusually high or low needs. In the light of contemporary genetic and physiologic knowledge and the statistical interpretations thereof, the typical individual is more likely to be one who has average needs with respect to many essential

nutrients but who also exhibits some nutritional requirements for a few essential nutrients which are far from
average."[5]

If we gear all our thinking and our investigations to
the concept of the "normal man" who is approximately
average in every respect, we are probably leaving out
of our thoughts and investigations the very individuals
who are vulnerable to heart attacks. This is an inde-
fensible modus operandi.

One thing that all hearts and blood vessels have in
common is that they need a continuous supply of
energy. This is derived from metabolism—the biological
burning process—which in turn requires fuel, oxygen,
and the necessary metabolic machinery. This metabolic
machinery must be kept in working order so that it
never fails, for failure means death. The blood which
furnishes the fuel and the oxygen also carries with it—
if we put the right things into our open mouths—the
wherewithal to keep the metabolic machinery in constant repair. If we can contrive with expert help to give
ourselves excellent nutrition, we will have gone a long
way toward keeping our hearts well.

This objective, excellent individual nutrition, cannot
be attained by concentrating upon the needs of a statistical "average" or "standard" man. If the recommended intake of vitamin B_6 for standard man is 2
milligrams daily, this is irrelevant except as a very
rough approximation. What a particular individual
needs may be far from average. Furthermore, how much
vitamin B_6 one needs depends markedly upon the
amount of fat and protein (tryptophan) he consumes,
as will be made clear in later discussions.

People for whom heart attacks are imminent—
whether they are aware of the danger or not—are
among those who may have special needs, and these
special needs may involve *any* nutrient. A higher than
average special need (for magnesium, for example)
may not show up in a statistical study as significant,
yet for the individual concerned it may easily make the
difference between life and death. Statistics may be
able to predict with respect to populations, but not for
individuals.

The most common form of heart failure involves obstruction of the coronary arteries which feed the heart itself. This is a localized event which, however, is part of a much broader picture. Practically all of us who have reached adulthood are afflicted, at least mildly, with a diseased condition known as atherosclerosis.[6] As we age, the insides of the blood vessels tend to accumulate deposits which hinder blood flow to every part of the body. This makes it harder for the cells and tissues to get the oxygen and the nutrition that the blood carries. When the coronary arteries get badly encrusted, the fatal danger of clotting and stoppage becomes acute.

These encrustations (plaques) are fatty in nature, but as they become more established they come to contain mineral matter (calcium) and become hard.[7] Thus arises the expression "hardening of the arteries." Cholesterol has long been known to be a prominent constituent of these fatty deposits.

The prevalence of cholesterol in these obstructing deposits has given rise to the idea that cholesterol is perhaps the villain.[8] This apparently obvious clue is, in fact, misleading. Cholesterol is an absolute essential for our bodies all through life. It is produced in our bodies by many types of cells and has functions associated with the very best of health.[9] Cholesterol in its proper place is good, not bad, but the deposit of cholesterol on the inside of artery walls is a source of trouble.

How can this depositing of cholesterol be prevented? The most obvious answer is: "consume less cholesterol."[10] Superficially, this sounds like a good suggestion; actually it is a poor one. Most of our good foods contain substantial amounts of cholesterol, and if we try to eliminate cholesterol consumption we sacrifice good nutrition.[11] In effect we would throw out the baby with the bath water. Anyone who deliberately avoids cholesterol in his diet may be inadvertently courting heart disease.

As we shall see later, the evidence points to the conclusion that good nutrition, if it is really good, prevents cholesterol deposits from forming, even when our cholesterol consumption is moderately high. We must remember that cholesterol is made within our bodies, and that this "homemade" cholesterol can be deposited in the arteries of a person who consumes no cholesterol at all. Furthermore, the rate of synthesis of cholesterol in the body is inversely influenced by the available supply of cholesterol from the outside (feedback mechanism). Not consuming cholesterol may in effect "open the valve" which accelerates the production of cholesterol within the body thereby increasing cholesterol synthesis.[12]

A better answer to the problem of cholesterol deposits may be this: "Consume more lecithin." It is known that lecithin has soap-like characteristics, is a powerful emulsifying agent, and its presence in the blood tends to dissolve cholesterol deposits.[13] When there is substantially more lecithin in the blood than cholesterol—a ratio of 1.2 to 1 is said to be favorable[14] —the actual amount of cholesterol can be high without the blood plasma getting milky or showing a tendency to produce fatty deposits.[15] L. M. Morrison found that the cholesterol levels in the blood of twelve patients were lowered substantially when they consumed about an ounce of lecithin per day for three months.[16] Lecithin is an enemy of cholesterol deposits, and consuming more lecithin is a useful preventive measure.[17]

It would be surprising if eating lecithin were the only answer. Lecithin, like cholesterol, is made within our bodies, and there are ways in which the bodily production of this beneficial agent can be promoted. There are certain nutrients, sometimes called lipotropic agents, which are peculiarly effective in promoting the bodily production of lecithin. Three substances of this group are methionine, choline, and inositol.

There is evidence that deficiency of these nutrients may cause cholesterol deposition. At Harvard it was found that both cebus and rhesus monkeys were afflicted with atherosclerosis as a result of consuming a diet which was satisfactory in every way except for a deficiency of methionine.[18] Morrison and Gonzales tried the experiment of giving 115 of their heart patients extra choline, and allowing 115 others (a matched group) to go without this nutritional supplement. With similar treatment throughout a period of three years, there were twelve deaths among those getting choline and thirty deaths among those who did not receive it.[19]

All observations and experiments relating nutritional factors to atherosclerosis should be considered in the light of our central thesis: When we give the various cells with which we are concerned the best possible environment, we will probably have dealt with the problem effectively. The heredity of these cells is probably satisfactory enough so that an appropriate environment will insure that they maintain a healthy metabolic condition free from abnormalities.

One of the nutrients that may be in short supply and has been prominently featured by several physicians as being important in the prevention and cure of heart disease, is vitamin E.[20] The findings of these physicians has not always been above criticism, and in general the orthodox position frowns on their conclusions, partly because, as we have indicated earlier, nutrition (including vitamins) has gained a bad name. Individual patients seem to have benefited greatly by the use of supplementary vitamin E. This can readily happen even though a large number of patients may not benefit. Vitamin E is an essential nutrient for our bodies, and there is no reason to doubt that its lack can be a basic cause of atherosclerosis and heart disease.[21]

Folic acid is another nutrient which may be in short supply in the environment of the cells involved in atherosclerosis. Evidence that this is so is based on a medical report in which seventeen elderly patients were treated by administering 5 to 7.5 milligrams of folic acid daily.[22] As a result of this treatment, fifteen patients responded by increased capillary blood flow and improved vision. This measurably-improved vision was ascribed to diminished atherosclerosis and better blood supply to the retina. In many of the patients there was increased skin temperature, again associated with improved circulation. The lack of uniformity in response was to have been expected since, of course, individuals differ quantitatively in respect to their need for particular nutrients.

A large amount of information, based upon carefully

controlled scientific experiments, indicates very strongly
that vitamin B_6 (pyridoxine) is another key nutrient
which is often present in inadequate amounts in the
cellular environment of those whose atherosclerosis is
extreme.[23]

Experiments with monkeys have yielded clear-cut
results. When they are rendered vitamin B_6-deficient,
they develop atherosclerosis rapidly.[24] When monkeys
are fed diets supplemented with vitamin B_6, they have
much lower levels of cholesterol in the blood than
when these diets are not supplemented. The animals
on the supplemented diets eat much more food than
the others, and since the diet contains cholesterol, they
get far more cholesterol into their bodies. This does not
matter, however; the extra vitamin B_6 they get allows
them to dispose of the surplus, with the result that their
cholesterol blood levels are not as high as in those
animals that consume less cholesterol.

It is most interesting that vitamin B_6 performs the
same functions throughout the whole biological kingdom. When tryptophan, one of the essential amino
acids, is processed in a body deficient in vitamin B_6, a
yellow pigmented substance—xanthurenic acid—is
formed. This substance is formed almost universally
under these conditions, and is excreted in the urine of
rats, mice, dogs, pigs, and monkeys whenever insufficient
vitamin B_6 is supplied.[25] Even insect larvae appear to
produce the same substance from tryptophan when they
are deficient in vitamin B_6.[26] This xanthurenic acid is
easily spotted. It may be likened to smoke that results
from the incomplete burning of tryptophan.

It would be dangerous to subject human beings to a
vitamin B_6-free diet for long periods, but L. D. Greenberg and his associates at California have done this
for two or three weeks, and have found that lack of
vitamin B_6 causes the excretion of xanthurenic acid and
that returning vitamin B_6 to the diet causes a corresponding decrease in its excretion.[27] That it is produced in human beings (as in other species) from
tryptophan is shown by the fact that when tryptophan
is eliminated from the diet, even during pyridoxine

deficiency, no xanthurenic acid is excreted in the urine. When animals or human beings are given extra amounts of tryptophan—beyond their capacity to metabolize it —xanthurenic acid is always excreted.

This serves as an important test. It is found that when young babies are given an extra amount of tryptophan, they respond very differently, as individuals.[28] Some can burn up extra amounts readily; others fail to do so and excrete xanthurenic acid. Such results can only be interpreted to mean that some babies innately have much higher needs for vitamin B_6 than others.[29] This is in line with the other facts of biochemical individuality and suggests that vitamin B_6 may be a peculiarly important factor in atherosclerosis in those individuals who have high requirements for this vitamin. Studies have shown that cardiac patients as a group excrete more xanthurenic acid after tryptophan loading than those who are free from heart disease, thus indicating that among heart patients vitamin B_6 deficiency is actually prevalent.[29]

It may be that vitamin B_6 is an important factor in the majority of cases, especially among individuals who consume relatively large amounts of fat. A study of rats has been made in Japan which indicates that the ingestion of fats on a tryptophan-containing diet caused a five- to ten-fold increase in xanthurenic acid excretion.[30] The consumption of extra fat evidently promotes vitamin B_6 deficiency.[31] In other words, when animals or men consume more fat, they need more vitamin B_6. This in turn suggests that in many cases individuals can overcome the atherosclerotic effects of extra fat by getting more vitamin B_6 into their diet. It also appears probable that very high protein diets containing much tryptophan may increase one's need of vitamin B_6.[32]

Other evidence linking vitamin B_6 deficiency with atherosclerosis is the fact that this vitamin is a necessary cocatalyst for the production of certain important and desirable unsaturated fatty acids.[33] Rats given an abundance of vitamin B_6 produce in their bodies about ten times as much of these unsaturated fats as comparable rats which are B_6-deficient.[34]

No one can state specifically how great the human needs for vitamin B_6 are. That some people need, on the same diet, much more than others complicates the situation. And, of course, the basal requirement for vitamin B_6 increases whenever there is increased consumption of fat or any protein containing tryptophan. The fact that the vitamin exists in nature in three forms (pyridoxine, pyridoxal, and pyridoxamine) does not make the problem any simpler.

It has been estimated by Greenberg and his associates that human beings require 3.5 milligrams per day, which is said to be about two and a half times as much as people ordinarily get. The Food and Nutrition Board sets an "allowance" at 2 milligrams a day which, on the basis of the same estimate of intake, is about 43 percent more than people usually get.

Common foods are liable to be deficient in vitamin B_6. Years ago, Wisconsin investigators found highly processed army K rations—a mixture of forty-five food items—inadequate with respect to vitamin B_6 when fed to rats or to rhesus monkeys.[35] It has been found that heat-sterilized milk, canned evaporated milk, or heat-processed milk powders have a substantial amount of the vitamin B_6 content destroyed, and that experimental rats cannot thrive on milk treated in this way.[36] It has also been found that some infants on heat-sterilized milk formulas get convulsive seizures which can be eliminated by vitamin B_6 supplementation.[37] Canned foods in general are suspect because this vitamin often does not resist high temperature treatment and is unstable in light, especially when it is in solution.[38]

Probably the most important basis for thinking that vitamin B_6 deficiency is widespread lies in the fact that our flours and breads are almost always deficient. It was fully recognized about thirty years ago that highly milled (low extraction) flours had vitamins and minerals removed that needed to be restored. Accordingly, "enriched" flour and bread came into existence. This flour and bread was enriched with thiamine (B_1), niacin, riboflavin (B_2), and iron.[39] No provision was made at that time for restoring vitamin B_6, pantothenic acid, vitamin E, or the other nutrients discarded during the milling process. It is therefore not surprising that rats fed enriched flours may develop convulsive seizures —a symptom of vitamin B_6 deficiency.[40] The widespread use of bread and flour which has been stripped of most of its vitamin B_6 is enough to account for a widespread deficiency.[41]

It is not certain that a modest increase in the amount of vitamin B_6 consumed would fill the needs of everyone, especially those who, like Jack Sprat's wife, eat a large amount of fat. Greenberg and his associates found that rhesus monkeys on high-fat, high-cholesterol diets were not protected by 1 milligram of vitamin B_6 a day, but *were* protected by 5 milligrams per day. If these observations are translated into human terms (men weigh about 5 times as much as rhesus monkeys), 5 milligrams of vitamin B_6 per day might not protect men on a high-fat, high-cholesterol diet. Twenty-five milligrams per day might be necessary.

Observations on human infants show conclusively that some infants have very high vitamin B_6 requirements. Some appear to need even eight to forty times as much as is usual. The term "pyridoxine-dependency" has been used to designate this condition. This is an unfortunate expression because all human beings are pyridoxine dependent; it is a matter of the *amount* needed. According to the principle of genetic gradients,[42] if some infants require eight times the average amount, it is to be expected that there will be others that require two, four, or six times the average.

All of these considerations lead us to conclude that in order to prevent atherosclerosis and heart disease, the avoidance of vitamin B_6 deficiency has a very high priority.[43]

The possibility that magnesium deficiency may also be implicated in coronary heart disease arose when it was reported that injections of magnesium sulfate brought about "dramatic clinical improvement" in patients who had suffered from angina pectoris and coronary thrombosis, and that the lipoprotein levels were brought to normal in many cases.[44]

It is not safe to draw conclusions from a single medical report. Since there has been corroboration from animal studies,[45] however, I think this report is worthy of attention, especially when one considers the possibility that such a deficiency might be the dominant cause of disaster in some cases, and yet not affect *all* heart patients. It may not even be statistically important, yet there may be some people whose biochemical individuality makes them peculiarly vulnerable to this lack.

It has been found that rats fed diets that ordinarily produce atherosclerosis were protected from it completely by increasing the level of magnesium consumption up to eight times.[46] There is evidence that the balance between calcium and magnesium is important.[47] If the levels of calcium consumption are high, the magnesium levels need to be high also. The consumption of an atherosclerosis-producing diet increased the magnesium requirements of rats fourfold.

Magnesium has been recognized as a vital element for many decades. It is known to be involved in many essential metabolic processes. Yet little attention has been paid to the question of how much we human beings need. It was not until 1968 (seventh edition of its publication) that the Food and Nutrition Board included "recommended allowances" for magnesium. Although our bodies contain less than one-fiftieth as much magnesium as calcium, the daily magnesium "allowance" for young men eighteen to twenty-two years of age is 0.4 grams—one-half as high as is that for calcium. Calcium is largely in the bones (though also indispensable elsewhere), while only about one-half the magnesium of our bodies is located in the bones.

We cannot assume that people automatically get as much magnesium in their food as they need.[48] Mild magnesium deficiency may be widespread, and a disastrous deficiency may not be uncommon among those suffering from heart attacks.

A consideration in connection with the possible existence of widespread magnesium deficiency is the fact that when flour and bread "enrichment" was instituted, it was made optional to add about three times as much calcium to the bread as is lost in milling the flour. Some bakers do this; some do not. But no provision was made for adding magnesium. For those who consume large quantities of calcium-enriched bread, this must create an imbalance with respect to these two elements. We have previously noted that when the calcium intake rises, the requirement for magnesium rises. The effect of the use of calcium-enriched bread would be to increase the need for magnesium while at the same time decreasing magnesium consumption.

The subject obviously needs further exploration, but it seems clear that magnesium deficiency is not only a possibility but a probability. There is evidence that women utilize magnesium more effectively than men, and this may be one reason for the lower incidence of heart disease in women (in addition to the protective effect of estrogen hormones in premenopausal females).[49]

No discussion of heart disease would be complete without mention of the question of saturated fats. It has come to be almost an orthodox position that if one wishes to protect oneself against heart disease, one should avoid eating saturated (animal) fats. While this idea may not be entirely in error, it is misleading in its emphasis. The evidence shows that high fat consumption, when accompanied by plenty of the essential nutrients which all cells need, does *not* cause atherosclerosis or heart disease.

Rats have been used extensively to study the effects of diet on atherosclerosis. Under *ordinary* dietary conditions the inclusion of saturated fats in their diet will consistently promote the deposition of cholesterol in their arteries.[50] For 285 days rats were fed a diet containing 61.6 percent animal fat, but highly superior with respect to protein, mineral, and vitamin content, without producing any pathological changes in the aorta or in the heart.[51] The animals did, to be sure, become obese, as much as three to four times their normal weight. Animals fed vegetable fats at the same level fared essentially no better and no worse. These findings were based upon extensive long-term experiments at Yale, using a total of 600 rats, which were observed for as long as two years. There were *no* findings suggestive that either high animal fat diets or high vegetable fat diets were conducive under these conditions to atherosclerosis.

These animals represented an extreme condition, since 81 percent of their energy came from fats. Their diets otherwise were extremely good. The protein was of high quality (casein) and was kept at a high level (20 percent); the vitamin levels were double those ordinarily used in this laboratory. The Yale findings were corroborated almost a decade later (1965) at Tufts University School of Medicine.[52]

That cardiovascular disease is not associated with high fat diets is also shown by a comparison study of matched groups of twenty-eight railwaymen from North India and twenty-eight from Southern India.[53] The consumption of fats, mostly of animal origin, was ten times higher among the North Indians than the South Indians, but there were no significant differences between their lipid and cholesterol levels. Among the South Indian population, the incidence of heart disease is said to be fifteen times as high as among the North Indians where the fat content of the diet is ten times higher. Dietary factors are doubtless very important in connection with the incidence of heart disease, but fat is only one factor, and other dietary factors are considerably more important.

This is also corroborated in a study of 400 Masai men in Tanganyika.[54] In spite of the fact that the diet of these men is almost exclusively milk and meat (consumption of whole blood is relatively rare), both of which contain much fat and plenty of cholesterol, the cholesterol levels in the blood of the Masai are extraordinarily low, and there was "no evidence of arteriosclerotic heart disease." It should be noted that a diet containing large quantities of milk and substantial quantities of meat is free from "naked calories," and is certain to supply an assortment of amino acids, minerals, and vitamins in liberal amounts. Though the

Masai have other health disorders—many of infective origin—they probably escape heart disease because their body cells are furnished with an environment that is adequate enough to protect their hearts and blood vessels.

A corollary of the notion that saturated fats are archvillains is the idea that one should eat substantial amounts of polyunsaturated fats. (The phrase "polyunsaturated fatty acids" has become virtually synonymous with "heart protection" in both popular and orthodox medical thinking.) While everyone should have unsaturated fats in his diet, their presence does not by any means afford adequate protection against atherosclerosis and heart disease. The current consumption of polyunsaturated fatty acids in the U.S.A. is higher than it has ever been, yet this does not curb heart disease.[55] There are many reasons on which to base our conclusion that other factors are far more important.[56] When other deficiencies are eliminated, the amount of unsaturated fat and the ratio of saturated to unsaturated fats is of secondary importance. If there is plenty of vitamin B_6 in the diet, fat metabolism tends to take care of itself.

I have said a good deal about vitamin B_6, but I do not mean to imply that it is, by itself, the answer to heart disease. All the nutrients contribute to the prevention of heart trouble.

Vitamin C is essential for the building of collagen, the most abundant protein built in our bodies and the major component of connective tissue.[57] This connective tissue has structural and supportive functions which are indispensable to heart tissues, to blood vessels,—in fact, to all tissues. Collagen is not only the most abundant protein in our bodies, it also occurs in larger amounts than all other proteins put together. It cannot be built without vitamin C. No heart or blood vessel or other organ could possibly perform its functions without collagen. No heart or blood vessel can be maintained in healthy condition without vitamin C.

Victims of prison camps who have suffered from vitamin C deficiency have been found to have widespread fatty deposits (atherosclerosis) in their arteries.[58] It is possible that vitamin C deficiency is directly implicated; it is unlikely that such deposits could have been due to too much fat or cholesterol in the diet.

Strong evidence has recently been presented that individual needs for vitamin C vary widely, and that some individuals have much higher needs than has hitherto been supposed.[59] While the functioning of vitamin C, except for its role in building collagen, is obscure, it is quite possible that many hearts and blood vessels would be better protected if an abundant environmental supply of this vitamin were available in the circulating fluids that bathe the tissue cells.[60]

Nothing we have said about specific deficiencies should obscure the fact that heart and circulatory diseases *may* have their roots in *any* nutritional deficiency. Though I will not give a detailed justification of this statement, I will mention that vitamin B_1 deficiency (beriberi)—if prolonged—seriously damages the heart.[61] No essential mineral, amino acid, or vitamin can safely be excluded from consideration in connection with heart disease.[62]

The heart and blood vessels are structures which require long range nutrition for continued maintenance. When one needs energy for an immediate task, a candy bar or a soft drink may provide the fuel to supply this energy. But nutrition for the long pull needs to be thought of in terms of the gradual building of healthy heart and blood vessels. Intravenous feeding of glucose may serve to keep a patient temporarily supplied with energy, but this kind of nutrition cannot keep the metabolic machinery of the heart and other internal organs in working order. To paraphrase a biblical saying, "man shall not live by fuel alone."

Animal experimentation has shown us convincingly that almost any energy-yielding food will serve to keep a healthy mammal alive for a few days or weeks. The animal's metabolic machinery is intact at the start, and its reserves of minerals, amino acids, and vitamins are such that it can function, after a fashion, even if the diet is badly deficient. If we prolong the feeding experiment month after month, we find that the food must be more and more complete if the animal is to survive. If the heart and blood vessels are to be kept healthy from youth to maturity, the diet must be a very good one. If the animal is to reproduce generation after generation, the food intake must be of the highest quality.

In our affluent society, where the fundamentals of nutrition are not stressed, our per capita sugar consumption is about twice what it was in 1900 when our society was more primitive.[63] Some individuals, of course, consume much more than even this high norm; they concentrate on short-range nutrition which includes few of the vitamins, minerals, and amino acids so vital in keeping heart and blood vessel tissues healthy. The consumption of naked calories not only does little for one's health, it tends to diminish the consumption of clothed calories available in other foods.

In England recently, evidence has been put forth by Yudkin and his coworkers that excess sugar consumption is statistically associated with atherosclerosis and heart attacks.[64] On the basis of their studies Yudkin states: "It would mean, for example, that a person assessed by our dietary history as taking more than 110 grams of sugar a day (4 ounces) was perhaps five or more times as likely to develop myocardial infarction as one taking less than 60 grams a day."[65]

Since Americans are estimated to consume about 140 grams of sugar per day (including syrups), one may not safely dismiss excess sugar consumption as a factor in heart disease. In another study, it was reported that on a statistical basis, sugar consumption was highly correlated with heart disease, and that coffee or tea consumption (in which sugar is often used) was *not* so correlated.[66]

Sugar seems to have deleterious effects in addition to its being a source of naked calories, in that its consumption appears to be statistically more conducive to atherosclerosis than is starch consumption.[67] At least partial explanation of this finding is to be found in the excellent work emanating from the University of Pennsylvania.[68]

Here it was found that fructose is highly distinctive metabolically as compared with glucose. Since starch yields glucose only and sugar yields fructose as well as glucose, it follows that starch and sugar are not nutritionally equivalent. Kuo and his coworkers found that the liver tissue of individuals with high blood-fat levels took up fructose five times as rapidly as individuals whose blood-fat levels were lower. Fat tissue from individuals with high blood-fat levels also took up fructose seven to eight times more rapidly than the fat tissues of individuals with low blood fat levels. This shows how biochemical individuality comes into the problem and gives us a lead as to how some individuals may be adversely affected by the fructose content of sucrose.

Is excessive salt consumption an adverse factor in heart disease? While many individuals are thought to consume far more salt than they need and feeding extra salt to animals may frequently cause higher levels of cholesterol in the blood[69]—I do not find much justification for the general use of so-called salt-free diets, in order to protect one's heart. If high blood pressure is also involved, however, the case against salt is stronger.[70] In my opinion everyone should be temperate in the use of salt; some may benefit greatly by consuming diets low in salt. This is a matter that needs to be decided for individual cases.

Can eating more frequently help reduce heart attacks? Probably. Heart attacks are often precipitated by the consumption of a heavy meal. When food is being digested, the blood is drawn to the gastrointestinal tract, and the heart, especially if its arteries are corroded, is liable to get shortchanged. There have been investigations that suggest that full meals should be replaced by more frequent consumption of less food and that this measure serves as a protection against heart attacks, and improves the functioning of appetite mechanisms.[71]

There are a number of other nutritional factors which may be involved in heart disease. In the Reference Notes we have added brief discussions of several of these.[72]

Body wisdom, which is cultivated from childhood, is

doubtless an important factor in helping people eat the kind of food they can tolerate. This, like so many other ideas connected with the nutritional prevention of heart disease, needs to be more thoroughly investigated. It may even be that the most important steps that need to be taken to prevent heart disease should be taken during the period from infancy to adulthood.

It is not my purpose here to discuss the entire subject of heart disease and its prevention. There are preventive measures other than nutritional ones that are important and effective. Conspicuous among these is getting suitable exercise and recreation, and the avoidance of tobacco, particularly cigarettes. Also there is the problem of avoiding or forestalling infections (rheumatic heart disease). While these matters need more exploration and better application, they go considerably beyond the scope of this book.

It is generally futile to make recommendations unless the individuals understand why the recommendations are valid. If an individual likes to eat candy (or smoke, or drink, or eat plenty of fat) he may have a tendency to shop around until he finds a physician who will at least mildly approve of what he likes to do. When there is no immediate crisis, people tend to follow their habitual patterns unless they are fully convinced that they should do otherwise. This is why it is crucially important for the public to be educated with respect to the needs of living cells for a continuously adequate environment. Nothing in nutrition can take the place of the intelligent interest of the person directly involved.

In order to provide long-range nutrition which will promote the healthy functioning of our hearts and blood vessels, we need continuously to watch the *quality* of our food. Good wholesome foods such as milk, eggs, cheese, meat, seafood, and vegetables are of high quality. Candy, starches, alcoholic beverages, soft drinks, and many processed foods—including those made from white flour—are of poor quality (in varying degrees) and should be used with caution. People may think that when they eat candy or drink an alcoholic beverage they will make up for it later by eating good wholesome food. It doesn't work out that way. It is as though we had within us a self-registering calorie tank; when we consume naked calories, the tank becomes occupied and leaves less room for well-clothed calories. A combination of poor foods can never fill the bill. This is one of the reasons why people who are concerned about the long-range nutrition of their hearts and blood vessels should restrict themselves in the consumption of all naked calories including bakery goods which are predominantly made from "enriched" white flour.

A partial way out of the difficulty, incidental to the poor quality of so many foods that are offered us, is to carry insurance by using nutritional supplements. This problem has already been discussed by the author in Chapters VIII and IX of *Nutrition in a Nutshell*.[73] The discussion will not be repeated here. I should emphasize, however, that no supplement offers complete nutrition, nor should a supplement be expected to do more than *add* to sensible eating. Amino acids, for example, are needed in too large amounts and are too expensive, on a practical basis, to be used in supplements. Therefore, good proteins must always be a part of the diet.

The makeup of nutritional supplements always needs to be scrutinized carefully. Many supplements, the names of which are almost household words, are compounded to be sold only to naive and undiscerning customers. One milligram per day of vitamin B_6, for example, is not enough for a supplement. Six milligrams of magnesium is used daily in one supplement; this is a ridiculously small amount, when a "normal" young man is supposed to need 400 milligrams per day. Another supplement on the market makes the magnificent daily contribution of 5 milligrams of potassium. This is about the amount present in one lima bean!

The need for continuing research in the matter of nutrition and heart disease is well illustrated by the problem of coenzyme Q. Very recent work reinforces the supposition that heart disease may be caused by the poor nutritional environment of the heart tissue. It has been found that coenzyme Q, a vital link in the metabolic machinery of living cells, is often deficient in the heart tissues of cardiac patients, while in the heart tissues of patients whose hearts are healthy (biopsy specimens), this deficiency does not exist. Coenzyme Q is not included in the nutritional chain of life because it is normally produced in our well-nourished tissues. However, under various conditions it may be produced in deficient amounts; in this case a nutritional supply may be effective. Coenzyme Q is essential to the life and health of the cells, and it is one of the things the cells in heart tissues cannot make in sufficient amounts unless the complete nutritional chain of life is supplied. The deficiency of coenzyme Q in heart tissues may be due to any one of a number of different nutritional deficiencies. Plainly, this is a matter that cries out for further investigation.

Personal experiences—singular and uncontrolled as they are—make for very weak medical evidence. But because it is relevant and suggestive, I cannot forbear from relating one of my own. For years I experienced angina distress (not pain, but numbness in the hand and arm and tightness in the chest—a feeling of being out of breath) when I exercised too vigorously or ate too heavy a meal. Such distress is due to the blood being drawn away from the heart, so that the pump itself is being deprived of oxygen and nourishment.

This condition started to develop because of advancing atherosclerosis. The blood vessels in my body which supply the heart and the other blood vessels, have tended to close down with age and to supply nourishment less effectively. In the summer of 1968 I began to lose the macular vision in my left eye. This may have been due to other precipitating factors like an infection —no eye doctor has been able to say with assurance— but advancing atherosclerosis was undoubtedly a contributing factor. At this time I began to be concerned; some infected teeth were removed in the fall of 1968, and I began to take seriously, with respect to its meaning in my own case, the material which coincidentally was being collected for this chapter. As a result, I began, early in 1969, doing some things for myself that

I had not done before. I took extra vitamin B_6 and folic acid, and increased my magnesium intake. (Previous to this I had for several years taken a good general nutritional supplement as well as extra amounts of vitamin E and vitamin C.)

Several improvements in my condition appeared to follow on the heels of these nutritional innovations; some were entirely unexpected, and none of them were specifically looked for. Some improvements could only be judged subjectively; others could be judged more objectively.

First, I gradually began to be able to walk farther and faster without shortness of breath. I have always walked for exercise, and earlier I would often be glad when a traffic light would turn red so that I could rest a little and recover from mild symptoms. This need for rest disappeared, and I became able to walk rather briskly—faster than most pedestrians. I felt that there had been definite improvement when, after several weeks, I could progressively walk without discomfort at a much faster pace over a particular path nearly two miles in length.

I did not notice a second improvement until two or three months after my walking capacity began to improve. I found that I did not need to watch my meals quite as carefully as before. Earlier I had often hesitated to go out to a restaurant because I knew I could eat only about a half or a third of what was set before me without suffering angina distress shortly afterward. This has gradually but markedly changed so that now I can eat a regular meal without distress.

A third improvement came quite unexpectedly. I noticed that I became tolerant and comfortable in cool rooms and that I used much less bed covering on cool nights than I had needed previously. This was due, presumably, to improved circulation.

The fourth improvement was observed when I began watching and testing carefully the condition of my right eye. My hope was that it would not suffer the fate of my left eye. As a result of almost daily testing, I found that the vision in my right eye actually improved so that in a couple of months after starting the nutritional innovations, under the same conditions, I could read about two lines farther down on the opthamologist's testing chart than before.

Subjectively, my health and mental vigor also seemed to improve; my golf handicap dropped two strokes, and at the end of the 1968–1969 school year, I still felt full of pep and did not have the dragged-out feeling that I had often experienced in previous years. This carried through the following year and I have been able to do what is, for me, a prodigious amount of work.

I fully realize that I have performed no scientifically controlled experiments on myself, and that I cannot offer scientific *proof* as to my exact condition, nor exactly what brought the observed improvements. I can say, however, that I am highly pleased with the results and that most probably my atherosclerosis has markedly improved in spite of the fact that angina distress is often an unreliable symptom to follow. None of this, incidentally, bears on the cholesterol problem. I have paid little attention to the cholesterol level in my blood because it has never been high.

This personal digression is not important in itself. What is important is the weight of evidence that impelled me to take the steps I did. On the basis of this evidence it seems highly probable that millions of hearts *can* be protected when serious attempts are made to give the body cells, including those in the heart and blood vessels, a fully adequate microenvironment. My personal actions may not have justified the evidence, but I think the evidence justified my actions.

6 The Fight Against Obesity

Public knowledge of why people become obese is now about at the kindergarten stage; it has not kept pace with the rapid spread of the valid doctrine that obesity is a health hazard to be avoided.

The public has been effectively indoctrinated, for example, with the simple but misleading idea that "eating fat makes you fat." People sometimes try to avoid eating fat as though it were poison, not realizing that fats often have protective food elements in them, while carbohydrates not only lack these elements but, at the same time, are extremely effective fattening agents. The secret of avoiding obesity does not, however, lie in the avoidance of either fat or carbohydrate, but in providing oneself with the full nutritional chain of life.

It is seldom appreciated that obesity must result essentially from a disordered appestat mechanism. The cells in the midbrain that constitute the appestat mechanism are like other cells in our bodies—they have definite functions, and if they are provided with a good environment, the chances are excellent that they will do a good job. Of course, if there is something inherently and unalterably wrong with the particular mechanism —its detailed microstructure, for example—then it may not be possible to furnish an environment good enough to correct the failure.

If we do our utmost by contriving in every possible way to provide these cells and tissues with a good environment—including fully adequate nutrition—we have perhaps done for them all that can be done. Until we do this we should not think of giving up.

We need to concentrate on the health of the appestat mechanisms instead of calorie counting and the sheer exercise of willpower. Fighting obesity without nature's help—without an adequate appestat mechanism—is like traveling up a swift-flowing river in a rowboat. Nature's way of preventing obesity needs to be understood and utilized. It has worked for billions of people (and animals) and always involves a healthy appestat mechanism. If this mechanism is disordered, consumption of fat and carbohydrates can indeed make one fat. Under such circumstances even protein consumption can do so.

In the war against obesity our objective has been foggy. We should not concentrate on the question, Why does "normal man" become obese? Instead, we should be seeking the answers to the questions, Why do vulnerable individuals tend toward obesity? and, What can be done to overcome this vulnerability?

If we knew the full answer to these questions, we could immediately bring relief to millions. In the meantime, anyone who claims he knows the full answer is deluding himself. We are certain that obesity cannot be described, as it often is, in terms of "over-nutrition." From the standpoint of *quantity,* the nutrition is *over* what it should be; from the standpoint of *quality,* the nutrition is *under* what is necessary to give the appestat cells a good environment.

Everyone, even those who tend to be obese, has an appestat, or control, mechanism which tells him to eat when his tissues need nourishment, and to stop eating when the requirements are satisfied. In human beings, and indeed in all animals, this mechanism is indispensable, and operates not only day by day but week by week and month by month. If mechanisms were not present to impel them to eat, animals, in the presence of food, would die of starvation. If mechanisms were not in operation to tell them when to stop eating, they would gorge themselves whenever they could.

The fact that such inherited mechanisms exist does not mean that they are rigid in their operation—that we are trapped in a situation beyond our control or that psychological factors are without influence. We can eat when our bodies are not crying out for food, or we can desist from eating when our bodies need nourishment. We can go on hunger strikes if we wish. Anxiety or excitement may temporarily take away our desire for food, or a relaxed atmosphere may stimulate this desire. The mechanism we possess, however, "remembers" what the food intake has been and is able to keep track of the state of nourishment of our tissues so as to insure that over a period of time we get about the right amount of food to keep us going.

The mechanism that governs food consumption is similar in principle and operation to the inherited mechanism that controls the breathing process. If there were no bodily mechanism to impel us to breathe, we would all die of suffocation. This does not mean that we lack voluntary control. We can hold our breath for a time if we choose, or we can breathe deeply and rapidly when our bodies do not demand it. Also, psychological influences may intervene: a beautiful sunset or a sudden surprise can "take our breath away," or emotional excitement may cause us to breathe heavily. But day by day, when we are preoccupied, and night by night, when we are asleep, the automatic breathing mechanism insures us against a pile-up of carbon dioxide and a lack of oxygen. We need not worry about the possibility of forgetting to breathe.

The mechanism that controls our overall food consumption can be a most marvelous and precise one.

There are some adults who depend solely on this mechanism. They do not "count their calories" or bother to weigh themselves periodically. Yet in the course of twenty years, their weight may stay at the same level, plus or minus a few pounds. Such an individual may easily consume during this twenty-year period 25,000 pounds of moist food. If he gained or lost five pounds during this time, it would mean that the amount of food assimilated matched the amount burned up, with an error of about 1/50 of one percent. If the mechanism were to make a one percent error consistently during this time, this would mean a gain (or loss) of about 250 pounds!

The mechanism for the control of total food consumption in relation to the total food burned up is universal. All animals use it to govern their long-range food consumption, and it functions surprisingly accurately, even in those individuals who have a mild weight problem. Even if such an individual were to "let himself go," the mechanism would usually not permit a weight gain, over a period of ten years, of as much as 100 pounds. Such an impaired mechanism would be "off" by less than one percent. Even those individuals who have trouble holding down their weight have working mechanisms. If they had no brakes at all, they might easily die of overeating the first time they went into a restaurant with a pocketful of money. There are many people in our affluent society who could afford to have five-course meals three times a day, or five times a day, or even all day. The reason this doesn't happen is that people in general possess internal braking mechanisms which effectively shut off the desire for food and do not permit continual engorgement.

Medical records show that there have been individuals afflicted with bulimia who have very ineffective brakes for the control of their eating. For example, a ten-year-old boy in England consumed enormous amounts of food (373 pounds during one week) for periods of months.[1] In this case, as well as in a number of similar ones, the body has a second line of defense—vomiting. The boy had an insatiable hunger, but he vomited most of what he ate. It is worth noting that those who have defective brake mechanisms in their appestats may also have other impairments in their brains; they are often mentally defective.[2] Medical records concerning individuals whose starting mechanism is very weak (anorexia) are relatively common. Such individuals may have almost no appetite for food —in fact, they may have an aversion to it—and go for weeks in a highly emaciated condition with hardly anything to eat.[3]

Another activity we often take for granted as "just happening" is that of the consumption of water. This too is under the control of a mechanism similar to that which controls the consumption of food.[4] When we exercise and perspire, we become thirsty; and if our control mechanism is working properly, we drink enough water to bring our dehydrated tissues back to normal. It can, if need be, even awaken us at night with a sense of thirst.

Defective water consumption mechanisms are by no means unknown. So-called polydipsia cases exist in which people may drink twenty-four to thirty-two quarts of water each day and pass correspondingly large amounts of urine. This water consumption mechanism may also be faulty in the opposite direction, in which case the individual has little or no sensation of thirst (hydroadipsia), and is only with difficulty induced to drink any water at all.[5]

Where are food consumption mechanisms located? It is not possible to delineate or describe succinctly the structures that are involved. They are primarily, but not solely, in the hypothalamic region. This is situated in the basal part of the diencephalon (or interbrain) and is close to the third ventricle (cavity) of the brain.[6] There are several clusters (nuclei) of cells in this region which are included in the hypothalamus. Experimental damage in the region of the cluster of cells designated as the ventromedian (front-middle) nuclei, results in increased food intake in cats, dogs, rats, mice, and monkeys.[7] All of these animals become obese as a result of this damage.

Under these experimental conditions, increased food intake and rapid weight gain are not maintained indefinitely. A plateau is reached, food intake tends to level off, and the experimental animal tends to maintain itself at a higher weight.[8] If the animal is fasted for a time, so that its weight is brought back to the non-obese level, it will, when allowed free access to food, build its weight back up to the obese level.[9]

Experimental damage to another area on the side of the hypothalamus has the opposite effect: the experimental animal loses its desire for food and will starve.[10] Thus two areas of the hypothalamus are involved in the control of food consumption. One area (lateral) contains an inciting mechanism which induces food consumption; the other (median) area contains a braking mechanism which stops food consumption when the body has enough. Injury to the median area causes the animal to eat too little. The functioning of these two areas has been further confirmed by installing tiny electrodes in them and mildly stimulating them electrically.[11]

The appestat is a double-acting mechanism located in the midbrain. In a healthy person there is an accurate balance between the two, so that while one cluster of cells induces the individual to eat, the other shuts off the eating. On a week-to-week and month-to-month basis *if* the appestat has been performing correctly, a person's intake of food will be exactly what it should be.

Animal experiments throw light on the problem of obesity. Rats and other animals can be made to become obese by surgically injuring the ventromedian cluster of cells in their appestat mechanisms. Such animals have been studied by many investigators with the general finding that such animals have lost many of their internal controls.[12]

Surprisingly, such obese rats will not make the same effort to get food as nonobese animals.[13] This was tested in several ways, including putting them into especially designed harnesses and registering their pull in the direction of food. The result seem unequivocal.

Furthermore, when barriers were put in their way (in effect, electric fences which shocked them) the obese animals were stopped by low voltages, whereas the nonobese animals were not. When the food was doctored with a little quinine to make it taste bitter, the obese animals tended to shun it more than did the healthy nonobese rats.[14] When the food was diluted with tasteless inert cellulose (25 to 50 percent) which decreased its calorie value proportionately, the nonobese healthy rats ate more, so that they would get about the right number of calories to meet their needs. The obese animals, which seemed to have lost their calorie sense, ate about the same amount of the diluted food as they did the undiluted.[15] This, of course, inadequately nourished them. The loss of internal control mechanisms was enough to change the animals natural time sense. Rats are nocturnal by nature—they do most of their eating at night. As a result of the lost time sense, they would eat about the same day and night. Most interesting of all, the obese animals revealed a lack of internal control by tending to eat on and on once they got started. Nonobese rats, on the other hand, characteristically eat a little, then leave the food until the appestat mechanism impels them to come back later for more.

It is apparent that obese animals do not lose *all* their internal controls, because they do not gorge themselves to death. After they become obese, they level off and tend to eat enough to keep them at about the same obese weight.

Evidently obese people similarly lose their internal controls. In obese people, as in the nonobese, hunger contractions of the stomach take place; but strangely the obese people do not feel hunger at that time.[16] In nonobese individuals, hunger is experienced when the glucose level of the blood is low but in obese individuals, this mechanism appears not to operate.[17] It has been found by ingenious experiments that obese individuals who had partaken of a full meal ate more crackers than a similar group that had empty stomachs.[18] This indicates a lack of internal control and a weakness of the internal braking mechanism—a tendency to eat on and on regardless of the fullness of the stomach. It was also found that fear—which usually raises the blood-glucose level and takes one's appetite away—did not operate this way in obese individuals.[19] They actually ate a little more when they were subjected to fear. It seems clear that while obese individuals do not fail to eat, they tend to eat for different reasons than do nonobese individuals.[20]

As in the case of the obese rats, obese human individuals are highly responsive to external stimuli, such as the taste of food,[21] but are unresponsive to internal stimuli.[22] They have lost their internal calorie sense, and if the food is unattractive, they eat less than they need.[23] They also lack a good braking mechanism to tell them when to stop eating.

Since the eating behavior of obese human individuals exhibits striking parallels with the eating behavior of rats whose appestat mechanisms have been injured surgically, it follows that the appestat mechanisms in obese humans are probably out of order.

How do control mechanisms get out of order? It remains to be proven that proneness toward obesity may be due to an impaired appestat mechanism induced by poor prenatal nutrition. Certainly it is a possibility, and another reason for paying more attention to prenatal nutrition.

We need, however, to face—in a matter-of-fact manner—the reasonableness of the idea that some individuals are born with appestat mechanisms that are more effective than others. We do not flinch at the idea that each of us is born male or female, or that some of us have blue eyes and some brown, that some are likely to be tall and some not so tall. We even accept the fact that some of us are born to be better looking than others. There is no good reason why we should flinch at another obvious truth: Some individuals are prone to be more plump than others. Some individuals may be born with many more adipose tissue cells than others.[24]

This is not to say that they *must* be far more plump

than others. Proneness is only a *leaning* or an *inclination* which can often be changed. The brain structures of different human beings are by no means identical. In fact, the numbers of different kinds of cells vary greatly from individual to individual,[25] and the reason that some individuals are prone to be more plump than others may be due to the fact that some appestat mechanisms are built more effectively than others. This does not mean, however, that a person whose innate appestat mechanism is not of the highest quality cannot—through care and training—learn to control the situation.

Human beings are extremely adept at contriving to circumvent what may be regarded as hereditary limitations. We not only have some success in trivial matters like the changing of the color of eyes and hair, but we regularly correct hereditary vision defects by the use of eyeglasses or contact lenses. We humans cannot see ultraviolet light as insects can, but we have other ways of detecting its presence, and we know a great deal about how to use it. We do not have the keen sense of hearing of dogs, so we invent telephones and, as a result, can hear each other talk around the world. We are not endowed by nature with wings, so we build wings and invent jet engines to propel them. Because we are born without much hair on our bodies to keep us warm, this does not mean that we must sit and shiver helplessly when the cold wind blows. There is no reason whatsoever to assume that an obese-prone individual is beyond help. When we know just what his problem is, surely we can find a way to circumvent it. This is not likely to happen, however, until we learn to cope with the environmental factors that influence the operation of individual appestat mechanisms.

Most of use are born with appestat mechanisms that are, or can be made, entirely serviceable. When they are not serviceable, something may have intervened to make them faulty. Lack of exercise has a crippling effect on appestat mechanisms. When rats, which otherwise have no tendency to become obese, are kept in a warm room in a very small cage where they can move very little, they invariably become obese.[26] They may eventually weigh two or three times as much as rats that are allowed to exercise by having larger cages. If the animals are kept in very small cages in a *cool* room, they get enough exercise by wiggling and shivering to prevent extreme obesity. These experiments are in line with long-recognized practical experience. When it is considered desirable to fatten geese, cattle, or hogs for butchering, it is a common practice to confine them and not allow them to exercise.

"Get plenty of exercise" is therefore good advice to give those who want to prevent obesity. This advice probably needs to be followed from an early age. Some individuals have an internal drive which constantly tells them: "Do something; don't just stand there!" On the other hand, there are other individuals who have an internal urge to "stand there" or, better still, "lie down."

In our studies on individuality in experimental animals, we have demonstrated that tendencies to exercise are inborn—or at least are present—at weaning time. Young rats of the same strain, when given a chance to use an exercise wheel, varied greatly from rat to rat in their use of such a device. Among a group of nineteen healthy rats of the same age, we found one that recorded almost no travel—an average of only 158 feet a day; while at the other extreme, one traveled on an average of nearly six miles per day. The other seventeen individual rats recorded traveling intermediate distance, scattered between the two extremes.[27]

If there is an "activity control center" (presumably in the brain where so many other control centers are located), it obviously functions quite differently in individual animals, but little is known about it.

The question arises whether a child who is predisposed to be inactive can, by training, develop a mechanism that will cause him to exercise more, and whether parents can help inactive children to become more active. We shall discuss shortly the role of nutrition in helping to alleviate inactivity.

Why is exercise so important for health? We do know that we are built to strive physically for food and other necessities, and that to get these necessities without any striving is not in accord with our biological background. It is probable that improved circulation, which is induced by exercise, is an important factor in promoting well being. It is also probable that exercise promotes an improvement in the quality of our blood. Valuable hormonal substances may be released as a result of exercise, and these substances may contribute to an improved cellular environment for the appestat and other mechanisms.

In any event, the fact remains, as Yudkin has pointed out, that "The appestat only works well with at least a moderate amount of physical activity."[28] What might be adequate exercise for one individual might be inadequate for another.

One of the ways of damaging a tissue is to poison it, and many people are finding new evidence that they have been unwittingly poisoning their appestats by cigarette smoking. It appears that people who have had no tendency toward obesity may find that they tend to gain weight when they stop smoking. It is possible that continued smoking over the years has mildly poisoned the whole balanced mechanism. Gold thioglucose selectively poisons the braking mechanism when it is administered to animals,[29] and when it is withdrawn, the braking mechanism is impaired. If this is the case with nicotine, the best bet such individuals have for preventing the obesity which follows giving up smoking is to watch carefully the *quality* of the food that they eat over long periods of time and to avoid empty or naked calories as much as possible. As we will explain later, it is probable that eating good food, over a period of time, can repair the damaged mechanism.

Bland diets may be helpful in combating obesity. There is evidence that the eating habits of obese individuals are often controlled not by the status of their internal body chemistry but by external factors such as attractiveness of the food. It follows, therefore, that one of the prime possibilities both in the treatment of obesity and in its prevention is the use of bland and uninteresting foods. On this basis, not only should obese or potentially obese individuals avoid gourmet eating, they should avoid being stimulated by the sight and smell of tasty food. It seems very likely that anyone who wishes to reduce badly enough can do so by following this expedient, especially if, at the same time, he consumes well-rounded diets relatively free from naked calories.

Of course this is not an easy prescription to follow. Some people would regard the cure as worse than the disease. For a substantial percentage of people, eating is one of the prime pleasures in life.[30] Such people may feel that to avoid pleasurable foods is far too great a price to pay for the avoidance of obesity. If one has and retains this attitude, it may work against his health, but preachments do little good.

Frequent consumption of small amounts of food may help prevent obesity. This expedient may be important. We have heard obese people boast that they eat only one meal a day. If so, this may be the very worst regimen for them to follow. Five or more snacks a day might be vastly better. Experiments with rats, which are by nature nibblers, have shown conclusively that if they are forced to abandon their nibbling behavior by being given access to food only two hours per day (one meal a day), they became obese.[31] In one experiment after ten weeks of such treatment, they weighed 30 percent more than rats that were allowed to nibble.[32]

Somewhat similar results have also been obtained with chickens,[33] dogs,[34] sheep,[35] and monkeys,[36] so it appears to be a general biological phenomenon. The satiety (braking) mechanism in the appestat appears to be impaired by engorgement with food, and the effect is prolonged beyond the time when the engorgement takes place.[37]

In order to investigate the effects of nibbling and gorging in humans, five subjects were studied over a period of a few weeks at the Ohio State University Health Center.[38] As might be expected, there were some substantial inconsistencies. However, gorging increased the cholesterol and phospholipid levels in the blood consistently, and nibbling had the opposite effect. In four cases, the gorging appeared to be accompanied by some gain in weight and the nibbling by loss in weight. It seems probable that the experiment was not of long enough duration to show clear-cut effects on body weight. In the experiments with rats, the gains in weight (averages) due to having one meal a day did not begin to show up for about four weeks. The contrasts were very strong after eight or ten weeks. Since the time scale for humans is about thirty times that for rats, results with human beings, comparable with those obtained with rats, should not be expected in less than a few years.

The results obtained up to now indicate clearly that obese individuals should eat light meals frequently and not try to limit food consumption by eating only one meal a day.

The "quick weight loss" diet described by I. M. Stillman[39] has a reasonable scientific basis, and I know from my own observations that it can be successful in at least some cases. This diet excludes nearly all carbohydrates and fats, and the individual limits himself essentially to lean meats, poultry, fish, seafood, eggs, cottage cheese, fat-free broths, and low-calorie (artificially sweetened) gelatin desserts. *Plenty of water* (eight or more glasses per day) should be consumed over and above other liquids such as coffee, tea, or soft drinks (provided they are free from carbohydrate), and a good mineral-vitamin supplement should be taken daily.

The protein-rich foods listed above are sources for many nutrients other than the amino acids. In our laboratories we have assayed many "proteins" and protein foods and found all of them to contain substantial assortments of B vitamins. Since many of the foods mentioned above are derived from living tissues, they also contain some of all the minerals needed by cells. What one is consuming on this diet is essentially the nonfuel components of good food. Since these nonfuel ingredients are not diluted with fuel in the form of carbohydrate and fat, the body cells and tissues—including those in the appestat of the brain—get a much better supply of amino acids, minerals, and vitamins than usual. This is especially true if the supplement—minerals and vitamins—is a good one. Under these conditions the dieter may be feeding his brain cells better than they have ever been fed before.

No restrictions are placed on how much of the various foods should be eaten in this diet. The dieter merely avoids deliberately stuffing himself or herself on any occasion, but eats temperately as much as he or she wants.

This "quick weight loss" diet is not recommended for continuous use over long periods of time, but only when one wishes to lose about ten to fifteen pounds in a period of a few weeks. For those who have a continuous obesity problem, the diet would probably have to be modified to include minimal amounts of carbohydrate and fat.

The prevention of the development of obesity is the principal goal toward which our discussion is pointed. Assuming that proneness to obesity may become evident in early childhood, is it possible that means can be instituted that will prevent obesity from developing? I believe there are. One of the most important expedients is making sure that the growing child gets the right food; no deficiencies should be allowed to perpetuate themselves. Feeding a child who is prone to become obese may require expert attention comparable to that which is needed for phenylketonuria babies. Certainly the use of naked calories—particularly sugar—should be discouraged. We have already noted that nutritional deficiency leads to "sugar hunger" and that a vicious cycle is thus established. Poor nutrition fosters worse nutrition.

We have already seen evidence that the nutrition of babies and young children is crucially important for brain development. Since the appestat is a part of the brain, it seems reasonable to assume that it, too, needs adequate nutrition throughout life. Is this a reasonable assumption? The fact that children sometimes outgrow obese tendencies (or that sometimes obesity develops later in life) suggests that nutritional factors may be at work. It also suggests that if these are properly directed, children who tend to be obese can grow up without being plagued by this difficulty. But there is also more direct evidence.

Anyone who is acquainted with the history of the discovery of vitamins knows that furnishing an animal with a low level of vitamin B_1 causes the appetite mechanism to be deranged. As a result, animals will cease to eat. Evidently, the cells in the appestat mechanism that incite an animal to eat are highly susceptible to a lack of this particular vitamin. The effect is striking. If the animal is force fed, it will live, but its desire to eat will be gone, and it will die without the force feeding. Most dramatic, however, is the effect of giving such an animal a good supply of vitamin B_1: The animal bounces back immediately with its appetite restored.

When animals are injured experimentally in the lateral portion of the hypothalamus (where the inciting mechanism is located), they lose all appetite for food and will die of starvation unless exceptional measures are taken. That nature can often repair these injured tissues is indicated by the fact that when such animals are fed, by a stomach tube, a good nutritious liquid diet made from eggs, milk, and supplementary vitamins for about two weeks, they began to show signs of recovery and will drink a little milk.[40] The duration of feeding necessary to induce recovery of their appetite mechanisms varies—in one group from six to sixty-five days. Presumably this variation is due, in part, to the fact that the damage done by the operation is not always uniform. But the point to note here is that all the experimental animals eventually recovered their appetites. Sixty-five days for a rat, incidentally, would be equivalent to about five years on the human scale.

If the inciting mechanism recovers from damage by good feeding, it seems reasonable to suppose that injury to the braking mechanism could also be overcome by similar measures. This, so far as we know, has never been tried—but it should be.

Experimenters at Harvard have found that obese mice could be made to stop eating by making them deficient in vitamin B_1, while vitamin A deficiency greatly enhanced the effect of surgical injury (lateral) to the hypothalamus and made the animals eat even more than otherwise.[41] There can be no doubt, I believe, that nutritional factors greatly influence the operation of the appestat mechanism.

Altogether, the situation seems rather hopeful. It seems highly probable that individual children who are prone to obesity can be prevented from becoming so by the use of high quality, well-balanced nutrition, tailored in some cases to individual needs. It also seems probable that if inactive children can be trained to become more active, they will eat better and their appestat mechanisms will be improved.

Do hormones have anything to do with obesity? Since hormones are numerous and have many regulatory functions in our bodies, it seems obvious to assume some connection. But while there is suggestive evidence that pituitary hormones, the thyroid hormones, adrenocortical hormones, pancreatic hormones, and sex hormones are implicated in obesity, the evidence is not clearcut.[42]

Insulin administration, which lowers the blood glucose level, has been shown to induce hunger and food consumption.[43] Glucagon, another pancreatic hormone, is antagonistic to insulin and in many experiments has been found to abolish hunger contractions and hunger sensations immediately.[44] Such observations are striking enough to show that hormones may be involved in obesity, but the present status of our knowledge about hormones and particularly about the individuals who may need hormone administration, is such that no practical recommendations or suggestions can be made. Bona fide discoveries may yet be made in the future. It is entirely possible that hormones not yet recognized are involved and that they enter into the complete environment of the cells in the appetite center.

Do emotions have any relation to obesity? The answer to this question is yes. We human beings are not built in compartments. Our bodily processes affect our minds and emotions, and, contrarily, our mental and emotional processes affect our bodies. When we harbor anxiety, fear, or hostility, there is little question that these emotions—probably by hormonal mechanisms —alter the microenvironment of the cells which make up our appestat mechanisms. It has often been suggested that individuals overeat and become obese because they are bored, unloved, insecure, or under tension. While these are doubtless some of the factors involved in individual cases, the practical means of avoiding such feelings is far from obvious. The psychiatric approach to the problem of obesity has not been crowned with conspicuous success.[45]

Should one use weight-reducing drugs? My approach to the prevention of obesity would certainly exclude the administration of most drugs to young people. By drugs, I mean substances foreign to our bodies, in contrast to nondrug items such as minerals, amino acids, vitamins, and hormones.

Drugs, if they are effective, must interfere with or influence enzymic reactions on our bodies. Even if they do this and confer temporary or local benefit, their continued use is liable to cause trouble elsewhere in the body. In general, such drugs are unsafe for continued use, and since there are so many other potential ways of bringing about the prevention of obesity, I would give drugs a very low priority.[46] I suspect that the majority of physicians feel the same way, for weight-reducing drugs are seldom prescribed on any but a temporary basis.

Why is calorie counting often ineffective? One reason is that it cannot be accurate enough. If someone were consistently to count all the calories he consumed, but missed his count by leaving out the equivalent of three peanuts each day, his mistake could theoretically result in a gain of eighty-eight pounds in twenty years. The idea that "a piece of pie" or "a slice of bread" or "a hamburger" contains a specific number of calories and that these figures can be used to calculate one's calorie consumption is ridiculous.

If the amounts we eat could be planned by calculation, disregarding our inner urges, it would be easy to gain or lose weight at will. To lose at the rate of two pounds a month (twenty-four pounds a year) it would merely be necessary to eat *exactly* as before and take an additional short walk every day. Such a scheme will not work because our inner urges change with the exercise and we have no way of eating *exactly* as before. Alternatively, in order to lose two pounds a month, one could eat exactly as before except for the elimination of the equivalent of fourteen peanuts a day. This will not work either, and for the same reason. The elimination of the equivalent of fourteen peanuts a day would immediately be "noticed" by the appestat mechanism, and the desire to eat would accordingly be stepped up to compensate for the missing peanuts.

Weight watching can be confusing. People who watch their weight carefully are often bewildered by the erratic pattern that shows up on the scales. Sometimes, when they abstain, the scale shows an imperceptible loss or even a slight gain. On the other hand, when they eat carelessly, their weight may go up very little, or it may even go down.

The major reason for such discrepancies is the variation in the water content of the body. When a 150-pound man steps onto the scales to weigh himself, he is weighing, on the average, about 93 pounds of water, along with 57 pounds of water-free material—proteins, fats, and minerals. The next time he weighs himself, the proteins, fats and minerals may weigh exactly the same, but the water may weigh 100 pounds. He now weighs 157 pounds and has gained weight.

The water content of individual human bodies varies from 45.6 percent up to 70.2 percent. Men's bodies are, on the average, about 10 percent higher in water content than those of women.[47] A human body weighing 150 pounds may contain as much as 81 pounds of solids: proteins, fats, minerals, etc. Or it may, at the other extreme, contain only 45 pounds of the same water-free material.

People who tend toward obesity probably tend toward unstable control of the water content of their bodies. Thirst mechanisms are often impaired when the appetite mechanisms are awry. In individuals whose water-control mechanisms are imperfect, it is difficult to say just what is being weighed when they step on the scales.

Although we know many things about obesity, there are many things we do not know. As L. V. Kinsell has pointed out, there are internal, organic factors "as yet by no means well understood, which on occasion will enable two individuals of approximately the same size and age, having 'normal metabolic rates' and indulging in about the same amount of daily activity, to move in different directions in regard to weight even though their food consumption is identical."[48]

Such differences among individuals should probably be reflected in differences in the levels of the various enzymes that catalyze biochemical transformations. But we do not know for sure. Little attention has been directed toward the problem of obesity from this angle, largely because of inadequate appreciation of the role that heredity may play.[49] Wide differences in the enzyme levels of "normal' individuals have, however, been observed.[50]

This biochemical individuality, which seems to involve the ready laying down of fat by some and not by others, can be seen in farm animals. Individual steers in the same pasture or feed lot do not become uniformly fat, even when they are bred to be uniform (which humans are not). The same thing holds true when obesity experiments are carried out with laboratory animals.

Finally, there remains the question of what our attitude ought to be towards obesity itself. There is some truth to the statement, "Obesity is a disease if we make a disease out of it." This is not to deny that obesity is a complicating factor in many other diseases,[51] or that it should be avoided when possible; but I agree with Hilde Bruch, the Columbia psychiatrist, who said: "I have come to the conclusion that it is basically wrong and leads to a biased misinterpretation of the whole problem to start with the a priori assumption that overweight is invariably harmful and an unmitigated evil, without any positive value for the carrier. . . . Despite the handicap which overweight implies, there are people who function better when they are heavy."[52] Bruch adds, "One great difficulty that interferes with a more meaningful and rational approach to the whole obesity problem is the current cultural attitude which condemns mild degrees of overweight as ugly signs of greedy self-indulgence."

If people generally were aware that every individual has distinctive features in his metabolism—in other words, everyone has a heredity—we could look with more tolerance on those who have a configuration different from our own. The fight to be "normal"—in which so many are engaged—is in itself a disease which can be eradicated only by education and acquaintance with the facts of inborn individuality as they exist in the entire human race. Differentness should not be stigmatized; we all exhibit it in one way or another and should be very glad that we do.

Nevertheless, extreme obesity can be a harmful condition, and I have tried to set forth in this chapter the best means available at present to prevent its occurrence. The findings all point in one direction: The appetite mechanism must be provided with the best environmental brakes possible—that means continuous good nutrition and care, as well as beneficial exercise.

I should be less than honest if I were to make a positive guarantee that following certain suggestions would eliminate or prevent obesity. I shall say, however, that the probability is high that superior nutrition, including plain wholesome high protein foods and excluding naked and semi-nude calories, consumed at frequent intervals, will prevent children from becoming obese and help bring about adjustment in appestats that are already slightly awry. I wish I could say this has been tried in 100 cases and that the results have been favorable in a high percentage of them. The truth is that so far as I know, this regimen has not been tried in any bona fide experiment. It is my opinion that this measure, including the use of nutrient supplements for insurance, affords the best chance of getting at the root of the trouble. When the trouble is really corrected, the individual concerned will automatically eat—within narrow limits of error—the right amount of food because his appestat is healthy and functioning well. This is, and always has been, nature's way of preventing obesity.

7 Prevention of Dental Disease

Vast sums of money could be saved and colossal miseries could be avoided if we approached the goal of dental health on two legs instead of one. We seem to go all out for oral hygiene, the *external* environment of the teeth, while we neglect the *internal* environment—the nourishment of the cells and tissues which form, support, and maintain the teeth.

Teeth are an integral part of our bodies. They are built by living cells, and are affected by living cells throughout their existence. There are no living cells in the outermost layer—the enamel—or in the dentin which constitutes the bulk of the tooth; but a small percentage of organic matter is nevertheless present. Calcium and phosphate ions, among other things, move to and from the teeth through minute channels in this organic material.

Bones are, in a sense, more alive than teeth, because in bones the living cells intermingle with the mineral deposits, and bones can mend themselves when they are broken. Teeth cannot. But this does not mean that the living cells in the pulp of the tooth and in the periodontal membrane, which is between the root of the tooth and the bone of the jaw, are inert, or that teeth are mere chunks of mineral, discrete from the living tissue surrounding. The nonliving parts of the teeth are in contact with living cells. These cells need an adequate environment so that they, in turn, can give the teeth the maintenance they need.

In the early stages of development, when the teeth are growing in size, the role of living cells in furnishing raw materials and in actually building the teeth is an obvious one. But living cells also play an essential role during the maturation of the enamel and the accumulation of the different layers of dentin. The latter is a complicated process which certainly does not take place automatically; it involves the functioning of living cells. According to some authorities,[1] healthy resistant teeth can, if incipient decay starts, throw up a wall of hardened dentin (sclerosis) which protects against further advance of the decay. It seems clear, therefore, that living cells play an essential role during the entire life of the teeth.

That teeth are not inert mineral deposits is also made obvious by the fact that if the body does not get enough calcium, the bones and the teeth are called upon to release some of their supply. When the body once again gets enough, the calcium borrowed from the bones and teeth can be restored. During pregnancy there is often a drain on the mineral reserves of the body. It was found by investigators in Norway that during the later months of pregnancy, women often need more calcium than they normally consume and a deficit tends to build up.[2] This fact is reflected in the old adage, "A tooth for every child," which refers to the observation that women who bear children are liable to lose teeth as a consequence. This observation has never been confirmed in statistical human studies. Animal experiments, however, which can be carefully controlled, indicate that the old adage probably has a substantial basis.

When the teeth of female rats of comparable age have been compared and analyzed, it was found that those that had borne no litters had teeth that were a little harder and had higher ash, calcium, and phosphate content.[3] The teeth of rats that had borne one and two litters were progressively softer and had lower mineral content. All the animals had consumed the same food.

Women do not have to lose teeth as they bear children. If the internal environment of women's teeth is maintained by complete nutrition of the associated living cells—this nutrition, of course, includes enough calcium, phosphate, and vitamin D—the bones and teeth will not become depleted during pregnancy.

A kindergarten approach is to say, "Calcium and phosphorus are needed for tooth building." Of course they are; teeth have large amounts of calcium and phosphate in them, but the kindergarten approach is not enough. Absolutely essential to the building of teeth are the living cells and tissues that support the teeth both physically and nutritionally. These living cells cannot do an adequate job unless they are sustained in healthy condition by an ample supply of all the amino acids, minerals, and vitamins that every living cell needs. If these cells and tissues get an inadequate supply of any one or more of the nutrients they need, they build and sustain teeth as best they can; but the resulting teeth may be of poor quality, comparable to the ears of corn that result when the corn has been planted in stony ground with no fertilizer and little water.

Iron, copper, tryptophan, pantothenic acid, and dozens of other nutritional elements are needed for tooth building, not because they are conspicuous constituents of teeth, but because they are *absolute necessities* for the living cells that do the building.

The formation of teeth begins very early in the life history of each individual. Even the permanent teeth which are to replace the baby teeth in later years begin their existence five months before a child is born. The cells responsible for tooth production during these early stages need complete nutrition, not only at that time, but for many years to follow.

That prenatal and early nutrition are essential for building strong teeth has been demonstrated in experimental trials. Rats of differing ancestry have been found, in many experiments, to produce young with healthy, decay-resistant teeth when their diets are good.[4] When prospective mothers are given diets that are inferior, however, the infant rats grow up to have teeth that are subject to decay.[5]

Similar conclusions regarding the development of bones and teeth have been drawn from careful, extended human studies involving very young infants and their mothers. In one study, "protein" nutrition was emphasized.[6] This, in reality, means more than the word protein implies, because the proteins that are used for food are always associated with a considerable assortment of B vitamins.

It should be appreciated in interpreting the experiments we are presently citing that completely ideal nutrition is never realized, and that we are not able at this stage of our knowledge to evaluate with exactness the diet of any given person. Despite this, protein nutrition alone can be evaluated with fair precision, and the mothers involved in these observations were rated as having either excellent protein nutrition or poor protein nutrition.

The mothers who had excellent protein nutrition produced babies 57 percent of whom had excellent bone development and 14 percent "retarded" bone development. The rest were about average. The mothers who had poor protein nutrition, on the other hand, produced *no* babies with excellent bone development; 71 percent had retarded bone development.

By taking X-ray pictures of the jaws of the same newborn babies, it was found that if the mothers had received what was regarded as excellent protein diets, 37 percent of the infants had excellent tooth development; in 47 percent, the development was about average; and in 16 percent, the tooth development was retarded. In contrast, the mothers who had poor protein nutrition delivered babies *none* of whom had excellent tooth development; 29 percent were about average; and 71 percent showed retarded tooth development.

The nutritional situation remains critical all through the period of tooth development and maturation. It has been well established in animal experiments that tooth resistance to decay (this is most commonly studied) depends on the diets the young animals are fed. It is possible to feed groups of young animals in such a way that most of their teeth will be sound and free from decay. On the other hand, they can be fed diets which cause a high prevalence of decay. Since such diets may affect the external environment of the teeth (this has received more than its share of attention) as well as the internal environment, experiments of this sort cannot be interpreted with the same certainty as those involving prenatal nutrition where the external environmental influences are ruled out, because the teeth have not yet erupted. The conclusion in the case of prenatal nutrition is clear: Teeth will be of good quality if the nutrition is fully adequate for the individual mother.

The nutritional status of an individual may change from week to week or month to month depending on the season and how wisely one eats. In a study of 942 school children in New York City, it was found that teeth erupting at about the same time tended to be of similar quality with respect to their resistance to decay.[7] It appears that during periods when the children were relatively well nourished, they produced resistant teeth, but when they were poorly nourished, the teeth eruptions at this time were poor.

Under prevailing conditions, the nutritional status of women tends to deteriorate as they give birth to more children. In line with this observation is the finding that there is a tendency for first-born children to have better teeth than siblings born later.[8] This deterioration is unnecessary. Well-rounded nutrition should keep mothers in such condition that they can continue to produce babies with excellent tooth development.

Underlying all these considerations is the fact that because of hereditary factors each individual has a biochemical individuality, and the quality of the teeth that he or she produces depends on the hereditary background as well as the environment encountered. Some tooth enamels are much harder and thicker than others; some dentins are far less destructible than others.

The effect of hereditary background on dental decay was discovered early in studies involving experimental animals. "Norway" rats fed the prevailing diets were initially found to be resistant to tooth decay, and there was a tendency to shift to the use of other animals. Cotton rats fed similar diets produced teeth that were far more susceptible to decay.[9] Slowly it became evident that not only is diet an important factor, but the resistance of teeth to decay varies greatly from strain to strain, from animal to animal, even when they are fed the same diet.

Several investigators have developed resistant and susceptible strains of Norway rats.[10] In one case, the eleventh generation of susceptible rats showed dental decay, on the average, in twenty-eight days, while in the resistant group, eating the same food and handled in the same way, decay did not appear, on the average, until 240 days.

In this study of Norway rats, although all the rats were consuming a diet that had been found to promote tooth decay, there were wide strain differences. One strain was most resistant, one was most susceptible, and the third was intermediate between the two. In two extreme groups there were, on the average four times as many cavities per rat as in the other. The three inbred strains of rats used in these experiments had not been bred to be different in their inherited tooth resistance, but they nevertheless turned out to be so.

One of the more careful and thorough studies involving Norway rats included 401 animals. In one group of ninety-one animals, the number of cavities averaged seventeen per animal after seventy-seven days on a particular diet. Yet there was one animal in this group that had no sign of a cavity. It becomes evident that each animal (and each human being) even though treated and fed the same, has its own inborn tendencies.[11]

According to the genetotrophic principle, proneness to possess teeth that are susceptible to decay can be overcome by furnishing the teeth with nutrition of the highest quality. Even if a developing human being has a tendency to have poor teeth when ordinary diets are used, this tendency can be overcome by furnishing nutrition that is better suited to the individual's peculiar needs.

To illustrate, some individuals need approximately five times as much calcium as others.[12] A woman may be getting less calcium than she needs, and for this reason her developing child may be producing teeth that are susceptible to decay. If she were given extra calcium (above average needs), the teeth might be strong and resistant. It should not be forgotten that *every* nutrient is necessary for tooth building.

There are two obvious things that can be done about poor teeth: Practice good oral hygiene and see a dentist regularly.

Less obvious to most people is the desirability of long-range nutrition of the best quality. Plenty of calcium and phosphate and ample vitamin D are clearly needed for maintenance. But other nutrients must also be furnished. There is strong evidence that vitamin B_6 needs to be thought of in this connection.[13] In one experiment, dental decay was decreased 40 percent in a group of children when they were given 3 milligrams of vitamin B_6 daily.[14] Fluoride is present in tooth enamel, and is a trace element needed for the production of good teeth.[15] Providing fluoride in the water supply is one method of taking care of this need.

On the negative side, the use of sugar should be restricted. In experimental animals and humans alike it is a commonplace that sugar consumption, particularly in solid form, promotes tooth decay.[16] It affects adversely both the external and internal environment of the teeth.

Periodontal disease is a real tooth killer. While tooth decay is an affliction to be avoided, dentists find it necessary to extract teeth largely because the living tissues around the teeth are diseased (peri = around). Records of treatment of beneficiaries of the U.S. Public Health Service reveal that more teeth are extracted for this reason than for any other. After the age of forty-five, eight out of ten teeth extracted are taken out because of diseased tissues around the teeth.[17]

It is well known that the gums are affected by poor nutrition. One of the classical symptoms of scurvy (lack of vitamin C) is soft, bleeding gums. As we have indicated, vitamin C is essential for the building of collagen, the substance that acts throughout our bodies as a framework, and holds the cellular structures in place.

It cannot be too strongly emphasized that all living cells associated in any way with the teeth, those in the gums, in the pulp of the teeth, in the periodontal membrane which lies between the teeth and the bone of the jaw, and those in the salivary glands, all require *complete* nutrition. If all these cells are kept well and functioning, the teeth have maximum protection.

Those who dwell exclusively on such subjects as oral hygiene, dentifrices, efficient toothbrushes, etc., in connection with protecting the teeth, are attempting to make progress by traveling on one leg instead of two. This approach is exemplified by the mother who furnishes her youngster with the most advanced toothpaste, and sees to it that he uses an electric toothbrush to keep his teeth clean, then turns around and more than cancels out all her good efforts by allowing him to substitute a Coke for milk at lunch. While she takes care of the external environment, she neglects the internal microenvironment of the crucial living cells. It is worth remembering that animals on excellent diets can maintain sound teeth without any brushing.

Everything that contributes to the health of teeth can be obtained from good wholesome foods: eggs, milk, cheese, meat, seafood, fruit, and vegetables. These foods are far more likely to furnish what is needed than standard bakery goods and processed foods, to say nothing of sugar.

Thus, by attending to the external environment of our teeth through sensible programs of oral hygiene, and to the internal environment through high-quality nutrition, we can expect to have healthy, long-lasting teeth. But if we attend to the external environment alone, we can expect trouble.

8 The Nutritional Approach to Arthritis and Related Disorders

Even though attempts to treat arthritis and related troubles by nutritional means have so far been limited and inexpert, the results have been exceptionally promising.

These are very difficult diseases to treat and in no area of medicine is there more of a tendency to treat symptoms and neglect underlying causes. Aspirin is used extensively and over long periods of time. It helps relieve the pain, but does nothing about what may cause the pain. If better "pain relievers" could be found, they would probably be adopted with enthusiasm.

Injuries, infections, allergic reactions, and psychological stresses may all play a part in the cause of arthritic disease, but the most probable underlying cause —poor nutritional environment for the cells and tissues involved—has, as usual, been neglected.

To illustrate how public thinking has become per-
meated with the idea that nutrition can be taken for
granted (and not even worth thinking about if one has
an arthritic or related disease), a *Consumer Reports*
bulletin (1970), supposedly written by informed experts, dismissed the whole subject of vitamin pills with
an airy "healthy people who eat balanced diets don't
need them."

This statement is both literally true and misleading
at the same time. If most people were healthy, there
should be no general concern about vitamins or nutrition. Babies would not be born deformed or retarded;
people would show no sign of atherosclerosis, nor
would they die prematurely of heart disease; there
would be no trouble about obesity; people would have
perfect teeth, and no one would age prematurely;
people would be free from stiff and disabled joints, and
there would be no mild or severe mental disease; people
would not become addicted to alcohol, tobacco, or
drugs. Anyone who implies that this is a description of
the real world is simply wasting our time.

I take it for granted that people who are perfectly
healthy in all respects and have a good prospect of
maintaining their good health consume balanced diets.
It happens, however, that among many hundreds of
friends and acquaintances, I can hardly think of any
who might remotely qualify as being "perfectly
healthy." I know of very few people who should be
unconcerned about the quality of their food.

Earlier in this book, speaking of the onset of disease,
I proposed the motto "If in doubt, try nutrition first." I
think this motto is apt in connection with the problem
of arthritic diseases, where there are oceans of doubt,
but few physicians would endorse it. Most of them
seem quite content to accept the Food and Drug Administration's almost meaningless assertion that "vitamins and minerals are supplied in abundant amounts
by commonly available foods."

Many of the difficulties associated with arthritic diseases stem from what in popular terms we may call
poor lubrication. Our joints and all other movable

structures in our bodies must be lubricated, and the lubricant used commonly is called "synovial fluid." Although the form of this fluid differs somewhat, depending on whether it is found in joint cavities, tendon sheaths, or in bursae (sac-like cavities between muscles, etc.), all forms seem to have properties in common, regardless of location. Synovial fluid is viscous, mostly a dilute water solution of various mineral salts, but containing about one percent of mucinous protein (mucoprotein) that gives it lubricating properties. It is closely related to interstitial fluid and to lymph, which together may make up 15 percent or more of the body weight.

We cannot effectively drink synovial fluid or its equivalent to improve lubrication. The water in the fluid, of course, comes from the water we drink, and the minerals are supplied by our food. But the effective mucoprotein, like other body proteins, must be produced in our bodies by living cells (in the synovial membranes) from raw materials furnished by food. If any mineral, amino acid, or vitamin is in deficient supply, or if the cells are poisoned by bacterial toxins or allergens, this can partially incapacitate the cells, and can lead to poor lubrication, with every movement accompanied by friction and pain.

Of the medical investigations that bear upon the problem of maintaining a healthy environment for the synovial and related cells, the most ambitious was made by a New England physician, William Kaufman, who made extensive use of the single nutrient niacinamide.[1]

Kaufman started out measuring the flexibility of each of twenty joints in 455 of his patients of all ages, regardless of whether or not they compained of arthritic pain. From these measurements he derived a composite "joint range index" for each individual at the time of the measurement.

Almost all individuals—young or old—exhibited some evidence, on Kaufman's criteria, of joint dysfunction. For youngsters, the composite index was often as high as 90 to 96 (100 highest possible); for the elderly (over sixty years old) the indices were often in the 60s.

Extremely arthritic individuals might have indices below 50—in two cases 31.5 and 32.6.

Many of these patients (for reasons best known to Dr. Kaufman) were induced to take, over a period of time, massive doses of niacinamide—400 milligrams to 2250 milligrams per twenty-four hours. The amount prescribed was adjusted to the severity of the case. The results were, on the average, remarkably beneficial. The average index rose for every age group, and for those over fifty, the indices rose on an average of about 12 percent within two months. The severely affected individuals improved their indices by 31 percent and 19.2 percent in the same time.

These results can best be interpreted to mean that the cellular structures involved in the impaired joints were often limited with respect to their niacinamide supply (something that all cells need) and that massive doses somehow get beneficial amounts of this one nutritional element to these cells. Such a result should not generate complete scientific surprise, any more than would the finding that the yield of a field of corn is improved when given more potash. It is interesting and understandable that the niacinamide did not bestow uniform benefit. Neither did it bring complete alleviation: the average range indices remained below eighty-five for all those over forty-five years of age.

Criticisms can be leveled at Kaufman's work; in fact, he mentions some limitations himself. Those who emphasize psychological factors will be inclined to discount his conclusions because he did not give some patients blanks (placebos). Some people show a marked improvement simply because they are receiving medication and attention, even when the "medication" is in dummy form. Furthermore, Dr. Kaufman's results— especially those involving relatively small improvement —may be questioned because his measurements were not purely mechanical and probably not completely free from personal bias. Yet the whole report is an honest attempt to arrive at the facts, and it seems clear (unless one wishes to assert that the grossest self-deception occurred) that great benefit was obtained by many of his patients. Dr. Kaufman's work has received scant attention, but he undeniably hit upon one nutritional measure that appears both to prevent and alleviate joint stiffness.

Another of the B vitamins that may be important in preventing arthritis is pantothenic acid. As the result of a study carried out in London, it is reported that the levels of pantothenic acid in the blood of arthritic patients was consistently lower than that of a control group, and that the severity of the rheumatoid arthritis was related to these levels.[2] The average level of pantothenic acid for the arthritis patients was about 65 percent of that of well individuals. Those whose levels were about 400 percent were severely crippled, and in two cases bedridden.

Treatment with pantothenic acid consistently brought relief after seven days, but improvement did not continue. The investigators concluded that some other essential factors were involved and that pantothenic acid was not a complete answer. This is precisely the kind of result that might be expected on the basis of the nutritional concepts we have been presenting. The whole nutritional chain of life is needed by cells with a deficient environment. What would have happened if the patients in London had also received an abundance of niacinamide and other essentials? We do not know. But regardless of what else the ailing cells may need, it appears likely that pantothenic acid is one of the nutritional elements that is often in short supply.

Arthritic patients often have anemia.[3] Experiments with folic acid showed that its administration improved this blood situation in all twenty cases of rheumatoid arthritis on which it was tried. Folic acid failed, however, to bring direct relief to the arthritic condition itself.[4] Presumably folic acid is only a partial answer. In another report, riboflavin was found to be lower than normal in blood plasma in 61 percent of rheumatoid arthritis patients.[5] This suggests that riboflavin may be a nutritional weak link in a substantial number of cases. It should be emphasized again that if any link is weak, lubricant-producing functions as well as others may be impaired. In still another study it was found that vitamin A was below normal levels in the blood of fifty-two out of fifty-eight rheumatoid arthritis patients.[6] This strongly suggests another weak link. Vitamin A's functions are incompletely known, but it is not at all impossible that its lack may cause arthritic conditions.

Other findings suggest the possibility that vitamin B_6 may also be a weak link in the chain. In more than one study[7] tryptophan metabolism has been found faulty in arthritic patients. We have previously noted that xanthurenic acid excretion results from faulty tryptophan metabolism, and that vitamin B_6 is effective in remedying this condition.

More direct evidence of the value of vitamin B_6 in correcting some arthritic and similar conditions comes from Mt. Pleasant in northeast Texas where John M. Ellis has been treating patients with this vitamin for about eight years.[8] He finds it to be particularly effective in relieving the pain, stiffness, and "locking" of finger joints, and also to be an effective agent for abolishing parasthesia (numbness), nocturnal paralysis of the arm, nocturnal muscle cramps, and pain in the shoulders, hips, and knees. The dosage he uses is 50 milligrams per day, and in his community of 14,000 inhabitants, he says five pharmacies have sold 100,000 such doses a month for three years. No undesirable side effects have been observed—only benefits.

From the scientific standpoint, such observations from physicians who do not have the time or facilities to do refined investigations must be accepted with caution. There were no control patients who received placebos to see if, under the prescribed conditions, blanks would not also confer benefit. Presumably some patients would, as usual, have appeared to have been benefited by placebos; but this does not rule out the probability that vitamin B_6 confers real benefit for the conditions Ellis describes. He does not claim that rheumatoid arthritis was cured by vitamin B_6. In making this statement Dr. Ellis is exercising caution because he knows the bad effects of extravagant claims. According to his interpretation, patients with rheumatoid arthritis might be benefited in their finger joints, but that the carpal joints of the hand and wrist did not receive benefit. Bursitis caused by injury was not benefited, according to his cautious observations.

Yet it seems very likely indeed that vitamin B_6 is another nutritional link that is probably weak in many sufferers from arthritis and kindred ailments. From our discussion up to this point, it would seem that a prudent individual who has trouble with arthritis would be sure that he has provided his internal environment plenty of niacinamide, pantothenic acid, riboflavin, vitamin A, and vitamin B_6. Why not?

Since enlargement of bones near joints and mineral deposits in cartilage are associated with arthritic disease, it seems likely that mineral imbalances may be involved as well. In this case mineral nutrition may be a key factor.

This is a field that will necessarily be difficult to explore because of the facts of biochemical individuality. Several years ago, in the author's laboratory, repeated samples of blood, urine, and saliva were collected under basal conditions from each of nine healthy young men eating their customary food. These samples were analyzed for the following mineral elements: sodium, potassium, calcium, magnesium, and phosphate.[9] These young men had average sodium levels that differed from each other by about 6 percent; their calcium and phosphate levels differed by about 30 percent; and the magnesium level in one was 208 percent higher than in another. Since the blood plasma is relatively stabilized in composition, it becomes evident that there are substantial differences in the handling of specific minerals by different healthy individuals.

It has been found that the calcium needs of "normal" young men vary about five-fold,[10] and that a careful study of the bone densities (with respect to the passage of X rays) of over 10,000 people revealed enormous differences. Far from being a uniform product, the bones of young men vary in density from one individual to another over a 5.7-fold range. This density was measured by determining the ability of a given thickness of bone to stop X rays—largely a function of the amount of apatite (a calcium phosphate mineral) present.[11] From these facts and those cited above, it is clear that the human factor in arthritis must be exceedingly important, and that proper mineral balances must often be considered on an individual basis.

The lubricating quality of synovial fluid is certain to be greatly influenced by the minerals that are in it, and it is quite conceivable that in some individuals the arthritic condition may be largely due to an inappropriate mineral balance.

The nodes or knots which often form near arthritic joints sometimes contain cholesterol deposits, and individual arthritics often have severe atherosclerosis in the aorta.[12] These findings suggest that in attempts to prevent arthritis, the same measures should be used as those which help prevent atherosclerosis. One of these is the avoidance of magnesium deficiency. Studies on the relation of magnesium deficiency to mineral balances in experimental animals make this seem reasonable.[13] In view of the likelihood of magnesium deficiency in the general population, we must regard this as potentially important.

Stiffness can be induced in the joints of guinea pigs by feeding them certain diets. Just what is wrong with these diets is not clear, nor have the nutritional factors responsible for the trouble been identified.[14] It has been shown, however, that when guinea pig diets are supplemented generously with egg yolk (which is rich in many nutritional factors), they are protected from allergically-induced arthritis.[15] Both these observations emphasize the desirability of approaching the problem of arthritis from the nutritional standpoint. Arthritis is a disease in which cellular environments probably play a leading role.

Gout is an arthritis-like disease which is characterized by deposits of uric acid salts in and near the joints. This, among other things, impairs lubrication. Gout has long been thought of as resulting from "high living," particularly intemperate eating. Biochemical individuality enters here also, and makes some individuals peculiarly susceptible (gouty diathesis). In a study in my laboratory, one individual in a group of eleven healthy young men showed, upon repeated tests, uric acid levels in his blood 26 percent higher than the average of his fellows, and 50 percent higher than one of them.[16] The mere presence of high uric acid in the blood is not enough to cause gout; its salts must be precipitated in and around the joints, and this does not always happen in individuals who have a high content of uric acid in the blood.

One of the time-honored measures to be taken in the case of gout is to avoid consuming food that contains substantial amounts of nucleic acids (sweetbreads for example), because nucleic acids give rise to uric acid in the body. Nucleic acids and uric acid, like cholesterol, are produced in the body (endogenously), however, and their avoidance in food may not effectively prevent uric acid piling up in the blood or its salts from being precipitated to settle in the joints.

The same measures that may be used to prevent arthritis may also be used to prevent gout. Gout is closely related to arthritis, and in some cases arthritic deposits are suggestive of gout. There is nothing which prevents people from having both gout and arthritis at the same time.

Back pain may have its origin in arthritis, but this condition, for which vitamin C appears to be very effective, may be only distantly related. Whatever it is, a pain in the back or neck is something to be avoided, and the usefulness of vitamin C in this connection was discovered by a Houston neurosurgeon. James Greenwood found that high doses (about one gram per day) were beneficial to himself when he was disabled by back pain. He began trying it on large numbers of patients and found that most of them gained substantial relief.[17] Since vitamin C can be purchased without a prescription and is harmless, Dr. Greenwood's remedy would seem to be worth trying.

It is possible that the benefit of vitamin C in this case is connected with its indispensability for the production of collagen, which is so important for all body structures and is essential to maintain the structure of intervertebral disks. We have already referred to the studies that showed that some guinea pigs require much higher levels of vitamin C than has been commonly supposed.[18] Some individuals are also evidently benefited by large amounts—far above what has been thought of as "normal" human requirements.[19] When relatively large amounts of this harmless nutrient are taken by mouth, the cells that produce collagen are able to appropriate it and are helped to do a better job.

While medical education has put a damper on experiments in which the nutrition of arthritics might have been studied and manipulated in an expert fashion, there is excellent reason for thinking that if this were done, sufferers could get real rather than palliative relief. There is even a good possibility that individual arthritics will be able—if they are lucky and make intelligent trials—to hit upon particular nutrients or nutrient combinations which will bring benefit.

I certainly would not want to give the impression that the management of these diseases is simple. But I do reaffirm the dictum that nutrition should be tried first. On the basis of reports presently available, the items that certainly need to be considered are niacin, pantothenic acid, riboflavin, vitamin A, vitamin B_6, vitamin C, magnesium, calcium, phosphate, and other minerals. The objective is to feed *adequately* the cells that are involved in producing synovial fluid and in keeping the bones, joints, and muscles in healthy condition.

In an earlier chapter I resorted to the device of personal anecdote in connection with the heart problem. With all the proper caveats, I should like to do so again, with respect to arthritis. This is something more than self-indulgence and less than science. I hope only that it will be interesting.

About two years ago, during a period of nearly a month, I was afflicted with cramps in my legs at night. These were often extremely painful, and I would have to get up and hobble around until the pain eased.

My doctor was on a temporary vacation at the time,

so I began looking up the subject myself, and came to the tentative conclusion that calcium deficiency probably had something to do with my trouble. Accordingly, I began dosing myself with precipitated chalk (calcium carbonate) at the rate of about 2 grams per day. Immediately after the first dose, the cramps disappeared and did not return.

About this time my doctor returned and made a blood analysis. The results showed that my calcium level was "normal," which was not surprising since I had been dosing myself with calcium carbonate. The report also stated that my phosphate level was "normal." I was suspicious of this and asked to see the laboratory report. This showed the phosphate level in my blood to be within what was thought of as the "normal" range, but at the very lowest level of normality.

At this time my nightly leg cramps had completely disappeared, but my legs did not feel entirely at ease or comfortable at night, for there was a dull, persistent discomfort. When I saw how low the phosphate level of my blood was, I substituted calcium hydrogen phosphate for the calcium carbonate, and immediately my leg discomfort disappeared. Since that time I have no trouble at all. I continue to take calcium hydrogen phosphate, but only when needed.

Soon after this, I noted a card-playing friend of mine having difficulty in shuffling. In fact his hands had become so uncertain in their operation—cramped and painful—that he had to ask someone else to shuffle for him. I volunteered (which I rarely do) by suggesting that he try some calcium hydrogen phosphate for *his* condition. I thought there was a chance that his condition might respond as mine did. As luck would have it, when he took a few tablets, his trouble disappeared completely. He purchased a supply of the tablets and takes them periodically as needed, and has had no recurrence.

To some, this may seem a trifling incident; and in a sense, it is. Yet when one remembers that suicides have resulted from very similar afflictions, the situation looms rather larger. Incidents apart, the conquest of arthritis and related diseases remains a major goal of medicine. And until a more promising alternative appears, I shall continue to invoke the motto, "When in doubt, try nutrition first."

9 How Can We Delay Old Age?

Some individuals don't seem to lose their youthful faculties despite their advanced years: Titian, the Italian painter, did work of high quality nearly up to the time of his death at ninety-nine; Roscoe Pound wrote a five volume work on American jurisprudence *after* he was eighty-six; Alonzo Stagg still used a hand-operated lawn mower when he was ninety-eight; Thomas Parr ("Old Parr") was able to thresh grain at 130, and when his body was autopsied at his death at 152, his internal organs were found to be in excellent condition. His tomb may be seen in the Poets Corner in Westminster Abbey.

Why do most of us fall so far short? Why can't all of us retain our faculties until ripe old age?

Hereditary factors are doubtless involved, but there is more to the story than that. According to the genetotrophic concept, an individual's heredity may be a serious stumbling block to his continued good health and longevity because his inborn nature requires unusual environmental conditions that are difficult to meet. The most important of these environmental demands are the nutritional needs of his body cells and tissues. If these are unusual, he may be barred from longevity, *provided* he lives and eats very much like his neighbors. If, however, by using unusual expedients he can get a suitable assortment of everything his bodily cells need, he may be able to retain a measure of youth until old age, even though initially he may have been handicapped by heredity.

Incidentally, I am making, in connection with this discussion, the important assumption that it is a *good* thing for every baby brought into the world to be given a chance to live his or her full life span. We are increasingly made aware of the existence of a population problem which must somehow be solved. If, along with appropriate sanitation and medical care, everyone in the world had room to live, good food to eat, water to drink, and air to breathe, the population could easily double every twenty years. If such conditions continued to prevail, the world population in 200 years would be over 1000 times what it is now. Every hamlet of 100 people would be a city of 100,000; every town of 1000 would be a city of 1 million; every city of 100,000 would be a megalopolis of 100 million; Tokyo, New York, and London would each have populations several times that of the entire present world population.

In past centuries infant mortality, infectious diseases, poor nutrition, etc., were successful in imposing limits on the quantity of human beings allowed to populate the surface of the earth. In the measure that these limitations are scientifically removed, we are forced to discover and explore humane methods to keep the population within manageable proportions.

If society elects to adopt a laissez-faire attitude toward this problem, life will eventually become so intolerable that people will not want to bring babies into the world; they will fight among each other for food and places to live, and population, pestilence, poor nutrition, and starvation will be among the inhumane ways by which population is controlled.

An extended discussion of the population problem would be out of place here. It is interesting to note, however, that the author of *The Geography of Hunger,* Josue de Castro, thinks that hunger, particularly protein deficiency, is an important factor in creating the problem of overpopulation.[1] In support of this thesis he cites several observations; for example, "Cattle raisers have long known that animals that get too fat may become sterile, and that reduced rations will reestablish fertility." He cites the following table (from unspecified sources) which indicates that there is an inverse relationship between birth rates and the amount of animal proteins consumed.

	Birth Rate	Daily Consumption of Animal Proteins (in grams)
Formosa	45.6	4.7
Malay States	39.7	7.5
India	33.0	8.7
Japan	27.0	9.7
Yugoslavia	25.9	11.2
Greece	23.5	15.2
Italy	23.4	15.2
Bulgaria	22.2	16.8
Germany	20.0	37.3
Ireland	19.1	46.7
Denmark	18.3	59.1
Australia	18.0	59.9
United States	17.9	61.4
Sweden	15.0	62.6

Furthermore, de Castro cites extensive experiments of J. R. Slonaker of Stanford University who, for several years beginning in 1925, fed rats diets containing several levels of protein intake, and made extensive observations with respect to them.[2] Among other observations, he found that with higher levels of protein intake the number of young produced was somewhat decreased. Slonaker's experiments cannot be accepted as conclusive evidence, however, because his basal diets were not good enough by modern standards to permit the animals to grow rapidly, and it may be suspected that his observations applied to his particular diets and therefore may not be applicable to other diets of varying protein content.

There seems, however, to be an interesting principle involved which should be further explored. Nature does take measures to prevent the extinction of a species, and when extinction is threatened—by starvation for example—it may be that an exaggerated sex urge is one of the devices used to perpetuate the race. It may be that this contributes to the high birth rate among people who are ill fed. A parallel is found in the area of plant physiology where it has been observed that plants often grow vegetatively as long as well fertilized, and tend to go to seed (reproduce) only when conditions become adverse.

The contrary possibility that a decrease in human birth rates could automatically be brought about by the provision of certain nutritional factors is at least worthy of study.

Yet while the population problem must be faced, for the time being we will limit ourselves to the assumption that babies already in the world should be treated humanely and that every living person may harbor a legitimate wish to live a long and useful life.

There are many ways in which people can age, and under the prevailing conditions each of us tends to have a unique pattern of aging. Among the early signs of old age are partial loss of the sense of balance, partial loss of hearing, partial loss of vision or of accommodation, decreased muscular strength, decreased joint flexibility, loss of endurance, loss of pigment in the hair, loss of hair (baldness), loss of teeth, loss of a clear complexion, decreased sensitivity in the skin, and decreased libido. An individual may be relatively free from certain of these symptoms of old age, while in other respects, his aging may be conspicuous.

In all these cases, cells and tissues in the body have become impaired. It seems probable that many of these impairments are due, at least in substantial degree, to poor blood supply. Blood supply can be poor in two different ways: it may be low in quantity because the blood vessels that carry it are ineffective, or it may be poor in quality because of the inadequacy of what we eat.

By greatly improved prenatal nutrition, it is probable that later generations could have much better balanced circulatory systems. There is little doubt that by paying more attention to continuous good nutrition (and using blood vessel surgery when necessary) that the impairment of specific cells and tissues in aging individuals can be greatly lessened. As individuals we are not tied inexorably to a particular pattern of aging.

On general biological grounds, it seems inevitable that longer life will be a direct consequence of better environment. Every kind of organism has to have an environment that is suitable for it; otherwise, it cannot live. The more suitable the environment is, the better the organism will fare. The cells in our body are no exception; they too will function longer (and our health will be maintained longer) if these cells are provided an environment, nutritional and otherwise, that is more suitable to their needs.

Obviously, anyone who aspires to a long life should begin by providing his cells and tissues with the whole chain of life and not an abbreviated or mutilated substitute. This will help him to avoid arteriosclerosis and many other degenerative diseases[3] and will provide his body with better ammunition to fight off foreign organisms.

Beyond this there is the possibility that the natural—and presumably inevitable—aging process can be slowed down. It seems probable that those who live up to 100 or beyond do so largely because they have unusually well-balanced circulatory systems, and their nutritional needs are met without any particular conscious effort. In other words, they flourish because their cells are provided environments suitable to their particular needs. The majority of people on the other hand may have special demands for certain nutrients, and these demands may not easily be met.

Science has not yet solved the problem of aging and

we cannot be certain just what happens or why it appears to be an inevitable process. But we may nevertheless make some speculations on the basis of the evidence we have. First, there is the finding that crosslinked molecules of various types are characteristically found in "old" tissues.[4] Large protein molecules lying close together for long periods become, in effect, "sewn" together. This chemical sewing together causes the structures involved to become rigid and lose elasticity. Also, the process may decrease the ability of certain protein molecules to act as catalysts (enzymes).

The presence of reactive "free radicals" in tissues can be detected by electron spin resonance (ESR) measurements, and are thought to contribute to the aging process by causing cross linking and other cumulative disturbances which clog the metabolic machinery.[5] Some of these free radicals are formed by the interaction of oxygen with polyunsaturated lipids, and result in the production of semistable peroxides which can be damaging to proteins.

These observations have prompted the speculation that when cells get old, errors may creep into the mechanism of protein construction.[6] Protein construction (protein synthesis) takes place continuously during our entire lifetime. The structure of proteins is coded in the DNAs (desoxyribonucleic acids), and the information is carried by messenger RNAs (ribonucleic acids), to the building sites. Possibly, as a result of aging, this mechanism may become imperfect. The messenger RNA may become slightly defective and lead to the production of proteins that are slightly altered—not quite as effective as they should be. The result is that as time goes by, the body eventually may reach a point when repair is so imperfect that vital functions are affected.

Correlated with this idea of cumulative errors in protein building are the observations that mild irradiation (with X rays, for example) of animals causes their life span to be decreased in about the same proportion to the amount of radiation used, and that radiation also causes chromosome aberrations (which can be observed in regenerating liver cells) in a parallel fashion. Mutations are in a sense reproductive errors, and the mutagenic effects of X-ray radiation have long been recognized. Since every organism is subjected to some radiation (traces of radioactivity and cosmic rays are ubiquitous and always have been), this may be regarded as one possible cause of aging.

Aging, as I have said, is inevitable, and all we can hope to do is delay the process by taking advantage of the understanding of the mechanisms involved. Providing cells and tissues with the best possible nutritional environment would seem to be an obvious expedient. Evidence about the relationship between nutrition and aging is scanty, but it is nonetheless suggestive. Here are some of the potentially more important findings.

C. M. McCay and his coworkers at Cornell demonstrated many years ago that by underfeeding rats—giving them less food than they normally would eat—their life spans were about 33 percent *longer* than when they were fed all they wanted.[7] This long-but-hungry-life solution to the longevity problem would not have a great appeal to people, and it may not even be applicable; but a lesson may be learned from it, namely that it is healthy to be hungry part of the time. It is probably true that striving for food is biologically advantageous.

Extending life by underfeeding might not work out as well for human beings as it did for McCay's rats because of differences in physiology of growth and development. When rats are underfed, they grow and mature more slowly, and their prolongation of life is an accompaniment of this delayed development. Rats under all conditions tend to grow during a much larger part of their life span; in fact it has been said that some growth takes place as long as they live. With human beings, underfeeding with good food might result in a delay of maturity (perhaps it would be necessary to raise the voting age to thirty). The social practicality of increasing life span in human beings by underfeeding seems dubious.

Another interesting observation regarding aging is the fact that every species tends to have its own characteristic life span. Among insects the life span may be greatly altered depending on the character of the nutritional environment provided the developing larvae. If a bee larva (female) is fed in a routine manner, an infertile worker bee is produced. It has a life span of a few weeks during the summer, but may live longer (through the winter) when its metabolism and body temperature is low. If exactly the same kind of bee larva is fed extraordinarily well (with a mixture called royal jelly) there results a queen bee which is not only fertile, but may have a life span of at least six or eight years.

I became interested in royal jelly because for years it was the richest known natural source of pantothenic acid. While direct comparisons between human beings and honey bees seem far-fetched, the possibility that royal jelly (or more specifically pantothenic acid) might prolong the life of mammals seemed to be a speculation worth exploring.

To find an answer, I carried out an experiment involving mice that were kept on a standard chow diet for their entire life span.[8] This diet, it could be stated, was one formulated by experts, and as I have previously indicated, such diets are far superior to what human beings customarily receive. It had in it what was regarded as an abundant amount of all the minerals, amino acids, and vitamins (including pantothenic acid), all of which mice need.

The mice were divided into two groups and were treated alike except that in one group each animal received 0.3 milligram of extra pantothenate per day in its drinking water. This amount of pantothenate was several times the amount that mice are supposed to require.

The results were striking: the forty-one mice on the complete chow diet lived an average of 550 days, while the thirty-three mice that got the extra pantothenate lived an average of 653 days. If the 550 days is regarded as equivalent to seventy-five years for a human, then the 653 days would be equivalent to eighty-nine years.

My interpretation of this experiment is certainly not that pantothenic acid is a miracle food. Probably a large number of the mice received all the pantothenic acid they needed in the chow diet and were not substantially benefited by the supplementary amount. However, some animals had, in effect, cells and tissues with higher requirements, and their lives were greatly prolonged by the supplement. This increased the average life span of the whole group nearly 19 percent. On a purely statistical basis, I would be willing to wager that if a large number of weaned babies were given 25 milligrams of extra pantothenate daily during their lifetime, their life expectancy would be increased by at least ten years. A similar bet might be made by an agronomist who, based upon his knowledge of the soil in a particular area, might wager that the corn crop on a given acreage would be increased by 10 percent if additional phosphate were used as a fertilizer.

Vitamin C (ascorbic acid) is a nutrient that has often been mentioned in connection with aging, and the abundant use of this cheap and harmless nutrient has been strongly suggested, particularly for those who are past middle age. Yet the crucial experiment of giving guinea pigs different levels of ascorbic acid to see how their longevity might be affected has apparently never been performed.

There are nevertheless reasons for thinking that vitamin C is important. One phase of aging is the stiffening of joints, and this is probably related to the fact that collagen production takes place more readily in the young than in the old. Since ascorbic acid is absolutely essential for the building of healthy collagen, it seems probable than an abundant supply of this vitamin would tend to slow down the form of deterioration which accompanies impaired collagen production.

Other observations which relate vitamin C to aging include the findings that ascorbic acid, when administered to rabbits, rats, and human beings, altered the blood composition in such a way as to decrease atherosclerosis.[9] Also in line with the probable protective effect of ascorbic acid against aging, is the finding that in old age, human tissues and body fluids are often very low in ascorbic acid.[10]

Ascorbic acid may delay old age because it has strong antioxidant properties (prevents unwanted oxidations). This possibility is related to the action of other agents, particularly vitamin E, which function in a similar manner. Vitamin E deficiency has often been observed to cause biochemical and physiological changes similar to those that occur in old age. Like ascorbic acid, the most prominent known characteristic of vitamin E is its ability to act as an antioxidant.

Lipid peroxidation, the formation of harmful peroxides, from the interaction between oxygen and highly unsaturated fats (polyunsaturates) needs to be controlled in the body. Both oxygen and the polyunsaturated lipids are essential to our existence, but if the protection against peroxidation is inadequate, serious damage to various body proteins may result.

Vitamin E is thought to be the leading agent for the prevention of peroxidation and the free radical production which is associated both with it and with radiation.[11] Vitamin E, along with a relatively large number of other antioxidants—ascorbic acid, ubiquinones, sulfhydryl compounds, and the trace element selenium —do their jobs in a complicated manner. They protect the body against the damaging products formed when oxygen reacts directly with the highly unsaturated fatty substances which are essential parts of our metabolic machinery.

We do not know all the details of how these antioxidants do their work in practical situations, and the information probably would not be of interest to laymen anyway. As a practical matter, providing plenty of vitamin E and ascorbic acid—both harmless antioxidants—is indicated as a possible means of preventing premature aging, especially if one's diet is rich in polyunsaturated acids.

A visible result of the harmful effects of peroxidation is the production of brown (lipofuscin-like ceroid) pigments which are deposited in various tissues, including the brain and heart. In one study, it was found that in vitamin E-deficient rats three to three and a half months old, the accumulation of these brown pigments in the adrenal glands approach that present in twelve-month-old animals fed an ordinary diet.[12]

While no one seriously entertains the idea of a philosopher's stone which will prolong life indefinitely, the evidence at hand indicates that well-rounded nutrition, including generous amounts of vitamin C and vitamin E can contribute materially to extending the healthy life span of those who are already middle aged. The greatest hope for increasing life spans can be offered if nutrition—from the time of prenatal development to old age—is continuously of the highest quality.

10 Environmental Control of Mental Disease

Millions of families at one time or another are stricken—often devastated—by mental disease. At the same time highly promising and harmless means of prevention go unexplored and untried simply because current medical education has been so bound by tradition.

Because of the biases of current medical education, no one is induced to face squarely the commonsensical question, If the environment of the brain cells is at fault when mental disease strikes, what steps can be taken to improve this environment?

No intelligent student of mental disease will question the probability that the brain environment is at fault; but who has canvassed in a scholarly, scientific way all the possible ways of improving this environment?

One possible way is to give the afflicted or threatened person love, security, and, through psychoanalysis, an understanding of the sources of his own trouble. This, in turn, may help to stabilize his internal chemical environment (e.g., prevent the stirring up of unwanted hormones) and so bring him a measure of peace and tranquility of mind. This avenue of approach is basic to traditional psychiatric training. It has been explored for decades, and has been the subject of voluminous discussions and writings.

Another way of improving the environment of the brain cells is to exclude foreign organisms and poisons. Krafft-Ebing, nearly seventy-five years ago, found that paresis (a disease with severe mental symptoms) was caused by syphilis spirochetes. The successful combat of these organisms with antibiotics now makes it possible to prevent this mental affliction. The "mad hatters" of France got that way because they used mercuric nitrate to process the felt in hats, and some of the poisonous mercury ions got into their brains. This kind of poisoning we have learned to control. With marvelous inconsistency, of course, we cook up and consume many drugs which actually do or potentially may cause mental trouble.

The third and most important way of improving the environment of the brain cells of the afflicted or threatened individual, is to give them an opportunity of receiving the full nutritional chain of life—not an abbreviated or mutilated version. The brain cells ultimately get from the blood only those nutrient elements that are furnished in the food we eat.

Brain cells, like all other living cells, commonly live under conditions of suboptimal nutrition; to give them fuller and better-balanced nutrition seems like an exceedingly promising way both to prevent and to treat mental disease.

In traditional medical thinking it is taken for granted that if a person eats the customary groceries and has an adequate circulatory system, his or her brain cells will automatically get what they need. This point of view has some slight justification in the fact that the brain cells are so vital to life that they are, to a degree, protected by nature. If essential nutrients are to be had anywhere in the body, the brain cells are likely to get a reasonable share. It has long been known, for example, that in starvation other bodily tissues may gradually waste away, but the brain retains its approximate initial weight and integrity up to the point of death.

We must realize, however, that all living cells are continuously subject to imperfect nutrition and that overt mental disease is *known* to result from malnutrition, as, for example, in pellagra. In the light of these considerations, we would be foolhardy indeed to take for granted that the nutrition of the brain cells is automatically satisfactory in those who are afflicted or threatened with mild or severe mental disease.

I will barely mention those relatively violent methods of treating mental disease—lobotomies, electric shock, insulin shock, Metrazol shock—because we are concerned here with prevention. Such treatment methods, which will continue increasingly to be discarded, may sometimes be temporarily palliative, but they also do substantial damage.

Sigmund Freud was the leading exponent of the first approach to mental disease—that of giving the threatened individual security and understanding. He was the founder of Viennese psychiatry which emphasized the idea that the psyche at birth is like a blank slate on which various designs are etched as the child grows. The character of the child is, accordingly, molded by his parents, relatives, and society in general. This molding process may be defective and thus the seeds are sown for future mental trouble.

Seemingly this thesis has much to recommend it, but it leaves out a very important fact that was unknown in Freud's time, namely that individual infants' brains differ "enormously" at birth.[1] There are slates and slates.

This fact, brought to light by K. S. Lashley over twenty years ago, and strongly emphasized ten years later in my book *Biochemical Individuality,* has completely eluded traditional medical education. Widely used treatises still learnedly discuss "the brain" as if it were an assembly-line product.

If we turn to the animal world we find that there are also many types of "slates," each with its own susceptibilities to conditioning. Some slates are so constructed that they get meaning from certain kinds of messages but fail to register others. The brain of a newborn rat, for example, like that of a newborn infant, is a blank slate; but it is of a very different kind. So far as its conditionability to language, mathematics, music, art, and abstract thinking is concerned, the rat's brain is deficient. It is not only blank to begin with in these respects, it remains that way.

Freud lived at a time when modern biological knowledge was scanty; he was a noted professor before the existence of hormones were discovered and many years before vitamins were heard of. Yet he showed, at times, remarkable biological insight.

He knew intuitively that he did not have all the basic answers. He knew, for example, that heredity was involved in mental disease. As early as 1896 he wrote, "The importance of hereditary predisposition is demonstrated by the fact that the same specific causes operating on a sound person would produce no manifest pathological effect, while its presence in a predisposed person will precipitate a neurosis."[2]

His uncertainty about his own postulates was expressed when he said, "One might ask me whether and how far I am convinced of the correctness of the assumptions here developed. My answer would read that I am neither myself convinced nor do I ask that others shall believe them; or better stated, I don't know how far I believe them."[3]

Looking ahead, he foresaw the potentialities of what we now call biochemistry. "The future may teach us to exercise a direct influence, by means of particular chemical substances, upon the amounts of energy and their distribution in the apparatus of the mind. It may be that there are other undreamed-of possibilities of therapy. But for the moment we have nothing better at our disposal than the technique of psychoanalysis, and for that reason, in spite of its limitations, it is not to be despised."[4] By 1927 he had become positive enough to say, "Of course, you know, I am firmly convinced that one day all these disturbances we are trying to understand will be treated by means of hormones or similar substances."[5]

How can medical education overlook or evade the fact that Freud's prophecy is in the process of being fulfilled? How can it dismiss the need for watching carefully the brain cell nutrition of all who are threatened with mental trouble?

In recent years, of course, a tremendous development has transpired in the use of drugs to combat mental disease. Tranquilizers and related drugs are given widely and generously, not only to those who are afflicted with mental disease, but to others who merely need to be calmed down. These drugs do, of course, modify the chemical environment of the brain cells, and they often alleviate symptoms, but they do not get at the root of the trouble. Their use is largely empirical and artificial, and out of line with the basic philosophy of cooperating with nature.

We need to ask, What is *nature's* way of preventing mental disease? Can we, by cooperating with nature, prevent and treat mental disease successfully?

In my opinion the answers to these questions are obvious. Because of the indifference of orthodox medicine, the ways and means that are available have not been implemented in detail, but so many parts of the jigsaw puzzle have become visible that it is clear that they fit together.

If you who read these words have never been afflicted with mental disease, it is not because you have undergone shock treatments or have consumed the right tranquilizers; it is because you have received in your food enough of all the minerals, amino acids, and vitamins that brain cells need to maintain them in reasonably good working order. It is possible that some other cells and tissues in your body have not fared as well, but that your brain, protected by nature as it is, has come through unscathed.

If any one of a number of nutritional items had been received by your brain in, what would be for you, inadequate amounts, you would have been afflicted with mental disease.

Pellagra is a case in point. It is a disease caused by poor nutrition, originally discovered in Italy and Spain. It was notably prevalent early this century in this country's southern states among people whose diet consisted largely of corn. The description of the disease is sometimes given in terms of the four Ds—dermatitis, diarrhea, dementia, and death. These often occur in approximately the order listed, unless the disease is checked. The "dementia," which may be extreme insanity, is frequently preceded by nervousness, insomnia, loss of memory, confusion, irritability, suspiciousness, hallucinations, apprehensiveness, and depression.[6]

If you have never suffered from pellagra, it is simply because your body cells, including those in your brain, have always received, somehow, in some way, enough niacinamide (sometimes in recent years called vitamin B_3) to keep them in working order.

That insanity may accompany pellagra and may be cured by supplying the missing nutrient (niacinamide) is clear from the following case described by Tom Spies.[6] The patient, a woman, in addition to her many other symptoms, was mentally distressed. She saw and heard monkeys, rats, and cattle running around her; she felt bugs, worms, and snakes crawling on her; she thought she was being poisoned and persecuted by her neighbors; and when she was at home she could not remember what she was doing from one minute to the next. On admission to the hospital she was apprehensive, had maniacal outbursts, and was often so withdrawn that she would not communicate at all. About twenty-four to thirty-six hours after receiving niacinamide, her mind began to clear and she knew that the "craziness and foolishness in her head" was unreal. After forty-eight hours, her mind was perfectly clear, and she was able to tell in detail of the distress she experienced, and the crazed condition of her mind during the week previous to her hospital admission. She knew this insanity was a thing of the past—which indeed it was—because after consuming good food for a few days, all her pellagra symptoms left her.

It is a remarkable fact that pellagrins, even when

their mental symptoms are severe, may often become sane, free from mental distress, and perfectly rational within a week after they get an adequate supply of the missing vitamin along with their food.[7] This vitamin is absolutely essential for the metabolism of brain cells and, unless the nervous mechanisms have been damaged beyond repair, their function returns promptly once the malnutrition is corrected.

The full story of pellagra is a complicated one, and many details need not concern us. Other portions of the body besides the brain are impaired, and in actual cases the victims often are poorly nourished in many respects. In other words, niacinamide is only one of several nutritional items likely to be consumed in inadequate amounts by those who suffer from pellagra. In pellagra, as in many other diseases which have fully accredited names, the symptoms are often diverse and unpredictable.

What kind of evidence is there to support the general thesis that mental disease is caused primarily by nutritional deficiencies in the environment of brain cells? With respect to any nutrient, we may ask the following three questions: Does a deficiency of this nutrient cause mental disease? Is there evidence of this deficiency among those afflicted with mental disease? Will the administration of this nutrient have a curative effect on those who are mentally ill?

In the case of niacinamide, the answers to all these questions are positive. A deficiency causes mental disease; niacinamide deficiency exists among those who have this mental disease; administration of niacinamide may bring about remarkable cures.[8] The evidence with respect to a number of other nutrients is less complete, but, as we shall see, the amount of such evidence is large.

A few years ago Linus Pauling, a brilliant chemist (the only person ever to receive two separate Nobel Prizes), published a highly significant article in *Science* entitled "Orthomolecular Psychiatry."[9] *Ortho* comes from the Greek meaning "straight," and orthomolecular psychiatry is the kind that would be concerned with straightening out brain chemistry.

In his article Pauling stresses the importance of "the substances normally present in the human body" and of the "essential nutrilites"—the nutritional substances. Specificially, he mentions the nutrients vitamin B_{12}, niacinamide, ascorbic acid, thiamine, pyridoxine, folic acid, magnesium, tryptophan, and glutamic acid, as all being concerned with brain functioning and thus with mental disease. In the discussion he explains in scientific terms why nutrients may have to be administered in relatively large amounts to bring about beneficial results.

It should be noted that while Pauling is not a physician, nor would he claim to be acquiainted with all the psychiatric literature, it is obvious that he is in a position to know what there is to be known about brain chemistry. From this standpoint his discussion makes sense. He is well aware of the limitations of present knowledge and would not risk his reputation by dealing with a subject so far removed from his specialty as psychiatry—unless he were on solid ground and competent to make the suggestions he has made.

If niacinamide, for example, were the only nutrient needed by brain cells, the problem would be simple. Actually, however, brain cells, like the others in our body, need the whole nutritional gamut.

To clarify the complex situation, let us imagine a purely hypothetical case. Suppose that there are ten nutritional deficiencies any one of which can cause mental disease. To simplify further, suppose that 10 percent of the common cases of mental disease are caused by each of these deficiencies. If this were so, an examination of the whole population of people afflicted with mental disease would not yield impressive statistics with respect to the importance of any *one* lack, and yet in accordance with our supposition, every case of mental disease would be caused by nutritional lacks.

Conventional medical research is not averse to investigating single questions such as, Is a lack of vitamin B_{12} (or pyridoxine or niacinamide) a common cause of mental disease? When the question is asked and answered with respect to one specific nutrient, the results may be unimpressive. What needs to be asked—and almost never is—is the broader and more pertinent question, Do various nutritional lacks or combinations of them commonly cause mental disease? This is obviously a question which can only be answered by sophisticated exploration.

The relation between pellagroid insanity and niacinamide has been known to medical science for several decades. The question of whether niacinamide lack of itself is *the common cause* of mental disease has also been explored. The conclusion, which seems justifiable, is that it is not. But this conclusion should not be surprising in light of the fact that niacinamide is only one of many nutrients for which brain cells have an absolute need. Under chronic conditions of suboptimal nutrition, many other nutrients are likely to be in short supply.

The question still faces us squarely: Do various nutritional deficiencies—or combinations of deficiencies—commonly cause mental disease? That the answer to this question is yes is made very probable by the evidence to which we shall now turn.

Information with respect to the relation between thiamine (vitamin B_1) lack and mental disease is incomplete. Its lack is known to allow degeneration of peripheral nerves, and in Britain and some other European countries this vitamin is often called "aneurin" because of this association. An early symptom of thiamine lack is loss of appetite. This obviously involves malnutrition of cells in the hypothalamus of the brain. Other symptoms include mental depression, irritability, confusion, loss of memory, inability to concentrate, and sensitivity to noise. These symptoms are all associated with mild mental disease and can be cleared up when thiamine is administered. Thiamine is clearly one of the nutrients that needs to be supplied in adequate amounts to prevent mental disease. Yet a study of mental patients in general would not yield impressive figures with respect to the common occurrence of this deficiency, especially in countries where staple foods (such as bread and rice) are "enriched" with this vitamin.

Linking riboflavin (vitamin B_2) lack to mental disease is even more difficult, although there is evidence that inadequate amounts can cause mental depression.[10] There is no doubt whatever that brain cells need this vitamin and that it is a link in the chain which is required to prevent mental disease.

Pantothenic acid deficiency, *by itself,* is probably uncommon in mental disease. Yet pantothenic acid is essential to brain functioning. Its lack can cause nerve degeneration in animals, and prisoners placed on a diet deficient in this vitamin apparently suffered from profound mental depression as a result.[11] (Obviously, such experiments would be terminated before serious mental disease resulted.) The wide variance observed in a few subjects suggests that some may have much higher needs than others. The fact that both animals and humans are reported to stand stress better when they are administered large doses of pantothenic acid is pertinent to this problem.[12] Clearly, pantothenic acid is one more link in the nutritional chain needed to prevent mental disease.

Vitamin B_6 (pyridoxine) deficiency is still another factor. Lack of this vitamin can cause convulsions. Some children require vastly more than others. In a sample of 800 psychiatric patients, the pyridoxine need was said to vary from 5 to 400 milligrams daily.[13] The fact that this vitamin is concerned in tryptophan metabolism has already been discussed. It has been found in one study that nine out of sixteen psychotic children had abnormal responses when given oral tryptophan, and that the condition was corrected by administering oral pyridoxine.[14] These facts, coupled with the probability that currently-used diets are deficient in this vitamin (due in part to its absence in bread), demonstrate that vitamin B_6 is not only a link in the nutritional chain, but a link that is very likely to be weak.

Vitamin B_{12} is definitely a link in the nutritional chain that protects against mental disease. In pernicious anemia, caused by deficiencies of this vitamin, the mental symptoms are by no means uniform; they can range from such mild symptoms as having difficulty in concentrating or remembering to stuporous depression, severe agitation, hallucinations, or even manic or paranoid behavior.[15] Like the symptoms in pellagra, those caused by B_{12} deficiency may be very similar to those observed in schizophrenia. Yet the relationship between pernicious anemia and B_{12} is not simple; other factors may be involved as well. Sometimes administering B_{12} will clear up the mental symptoms associated with pernicious anemia rather slowly—and occasionally, incompletely. The relationship between vitamin and disease is not as direct as in the case of pellagra.

Biotin deficiency is rare, but has been induced in human volunteers by including avidin (from raw egg white) in their diet. Avidin combines with biotin and renders it unavailable.[16] As a result of this induced deficiency, mental symptoms were common: depression, lassitude, hallucinations, and panic. When biotin was administered, all these symptoms disappeared. Biotin is something that we expect to get as a matter of course, and usually we do, but there may be exceptions. It is clear, however, that if we do not get enough biotin, mental disease results.

In the past few years there have been a number of studies that implicate folic acid deficiency in mental disease. In one survey of fifty-nine elderly psychiatric cases (new admissions to the hospital), forty-eight had subnormal folic acid levels in the blood.[17] In another study involving seventy-five patients, thirty-seven had low levels.[18] In a third study, low folic acid levels in the blood were found in twenty-eight out of seventy-two cases.[19] The dividing line between low and normal values is uncertain, and the methods of determination are not well controlled, but there is no doubt that folic acid deficiency is common among elderly psychiatric patients.[20] It is also clear that anticonvulsants and other drugs contribute to the lowering of the folic acid values. Many individuals who have low folic acid levels are greatly benefited by folic acid administration.[21]

Vitamin C has become implicated in the mental disease problem in recent years. Even as early as 1940

it was found in a study in Germany that twelve schizophrenics excreted very little ascorbic acid in their urine,
and that when they were given large doses, nine showed
improvement and six were finally discharged.[22] More
sophisticated recent studies have confirmed and extended this finding. In one study it was found that on
the average schizophrenics burn up ascorbic acid ten
times as rapidly as do normal people.[23] In another
"double blind" study involving forty schizophrenics,
significant improvement was observed in those getting
ascorbic acid over those getting placebos.[24]

We cannot be absolutely certain yet that all mentally
diseased individuals have ascorbic acid deficiency and
are improved by massive doses. But the evidence points
strongly toward the conclusion that ascorbic acid is a
link in the chain and that giving the brain cells an
ample supply is one way to help insure healthy brain
functioning.

Nine vitamins have so far been mentioned as agents
that help protect against mental disease. Nutritional elements other than vitamins are also essential links in this
protective process. Iodine is one such element. In regions
where the soil and water have an extremely low iodine
content and iodine deficiency occurs, the thyroid glands
cannot develop and do their work. In extreme cases,
cretinism develops. Every person who is mentally sound
and well has had—of necessity—enough iodine to prevent this type of mental disability.

Potassium deficiency, like biotin deficiency, is rare in
the general population, but it may result from certain
diseases or in hospitals, through the prolonged intravenous administration of sodium chloride solutions
(saline) which induces potassium excretion.[25] When
potassium deficiency occurs, it causes increased nervous
irritability and mental disorientation.

Magnesium is another of the protective substances
necessary to maintain mental health. A case has been
reported in which a patient had paranoid psychosis and
accompanying magnesium deficiency; the psychosis
cleared up when magnesium was administered.[26] This
would appear to be a rare case, so far as the evidence

is recorded, but in the light of our early discussions about magnesium deficiency, it merits consideration.

To the vitamins and inorganic elements cited, we must add the essential amino acids. William Rose, who discovered the essential amino acid threonine, first observed that when he placed young men on diets deficient in specific amino acids for a short time, they sometimes became irritable and hard to get along with. Their symptoms disappeared when the missing amino acid was returned to the diet.[27] At Purdue University, volunteer students were observed subsisting on different levels of lysine, one of the essential amino acids. One of the students had to withdraw from the experiment because the low level he was getting diminished his concentration, and he was in danger of failing his examinations. When a fully adequate level of lysine was given him, all complaints ceased accompanied with an increase in his bodily retention of nitrogen.[28]

Taking into account all that we know about the chemistry of nervous tissue—the dry material in the brain is over one-third protein—and nutrition in general, it seems safe to say that every essential amino acid is necessary to protect against mental disorders. Life itself cannot be maintained without these nutritional elements. It seems obvious that brain function depends upon them[29] and that poor protein nutrition in general may be a contributing factor in many cases of mental disease.

All this may sound as though no nutrient is excluded from this survey. In a sense that is perfectly true. I have failed to mention certain nutrients such as vitamin A, vitamin E, copper, manganese, zinc, etc., as being deficient in mental disease, but I certainly would not exclude these nutrients simply because evidence is unavailable. The safest assumption we can make is that every essential nutrient is needed by brain cells and that the inadequate supply of any one will cause trouble.

But it is also true that some nutrients are of special interest because they are peculiarly associated with brain metabolism. Such a nutrient is the amino acid, glutamic acid. While it is nutritionally nonessential for the body as a whole, it is a unique substance in that it can be used in addition to glucose, as a fuel by brain cells in their very active metabolism. To be sure, like most of the amino acids, glutamic acid itself does not readily pass the "blood-brain barrier." It may be in the blood plasma at relatively high levels and yet get through to the fluids that bathe the brain cells in only small amounts. The amide of glutamic acid, glutamine, however, can readily pass the blood-brain barrier. After it gets to the brain, it is transformed into glutamic acid and is then used as a fuel.

There has been a protracted dispute in medical literature over the thesis that "intelligence" and brain functioning are enhanced in mentally retarded patients by the administration of large doses of glutamic acid. Without entering deeply into this dispute, I should like merely to suggest that where there is so much smoke, there is probably some fire. The essential and suggestive fact to remember is that glutamic acid is *uniquely* a brain fuel.

Approximately twenty years ago, a leading psychiatrist told me of experiments that he had performed in which schizophrenic patients were administered glutamic acid. The results were remarkably favorable, but the effect lasted only a few days. The whole idea was abandoned, and the observations were not, I believe, ever published.

It seemed to me at the time (and still does) that the findings strongly suggested that a metabolic lapse in brain metabolism was present in schizophrenics and that further biochemical exploration was emphatically called for. What would have happened if glutamine (which readily passes the blood-brain barrier) had been used? What would have happened if other nutritional items had also been administered? What would have happened if in addition to all of this, the patients had also been administered extra amounts of oxygen? The answers to these questions could be very important indeed.

Another nutrient, inositol, may not be nutritionally essential for the body as a whole, but may be of special value in brain-cell nutrition. This substance is present in some of the phospholipids in the brain, and in experiments performed on animals it has been found to be nutritionally helpful.[30] A. Hoffer, a nutritionally-oriented psychiatrist, tells of a preparation available in Canada that contains niacin and inositol. This is used to treat mental illness and is tolerated by individuals who cannot take niacin or niacinamide in large amounts. It is presumed that inositol, a natural substance present in many foods, functions nutritionally.

There is vast room for exploration with respect to essential nutrients which may be peculiarly valuable in brain-cell nutrition. I believe not only that most mental disease can be prevented by careful expert attention to the brain-cell environment, but that means can be found whereby mental disease can be treated successfully—continually using measures which are in line with the basic philosophy of cooperating with nature.

Physicians have at their disposal means of administering nutrients that are not available to laymen. It is, for example, entirely probable that a nutritional deficiency can occur even when an individual consumes food containing enough of the nutrient in question. Faulty digestion may be responsible, or it may be that absorption of the needed nutrient through the intestinal wall is inadequate. Both digestion and absorption involve enzymatic action, and as we have indicated, differences in enzyme efficiencies is an important aspect of biochemical individuality. It may therefore be necessary, in the treatment or prevention of mental disease (and other diseases), that certain nutrients be injected rather than ingested.

Even with our present state of knowledge, however, it should be possible both to prevent and to treat mental disease by attempting to furnish to the patients everything needed for good brain nutrition. I can imagine that some physicians may be inclined to dismiss this suggestion as a shot-gun approach. My answer is that when we eat good wholesome food we never consume just one vitamin, one mineral, or one amino acid. We eat a broad assortment of all of them in one meal. If nature uses a shot-gun approach, it seems that medicine would not be ill-advised to follow nature's example.

The best time to begin a nutrition-based program of preventing mental disease is the earliest time. We have already called attention to the probability that inadequate prenatal nutrition is responsible for the creation of mentally retarded children, and that mental development during infancy is fostered only if the nutrition is good. Nutrition probably hits one of its low spots during adolescence. Children assume during these years that they can survive by consuming large amounts of soft drinks, candy bars, potato chips, and other "fun" foods. As a result they may actually be making themselves more vulnerable to mental disease in the days to come.

As old age approaches there is an increasing tendency for people to be afflicted with mental disease. This suggests that the cumulative effect of some nutritional deficiencies may be involved. By the same token, elderly people are often benefited by nutritional supplements.

I might point out here that, so far, we have been discussing the kind of extreme mental diseases that in ordinary language is included in the term "insanity." It is well recognized, however, that many people suffer from milder mental disorders. Paul Dudley White and his Harvard colleagues found that "anxiety neuroses" occur in about 4.7 percent of the general population.[31] In addition, these individuals will have other outward symptoms such as palpitation, breathlessness, fatigue, chest pain, dizziness, faintness, headache, weakness, vomiting, or loss of appetite from two to ten times more often than other members of the population.

A particularly interesting result of this study was the Harvard investigators' discovery that mild or heavy exercise produced substantially higher levels of lactate in the blood of individuals with anxiety neuroses than in members of control groups. This has been amply confirmed by several other studies.[32] Exercise (or the secretion of adrenaline into the blood) always causes an increase of lactate levels in the blood, but in certain individuals there is a tendency to release far too much.

This correlates with a study at Washington University Medical School in St. Louis, in which it was demonstrated that typical anxiety attacks can be brought about by the infusion of lactate into the blood of susceptible individuals.[33] Interestingly, when calcium ions were infused along with the lactate, the individuals were largely protected from the excess lactate and did not evince anxiety symptoms.

A technical discussion of the possible interpretations of these results would be out of place here, but certain conclusions seem safe. In the first place, there is unquestionably a biochemical basis for at least some anxiety neuroses; secondly, there is a strong familial tendency to be vulnerable to anxiety neurosis, and inherited biochemical individuality is a factor; thirdly, there is real hope that the condition can be alleviated by nutritional means. We know that some individuals need five times as much calcium as others. Perhaps the victims of anxiety neurosis are among these. Or perhaps excessive metabolic lactate production may itself be the source of the trouble. Or it may be that excess adrenaline secretion is a metabolic fault. Or perhaps unusual sensitivity to lactate is involved. In any case, nutrition seems to be implicated and probably should be adapted in an expert way to the peculiar needs of individuals who are afflicted with this disorder.

Because of the prominent involvement of fatigue in anxiety neurosis, the nutritional factors involved in fatigue also require attention. Investigators in India have found that ascorbic acid is an antifatigue factor.[34] This is particularly interesting in that the needs of different individuals for ascorbic acid probably varies extremely. It is possible that some who have anxiety neurosis need, among other things, an extra supply of ascorbic acid.

I am not here suggesting a specific treatment for anxiety neurosis; that would be premature. But I do strongly suggest that anxiety neuroses and other mild forms of mental trouble—including emotional instability and depressed spirits—may prove to be treatable by paying expert attention to nutritional factors.

Many people continue to believe that most mental diseases are primarily psychic (i.e., nonphysical) in nature, while an increasingly popular school of thought holds that biochemical changes are basic to all mental disease. Actually, these two schools of thought are not fundamentally incompatible. It is not at all impossible for brain biochemistry to be influenced and helped by psychotherapy, nor is it impossible for biochemical changes to influence and help one's psyche.

It is well known that emotional states such as fear, hate, love, and stress cause biochemical changes to take place in the body, primarily through the operation of the endocrine glands. It has been found that even loneliness can cause biochemical changes in rats kept in isolation.[35] Our knowledge of the dynamic biochemical changes that take place in the brain is very scant, but there is no doubt that these changes take place all of the time. I have spoken of brain cells becoming incapacitated because of poisons. There is reason to think that these poisons may be released by emotional and psychic changes. Hence, on logical grounds, even if one adheres strictly to the idea that deranged biochemical processes are fundamental to mental disease, psychotherapy cannot be ruled out as one possible means of treating and preventing mental disease.

That psychoanalysis is effective as a treatment for serious mental disease has been questioned many times by eminent authorities. Freud himself wrote, "You know that the theory of psychiatry has hitherto not been able to influence obsessions. Can psychoanalysis perhaps do so, thanks to its insight into the mechanisms of these symptoms? No . . . it cannot; for the present, at least, it is just as powerless in the face of these maladies as every other therapy."[36]

Toward the end of his life Freud stated that psychoanalysis would be remembered as a psychology of the unconscious and not as a method of treatment.[37] Methods of psychotherapy have, in general, yet to prove themselves.

In view of the failures of other methods of prevention and treatment, and in light of its obvious applicability, I can see no reason why improving the brain-cell environment should not become a prime objective of those who want to prevent or cure mental disease. On the contrary, I think there is every reason to believe that giving the brain-cells *complete* nutrition will yield phenomenally successful results.

11 The Battle Against Alcoholism

No informed person today believes that we are winning the battle against alcoholism. W. B. Terhune has stated that in New York state alone the alcoholic population is increasing at the rate of 20,000 per year.[1] Alcohol consumption may seem to provide pleasant warmth, relaxation, and euphoria, but if it develops into alcoholism, it is like a slow fire which tortures and eventually destroys its victim.

In trying to put out these alcoholic fires we have been largely unsuccessful because we depend on using the wrong weapons and at the wrong time—after the fire has done serious damage.

Alcoholism is the only disease in existence for which the treatment is commonly referred by physicians to laymen. Admittedly, members of Alcoholics Anonymous have a firsthand knowledge of the disease, and have helped thousands of fellow alcoholics to become abstainers; but they do not help an individual who is on the long trip (usually seven to ten years) *toward* alcoholism; he or she must first go over the hill.

Fighting fires that have already done serious damage will always be necessary, but fire *prevention* is surely preferable. Every possible prevention measure needs to be taken. If we wish to prevent alcoholic fires, we should do a thorough job and eliminate all the causes, whether they seem at the moment important or unimportant. Many different ideas have been expressed with respect to the basic cause of alcoholism. Since we cannot at this time be sure which ideas are the most valid, we should not disregard any of them. Physiological and biochemical factors—such as endocrine imbalances and poor nutrition—are thought by some experts to be involved in the development of the disease. We cannot afford to neglect any of these physiological matters simply because they involve technical knowledge and do not readily lend themselves to easy handling in "workshops" or discussion groups. Alcoholism needs all-inclusive rather than one-sided attention because it is one of the most devastating diseases known.

Much confusion exists in the minds of those studying alcoholism. Some people are tempted to look for the culprit in social situations involving poverty, affluence, marital and family relations. Others discuss at great length the stages through which a hypothetical individual passes to become a typical alcoholic, knowing full well that there is tremendous variability with respect to these stages, and that there is no such thing as a "typical" alcoholic.

All these considerations may have merit, but unfortunately they fail to strike at the central fact of alcoholism: Some individuals, when they consume liquor over a period of time, become compulsive drinkers.

The fact that some individuals become alcoholics and others—under similar circumstances—do not is inescapable and is of the utmost importance in understanding the disease. When alcoholism strikes, whether its victims are male or female, married or unmarried, charming or repulsive, moral or immoral, rich or poor, gifted or ungifted, extraverted or introverted, it always

only strikes *certain individuals,* while others remain un-
touched. Furthermore, it strikes with essentially the
same result; the victim becomes a compulsive drinker.

From what I have written up to now, it should be
obvious that my own scientific orientation would inevitably make me turn to the brain as being the most
probable location of the alcoholic difficulty. If this
suggestion has any merit at all, then any comprehensive
attempt to prevent alcoholism will most certainly include measures designed to protect our brains from
whatever it may be that leads to alcoholic trouble. In
the paragraphs that follow, I will present evidence that
this may be possible.

The brain is an organ highly involved in all sorts of
regulatory mechanisms: temperature regulation, blood
flow, functioning of internal organs, breathing, as well
as water and food consumption, which includes specific
appetites. The fact that compulsive alcohol consumption is often accompanied by indifference or aversion to
food is a strong indication, in itself, that the appetite
center in the brain is out of order.

When the effect of drinking alcohol is described in
purely biological terms, it seems in principle to be very
simple. Alcohol at low concentrations is a fuel which is
used by cells and tissues with little or no damage. At
higher concentrations alcohol is a poison. About this
there is no question. The toxic effects of alcohol (in*toxic*ation brought about by alcohol) manifest themselves
in many ways, due in part to innate differences in our
biochemical makeup. Some individuals become dizzy
and unsteady; some have slurred speech; some become
joyous and noisy; some have a tendency to vomit; some
develop double vision and some, in time, have their
appetite mechanism impaired so they have an aversion
to food and want only alcohol. When any of these
symptoms appear, specific bodily tissues are being affected. In some individuals the speech mechanism is
most vulnerable; in others the vomiting reflexes are
touchy; in some the appetite mechanism may be easily
upset.

In no case do the symptoms of intoxication come in

regular order; there is no uniform progression for all individuals. Some people can consume large amounts of alcohol without having their speech impaired; some practically never stagger or show signs of dizziness; some never vomit. Some, fortunately indeed, never have their appetite mechanisms impaired to such an extent that they become compulsive drinkers and lose control. Whatever else may happen to consumers of alcohol (and a great many things may happen) only those whose appetite mechanisms are deranged become alcoholics.

If the alcohol content of the blood could be maintained at a high enough level for a long enough period, it may be presumed that anyone could become an alcoholic. Practically speaking, however, some individuals tend to consume so little that they are in no danger. Some individuals are protected from becoming alcoholics because they vomit readily even when they consume relatively small amounts.

The fortunate individuals may be those for whom alcohol produces only the outward symptoms: dizziness, slurred speech, double vision, vomiting, etc., and no loss of appetite control. The unfortunate ones may be those who carry their liquor very well without staggering, slurred speech, or vomiting. Instead, the alcohol level in the blood and in the brain may continue to build up until they run a strong risk of being poisoned in a more vital and lasting way. I remember being told by an alcoholic that from the first relatively large amounts of alcohol he consumed, he showed none of the common signs of drunkeness—only pleasure and euphoria. Before long, however, alcoholism, an insatiable craving, dominated his whole being—a far from pleasurable condition. The only escape, ultimately, was total abstinence.

The case I have just mentioned is an extreme one. At the other extreme there are those who occasionally, but not habitually, get into the position where one drink calls for another to such an extent that the individual is temporarily incapacitated. It is usual to draw the line between an alcoholic and a nonalcoholic at the point where loss of control is frequent and drinking interferes with the performance of a job or of "normal" activities. Of course, some individuals move gradually, almost imperceptibly, toward alcoholism. The "just one" martini is replaced by "just one more." A prudent individual will see the signs ahead and will institute prevention before it is too late.

In traditional medical education, alcoholism is thought of as a primarily mental disease involving a personality disorder or weakness from which an "escape" is sought. While medicine fully recognizes that alcoholics who follow their usual bent are malnourished, this is commonly regarded as a *result* of their alcoholism. Many physicians have been led to accept as axiomatic the idea that nutrition is of concern only in "deficiency diseases." That alcoholism might be caused by malnutrition of the brain cells has never been thought worthy of consideration. It is quite possible, of course, that malnutrition develops as a forerunner of alcoholism, and that it is only when malnutrition of the brain cells becomes severe that true alcoholism appears. Becoming an alcoholic is a gradual process.

I will, however, herewith positively assert that *no one who follows good nutritional practices will ever become an alcoholic.* This is obvious, when you think of it. It usually requires seven to ten years of heavy drinking to produce an alcoholic, and during the time of heavy drinking, the alcoholic-to-be is violating the most basic rules of good nutrition by ingesting far too large a proportion of his energy in the form of naked calories.

Alcohol is double barrelled in its effect. In moderate amounts, it does furnish fuel for the body, but it is fuel only (it requires and uses up other nutrients for its metabolism). In higher concentrations, it acts as a poison. Alcohol consumption thus tends not only to deprive the brain cells of the items in the nutritional chain of life, it also may, if taken in large enough quantities, actively damage the brain cells. The poisoning effects may be caused by alcohol acting independently, or it may be brought about by products of alcohol metabolism, or by poisons formed from alcohol metabolites joining with others to produce new types of poisonous agents.[2]

Excessive sugar consumption can be a somewhat similar nutritional fault in that it provides only naked calories. It too can arise from a derangement of the appetite mechanism, as in diabetics who often have an intense craving for the sugar that their bodies metabolize poorly. Children who are malnourished have had their appetite mechanisms impaired so that they have a tendency to eat more sugar (candy) than those who are well nourished. But sugar does not have poisonous effects comparable to those of alcohol, and in this respect it is relatively harmless. Furthermore, by education or instinct, most of us know enough not to drink several cokes or to eat several candy bars before meals. Alcohol, on the other hand, often has the deceptive effect of stimulating appetite. It may do this temporarily, but in the long run our appetite mechanism will see that we take in approximately the necessary amount of calories to keep our bodies going week after week. When we consume calories in the form of alcohol, we eventually crowd out of our diet about the same number of calories we would be getting from wholesome food.

There can be no doubt that a prealcoholic—as he passes down the road toward alcoholism—becomes progressively worse off nutritionally month by month. As he consumes more alcohol, he not only gets less good food, but he also gets increased effects of alcohol poisoning.

There is much evidence that serious brain damage actually does result from heavy alcohol consumption. One of my coworkers, Mary Kay Roach, carried out a careful biochemical study that showed conclusively that alcohol consumption (whether voluntary or forced) on the part of experimental animals (hamsters) resulted in a substantial loss of the brain's ability to use glucose as a fuel.[3] We have previously pointed out how very active brain metabolism is. There is every reason to believe that this rapid metabolism is necessary for health. It may be taken for granted that anything that impairs glucose metabolism in the brain has serious consequences.

Additional light has been thrown on alcohol and brain damage in a study recently carried out in South Carolina.[4] By microscopic examination of the condition of the tiny blood vessels visible on the surface of the eyeball, it was found that among individuals with a high alcohol content of the blood, these vessels were often filled with agglutinated blood masses which tended to stop blood flow. A close correlation was observed, in thirty adult cases, between the condition of these tiny blood vessels and the alcohol content of the blood of the person under examination. In healthy individuals whose blood vessels were examined before and after alcohol consumption, the vessels became increasingly clogged as the alcohol content of the blood was raised.

Similar clogging of small blood vessels takes place all over the body when the blood alcohol level becomes too high. One result is that the nerve cells in the brain are partially deprived of oxygen and food. The brains of alcoholics upon postmortem examination are often seriously damaged.[5] They may be edematous ("wet brain") or they may have areas that are atrophied, with numerous small blood vessels that are clogged and multiple hermorrhages.

Alcohol consumption, at high levels, undoubtedly acts in several ways to damage brain cells: stopping blood flow; direct or indirect poisoning of the brain cells; deprivation of the brain cells of minerals, amino acids, and vitamins by substituting naked calories for good food. Whatever the mechanisms are, the effect is the same. The brain cells are impaired and they die off with greater rapidity when the alcohol level of the blood is allowed to remain at a high level.

From these facts it seems a reasonable deduction that alcoholism probably results from an impairment of the cells in the appetite-regulating mechanism in the hypothalamus region of the brain. In individuals who are prone to become alcoholics, these cells are vulnerable, and may become so seriously damaged that the sight or thought of food is nauseating, and only alcohol has an appeal.

What practical things can be done for those who are on the road to alcoholism? Everyone has in his own hands two vitally important keys, food and drink. If these can be controlled, the battle can be won. If drink cannot be controlled, the individual has arrived at the state of being an alcoholic—rehabilitation rather than prevention is in order. First, the alcoholic should get help from Alcoholics Anonymous or any similar organization that prohibits drinking; then every effort should be made to provide the alcoholic with the *best possible food*—not just something to eat—so that the brain cells will have the best chance of becoming rehabilitated.

Since the best possible food is not always easy to get, and alcoholics are chronically malnourished and need to make up for the years of past deficiency, an alcoholic should supplement his diet with a good assortment of minerals and vitamins—and even amino acids if it can be ascertained what he particularly needs. Usually, however, the amino acid needs are best taken care of by concentrating on good protein foods, lean meats, fish, eggs, and cheeses. Under these conditions carbohydrate foods should be largely avoided.

This good nutrition will help the brain (and other organs) both directly and indirectly. Liver cells may be damaged by what many would consider moderate drinking,[6] and since the liver furnishes the brain cells their glucose and protects them from accumulating metabolic poisons, anything that will help the liver will also help the brain.

If it were true that alcoholic difficulties are due to the lack of a single amino acid, mineral, or vitamin, then the solution would be easy, and the particular nutrient in question could be supplied. Usually more than one nutrient is involved. There are many findings, however, which suggest that in some individuals certain nutrients are more crucial than others.

Years ago Boston investigators tried administering an assortment of vitamins to alcoholics, with results that indicated that some patients were definitely benefited.[7] Of the twenty-five patients who had vitamin medication for thirteen months or more, "seven patients were abstinent, seven were controlled, two were improved, and nine exhibited no change." Considering that the vitamin supplement and dosage could have been substantially improved, and the administration was cumbersome, it is probable that a relatively small percentage of the patients got the prescribed supplements regularly.

It seems likely that the vitamins contained in Tycopan (a brand name of E. Lilly, based on a supplement that I formulated about twenty years ago) are very often of crucial importance, because hundreds of alcoholics have claimed benefit, many of them indicating dramatic results.[8]

There are, however, other nutritional factors which are extremely interesting. My colleague, William Shive, looking at the problem of alcoholism in a broad biological perspective, became interested in a certain "unknown"—a substance to be found in many plant and animal extracts which protected microorganisms from alcohol poisoning. He argued that this substance might have something to do with alcoholism. The unknown was isolated, and turned out to be glutamine—an amino acid present in proteins but often destroyed (converted to glutamic acid) when proteins are broken down.

This substance strongly protects bacteria against alcohol poisoning. It is unique among amino acids in that when it is given to rats, it decreases their voluntary alcohol consumption.[9] Presumably glutamine gets to a rat's brain and there protects the cells in the appetite center just as it does bacterial cells in a test tube. The result is that the alcohol ingested does not upset the rat's appetite mechanism and cause it to consume more alcohol.

Human trials of glutamine have been limited, partly because of lack of interest or expertness in nutritional approaches, partly because of its high cost, and partly because of misunderstandings. One of the top medical leaders in the area of alcoholism told me many years ago that he tried out glutamine and got no positive results. It was a hasty conversation, and I was not well enough acquainted with him to quiz him in a pointed manner. In retrospect I became convinced beyond all reasonable doubt that what he had tried was glutamic acid (earlier called glutaminic acid), and that he had not tried glutamine at all. Glutamine was not available to physicians at the time, and if it had been, it would have cost at least $12 per day per patient to make trials. Glutamic acid (which was available and cheap) will *not* protect bacteria from alcohol poisoning, and will *not* cause a decrease in voluntary alcohol consumption in rats, so it is not surprising that negative results came from his experiments.

Years later, another physician high up in the alcoholism councils of the United States told me of trying glutamine with negative results. In this case I did inquire as to the source of the material. I eventually found out—not much to my surprise—that what was used was a preparation containing glutamic acid but not glutamine. The firm from which the material was obtained wrote me that they had no glutamine on hand nor had they ever carried it. Again, there can be no surprise about negative results.

Enough trials of authentic glutamine have been made, however, to yield some highly suggestive results.[10] The most striking single case was described by J. B. Trunell who gave glutamine to an alcoholic patient under conditions that kept the patient unaware that anything at all was being given. (Glutamine is tasteless.) The result was dramatic; the individual *voluntarily,* with no other apparent reason, promptly stopped drinking, got a job, and at last report, two years later, no longer craved alcohol.

The evidence indicates, however, that glutamine does not work in a uniform manner. The responses of individual alcoholics are inconsistent and sometimes negative. More extensive trials have been hampered by the unavailability of glutamine at a reasonable price. It is only recently that glutamine has become available at a low retail price—about 5 cents a gram.[11] This will allow a person to take as much as 4 grams daily at a cost of about 20 cents per day. Even half this amount may be enough to bring benefit. I hope that extensive trials

will be made now that this harmless and potentially
valuable food substance is available.

In recent years, strong evidence has accumulated
indicating that magnesium lack may be an important
factor in alcoholism. It has been found that the magnesium levels in the blood[12] and in the muscles[13] of
alcoholics are often low, and that unlike well individuals, alcoholics tend to retain administered magnesium. Low levels of this element are often associated
with withdrawal symptoms.[14]

I have before me a confidential document dealing
with vitamin B_3 (niacinamide) therapy. It describes the
treatment of 507 confirmed alcoholics with large doses
of niacin or niacinamade, and reports that 87 percent
received benefit. While this experiment can be criticized
because of lack of controls, the fact that large numbers
of reports have indicated that alcoholics are benefited
by this type of "megavitamin" therapy should provoke
serious investigation of the question.

The relationship between alcoholism and anxiety
neurosis has not been adequately explored. Some authorities have assumed that men and women are afflicted with anxiety neurosis equally, but that men are
more likely to become alcoholics, thus diminishing the
number of men who have the more typical anxiety
neurosis symptoms.[15] The connection between the two
conditions is questionable, but, as we saw in the last
chapter, it is interesting that anxiety neurosis does have
a biochemical basis.

From all the facts relating alcoholism to biochemical
factors and nutritional deficiencies, it becomes clear that
whatever measures may be taken to prevent alcoholism,
the neglect of the nutritional approach cannot be
justified.

Anyone who feels himself threatened with alcoholism
should, as the most elementary precaution, begin to take
steps to improve his diet. In addition to paying attention to the quality and quantity of his normal food intake, he should probably make use of suitable nutritional supplements, including glutamine. Sources of
such supplements are listed in the Reference Notes.[16]

The question naturally arises: Is it possible to tell in advance whether a young person is alcoholism-prone, so that in individual cases concerted efforts can be made to head off the disease? Although a number of studies, psychological and biochemical, have been made seeking to find the answer, this subject has not received as much attention as it merits.[17] In our laboratories, several efforts in this direction have become complicated by the interference of ethnic differences.[18] One study of blood amino acid patterns, however, strongly indicates that the answer can be found. The fasting blood levels of the different amino acids form unique patterns which reflect one's biochemical individuality, and the indications are that alcoholism-prone individuals have patterns that are affected in a characteristic manner when alcohol is consumed. These patterns can at present be explored only by relatively expensive methods; but as techniques improve, these methods may become more accessible.

When the incidence of alcoholism decreases in the United States, it will be because medical education has undergone considerable reorientation and change. Physicians—and people following their lead—will have become more nutrition-conscious and more aware that the environmental conditions under which we ask our brain cells to live really make a difference.

12 How Is the Cancer Problem Related?

Because thousands of man-years of effort have gone into the problem of understanding cancer, a prudent scientist will hesitate before attempting to make any new suggestions or contributions in this area.

The two crucial questions so far as this book is concerned are: Has the big failure in medical education had a damaging effect on cancer research? and, Will increased attention to cellular nutrition increase the chances of success in cancer research? Since the answers to both of these questions are emphatically in the affirmative, it appears desirable to explain why, and in what particulars.

Cancer research is directed in three general directions: *prevention, detection,* and *treatment.* These are interrelated, and all require, ideally, an understanding of the disease. Our concern is prevention, since that is the primary subject of this book.

We have already indicated that in human development from a single fertilized egg cell, an early and stupendous event is the production of many different kinds of cells which eventually make up our tissues and organs. This process is called "differentiation." In spite of having a name for the process, we have little idea—in terms of mechanisms—how or why it takes place.

Related to this differentiation process is the fact that the cellular multiplication takes place in a controlled, orderly fashion. The various tissues and organs grow to a certain size when cell multiplication stops, and further growth is thereafter checked. The liver, for example, grows to a certain size and does not continue to expand as it would if the multiplication of liver cells were not held in check. If part of the liver is removed surgically, liver cells do multiply, and the liver is regenerated, but only to its original size. The controlling mechanisms involved in determining how large bodily structures and organs will ultimately be, and the mechanisms for keeping the cells from multiplying unduly, are almost completely unknown. We only know that these mechanisms exist and that "population explosions" all over our bodies are continually being prevented.

If we understand the mechanisms which determine organ sizes and keep cells from multiplying out of bounds, we would be in a vastly better position to tackle the cancer problem, because cancer cells actually do get out of bounds and grow wildly. We do not know why they do, nor do we know why other cells do not. We know that different cells and tissues differ in their reproductive powers. The situation in the brain for example, is quite unlike that of the liver. If part of the brain is removed, the brain cells do not multiply to fill the gap. Nerve cells in general lose their power of multiplication.

What are cancer cells, and what is their origin? They arise ultimately from healthy cells of various types—particularly from cells that are capable of multiplying, like those in the skin—not from cells that are incapable of multiplying, like ordinary nerve cells. Brain tumors occur, but they are rare and sometimes involve cells other than neurons. If by some magic we were able to stop all multiplication of cells in our bodies, there would be no more cancer. Of course, such a thing is impossible, because our skin cells, for example, slough off and have to be replaced. Shortly we would be without any skin.

Why do certain cells multiply to produce the outlaws we call cancer cells? We don't know. But we do know, for example, that light, particularly in the ultraviolet region, can induce the production of skin cancer. We know of a host of chemicals called carcinogens which are capable of inducing cancer when they come in contact with the skin or with other tissues. Some of these agents are present in tars and smoke. We know also that continual mechanical irritation may induce cancer.

It has been established also that some cancers—the evidence is clear-cut with respect to some animal cancers—are induced by virus-like agents which invade cells and cause their progeny to become outlaws.

On the basis of these recognized facts, we can set up a program for preventing cancer which involves avoiding ultraviolet light, tars and carcinogens, mechanical irritation, and cancer viruses. All of these are practical expedients except the last. It may be that cancer viruses are extremely widespread, and since there is no practical means of detection, we are, at present, at a loss as to how they can be avoided.

There is, however, a great deal more to cancer prevention than these remarks would indicate. The matter of individual susceptibility cannot be left out of the picture. Light, carcinogens, mechanical irritation, and viruses do not yield the same results with different individuals, and there must be basic reasons why this is so. If we knew why certain individuals are resistant to various cancer-producing agents, we might be able to confer this resistance on others, and thus prevent cancer from developing.

Two basic factors must enter into determining whether or not a particular healthy cell will give rise to cancer cells. One is its hereditary background; the other is the environment in which the cell lives. Even if the hereditary background seems to have a weakness, this does not mean that this weakness cannot be corrected by adjusting the environment.

The cancer-inducing agents that we have mentioned are all a part of the environment of cells. Are there not environmental factors that work in the opposite direction to *protect* against cancer? We think there are, and that these have not been adequately explored.

The problem of cancer appears in one sense to be a single problem; in other words, we have strong reason to hope that if we can conquer the problem in one mammal, as it relates to a single tissue, this will throw important light on all cancers in all mammals. This hope is based in part on experiments done in the author's laboratory nearly thirty years ago. We assayed many tissues for eight different B vitamins and made many comparisons.[1] Included in the study were twenty-two different human cancer tissues, thirteen rat tumors, and fourteen different mouse tumors. The results showed that all the cancer tissues, regardless of source, bore resemblances to each other, and indicated that, to a degree at least, mammalian cancers constitute "a common tissue type." The same general conclusion has also been reached as a result of enzyme studies.[2]

All of the B vitamins which are present in all other living cells are found in cancer tissues. Perhaps the most consistent difference between the cancer tissues and the normal tissues was that the folic acid content of cancer tissues tended to be high. This finding has led to much experimentation on the supposition that the folic acid needs of cancer cells are high, and that folic acid antagonists (which tend to keep folic acid from functioning) would act as anticancer agents by starving the cancer cells with respect to this nutrient. A large number of reports, many of them favorable, have resulted.[3]

If cancer cells were found to have nutritional needs distinctly different from those of normal cells, it should be possible to starve the cancer cells while nourishing the normal cells in a satisfactory manner. In general, however, the nutritional needs of the cancer cells and the normal cells appear to be too much alike. While it is possible by nutritional manipulation to starve cancer cells and make them multiply more slowly, the animal that bears the cancer is generally being starved simultaneously, with no substantial improvement in the situation. Such measures as these, however, are treatment measures and are not concerned with preventing the initial onset of the disease. Prevention is the primary subject of our discussion.

What environmental influences can be brought to bear on healthy cells to help them resist the agents that cause the initiation of cancer? On logical grounds, and on the basis of our previous discussions, it would appear that the most important measure to be taken would be to improve the nutritional environment of the cells that are liable to yield cancerous progeny. Nutritional improvement is always possible—an idea that is patently true once one recognizes the fact that all living cells commonly exist under conditions of suboptimal nutrition.

What evidence, if any, indicates that improved nutrition might prevent the onset of cancer?

The females of certain strains of mice are highly susceptible to mammary tumors. What, biochemically, is different about these susceptible mice, and why certain ones—even in these susceptible strains—escape is unknown. That cellular nutrition greatly affects the initiation of new cancerous growth is shown by the experiments of White and his coworkers who found that giving the animals diets low in cystine completely prevented the tumors from developing.[4] It is true that the females exhibited little or no estrus, indicating that a hormonal imbalance had been produced; but the prevention of tumor growth wholly by nutritional means is in itself interesting. It suggests, of course, that other nutritional measures might bring the same result without inducing a hormonal imbalance. Cystine should not be regarded as a cancer-producing culprit except under very special circumstances and for particular animals.

It has been found that rats can be induced to develop cancers if they are fed diets deficient in choline. In one

experiment, fourteen out of eighteen rats developed
cancers on the deficient diet, while no rats had cancers
when the diet was supplemented with 0.2 percent
choline.[5] From these experiments, it cannot be concluded that choline is the only nutrient to be watched
in connection with cancer prevention. It is not that
simple. In these particular rats, choline may have been
a limiting factor, but in other animals or human beings
some other nutrient or nutrients might play a comparable role.

In California, recent suggestive experiments have
indicated the benefits of certain liver extracts (injected)
in preventing spontaneous mammary tumor formation.[6]
Nearly half of the untreated mice developed tumors,
compared with about one-sixth of those receiving the
liver extract. Liver extracts are conspicuously rich in
various B vitamins, and it may be presumed that oral
ingestion of the material might also have been effective.
In any event, the effect was probably due to some
nutrilites (known or unknown) present in liver.

At Minnesota experiments were performed that involved giving susceptible female mice diets restricted as
to calories but supposedly ample with respect to minerals, amino acids, and vitamins.[7] The result was that
the incidence of mammary cancers during sixteen
months was decreased from 67 percent to zero. Again,
this is a demonstration that the nutritional environment
of the body cells can be adjusted so as to prevent cancer formation.

Experiments on how to prevent the initiation of
spontaneous cancers by nutritional means need to be
greatly extended and amplified with the utmost sophisti-
cation.

Further evidence of the importance of the nutritional
environment of cells in preventing cancer has been obtained by the experimental use of known carcinogens.
Perhaps the most widely used carcinogen is p-dimethyl
aminoazobenzene ("butter yellow"). A Japanese investigator first found that when this dye is fed to rats,
it produces liver cancers.[8] That nutritional factors are
involved in protecting against this carcinogen is clearly

shown by the fact that feeding riboflavin,[9] nicotinic acid, casein, yeast, egg white,[10] and milk[11] all have marked delaying effects.

In one experiment the animals that were fed the unsupplemented diet containing the butter yellow began getting cancers at about forty days, and all were cancerous at about 120 days.[12] Supplementing the diet containing the dye with casein delayed the first onset to about sixty days, and only about 75 percent of the animals became cancerous. A combination of casein and riboflavin delayed the first onset to about 150 days, and only one animal out of twenty-six became cancerous. When 15 percent of a yeast was added to the diet, all animals were protected for 200 days.

In another experiment it was found that 15 percent yeast protected all animals;[13] when 6 percent of the diet was yeast, 70 percent of the animals were protected; when the yeast content of the diet was reduced to 3 percent, only 30 percent of the animals were protected; when no yeast was included, all the animals developed cancers.

These experiments demonstrate clearly that healthy cells resist becoming cancerous when they are furnished the full nutritional chain of life. The importance of yeast as a source of needed nutrients can be overemphasized, because while the particular yeast used (yeasts are not all the same) was completely effective in these experiments, other yeasts used with other animals might yield results far less impressive. It should be noted that the yeast, in order to be effective, had to constitute a substantial part of the diet. A little dab of yeast or a few tablets of yeast could not be expected to be of substantial value.

There are two other nutrients that, for special reasons, deserve mention in connection with cancer prevention. Vitamin C is interesting because of the possibility that the impairment of collagen formation may be a preconditioning factor for cancer initiation.[14] Collagen is, of course, a structural necessity in our bodies, and it seems very probable that its maintenance in healthy condition is part of the means by which cells are kept from growing wild. It has been observed that in guinea pigs, transplated tumors grew less rapidly when the guinea pigs had plenty of ascorbic acid, and that cancer tissue has no particular affinity (or perhaps use for) ascorbic acid.[15] Because it is probable that many people get far less than the optimal ascorbic acid, and also because it is harmless, its use as one possible preventive measure against cancer is strongly suggested.

Vitamin A is interesting because of its unknown but very real function in keeping epithelial tissue healthy. Epithelial tissues are subject to cancer. Whitish warty patches on the tongue, cheeks, and gums known as leukoplakia may become cancerous and have been successfully treated and caused to regress by vitamin A administration.[16] It seems a shame that our knowledge of the way vitamin A functions is so scanty—particularly the functions that can be performed by vitamin A acid—and that medical education tends to turn its eyes away from its importance. Since in moderately high doses vitamin A is harmless, its use as a possible preventive measure against cancer suggests itself. It is, of course, needed for many other reasons not associated with cancer prevention.

After cells have become cancerous, the situation changes, and it is not possible to curb the aggressive multiplying cancer cells by good nutrition. In fact, cancer cells often act as parasites and rob the healthy cells of what they need.[17] It was found, for example, in the experiments just mentioned (showing that butter yellow cancers are consistently prevented by excellent nutrition), that after cancers start, they cannot be stopped by similar means. It is then too late.

In the previous chapter we have decried the tendency to wait until the fires of alcoholism are raging before trying to put them out. Certainly, on the basis of our discussion, this situation is equally serious in the case of cancer. Instead of concentrating our efforts on ways of treating or curing cancer, we should be concentrating on ways of preventing cancer. This seems to be a more worthy and a more easily reached goal.

Medical education has neglected to perform a refined study of nutrition in all of its aspects and has diverted attention away from the most promising means of controlling cancer. That avenue is the nutritional approach which must encompass the human element of individual susceptibility.

This same deficient education has made it easier for people to accept the "waiting" philosophy: Wait until deformed and mentally retarded babies are born, then give them loving attention; wait until heart attacks come, then, if the patient is still alive, give him or her the best care possible; wait until mental disease strikes, then give considerate treatment; wait until alcoholism strikes, then turn to the task of rehabilitation; wait until cancer growth becomes apparent, then try to cut it out or burn it out with suitable radiation.

This same waiting philosophy applies in the area of pollution. We wait until pollution begins to be intolerable before we become concerned. A forward-looking and a preventive attitude could save us endless trouble.

The nutritional environment of our cells and tissues is of prime importance, and when attention is directed to this environment, there is excellent reason to hope for the day when there will be experts who can help us prevent the production of deformed and retarded babies, prevent heart attacks, prevent mental disease and alcoholism, and even prevent cancer. Although heredity may perpetuate certain weaknesses, the control of the nutritional environment can probably overcome these weaknesses, and prevention can become a reality.

13 Food Fads

In the preceding nine chapters we have been discussing the relationship between nutrition and a number of specific diseases and defects. The evidence that we have considered has, it seems to me, the profoundest implications for medical research, for medical practice, and the public health generally. Its immediate effect on laymen is worthy of special consideration.

It is not in the layman's power to make scientifically accurate analyses of his own individual nutritional needs. Nor is it possible for him to undertake the kind of carefully controlled research necessary to establish exact relationships between specific nutrients and the prevention of specific diseases. Since orthodox medicine gives him little or no guidance in the matter, what is he to do?

In the past, he has often prescribed for himself. The result, as the medical profession has been rather too quick to point out, may be what is called "food faddism." The term is usually applied contemptuously to describe what is certainly not science, but which, under the circumstances, is not always worthy of contempt.

Many food fads are, of course, simply rubbish. A few make a certain amount of nutritional sense, and a very few are far from nonsense. But inevitably, all food fads suffer from a couple of major defects. The first such defect was neatly summarized by Lucretius over 2000 years ago: "What is food to one man may be fierce poison to others." In other words, the fads tend to identify certain foods as good for all people at all times without making allowance for the tremendous variation in individual requirements. The second defect common to the majority of faddists is their lack of sufficient scientific background to appreciate the interrelationships between nutrients and how they work together. The faddists often have bizarre notions which cannot stand the light of scientific inquiry.

Yet faddists may display some intuitive wisdom. There is sometimes difficulty in drawing a line between a "faddist notion" and a perfectly valid observation which applies, however, only to a limited number of people. For example, a person who may or may not be inclined toward hypochondria experiments with goat's milk and finds that he not only likes it, but it also likes him. His health and digestion improve, and he begins recommending it to his friends. Some of them may thrive on it too, and as a result a fad is started. How important the fad becomes will depend on how many people seem to thrive on goat's milk, and how persuasive the proponents of the fad are. There is no question that goat's milk is of high nutritional value, and that for some people, as our later discussion will make clear, it may have distinct advantages over cow's milk.

One individual who takes the goat's milk recommendation seriously may find that his health doesn't quite click until he also consumes some old-fashioned black walnuts (or some equally improbable adjunct). This then potentially becomes a new variant of the fad of drinking goat's milk. Whether this variant is accepted at all depends largely on the eloquence of the proponents and whether other individuals—including highly suggestible ones—try out the new wrinkle and find in it some real or imaginary advantage.

Faddist attitudes toward milk cover an extremely wide range. Not a few faddists at one time or another have adopted the notion that milk and milk products constitute a superfood; therefore, milk should be consumed to the exclusion of other good foods. At the other end of the scale there are those—and this includes some physicians who are unusually poorly informed—who decry the use of milk by adults on the contention that nature intended it for babies and young animals and that it is therefore not suitable for adults.

Those who know and care about the chemical composition of milk—what food qualities it possesses—realize that it contains a most unusually well balanced assortment of minerals (except iron, which is a notable lack), amino acids, and vitamins, and that its chemical composition makes it an extraordinarily good food for old or young. Its origin—whether it grows on trees, is dug up from the earth, or comes from a cow's udders—is of no consequence in determining its food value.

Those who have experimented with feeding laboratory animals milk and milk products know that its value as a well-rounded food is outstanding and difficult to match with any other common food. Almost any animal consuming a diet free from milk or milk products will have its condition improved if some milk is added to its diet. This effect is brought about not only by the minerals and vitamins, which are extraordinarily well balanced, but also by the excellent balance of the amino acids in milk proteins. Proteins with nutritionally excellent amino acid makeup are hard to come by. Any extreme position with respect to milk—either that it should be used universally or that its use should be restricted to small children—is a faddist notion which cannot be defended scientifically.

In recent years, well substantiated evidence has been collected which demonstrates conclusively that the consumption of milk (by the glassful) can be harmful to 5 to 10 percent of Caucasian adults, and to about 70 percent of Negro adults (both in America and in Uganda) and to a large number of Oriental adults.[1] The reason for the difficulty lies in the fact that in these individuals, for hereditary reasons, the digestive enzymes (lactases) which split milk sugar (lactose) are almost absent.

There appear to be two different enzymes that accomplish the same thing: the juvenile type, possessed by everyone during early youth; and the adult type, which is possessed (and retained) by a large percentage of Caucasians and by a smaller percentage of those of other races. As a result of this enzyme lack, which may be accentuated as one ages, milk sugar is not digested and is not absorbed. Like any other unabsorbed soluble substance in high concentration (magnesium salts, for example), it has a strong osmotic attraction for water, and acts as a cathartic, causing abdominal pain and cramps. Of course the nondigestibility of lactose by those deficient in lactase causes them to lose a substantial part of the calorie value of the milk. Aside from its cathartic action, the undigested lactose in the intestine may have unfavorable effects on the bacterial organisms that ordinarily flourish there.

These phenomena constitute a clear-cut basis for at least one of the faddist notions about the use of milk. If any individual adult is observant enough to note that in his own case consuming milk causes even a mild discomfort (there are all degrees of lactase deficiency), he may wrongly assume that this is true for anyone. It then becomes reasonable to conclude that adults probably should not drink milk, and to find reasons why it should be avoided by every grown person.

If a physician himself appears to be among the small percentage of Caucasian adults who cannot tolerate milk, he may be human enough to be tempted to rationalize and find reasons why all adult people should not consume this food. If he makes similar observations among his patients, he may jump to the same erroneous conclusion—especially so because medical education has neglected to teach about nutrition and its relation to the needs of individuals.

Milk is such a marvelously complete food in so many respects that it seems a shame if its nutritional value has to be lost to any substantial part of the population. There are probably relatively easy ways to get around this difficulty. Cultured buttermilk, yogurt, and similar products retain much of the nutritional value of milk and at the same time are often very low in lactose. If they are palatable, people who are upset by milk may use them as a valuable substitute. People's taste reactions are by no means identical, however, and some would probably rather starve than drink buttermilk or any similar drink which contains substantial amounts of lactic acid.

There is another possible way out of the difficulty. Lactase-treatment of milk should not be impractical. The .product would not be soured milk; it would differ from ordinary milk only by the presence of glucose and galactose in the place of lactose.

In the above discussion we have noted the reasons behind several food fads—those involving the drinking of buttermilk or yogurt. These practices may be perfectly valid and extremely valuable *for certain individuals;* they take on a faddist color only when uninformed individuals recommend them as life-saving measures, to be used indiscriminately by anyone and everyone.

The studies that have resulted from the discovery that lactose is poorly tolerated by a substantial part of the adult population have opened up a whole new area of biochemical individuality which has hitherto not been recognized. This has to do with individual differences in the ability to digest specific foods.

In 1951 in the author's laboratory, studies involving the technique of paper chromatography showed that every healthy individual excretes in the urine a distinctive pattern of amino acids and other urinary constituents.[2] In 1952 in Germany, it was shown, using similar techniques, that each healthy person exhibits a distinctive pattern of amino acids in the digestive juice which is secreted in the duodenum (first portion of the small intestine).[3]

As a result of studies designed to clear up the milk tolerance problem, it has been found that healthy adult individuals have in their intestinal mucosa not only widely varying amounts of *lactase* which digests lactose, but also widely varying amounts of *sucrase* which digests ordinary sugar, and *maltase* which splits malt sugar. These variations among a group of 100 healthy individuals were in each case ten- to twenty-fold or more![4]

There is a great deal more to this finding than is superficially apparent. If these carbohydrate-digesting enzymes vary so enormously from one well individual to another, how can we escape the probability that other digestive enzymes vary in the same manner in "normal" people. It is very likely that each individual has a distinctive pattern with respect to the entire gamut of digestive enzymes which attack specific types of linkages in carbohydrates, fats, and proteins. This might give each individual an ability to digest only certain foods with great facility. Here we see what may be the scientific basis for an enormous number of food fads, each of which may be of great importance for the promotion of good health in some individuals. They cannot be condemned unless they are urged upon the general public.

That each individual does indeed have a distinctive enzyme pattern in his digestive juices is supported by conclusive evidence that individual enzyme patterns in the blood are often highly distinctive,[5] and by the widely observed fact, perhaps first enunciated by Lucretius, that individual people thrive on different types of foods. Peculiar eating practices may not always be based upon whim and caprice.

For the complete digestion of proteins, a large number of digestive enzymes are involved; each is most effective for certain types of linkages within the proteins digested. If each individual has a distinctive pattern of protein-splitting enzymes, it becomes reasonable to suppose that each may have a facility for digesting certain proteins and a lack of facility for others. This could help explain why some "normal" people have strong likes and dislikes for certain protein-rich foods—fowl, fish, eggs, mutton, pork, or beef. The proteins in these foods have distinctive structures. This same variation in digestive enzymes furnishes a basis for understanding why goat's milk may be a highly valued food for some individuals. The proteins in the milk of different animals are not the same.

In some cases, of course, definite allergies may be involved. In such cases the individual has become sensitized to a particular protein and is so conditioned that even traces of the protein may cause trouble. Allergies to milk and egg proteins, for example, have been observed many times. In the case of those adults who typically suffer from abdominal cramps as a result of drinking milk, no allergy need be involved since the same symptoms can be induced by the consumption of pure lactose.

Intolerance to wheat proteins is another problem brought to light in recent years, which involves individual differences in digestive enzymes. In some individuals who lack the necessary enzymes to break down wheat gluten or gliadin completely, there are evidently formed toxic polypeptides (partially split proteins) which damage the intestinal mucosa and prevent it from doing its highly specialized work of absorption. One of the prominent symptoms associated with this difficulty is the excretion by way of the intestine of large amounts of fat (steatorrhea). This cannot be induced in nonvulnerable individuals who possess the digestive enzymes to digest wheat gluten, even when they are fed large amounts of wheat protein for long periods of time.[6] An association between gluten intolerance and milk intolerance has been noted,[7] suggesting that deficiency in various types of enzymes may occur in the same individuals.

A vast amount of evidence suggests that digestive difficulties incurred by differences in the efficiency of various enzymes in the digestive tract are widespread and may be devastating. It can never be assumed that digestion is "no problem," and that all foods that are regarded as wholesome are forthwith readily digested by any individual that consumes them. The implication so often found in books on nutrition that "the normal person" automatically digests carbohydrates to an extent of about 97 percent, fats about 95 percent, and proteins about 93 percent, can be very misleading. We can have no certainty that Jack Sprat and his wife had intestinal lipases (fat-digesting enzymes) of similar efficiency. It seems probable that digestive deficiencies of one kind or another exist among a substantial part of the entire population, especially those who do not enjoy "perfect health."

The solution to these widespread digestive problems is not to find some foreign chemical that will stop "heartburn" and other digestive distress signals, but rather to find for the individual sufferer the right kinds of adequate food so that digestion and assimilation will take place easily and smoothly. Many people may find that it is possible, utilizing their own body wisdom, to solve these problems for themselves; many others, however, need the expert help of physicians who are trained to recognize the problems as they really exist, and to suggest practical ways of circumventing the difficulties.

It is easy to see, in the light of what we know about nutrition, the inherent limitations of food fads that focus on a single kind of food. Yogurt, honey and vinegar, blackstrap molasses, and sassafras tea may have some value, but individually or collectively they do not point the way to good health for everyone.

There are other widely prevalent ideas about foods, however, which relate to their handling before they are consumed. Among the laymen who have become fully convinced on intellectual grounds or through experience that proper nutrition is a key to good health, there are those who use the terms "natural foods" and "organically grown." These terms require clarification.

There is one sense in which the proponents of "natural food" are clearly in the right. Polished rice and white flour are not natural foods in that the germs of the grains have been removed. What is retained is largely the energy store of the natural grain with no substantial part of the nutritional chain of life retained.

No food prepared from white flour or white rice (and there are many) are natural foods. Many foods are processed in such a way (often involving heat treatment) that their natural food value is lost. These are no longer natural foods.

Yet one can carry the idea of natural food to extremes. One may say that it is not "natural" for a human being to drink *cow's* milk, or for an adult to drink milk at all. One could take the extreme position that a carrot pulled from the ground loses its "natural" quality when the bacteria-infested soil surrounding it is washed away, or if it is cooked. Such extreme ideas as these I cannot accept, because they fly in the face of scientific findings and centuries of experience. We must be temperate in our interpretation of the expression "natural foods."

We live in a practical world along with many hundreds of millions of other people. Many of these live in cities and in cold climates and unless ways of severely limiting populations and preventing congestion can be found, it is quite impossible for every family to have its own cow or goat (or yak) and chickens and to grow its own garden produce twelve months out of the year. Food preservation and transportation must be practiced on a grand scale as long as our world resembles the world of today.

All gardening is in a sense "organic" gardening. Anyone acquainted with the biochemistry of green plants knows that even the poorest soil abounds in bacteria, fungi (molds), and other forms of life, and that a growing plant always develops in symbiotic relationship with these soil organisms.

It is true that in a soil fertilized by manure, these soil organisms are more prolific, and if everything else the plants need is present, the plants are well nourished. But no plant—even corn growing in a stony unfertilized field—can develop unless it gets from its surroundings everything necessary to build its own metabolic machinery. No grain of corn ever developed or could develop unless it contained some of every necessary mineral, amino acid, and vitamin.

Whether corn grown under some conditions has a

greater quantity and a better-balanced assortment of these essentials than if it were grown under other conditions, is a separate question. We need first to dispel the idea that corn plants and other plants can ever grow "artificially," or in such a way that the grown plant is devoid of the minerals, amino acids, and vitamins capable of sustaining the life of mammals. Plans always grow "organically" (that is, in cooperation with soil organisms) to produce plants that have in their make-up all of the chemical links necessary to organic life.

The important fact is that plants vary in their nutritional value depending on the fertility of the soil in which they grow. The nutritional situations under which green plants grow are exceedingly complicated.[8] In the early stages of growth, very young plants need vitamins and other nutrients which may be supplied from the outside.[9] Later on, the green plant manufactures its own supply and stores these essentials in the seeds which pass them on to the growing seedling. The roles that symbiotic organisms play in furnishing various organic structures to the growing plantlets are often very poorly understood and differ from one type of plant to another.

The mineral content of the soil in relation to the growth of plants is easier to investigate. One thing is certain: Organisms cannot change one element into another. If a plant has iron, copper, zinc, calcium, potassium, and phosphorus in its makeup, these elements must have come from the soil in which the plant grew.

Manure abounds in microorganisms; its application helps make soil more porous so the roots can get needed oxygen and, in addition, it furnishes the minerals and nitrogen that plants need. Manures from different sources are not the same, however, nor does cow manure (or horse manure) have a constant composition. If, for example, the natural soil on which cattle graze is deficient or poorly balanced in trace elements, the manure from these animals will reflect these deficiencies. This is true in the Florida Everglades where the soil is low in copper and has a superabundance of molybdenum. When the soil conditions are corrected, the manure from the animals is likewise improved.

It is not certain that the element iodine is necessary for the healthy growth of plants, but it most certainly is essential for the life of the mammals. In "goiterous" regions (e.g., Switzerland, the Great Lakes area, and the Pacific Northwest), the vegetation is so low in iodine that some animals are affected by the lack of it. Manure from all animals in the area is very low in iodine because no animal can make iodine out of any other element. If the animals are artificially fed iodized salt, then their manure is improved as a fertilizer, and plants grown on the soil thus fertilized will sustain the life of animals and prevent the occurrence of endemic goiter.

Experiments with agrostis ("bent grasses")[10] have shown that the application of larger amounts of calcium and phosphate to the soil caused nearly a doubling of the content of tryptophan (one of the essential amino acids needed in the diet of mammals) in the grown plant. Experiments with Italian ryegrass showed that fertilizing the soil with ammonium sulfate or with sodium nitrate substantially increased the nutritional value of the grass with respect to the nutritionally essential amino acids arginine, leucine, lysine, phenylalanine, and tryptophan.[11] Experiments with leucine showed that increasing the boron supply caused a doubling of the production of tryptophan. (Boron itself is known to be necessary for green plants, but is not known to be needed by mammals.[12])

The vitamin contents of plants are likewise increased when the plants are given better nutrition. It has been found, for example, that when three plants—cocksfoot, white clover, and cow parsnip—were grown on soils fertilized with manure only, the carotene (provitamin A) contents were substantially lower than when the fertilizer was supplemented with a nitrogen-potash-phosphate mixture.[13] This experiment shows, incidentally, that manure fertilizer may be subject to limitations and can, in some cases at least, be improved by appropriate additions.

In Germany, studies have shown that fertilization with nitrogen, potash, and superphosphate increased the yield of oats over twenty times and at the same time doubled the level of thiamine (vitamin B_1) in the grain produced. The same experiment with millet showed a tripling of the yield and a 37 percent increase in the thiamine content of the grain produced.

From these and other experiments, it becomes clear that when plants are furnished better nutrition, the plants that result are superior in their nutritional value for animals and man. We can be sure that whenever food plants are able to grow, they will contain the essential food elements needed by mammals. If these plants are furnished the best possible nutrition, however, it is safe to assume that they will have higher nutritional value for animals and man.

There is really no escaping the fact that it is only through the intelligent and conscientious application of the lessons of science that we shall achieve the kind of improvement in nutrition necessary to raise significantly the general level of health and to prevent the onset of specific diseases. The hit-or-miss oversimplifications of the food faddists—and still less, the neglect of the medical profession—will not accomplish the task.

And still we are left with the question, "What can the layman do?"

Without succumbing to the extremes or the errors of food faddism, he can, of course, do many common-sense things to improve his own nourishment. He can pay attention to the quality of the food he eats. For insurance he can use vitamin, mineral, and amino acid supplements. And he can watch the intake of toxic elements such as alcohol, tobacco, and needless drugs.

But there is something he can do beyond ministering to his own immediate needs. He can bring pressure to bear on those who should be ministering to him. He can do so as a customer, as a client, as a patient, as a citizen, and as a voter.

Let us, for example, consider how we, as customers, relate to the food industries—how we are served and how we might be served.

14 What the Food Industries Can Do

The food industries, though based on science, have tended to stand still (or regress) with respect to performing their essential function in society, namely, producing food of better and better nutritional quality for the consumers. Because of long standing neglect of nutrition and the nutritional improvement of life, the food industries tend to take food quality for granted.

There is a sore need for a revolutionary change in attitude. The public, the medical profession, those who produce food by agriculture, and those who process, package, preserve, distribute, and sell foods, all need to realize that the quality of the food we eat is a problem that outranks even that of the quality of what we read in school books, newspapers, and magazines.

Scientific advances have made it possible for food to be vastly higher in quality today than it was ten, twenty, forty, or a hundred years ago; but in the food industry there has been a prevailing attitude of merely getting by the Food and Drug Administration and of waiting until some government committee prods them before trying to improve upon the food that grandma used to prepare. Even those citizens who are concerned about our food would often be content with nutrition as good as, or maybe a little better than, it was in the days of Queen Victoria.

We take it for granted that the other science-based industries will make substantial advances decade after decade. We see the development of TV and color TV, of beautifully recorded music, of transportation that can take us to the moon and back, and take it all in stride. The textiles of today are incomparably superior to what they were when the choices were between cotton, wool, and silk; the paint industry has been completely revolutionized; our present day lighting is a far cry from the glow produced by Edison's carbon lamp. We may swear at computers, but the industry that produces them has made unbelievable advances, and will continue to do so.

Furthermore, these advances have come from *within* the industries themselves. Can one imagine the Bell Telephone Laboratories waiting for the approval of a governmental committee before inventing the transistor? Can one imagine the textile industry sitting on its haunches for thirty years after its first production of rayon, waiting to see if vastly improved textiles might be in order? Does IBM wait for public or governmental advice as to the best ways of improving its products? If the food industries were to keep pace with the other science-based industries, they would employ experts of the highest quality who would put to shame any outsiders who might wish to tell them what to do. Where does one find outstanding experts in electronics, in textiles, in lighting, or in computer design? While academic men make their contributions, the men in the respective industries do not sit around waiting for developments to take place outside the industries.

How scientifically weak one segment of the food industry—the milling and baking industry—has been, is demonstrated when one considers the story of the "enrichment" of flour and bread.

White flour and bread, though supposedly relished and in demand, has been under attack by nutrition-minded people for several decades. It is well known that white flour keeps much better than whole wheat flour and that one reason for its better keeping quality is the fact that it will not support the life of weevils. Yet, during the milling process, the germ of the wheat grain is eliminated, and with it goes the fatty components and many of the items in the nutritional chain of life. What is left is largely starch and wheat protein; the latter, like many other vegetable proteins, is of relatively low nutritional quality.

In 1941, partially at the instigation of my older brother, R. R. Williams, now deceased, the "enrichment" of white flour and bread was instituted.[1] At that time it was decided, largely on the basis of expert help outside the industry, that thiamine, riboflavin, niacin, and iron should be added to flour and that calcium should be an optional supplement. These nutrients were added to restore, at least in part, those lost in the milling process. Many practical and technological considerations were involved in making these choices, including palatability, availability, cost, and evidence as to the probability of substantial nutritional improvement. As of the time of making these decisions, the choices were reasonable ones.

The sad part of the story is this: Since 1941, for a period of about thirty years, the milling and baking industry—lacking any substantial outside prodding—has rested quiescently on this early "enrichment." It has never made any significant attempt to improve further the nutritional quality of flour and bread.

Having become keenly aware of the situation and its importance through the preparation for the writing of this book, I performed the following experiment with the technical assistance of Charles W. Bode.

Young weanling rats of four different strains, 128 in number, were placed on two bread diets. One group of sixty-four was placed on commercial enriched bread still produced essentially in accordance with the practices of about thirty years ago. A matched group of sixty-four was given the same bread which had been

supplemented in accordance with more up-to-date
knowledge by the addition of small amounts of minerals,
other vitamins, and one amino acid, lysine.[2]

The two breads were indistinguishable in appearance,
and the added nutrients at wholesale rates would cost
only a fraction of a cent per loaf.

That the rats on the commercial enriched bread
would not thrive was to be expected. After ninety days,
about two-thirds of them were dead of malnutrition
and the others were severely stunted. The rats on the
improved bread did surprisingly well; most of them
were alive and growing at the end of the ninety-day experiment. Their growth and development on the improved bread was on the average seven times as fast as
on the commercial bread.[3]

It is my contention that the milling and baking industry should have been doing experiments like this for
decades, and should have been moving consistently in
the direction of better bread by whatever routes seemed
most appropriate to the experts. As a science-based
industry, the milling and baking industry should be expected to advance. Bread holds—or should hold—a
unique position as the staff of life, a staple basic food.
If the food industry is not interested in improving our
daily bread, it is not to be expected that it will be much
concerned about other foods.

Actually, "enriched flour" (it should, on the basis of
present knowledge, be called "deficient flour") is used
in the preparation of a multitude of other products such
as cakes, cookies, crackers, pastries, doughnuts, biscuits,
muffins, waffles, pancakes, macaroni, noodles. All of
these would be far better nutritionally if the flour were
not needlessly so deficient.

Furthermore, the complacent acceptance of the
limited "enrichment" with thiamine, riboflavin, niacin,
and iron, has held back the nutritional improvement of
all other cereal products. When corn or rice or breakfast foods are "enriched," the same four nutrients are
added, as though these constituted an exclusive "sacred
quartet," and no other nutrients could be of concern.
There are many other nutrients—pyridoxine, panto-

thenic acid, folic acid, vitamin B_{12}, vitamin A, vitamin E, magnesium, and the trace elements—that need to be thought of in any real enrichment program. Some of these are probably sorely lacking in many diets— especially when these diets include many products made from "enriched" flour. People who eat substantially more bread and related products than the average (often those with lower incomes) are liable to be badly deficient in the items that we used in our feeding experiments to supplement commercial bread.

I personally feel keen disappointment in the failure of the food industry to advance, because most of my scientific life has been devoted to exploring and increasing our knowledge about nutrition. My endeavors have resulted in the discovery, isolation, and synthesis of one key vitamin, pantothenic acid; I have named another— folic acid—and have contributed by the microbiological approach to our knowledge about many others. Yet the vast amount of information and insight into nutrition gained in the last thirty years by hundreds of investigators has netted very little in terms of improvement in the food industries. This is a disgrace.

When our experiment involving the improved bread was reported to the National Academy of Sciences in October 1970, and the story got into the newspapers, I began to get protests from the Millers' National Federation and the American Institute of Baking. Their arguments rested largely on the thesis that bread was not supposed to be eaten alone and that other foods fill in the deficiencies of bread.

While bread need not be by itself a perfect food, it is nevertheless about as basic as a food can be. If it is grossly deficient and the deficiencies can be readily and inexpensively corrected, it should be the self-imposed responsibility of the milling and baking industry to see that it is done.

The Millers' National Federation published an interview with its president, C. L. Mast, Jr., the day after my paper was given to the National Academy. Mr. Mast said, in part: "If competent nutrition authority recommends any other additions to enriched flour and bread, you may be sure that the milling-baking industry will do its utmost to meet what it considers its responsibility in providing essential nutrients in such form that they meet public acceptance."

This sounds encouraging, except that it is the milling and baking industry itself that should provide the authorities and not wait for outsiders to tell them what to do.

In the same statement, Mr. Mast said, "the Millers' National Federation and the American Bakers Association had petitioned the Food and Drug Administration, November 5, 1969, for permission to treble or quadruple the amount of iron in enrichment, and subsequently asked Food and Nutrition Board support of a proposal to increase by 50 percent the amount of thiamine, niacin, and riboflavin in the enrichment formula."

These requests, particularly the latter one, reveal a singular lack of understanding of modern nutritional principles. From the perspective of 1941, the suggestion that more thiamine, riboflavin, niacin, and iron be added may sound reasonable, but from the perspective of thirty years later, it is ridiculous to stutter like a broken record about the "sacred four." Thiamine, riboflavin, niacin, and iron are no more indispensable in the scheme of life than are pyridoxine, pantothenic acid, vitamin E, folic acid, magnesium, and the trace elements, all of which are lost to a substantial degree in the milling process.

In our rat feeding experiments, we left the iron, thiamine, riboflavin, and niacin strictly alone, and improved the bread enormously by adding minor amounts of *other* nutrients. These nutrients were either not readily available in 1941, or their importance was not fully recognized. A lot of things can happen in science in thirty years.

One bit of philosophy accepted by some of those who supported the "enrichment" program, involved making the white bread as nearly equivalent as possible, nutritionally, to whole wheat bread. I see no reason why such a philosophy should be adhered to today. Why shouldn't modern bread be vastly *better* than old fashioned whole wheat bread?

It is well known that wheat proteins are poorly balanced in amino acid content so far as human consumption is concerned.[4] The amount of lysine, one of the essential amino acids, is, for example, far too low; and the nutritional value of bread and the availability of the protein in it would be greatly increased if it were supplemented with lysine. Since this is an economical and completely harmless procedure,[5] I can see no argument against it. There is nothing sacred about the composition of whole wheat that should make us slavishly follow its dictates in our search for good food.

It would be out of place for me or anyone else who lays no claim to expertness in milling and baking technology to outline precisely how the industry should proceed. This is *their* business. They should greatly improve our daily bread by whatever means they can— by including the germ in the flour, supplementing with milk powder and/or soybean flour, adding vitamins, minerals, and amino acids, or whatever. Since they have already moved part way in the direction of supplementation with specific nutrients, it seems logical that they should try further moves in the same direction. Our experiment suggests one possibility, but it is only a suggestion. Every possible means should be explored. The important thing is that bread, a staple food, be improved nutritionally.

One of the weak links in the enrichment program has been lack of attention to newer knowledge about the calcium-magnesium situation. The addition of calcium to bread was placed on an optional basis. It still is; some bakers put it in, others do not. In 1941 the human requirements for magnesium were not known to be high, nor had a magnesium-deficiency disease been demonstrated in man.[6] The Food and Nutrition Board gave estimates of the magnesium needs of human beings for the first time in their 1968 edition of its publication on "Allowances."[7] For a young man, this need is set at 400 milligrams per day, about one-half of the calcium need!

If the calcium addition is made to "enriched" bread (it should be, and there should be uniformity), then by all means magnesium should be added also. Extra calcium calls for extra magnesium, since a balance needs to be maintained. As we noted in an earlier chapter, magnesium deficiency is probably widespread, and increasing the intake of magnesium is an important measure recommended for protecting against heart disease.

Trace elements need to be thought of also; many vital ones are present in whole wheat and are removed in the milling process.[8] All of these matters should be of great concern to the milling and baking industry.

A key to this entire problem lies dominantly in the area of public education. If medical scientists and the general public were aware that the nutritional environment of our body cells and tissues hinges on what we eat—every mouthful contributes—and that this environment determines the degree of health we possess, then the public would be continually complaining about the poor nutritional quality of the flour and bread, and the industry would be forced to act. When the best that the baking industry can offer an infant for a snack is a soda cracker or some other washed-out tidbit, it is time for a change.

I have dwelt upon the problem of "enriched" bread because it is such a staple food, and the neglect of it is accompanied by a disregard of the nutritive value of foods in general. Improvement of all present-day foods should be on our minds.

The canning industry has, on the whole, done a good job in preserving the better known nutrients from destruction during the canning process. What is needed now is attention to the nutrients that are just as indispensable as thiamine, riboflavin, niacin, and iron, but that have received far less attention. Tables designed to give information about the nutritive value of foodstuffs rarely mention such items as vitamin B_6 (pyridoxine, etc.), pantothenic acid, vitamin B_{12}, and folic acid, and yet these are indispensable to life, and there is evidence that deficiencies are commonplace.

Since two of these nutrients exist in nature in various forms, the problem of knowing precisely how they are affected by canning or other food processing is not simple. Part of the burden of proof with respect to their retention should rest with the food processors who need to be concerned about the loss of all essential nutrients.

We need to develop a different psychological attitude toward eating. Instead of reassuring ourselves by saying, "Enriched bread (or breakfast cereal) is harmless; it won't hurt me," we need to realize that we need to derive *help* and *benefit,* day by day and hour by hour, from the food we eat, and that anything that does not help *contributes* to our ill health.

We have developed something of this attitude toward our cats and dogs, who fare better at the supermarket than we do. They have fewer choices, but most of the foods offered them are compounded scientifically and are far superior nutritionally to what their owners eat. People who would not think of feeding a dog bread, doughnuts, and coffee, or waffles and syrup eat such foods with abandon.

We (and the food industry) need to appreciate that for young children the "headstart" we may attempt to give them educationally may be more than cancelled by the "hindstart" we give them nutritionally. The brain cells of children need to be furnished an adequate nutritional environment so that brain development can take place. As it is, the brain cells of many youngsters are forced to limp along as best they can in a poor environment induced by deficient nutrition.[9] This is a most serious situation.

Who in these days can say that the environment doesn't matter? Whenever we eat "enriched" bread or any other product that is needlessly deficient, we help along the development of a poor environment. Every food we eat should contribute *in a positive way* to the development of a better environment. At present it is easy in a supermarket to pick out hundreds of items which *detract from* rather than contribute to a good cellular environment. The entire food industry should have as its aim building up better internal environments for children and adults.

Agriculture, too, needs to join in the scientific quest

for better food. While it is impossible to produce, by agriculture, foods that are lacking in nutritional value, we have it in our power to grow vastly improved foods through better soil use and more intelligent fertilization.

This is a complicated field of endeavor since soils vary considerably, and require different fertilization for different plants. It may be that some plants can be improved in nutritional value far more than others by proper fertilization. But over the country we have a large number of agricultural experimental stations and regional laboratories, many of which should be directing their major energies precisely toward the unravelling of these problems. Because the whole science of nutrition (as it applies to real people) has lagged terribly, agriculture has tended to fall into the same rut as the rest of the food industry, and to be satisfied if the food it produces is about as good as our grandfathers had. Agriculture can and must move ahead in the production of better grains, better fruit, better vegetables, better melons, better meats, better eggs, better milk.

The food industry as a whole, including agriculture, needs to be increasingly concerned about the problem of contaminating the internal environment of our bodies by the free use of additives which have no nutritional value and are always capable of doing harm. *Lancet*,[10] a prominent British medical journal, points out that, on the average, one consumes in the course of the year about three pounds of chemicals that are not normal constituents of foods. Some of these—preservatives, coloring agents, and sweeteners—are deliberately added to food; while others, such as insecticides and antibiotics, may get there unintentionally.

It is too much to expect that the internal environment of our body cells and tissues will be completely free from all contaminants. (The air we breathe, and the water we drink, is never *absolutely* pure.) But it is the food industry's responsibility zealously to guard this internal environment not only by putting the right things into it, but also by leaving the destructive things out.

Food technology is far too complicated to make it possible for an outsider to discuss in detail just what the various branches of the food industry should do about specific additives.[11] What we need to develop in the food industry is adherence to the motto of the future: "Better and better food." When this is followed, additives will be held to an absolute minimum. The idea that an additive is acceptable if it helps sales and does not make the customer noticeably ill must be discarded. I believe an informed public will force this change in attitude.

Indeed, it is on the power of an informed public opinion that we shall probably finally have to rely to effect most of the significant improvements in our nutritional situation. I do not underestimate the difficulty of creating an informed opinion, but in view of the tremendous interest in our macroenvironment which has developed in a few years, it is by no means unreasonable to hope that a similar interest can be stirred up with respect to our microenvironments.

Of course, the teaching of nutrition to home economics students would be vastly simpler if there were fewer vitamins, minerals, and amino acids to worry about. But we have to take nature the way we find it. If we simplify matters too much, we do violence to truth.

In a booklet, "Eat to Live,"[12] put out by the Wheat Flour Institute of Chicago (1970), a deplorable full page illustration shows a pyramid of 10 children's blocks labelled: The "Key" Nutrients. These individual blocks represent vitamin A (at the top), then two Bs (thiamine and niamine) next, then beneath them C, another B (riboflavin) and D, and on the bottom row Protein, Calcium, Iron, and energy.

This is a most unfortunate picture, because what it says it fundamentally untrue. In order for our cells and tissues to have a proper environment, we need to have adequate supplies of a *team* of nutrients, and the team is as strong as its weakest member. Pyridoxine (vitamin B_6), pantothenic acid, cobalamine (vitamin B_{12}), and folic acid are absolutely essential nutrients, just as are thiamine, niacin, and riboflavin. Phosphate, magnesium, potassium, and the trace elements are just as indispensable as calcium and iron.

Abbreviated nutrition, which is adequate with respect to only some of the needed nutrients, can only lead to diminished health and early death. This kind of nutrition is easily attained; our children, with all their candy bars, potato chips, soft drinks, and "enriched" bread live with it all the time, and we adults sometimes fare little better. The kind of nutrition we crucially need, what the food industry should provide us, is *complete nutrition*—the kind that leads to abundant health.

15 New Developments in Basic Medicine

Informed public opinion is a powerful force that will not only help bring the food industries to acknowledge the nutritional facts of life, but it can be a potent factor in rejuvenating medical education.

We *know* that our nutrition can be improved and thereby our general health. We have presented overwhelming evidence that nutrition can play a vital role in the prevention of many diseases, both trivial and deadly. When this evidence becomes generally available, I predict it will have a profound effect on medical education. Medical people who have set ideas will resist, but the more alert minds, young and old, will be impressed, and will not be inclined to quibble over nonessential details.

In order to hasten the day when change will come in medical education, informed public opinion can play a tremendous role. Those of us who are outside the medical profession cannot be expected to do what physicians do, but we have a right to be interested in

215

the total environment of our bodies. We can recognize obsolete attitudes; we can be suspicious of the jargon that may be offered in lieu of intelligent knowledge about nutrition; we can *insist* that the doors of knowledge be opened to admit vital information related to nutrition. If we believe in the case for better nutrition, we should be prepared to put it forcefully and intelligently.

A good example of why the layman needs to be informed relates to the way in which statistics are often used in medical research. The so-called statistical approach is much used by medical researchers because, as a mathematics based method, it seems reassuringly scientific. However, it has a lamentable tendency to give answers only to those questions that are genuinely unimportant or that are so obvious that they hardly needed asking. The result is that all too often our attention is deflected from what might be significant to what is patently insignificant.

For the sake of clarity, and as an illustration, let us imagine we are living at the time when riboflavin, the yellowish pigment in milk whey, was found to be a vitamin. The traditional medical approach to this new substance, providing there was interest in it in the first place, would involve trying it out to see whether it had therapeutic or prophylactic value in connection with various diseases.

Let us imagine, as a purely hypothetical case, that one medical investigator suspected riboflavin might be valuable in preventing the production of malformed babies, that another investigator thought it might be valuable in treating heart disease, that another thought it might help solve the dental disease problem, and still another that it might help curb cancer.

If these possibilities suggested themselves strongly enough, the first thing to do, traditionally, would be to perform some preliminary animal experiments. Certain animals on basal diets would be given riboflavin in appropriate doses; other matched animals would not. Methods would then be devised for determining whether or not riboflavin had any beneficial effect. Such experiments would have been discouraging because, when analyzed, the results would undoubtedly have failed to be statistically significant. The investigators would rightly assume that if similar human experiments were done (these would be extremely expensive) the results would also be negative. Then the conclusion would be drawn that riboflavin probably has no value in connection with any of these diseased conditions because experimental design had a fatal flaw.

This conclusion would be completely unwarranted. The statistics are not in error; it is the biological thinking that is invalid.

In accordance with the way metabolic machinery works, no nutrient *by itself* can be effective. It is like a nut or a bolt in a complicated machine; by itself it cannot operate. This fact and its meaning need to be pondered. No investigator could validly report riboflavin to be ineffective in counteracting malformations, heart disease, dental disease, or cancer unless he had tested it under conditions appropriate for its functioning. If it is to carry out its functions, all other parts of the metabolic machinery must be in working order.

A more valid experiment designed to test the value of riboflavin in connection with the various diseased conditions mentioned would involve giving riboflavin *plus* all the other nutritional essentials to one set of prospective animal mothers while withholding riboflavin only from another set.

The results of such an experiment are already pretty well known. In the total absence of riboflavin, there would be no reproduction whatsoever, while if it was kept at a low level, the reproduction would be faulty (malformations, etc.) and the young, often with faulty hearts and teeth, would probably not live long enough to develop cancer. By more elaborate experiments, of long duration and involving several levels of riboflavin, not only would the beneficial effects of riboflavin be evident in connection with malformations, heart disease, and dental disease, but probably also in preventing cancer. Its preventive effect on cancer has actually been demonstrated when a cancer-producing substance is included in the diet.[1]

As always, in science, the validity of the experimental

method is crucial. Is riboflavin effective as a therapeutic or prophylactic agent in connection with malformations, heart disease, dental disease, and cancer? If the experiment involves administering riboflavin by itself as an isolated agent, the answer appears to be "no." If, on the other hand, the experiment is designed to give riboflavin a chance to work effectively (its functioning *must* be cooperative in nature), then the answer is "yes."

One of my highly reputable physician friends has written me: "Vitamins have been tried in the treatment of every kind of ailment regardless of rationale. A 'cure-all' in the public mind. Millions spent catering to this fad." This to me points to the crucial difficulty; riboflavin and other vitamins and nutrients have indeed "been tried," but only in a haphazard way, under conditions that often make it almost certain that statistically positive results will not be forthcoming. Testing nutrients adequately must take into account the inevitable teamwork involved.

Testing a drug is fundamentally quite different from testing a nutrient. If one wishes to know whether quinine is effective as a treatment for malaria, it is tested *by itself,* and one finds the answer. If one wishes to test the effectiveness of digitalis for certain heart conditions, one tests it *by itself* and gets a positive answer. If one wishes to test morphine for its effectiveness in relieving pain, one administers it *by itself,* and finds that the effect is remarkable. The testing of these drugs resembles, in a way, a coach trying out Olympic candidates for the high jump, pole vault, or shot put. The evaluation of the individual athlete is reached after he has performed by himself.

Drugs in general are *by themselves* effective agents which cause an interference with or modification of enzyme systems already in the body. The results of their action is not perfectly uniform because the enzyme systems in different individuals are by no means identical.[2] But the enzyme systems, whatever their exact characteristics, are preformed and ready to be influenced by the individual drugs.

Testing a nutrient for its effects is quite different

from testing a drug. When a nutrient is tested by itself, it is like a professional football coach trying out a quarterback without providing him a football team to work with.

Nutrients are effective because they are constructive; they enter into the makeup of enzyme systems and can function in this constructive way only when all the other building blocks are available. If only one link is conspicuously missing, then supplying this one link by itself will be effective. This is exceptional, however. Body cells live constantly under conditions of suboptimal nutrition, and for a given cell at a given time there is always a weakest link in the long nutritional chain. When a single nutrient is tested it cannot be effective unless it happens to strengthen this weakest link. For it to work, all the other members of the team must be playing ball. Historically there have been a few cases of flagrant nutritional deficiencies in which single nutrients have been effective. However, a victim of beriberi is never brought back to health by thiamine alone, a victim of scurvy needs good food in addition to ascorbic acid, and pellagra victims are practically always in need of several vitamins plus good protein food. Rickets is often benefited by vitamin D, but this vitamin (or its equivalent in sunshine) is absolutely worthless by itself. If calcium and phosphate, for example, are not furnished in suitable amounts, vitamin D is helpless. Teamwork is *always* involved.

As I have said, if riboflavin were administered by itself to animals in a traditional experiment, the statistical analysis of the results would probably have yielded negative answers. It is easy to see why this would be so; riboflavin deficiency is not that common. Riboflavin is only one of dozens of links that can be weak, and weakness in any one of these can cause an impairment of the metabolic machinery. It cannot be supposed that supplying riboflavin in the diet would strengthen the weakest link in more than a fraction of the cases.

In the experiment cited in a previous chapter, it was found that administering riboflavin alone to rats delayed the first onset of butter yellow cancers for about twenty-five days and decreased the incidence of cancers from about 100 percent to about 80 percent. This was a partial effect due to the fact that in about 20 percent of the animals the riboflavin was conspicuously deficient, so that when it was supplied, benefit resulted.

When casein, with its good supply of all the essential amino acids, was added to the diet, it also had a delaying action—about like riboflavin. But when casein and riboflavin were both added to the diet, the first onset of cancer was delayed nearly 150 days (equivalent to about eight years of human life) and then only 3 percent of the animals became cancerous. The teamwork was effective enough so that a large percentage of the animals were protected.

If some other carcinogenic agent were involved in the experiments, or if the rats were of a different strain or were on a different basal diet, the percentages would probably be very different; but the principle would be unchanged: The nutrients are constructive; they work together, and no one of them can be tested as though it were an independent agent working by itself.

There is a very broad principle involved here. What we have said about riboflavin applies to every other nutrient; each needs to be tested under appropriate conditions—conditions that will allow it to function. What has been said in connection with malformations, heart disease, dental disease, and cancer applies in principle to obesity, arthritis, mental disease, alcoholism, and any other disease one can think of. All diseases need to be explored from the standpoint of what various nutrients can do when tested under conditions that allow the nutrients to function cooperatively. This has not been done, and that is what this book is about.

Billions of dollars and many thousands of man-years have gone into the discovery of what we know about the essential nutrients that human beings need every day. Up to now much of this money and effort has been wasted simply because we have failed to appreciate adequately that nutrients are always involved in teamwork; we have allowed preconceived notions, gained from our centuries-old experience in testing drugs, to dominate our thinking. Nutritional benefits come from team play, and the *whole* team is needed—the nutritional chain of life.

Experiments need to be carried forward with these facts in mind. Contrary to views that have occasionally been expressed to me, meaningful human experiments are not, necessarily, prohibitively costly in money or manpower. For example, one experiment in prenatal nutrition might involve furnishing one population of brides with comprehensive nutritional supplements containing, as far as feasible, adequate amounts of all the nutrients that are likely to be furnished in too-limited amounts in common daily diets. For comparison, another similar population of brides should be allowed to go their own way without the special supplements.

In an experiment of this kind, it is obvious that imperfections would exist. Individual brides who should take the provided supplements would not do so; individual brides in the control group might occasionally get, on their own, something that would be just as effective—for them—as the supplements.

Records of the miscarriages, premature births, malformations, mental retardations, bone and tooth development, etc., would be kept, and it would be most surprising indeed if, in the light of animal experiments, there were not highly significant statistical differences between the two groups. The experiment would perhaps not be easy to administer, and the cost would be substantial, but the potential benefits would be tremendous. The experiment might point the way, for example, toward the elimination of the hundreds of thousands of mentally retarded babies born each year.

The formulation of a suitable supplement would not be a routine procedure. Supplements that are currently available through pharmaceutical houses are unsuitable, because in most cases they have several deficiencies. In order to be effective, *all the links* in the nutritional chain of life need to be provided either in the food or in the supplement. Such a supplement should include such items as calcium hydrogen phosphate, magnesium oxide, all the B vitamins in adequate and appropriate amounts, vitamin A, vitamin E, vitamin D, vitamin K, plenty of ascorbic acid, choline, inositol, linoleic acid, and possibly some amino acids such as lysine or methionine, and several trace elements in appropriately small amounts. The material would have to be provided in an easy-to-take and attractive form, and the formulation would have to take this factor into account. Yeast might be used to supply generous amounts of some of the nutrients, but in order to be effective, the amounts of yeast used would probably have to be large and hence not easy to take.

Similar experiments need to be done with populations of middle-aged candidates for heart attacks to see if a supplement (probably omitting vitamin K) would not bring a substantial decrease in the incidence of these attacks. Despite all the expensive experimentation done on heart disease, no one has tried, in a straightforward way, the prophylactic effect of a supplement that has been formulated in a sophisticated and comprehensive manner. We have presented evidence that the results should be strongly positive.

Other experiments could be performed with children, keeping an eye on dental health. Again, we have presented evidence indicating the likely results.

Experiments need to be performed to see if mental disease cannot be controlled by the same means. On the basis of the evidence presented in Chapter 10, there is strong reason for thinking that if two populations were compared, the incidence of mental disease would be greatly diminished in the nutritionally-protected group. Such experiments have never been done.

Alcoholism and its prevention should be similarly tested, in which case glutamine should be included in the supplement. Because alcoholism is usually kept under cover, and its incidence is subject to rumor and opinion rather than objective evidence, experiments are difficult. At Harvard, a curative experiment bearing some resemblance to those we are proposing was attempted about sixteen years ago.[3] This, in spite of difficulties, yielded some mildly favorable results. The populations were very small, and were made up of confirmed alcoholics. The supplement used was not a comprehensive one, and since the glutamine effect had not been discovered at the time, this amino acid was not included. Since the "nutritional team" sent in to do the job was an incomplete one, it is not surprising that the treatment was only partially successful. Curative and prophylactic experiments along these lines need to be continued and expanded.

In Harlem, thirty years ago, an experiment was performed that involved giving certain Negro families a limited nutritional supplement to see what effect it might have on the incidence of tuberculosis.[4] The one positive effect observed was that the incidence of new cases of tuberculosis was lower in the treated group than in the control group. However, the difference did not quite reach significance at the 5 percent level of probability. The supplement used was, however, conspicuously deficient by today's standards. It contained no vitamin B_6, no pantothenate, no folic acid, no vitamin B_{12}, and no vitamin E. With the incomplete nutritional supplement used, it is not surprising that the results of the team play were unimpressive.

In Altadena, California, a study was made a few years later in which great care was used to see that *all* the tubercular patients were, by prevailing standards, well-nourished.[5] The patients were secretly divided into two groups. One group (B) received daily nutritional supplements of 600 milligrams of ascorbic acid, 75,000 to 150,000 units of vitamin A, about 5000 units of vitamin D, about four grams of brewer's yeast, and six grams of dried liver; the control group (A) received placebos. None of the attendants or patients knew which individuals were getting the supplements and which the blanks.

After totaling up the reports from all the patients, it was found that those who secretly got the supplements were better off in many respects: There was more improvement in chest X rays; more patients were discharged as cured; most patients had improved appetites; as a whole, they gained weight about twice as fast as the control group; and they showed decreased restlessness and demand for attention. The control group was considered to be "exceedingly well-nourished," and the supplements used by the experimental group were not up to modern standards. Yet the contrast between the groups was impressive.

Sophisticated studies of this sort are not fostered by current medical education. Nutrition-minded physicians are, after all, considered suspect by the orthodox.

Implicit in all that I have said so far is the central idea that experiments should be performed to explore the uses of nutrients working as a team. Can elderly people be made more comfortable, more alert, and freer from all sorts of vexations by protecting them nutritionally? To what extent can allergies be prevented by fully adequate nutrition? Cataracts in the eyes are known to be produced in animals by nutritional deficiencies;[6] can they be prevented in humans by attention to complete nutrition? Experiments testing the effect of nutrients, working as a team, need to be extended in many directions. Unfortunately we cannot rely on most of the experiments done in the past because the cooperative aspect of nutrient functioning has almost never been taken into account.

Are there essential nutrients that are still undiscovered? Most investigators may be inclined to say "no" on the basis of the argument that animals can be successfully raised on synthetic diets. This is not a completely satisfactory answer. There has never been a successful continuous feeding of a synthetic diet to several successive generations of animals.

If it should be found that some unknown, which we shall call X, is needed in addition to those nutrients normally listed as necessary for mammals, then all the nutritional experiments done to date need to be reevaluated. It may be, of course, that this X is widely distributed in adequate amounts, and that deficiencies of it are rare. If this is the case, then the recognition of X might not be of such great significance. But if there are unknowns, then we can be sure that some otherwise well-conceived therapeutic and prophylactic trials will have yielded negative results because these lacks have not been recognized. The whole team is needed, and we dare not rely too heavily on the possibility that the present list is a complete one.

Another aspect of the general problem has to do with the existence of what we can appropriately call "symbiotic cell nutrients." These are nutrients that are not required by the body as a whole, but are produced by certain body cells and needed by others.

A case in point is inositol. It is not included in our basic list of items in the nutritional chain of life because there is definite evidence that it is synthesized in the tissues of higher animals.[7] That it is required by human liver cells and bone marrow cells in tissue culture has also been demonstrated.[8] Presumably, it is commonly produced by some cells in our bodies and furnished to others. This raises the question of whether endogenous inositol production may at times be too limited, in which case an animal or a human being may be benefited by an added amount in the diet. That this is the case has been shown by producing nutritional deficiency states in several animals which can be overcome by inositol feeding. It is because of this possibility that we have suggested the inclusion of inositol in a comprehensive nutritional supplement.

The importance of these observations lies in the fact that they raise a general question: May animals or human beings, under certain circumstances, benefit from having in their diet substances other than those listed as belonging to the group of basic nutrients? The answer to this question is yes.

Among the substances that are ordinarily synthesized within our bodies, but that may at times be nutritionally advantageous because their endogenous production is limited, are inositol, lipoic acid, glutamine, coenzyme Q, and probably several others. These need to be woven into the total nutritional picture—and the worth of each of these can only be established by testing it in conjunction with all other nutrients.

Here we find a vast unexplored territory.[9] Many

diseases which may not respond when the ordinary nutrients are fully supplied might do so when supplements containing "symbiotic cell nutrients," inositol, lipoic acid, glutamine, coenzyme Q, and the rest, are supplied in addition. A vast amount of experimentation along these lines is in order.

Are there additional cell nutrients (as opposed to general nutrients) which have not, up to now, been recognized? Yes, there are; and these will one day constitute additional nutritional ammunition for those engaged in the fight against disease.

One evidence of their existence is the fact that when we attempt to grow various body cells in tissue culture, we are continually up against the necessity of providing these cells with blood serum, embryonic tissue juice, or some other natural material that contains unknown chemicals and is indispensable precisely because of these unknowns. Tissue culture directed toward the identification of these unknowns should obviously be a matter of major concern for medical investigators. These unknowns are potentially essential members of nutritional teams which can be used to combat disease.

That unknown cell nutrients exist and may be highly protective in preventing infectious diseases has been shown by a long-range study carried out largely at the Rockefeller Institute (now Rockefeller University). This study, which has had many ramifications and has lasted at least twenty-seven years, showed conclusive evidence of the existence of a substance that, when added to the diet of mice (200 to 400 parts per billion), will protect them from salmonella infections (mouse typhoid) so that their survival is increased from 10 percent up to 90 percent.[10] The substance has not been completely purified, but it has a relatively low molecular weight (dialyzable), appears to have catechol properties and to have in it "some amino acids, especially serine." The substance is apparently not a vitamin, since it is not necessary for the growth of mice, but it acts nutritionally in a remarkable manner. In fact, mice that have had it in their diet all their lives and have been thereby protected from salmonella infection, become immediately susceptible if it is excluded from their diet for two days.

This material is widespread in various foods. It is produced, for example, by an aerobacter, and a source for it was devised by culturing this organism. The exact chemical makeup of this and similar protective agents in animals and men needs to be known, and such research should have high priority for medical scientists. Here again we have a vast territory related to nutrition which needs to be explored.

There is a form of "supernutrition" which obviously is not of general application, but needs to be considered in individual cases where the expense would not be prohibitive. This involves making as sure as possible that the individual concerned gets not only all the needed minerals, vitamins, and the other cell nutrients which *may* be needed, but also all the amino acids. It should not be taken for granted, for example, that an individual getting plenty of good protein food is, *ipso facto,* well supplied with all the needed amino acids; but, as we have seen, problems involving biochemical individuality in digestive (or absorptive) enzymes may intervene. Amino acids as such are available and can be supplied directly.

If I were afflicted with a disease of obscure origin that is virtually untreatable, or if I were a physician in charge of such a case, I would certainly wish first to see if "supernutrition" might help. This would involve expending every effort to improve the nutritional environment of the afflicted cells and tissues. Such measures need to be tried in connection with diseases like multiple sclerosis and muscular dystrophy. Particularly interesting from the standpoint of the theme of this book is whether nutritional means cannot be effective in *preventing* the occurrence of these diseases.

One of the complications in any attempt to apply nutritional knowledge to individuals in order to cure or prevent disease, is the possibility of imbalances. It would take us too far afield to go into detail about these possibilities, yet they must be recognized.

Too much of one amino acid can interfere with the teamwork of the other amino acids.[11] Fortunately, such interference is not conspicuous when the intake of amino acids is kept at reasonable levels. Nutritional imbalances between minerals may also exist; these have received some attention beginning with the classic observations with respect to relationships between calcium and phosphate in rickets. Imbalances between various vitamins, and between vitamins and other nutrients, is another possibility that cannot be entirely dismissed. Fortunately, however, decades of experience have shown that vitamins, individually and as a group, are most often inert unless they are used cooperatively in the body for constructive purposes. There is no vitamin that cannot be administered safely at a level ten times that of the usual supposed need.

It is true that when vitamin D was first produced by irradiation, it was exceedingly cheap, and uninformed persons took enormous doses (on the assumption that if a little is good, more is better). Some damage resulted; but the amounts taken were often hundreds or thousands of times as much as are ordinarily needed.

Similarly, "vitamin A toxicity," which has received an inordinate amount of attention, has been produced only when dosages have been extremely large as compared with ordinary needs. In one extreme experiment involving rats, for example, the animals were given 10,000 times what rats are said to need. Even at this level of dosage the symptoms were only moderately severe.[12] At current prices, to get a like amount of vitamin A, a human being would have to consume 1000 capsules each containing 50,000 units, and the cost would be about $65 per day.

While excessive dosage with vitamin A is undesirable, the danger from moderate dosage up to 50,000 units per day is minimal. More, however, needs to be known about the functions of vitamin A and vitamin A acid.

The situation with respect to folic acid is unusual. The Food and Drug Administration does not permit it to be put into vitamin supplements in substantial amounts (without prescription) because, in case one is inclined toward pernicious anemia, folic acid may cover up the condition without preventing it, and vitamin B_{12} deficiency may become serious. Both vitamin B_{12} and folic acid are needed. Thus, if vitamin B_{12} is supplied in abundance either by injection or by mouth (in the latter case along with the intrinsic factor, if necessary), then extra folic acid is harmless.

In general, then, one does not have to be much concerned, on the basis of present knowledge, about imbalances involving vitamins. High dosages, in doubtful cases, should not be taken over long periods of time without expert advice. It is, of course, physicians who *should* be able to give this advice.

The whole matter of imbalances, especially when it comes to individual cases, is a matter that will require much study in future decades. The more so, since the results are likely to be complex. Because of biochemical individuality, it is entirely possible for certain individuals to be susceptible to imbalances that will not disturb others.[13]

Another development in medical exploration and education will involve the expanded use of automated equipment to make all sorts of analyses, and computer techniques for analyzing the data obtained. Automated equipment and computer techniques are already being used in a number of hospitals, and rapid development is under way. But as this book has all too plainly indicated, we shall almost certainly have to modify the orientation of those who decide what tests are to be made and what new ones will be developed. One of the most encouraging aspects of this development is the fact that tests are becoming vastly cheaper as time goes on. I am informed that one laboratory is performing a group of tests for eleven trace elements for a fee to the patient of less than $1.00 per test.[14]

The number of tests that can be done is legion. Many of the tests that have a strong appeal on the basis of our discussions are those that will determine (by loading tests and the subsequent evaluation of blood and urine constituents, etc.) the nutritional needs of a particular individual, especially if some of these needs are unusually high.

It is obviously unthinkable that we should seek to learn "everything that can be learned about everybody."

We can study specific disease problems, however, and determine what factors of biochemical individuality are most likely to be involved in each disease. This is one of the important functions of medical research, and it cannot be accomplished without the use of the most sophisticated computer techniques.

Computerized information will be increasingly valuable in diagnosing diseases, and one of the outgrowths will be the recognition that many diseases that are often considered as single diseases will be found to include those with several different etiologies. For example, nearly twenty years ago one of my graduate students, himself a diabetic, made a study of the biochemical individuality existing in a series of individuals diagnosed as afflicted with diabetes mellitus.[15] His preliminary conclusions, based upon substantial evidence, were that there are several different types of diabetes mellitus associated with different sorts of metabolic peculiarities. There are a number of different reasons, in different individuals, why glucose is not well utilized and tends to pile up in the blood.

A statistical study of a treatment method for diabetes mellitus (I am told that a recent study of this sort cost $7 million) is relatively useless and meaningless if it merely answers questions about the statistical diabetic and does not answer questions for the different individuals who have the disease with diverse etiologies. If such an experiment is not refined in the biological sense as well as the mathematical sense, the final relatively worthless conclusion is liable to be "sometimes yes, sometimes no."

Not only will computerized analysis, taking biochemical individuality into account, be most valuable in diagnosing disease, it will also be invaluable for determining those "leanings," with which all of us are born, that tend to make us susceptible to certain diseases and resistant to others.[16] These innate susceptibilities and resistances can probably be spotted in healthy young people long before the diseased conditions arise. What is more important, by suitable expert nutritional manipulation, the onset of these diseased conditions may be delayed indefinitely.

I envisage the time when, as part of the obstetrical service in hospitals, there will be a computerized record of each newborn baby's pattern of biochemical peculiarities, serving as a basis for future nurture and treatment. It is highly probable that many of the individual's leanings and susceptibilities can be determined at that time, and that in some cases special nutritional treatment can obviate future trouble, just as at present we are able to prevent, in the rare case of phenylketonuria, the onset of mental retardation.

Because expertise in maintaining human health demands the recognition of inborn individuality and the ability to deal with it using highly sophisticated statistical techniques, the mathematical artifact—the statistical or standard man—will cease to be of absorbing interest. We will deemphasize the use of medicines which often do damage to individuals in spite of the fact that "statistical man" might appear to be benefited. We will concentrate on constructive measures—providing the cells and tissues of our bodies the best possible nutritional environment.

Yet to bring about these necessary and inevitable changes, the public must raise its voice. We must demand governmental attention to and endorsement of a program of environmental prevention of disease—much like that which the antipollution drive has received. We are actually concerned with a positive approach to the very same problem—our internal environments. Impure air and water would be harmless if they failed to pollute our internal environments. It seems ridiculous for us to be concerned exclusively with keeping the wrong things out of these environments when we should be concerned also about putting the essential things in.

Even cancer, against which President Nixon has recently called for a concerted attack, is related to internal environments. This disease, like others, cannot be dealt with successfully unless the positive approach to our internal environments is adopted.

I submit that the environmental prevention of disease is not only possible but that it merits high priority—along with pollution and cancer—in the public mind and in governmental concern.

Reference Notes

CHAPTER 1

The Flaw in Medical Education

1. Williams, R. R. *Toward the Conquest of Beriberi*. Cambridge: Harvard, 1966, p. 19.

2. Williams, R. J., Beerstecher, E., Jr., and Berry, L. J. "The concept of genetotrophic disease." *Lancet*, 287:Feb., 1950.

3. Williams, R. J. *Biochemical individuality: the basis for the genetotrophic concept*. New York: Wiley, 1956. Subsequently published in two paperback editions. Currently available at the University of Texas Press at Austin. This volume has attracted enough attention so that it has been translated into Italian, Polish, and Russian for scientists who do not read English.

4. Scrimshaw, N. S. Quoted in *Hunger U.S.A.: a report by the Citizens' Board of Inquiry into hunger and mal-*

233

nutrition in the United States. Washington, D. C.: The New Community Press, 1968, p. 40.

5. Sebrell, W. H. "Changing concept of malnutrition." *Am. J. Clin. Nutr.*, 15:111, 1964.

6. Stare, F. J. Quoted in *Hunger U.S.A.*, Washington, D.C.: The New Community Press, 1968, p. 40.

7. Sigerist, H. E. *The university at the crossroads,* New York: Shuman, 1946. p. 114.

8. Steiglitz, E. J. Quoted in *Time,* July 23, 1956.

9. Ryle, J. A. *Changing Disciplines.* London: Oxford, 1948, pp. v, vi.

CHAPTER 2

The Nutrition-Heredity Factor

1. Williams, R. J., et al. "Individuality as exhibited by inbred animals: its implications for human behavior." *Proc. Nat. Acad. Sci.,* 48:1461, 1962; *See also* Williams, R. J. "Biochemical and physiological variations within groups of supposedly homogeneous experimental animals." *Symp. on Factors Involved in Host-Agent Relationships,* Ames, Iowa, Aug. 1961.

2. Williams, R. J., and Pelton, R. B. "Individuality in nutrition: effects of vitamin A-deficient and other deficient diets on experimental animals." *Proc. Nat. Acad. Sci.,* 55:126, 1966.

3. Williams, R. J., and Deason, G. "Individuality in vitamin C needs." *Proc. Nat. Acad. Sci.,* 57:1638, 1968.

4. Storrs, E. E., and Williams, R. J. "A study of monozygous quadruplet armadillos in relation to mammalian inheritance." *Proc. Nat. Acad. Sci.,* 60:910, 1968

5. Goodenough, V. W., and Levine, R. P. "The genetic activity of mitochondria and chloroplasts." *Scientific American,* Nov. 1970.

6. Lashley, K. S. "Structural variation in the nervous system in relation to behavior." *Psychological Rev.,* 54:33, 1947.

7. Williams, R. J. "Heredity, human understanding and civilization." *Amer. Sci.,* 57:237, 1969.

8. Freud, S. "Heredity and the etiology of neurosis." In *The standard edition of the complete psychological works of Sigmund Freud.* (Vol. III.) London: Hogarth, 1962, p. 143.

9. Jacobs, E. A., et al. "Hyperoxygenation effect on cognitive functioning in the aged." *New Eng. J. Med.,* 281:753, 1969.

CHAPTER 3

A New Hope for Better Health

1. Yudkin, J. "Patterns and trends in carbohydrate consumption and their relation to disease." *Proc. Nutr. Soc.,* 23:149, 1964.

2. Consumer and Food Economics Research Division. "Food intake and nutritive value of diets of men, women and children in the United States, Spring, 1965." Agri. Res. Ser., U. S. Department of Agriculture; Consumer and Food Economics Research Division. Dietary levels of households in the United States, Spring, 1965. Agri, Res. Ser., U.S. Department of Agriculture.

3. Meiss, A. N., et al. "Effect of nutritive improvement of bread on growth." *J. Am. Dietet. Assoc.,* 48:409, 1966.

4. Burton, B. T., executive ed. *The Heinz handbook of nutrition: a comprehensive treatise on nutrition in health and disease.* H. J. Heinz Co., New York: McGraw-Hill, 1959, pp. 135–138.

5. Williams, R. J. *Biochemical individuality:* the basis for the genetotrophic concept. New York: Wiley, 1956, Chapter X; Williams, R. J. "Individuality of amino acid needs." In *Protein and amino acid nutrition,* A. A. Albanese (Ed.), New York: Academic, 1959, pp. 45–56; Williams, R. J., and Pelton, R. B. "Individuality in nutrition: effects of vitamin A-deficient and other deficient diets on experimental animals." *Proc. Nat. Acad. Sci.,* 55:126, 1966; Williams, R. J., and Deason, G. "Individuality in vitamin C needs." *Proc. Nat. Acad. Sci.,* 57:1638, 1967.

6. Pauling, L. *Vitamin C and the common cold.* Chapter 10. San Francisco: Freeman, 1970.

7. A newspaper report occurred in the *London Sunday*

Chronicle of May 3, 1953. Subsequently, the same Salvation Army group published a book, *We Are What We Eat*, by A. B. Cunning and F. R. Innes, and published by the Salvationist Publishing and Supplies, Ltd., 1958.

8. McCarrison, Sir Robert, and Sinclair, H. M. *Nutrition and health*. (3rd ed.) London: Faber, 1964, p. 29.

CHAPTER 4

Stillborn, Deformed, and Mentally Retarded Babies

1. Williams, R. R. (Ed.) *Appraisal of human dietaries by animal experiment*. A Conference Under the Auspices of the Williams Waterman Fund for the Combat of Dietary Diseases, Hotel Roosevelt, N.Y., 1947; *See also* Dalldorf, G., and Williams, R. R. *Science*, 102:668, 1945.

2. Eastman, N. J., and Hellman, L. M. *Williams obstetrics*. New York: Appleton-Century-Crofts, 1961.

3. Richmond, J. B. "Mental retardation," *J.A.M.A.*, 191:243; 1965.

4. Levinson, A., and Bigler, J. A. *Mental retardation in infants and children,* Chicago: The Year Book Medical Publishers, 1960, p. 29.

5. Wilson, J. L. *Congenital malformations*. New York: International Medical Cong., 1964.

6. Winters, J. C. "Some trials of human diets on lower animals." In Williams, R. R. (Ed.) *Appraisal of human dietaries by animal experiment*. A Conference Under the Auspices of the Williams Waterman Fund for the Combat of Dietary Diseases, Hotel Roosevelt, N.Y., 1947, p. 5.

7. Warkany, J., and Nelson, R. C. "Appearance of skeletal abnormalities in the offspring of rats reared on a deficient diet." *Science*, 92:383, 1940; Warkany, J., and Nelson, R. C. "Skeletal abnormalities in the offspring of rats reared on deficient diets," *Anat. Rec.*, 79:83, 1941; Warkany, J., and Nelson, R. C. "Congenital malformations induced in rats by maternal nutritional deficiency." *J. Nutr.*, 23:321, 1942.

As early as 1939, Warkany and Nelson reared and bred different groups of female albino rats of the Sprague-

Dawley strain on six different diets of varying nutritional value, with the predictable result that the offspring thrive in health relative to the nutritional quality on the diet. More than one-third of the females' offspring fed a suboptimal diet showed skeletal abnormalities and many other congential malformations, while this pattern did not occur with the offspring of the females fed a balanced stock diet.

8. Lefebvres-Boisselot, Jeanne. "The influence of a slight pantothenic acid deficiency on the results of gestation in the rat." *Compt. Rend.*, 238:2123, 1954; *See also* Pfaltz, H. "Effect of vitamin deficiency in rats upon fertility, gestation, and rearing of the young." *Intern. Z. Vitaminforsch.*, 25:148, 1954; Giroud, A. et al. "Relation of folic acid deficiency to a secondary pantothenic acid deficiency in the pregnant rat." *Intern. Z. Vitaminforsch.*, 25:153, 1954.

9. Unna, K., and Greslin, J. G. "Toxicity and pharmacology of pantothenic acid." *J. Pharmacol. & Exper. Therapeut.*, 73:85, 1941; Unna, K., and Greslin, J. G. "Toxicity of pantothenic acid." *Proc. Soc. Exp. Biol. Med.*, 45:311, 1940; Unna, K. "Pantothenic acid requirement of the rat." *J. Nutr.*, 20:565, 1940; *See also* Unna, K. *Am. J. Med. Sci.*, 200:848, 1940.

10. Beerstecher, E., *In the biochemistry of B vitamins*. New York: Van Nostrand Reinhold, 1950.

11. Williams, R. J. *Nutrition in a Nutshell*. New York: Doubleday, 1962, pp. 117–118.

12. Most any chemical may be harmful it the dosage is high enough. Four studies are cited in which tests were made for the possible deleterious effects of high levels of pantothenic acid on rats and guinea pigs. Z. T. Wirtshafter and J. R. Walsh reported (*Endocrinology*, 72:725, 1963) that at high levels it could produce liver damage. The smallest dosages used were about equivalent to 7 grams per 70-kilogram man. When rats were given 50 grams a day (Fridanza, A., et al. *Boll. Sci. Ital. Biol. Sper.*, 35:1774, 1959) it prolonged the estrus cycle in females and induced precocious sexual development in the young. Gonadal changes occurred and the 17-ketosteroid excretion was increased (*Ibid.*, 35:1776, 1959). This dosage, on a body weight basis, would be the equivalent of from 7 to 35 grams per day for a 70-kilogram man. Guinea pigs, when injected intramuscularly with 100 milligrams/100 grams of body weight, showed significant elevation of blood sugar and an increase in liver glycogen, but the animals were not seriously damaged (Fridanza, A., and Constable, B. J. *Boll. Soc. Ital. Biol. Sper.* 39:638, 1963). This dosage would correspond to 70 grams for a 70-kilogram man which is more than 100 times the perfectly safe daily dose proposed for our experiment.

13. Ralli, E. P., and Dumm, M. E. "Relation of pantothenic acid to adrenal cortical function." *Vitamins & Hormones,* 11:135, 1953.

14. Hale, F. "The relation of vitamin A to anophthalmos in pigs." *Am. J. Ophthal.,* 18:1087, 1935.

15. Hale, F. "Pigs born without eyeballs." *J. Heredity,* 24:105, 1933.

16. Williams, R. J. *Biochemical individuality.* New York: Wiley, 1963, p. 146.

17. Albanese, A. A., et al. "The effect of tryptophane deficiency on reproduction." *Science,* 97:312, 1943.

18. See especially Burke, B. S., et al. "Nutrition studies during pregnancy. IV. Relation of protein content of mother's diet during pregnancy to birth length, birth weight, and condition of infant at birth." *J. Pediat.,* 23:506, 1943; *See also* Cravioto, J., and Robles, B., "Evolution of adaptive and motor behavior during rehabilitation from kwashiorkor." *Am. J. Orthopsychiat.,* 35:449, 1965; Graham, G. G. "Effect of infantile malnutrition on growth." *Fed. Proc.,* 26:139, 1967; Editorial. "Nutrition and learning: a connection?" *J.A.M.A.,* 200:20, 1967; Cravioto, J. "Appraisal of the effect of nutrition on biochemical maturation." *Am. J. Clin. Nutr.,* 11:484, 1962; Schrimshaw, N. S. "Malnutrition, learning and behavior." *Am. J. Clin. Nutr.,* 20:493, 1967; Carson, N. A. J., et al. "Homocystinuria: a new inborn error of metabolism associated with mental deficiency." *Arch. Dis. Childh.,* 38:425, 1963; Stoch, M. B., and Smythe, P. M. "Does undernutrition during infancy inhibit brain growth and subsequent intellectual development?" *Arch. Dis. Childh.,* 38:546, 1963.

19. Kalter, H., and Warkany, J. "Experimental production of congenital malformations in mammals by metabolic procedure." *Physiol. Rev.,* 39:69, 1959.

Some references for vitamin E deficiency during gestation: Thomas, B. H., and Cheng, D. W. "Congenital abnormalities associated with vitamin E malnutrition," *Proc. Iowa Acad. Sci.,* 59:218, 152; Cheng, D. W., et al. "Gross observations on developing abnormal embryos induced by material vitamin E deficiency." *Anat. Rec.,* 129:167, 1957; Cheng, D. W., and Thomas, B. H. "Relationship of time of therapy to teratogeny in maternal avitaminosis E." *Proc. Iowa Acad. Sci.,* 60:290, 1953; Cheng, D. W., and Thomas, B. H. "Histological changes in the abnormal rat fetuses induced by maternal vitamin E deficiency." *Anat. Rec.,* 121:274, 1955; Cheng, D. W., et al. "Effect of variations of rations on the incidence of teratogeny in vitamin E-deficient rats." *J. Nutr.,* 71:54, 1960.

Reference to vitamin C deficiency during gestation: Martin, M. P., et al. "The Vanderbilt cooperative study of maternal and infant nutrition. X: asorbic acid." *J. Nutr.,* 62:201, 1957. Martin and his colleagues relate premature birth in humans to a vitamin C deficiency.

Some references to thiamine deficiency during gestation: Ensminger, M. E., et al. "Observations on the thiamine, riboflavin and choline needs of sows for reproduction." *J. Anim. Sci.,* 6:409, 1947; Coward, K. H., et al. "The influence of a deficiency of vitamin B_1 and riboflavin on the reproduction of the rat." *J. Physiol.,* 100:423, 1942; Coward, K. H., and Morgan, B. G. E. "The determination of vitamin B_1 by means of its influence on the vaginal contents of the rat." *Biochem. J.,* 35:974, 1941; *See also* Brown, M. L., and Snodgrass, C. H. *J. Nutr.,* 87:353, 1965.

Some references to riboflavin deficiency during gestation: Warkany, J., and Schraffenberger, E., "Congenital malformations induced in rats by maternal nutritional deficiency. V: effects of a purified diet lacking riboflavin." *Proc. Soc. Exp. Biol. Med.,* 54:92, 1943; Gilman, J. P. W., et al. "Some effects of a maternal riboflavin deficiency on reproduction in the rat." *Canad. J. Med. Sci.,* 30:383, 1952; Giroud, A., et al. "Chute du taux de la riboflavin au stade ou se determinant les malformations embryonnaires." *Int. Z. Vitaminforsch.,* 23:490, 1952; Deuschle, F. M., and Warkany, J. "Congenital dentofacial malformations induced by maternal deficiency." *J. Dent. Res.,* 35:674, 1956; Giroud, A., and Boisselot, J. "Repercussions de l'avitaminose B_2 sur l'embryon du rat." *Arch. Franc. Pediat.,* 4:317, 1947; Noback, C. R., and Kupperman,

H. S. "Anomalous offspring and growth of Wistar rats maintained on a deficient diet." *Proc. Soc. Exp. Biol. Med.*, 57:183, 1944; Warkany, J., and Nelson, R. C. "Congenital malfunctions induced in rats by maternal nutritional deficiency." *J. Nutr.*, 23:321, 1942; Warkany, J., and Nelson, R. C. "Skeletal abnormalities in the offspring of rats reared on deficient diets." *Anat. Rec.*, 79:83, 1941.

Some references to a nicotinic acid deficiency (induced by a niacin antagonist) during gestation: Chamberlain, J. G., and Nelson, M. M. "Congenital abnormalities in the rat resulting from single injections of 6-aminonicotinamide during pregnancy." *J. Exp. Zool.*, 153:285, 1963; Landauer, W. "Niacin antagonists and chick development." *J. Exp. Zool.*, 136:509, 1957; Pinsky, L., and Fraser, F. C. "Production of skeletal malformations in the offspring of pregnant mice treated with 6-aminonicotinamide." *Bio. Neonat.*, 1:106, 1959; See also Byerly, T. C., et al. *J. Agr., Res.* 46:1, 1933; Ruffo, A., and Vescia, A. *Boll. Soc. Ital. Biol. Sper.*, 16:185, 1941; Pinsky, L., and Fraser, F. C. *Brit. Med. J.*, 93:195, 1960.

Some references for pyridoxine (B_6) deficiency in gestation: Ross, M. L., and Pike, R. L., "The relationship of vitamin B_6 to protein metabolism during pregnancy in the rat." *J. Nutr.*, 58:251, 1956; Weinstein, B. B., et al. "Clinical experience with pyridoxine hydrochloride in treatment of nausea and vomiting of pregnancy." *Amer. J. Obstet. Gyn.*, 46:283, 1943; Willis, R. S., et al. "Clinical observations in treatment of nausea and vomiting in pregnancy with vitamins B_1 and B_6: a preliminary report." *Amer. J. Obstet. Gyn.*, 44:265, 1942.

Some references for pantothenic acid deficiency in gestation: Nelson, M. M., et al. "Teratogenic effects of pantothenic acid deficiency in the rat." *J. Nutr.*, 62:395, 1957; Hurley, L. S., and Volkert, N. E. "Pantothenic acid and coenzyme A in the developing guinea pig liver." *Biochem. Biophys. Acta*, 104:372, 1965; Hurley, L. S., et al. "Pantothenic acid deficiency in pregnant and nonpregnant guinea pigs, with special reference to effects on the fetus." *J. Nutr.*, 86:201, 1965; Barboriak. J. J., et al. "Effect of partial pantothenic acid deficiency on reproductive performance of the rat." *J. Nutr.*, 63:591, 1957; Boisselot, J. "Malformations congenitales provoquées chez le rat par une insuffisance en acide pantothenique du regime maternel." *C. R. Soc. Biol.*, 142:928, 1948; Nelson, M. M., and Evans, H. M. "Pantothenic acid deficiency and reproduction in the rat." *J. Nutr.*, 31:497, 1946; *See also* Boisselot, *J. Arch. Franc. Pediat.*, 6:225, 1949; Lefebvres, *J. Ann. Med.*, 52:286, 1952; Zunin, C., and Borrone, C. *Acta vitamin.*, 8:263, 1954.

Some references for folic acid deficiency in gestation: Nelson, M. M., and Evans, H. M. "Pteroylglutamic acid and reproduction in the rat." *J. Nutr.*, 38:11, 1949; Nelson, M. M., et al. "Multiple congenital abnormalities resulting from transitory deficiency of pteroylglutamic acid during gestation in the rat." *J. Nutr.*, 56:349, 1955; Monie, I. W., et al. "Abnormalities of the urinary system of rat embryos resulting from maternal pteroylglutamic acid deficiency." *Anat. Rec.*, 120:119, 1957; Johnson, E. M. "Effects of maternal folic acid deficiency on cytologic phenomena in the rat embryo." *Anat. Rec.*, 149:49, 1964; Johnson, E. M., et al. "Effects of transitory pteroylglutamic acid (PGA) deficiency on embryonic and placental development in the rat." *Anat. Rec.*,146:215, 1963; Johnson, E. M. "Electrophoretic analysis of abnormal development." *Proc. Soc. Exp. Biol. Med.*, 118:9, 1965; Sansome, G., and Zunin, C. "Embriopatie spermantale de somministrazioni di antifolici." *Acta vitamin*, 8: 73, 1954.

Some references for vitamin B₁₂ deficiency during gestation: Jones, C. C., et al. "Tissue abnormalities in newborn rats from vitamin B_{12} deficient mothers." *Proc. Soc. Exp. Biol. Med.*, 90:135, 1955; Woodard, J. C., and Newberne, P. M. "Relation of vitamin B₁₂ and one-carbon metabolism to hydrocephalus in the rat." *J. Nutr.*, 88:375, 1966; O'Dell, B. L., et al. "Vitamin B₁₂, a factor in prevention of hydrocephalus in infant rats." *Proc. Soc. Exp. Biol. Med.*, 76:399, 1951; Newberne, P. M., and O'Dell, B. L. "Histopathology of hydrocephalus resulting from a deficiency of vitamin B₁₂." *Proc. Soc. Exp. Biol. Med.*, 97:62, 1958; Dryden, L. P., et al. "The relation of vitamin B₁₂ deficiency to fertility of the female and birth weight of the young in rats fed purified casein rations." *J. Nutr.*, 45:377, 1951; Ferguson, T. M., and Couch, J. R. "Further gross observations on the B₁₂-deficient chick embryo." *J. Nutr.*, 54:361, 1954; Olcese, O., et al. "Congenital anomalies in the chick due to vitamin B₁₂ deficiency." *J. Nutr.*, 41:423, 1950; Dryden, L. P., et al. "The relation of vitamin B_{12} deficiency to ovarian function and reproduction in the rat." Abst., 116th meeting, American Chemical Society, p. 39 A; Lepkovsky, S., et al. "Reproduction in vitamin B_{12} deficient rats with emphasis upon intrauterine injury." *Am. J. Physiol.*, 165:79, 1951; *See also* Sillampaa, M. *Kinderaerztl. Prazis.*, 33:299, 1965.

References to biotin deficiency during gestation: Kennedy, C., and Palmer, L. S., "Biotin deficiency in relation to reproduction and lactation." *Arch. Biochem.*, 7:9, 1945; *See also* Cooper, W. A., and Brown, S. O. *Texas J. Sci.*, 10:308, 1958.

References to iodine deficiency during gestation: Kemp, W. N. "Iodine deficiency in relation to still-birth problem." *Canad. Med. Assoc. J.*, 41:356, 1939; *See also* Lotmar, F. *Z. Ges. Neurol. Psychiat.*, 146:1, 1933.

Some other references: Hughes, E. H. "Some effects of vitamin A deficient diet on reproduction of sows." *J. Agri. Res.*, 49:943, 1934; Scrimshaw, N. S., et al. "Serum vitamin E levels in complications of pregnancy." *Ann. N.Y. Acad. Sci.*, 52:312, 1949; Everson, G., et al. "Effect of ascorbic acid on rats deprived of pantothenic acid during pregnancy." *J. Nutr.*, 54:305, 1954; Alexander, G. "Influence of nutrition on duration of gestation in sheep." *Nature*, 178:1058, 1956; Ershoff, B. H., "Degeneration of the corpora lutea in the pregnant vitamin E-deficient rat." *Anat. Rec.*, 87:297, 1943; Macomber, D. "Effect of a diet low in calcium on fertility, pregnancy, and lactation in the rat." *J. A. M. A.*, 88:6, 1927; Warkany, J. "Manifestations of prenatal nutritional deficiency." *Vitamins and Hormones*, 3:73, 1945; Scott, J. M. D. "Studies in anemia." *Biochem. J.*, 17:166, 1923; Dutt, B., and Mills, C. F. "Reproductive failure in rats due to copper deficiency." *J. Comp. Path. & Therapeutics*, 70:120, 1960.

For further references on effects of deficiency states in gestation, see those cited below.

20. Hurley, L. S., and Swenerton, H. "Congenital malformations resulting from zinc deficiency in rats." *Proc. Soc. Exp. Biol. Med.*, 123:692 1966.

21. Daniels, A. L., and Everson, G. J. "The relation of manganese to congenital debility." *J. Nutr.*, 9:191, 1935; Orent, E. R., and McCollum, E. V. "Effects of deprivation of manganese in the rat." *J. Biol. Chem.*, 92:651, 1931;

Hurley, L. S., and Everson, G. J. "Influence of timing of short-term supplementation during gestation on congenital abnormalities of manganese-deficient rats." *J. Nutr.*, 79:23, 1963; Hurley, L. S., et al. "Disproportionate growth in offspring of manganese-deficient rats. I. The long bones." *J. Nutr.*, 74:274, 1961: *Ibid.*, "II. Skull, brain and cerebrospinal fluid pressure." *J. Nutr.*, 74:282, 1961; Hurley, L. S., "Studies on nutritional factors in mammalian development." *J. Nutr.*, Sup. 1, 91:27, 1967.

22. Caskey, C. D., et al. "A chronic congenital ataxia in chicks due to manganese deficiency in the maternal diet." *Poultry Sci.*, 23:516, 1944; Everson, G. J., et al. "Manganese deficiency in the guinea pig," *J. Nutr.*, 68:49, 1959; Hill, R. M., et al. "Manganese deficiency in rats with relation to ataxia and loss of equilibrium." *J. Nutr.*, 41:359, 1950; Asling, C. W., et al. "Abnormal development of the otic labyrinth in young rats following maternal dietary manganese deficiency." *Anat. Rec.*, 136:157, 1960; Hurley, L. S., and Everson, G. J. "Delayed development of righting reflexes in offspring of manganese-deficient rats." *Proc. Soc. Exp. Biol. Med.*, 102:360, 1959.

23. Nelson, M. M., et al. "Multiple congenital abnormalities resulting from transitory deficiency of pteroylglutamic acid during gestation in the rat." *J. Nutr.*, 56:49, 1955.
See also Nelson, M. M., et al. *J. Nutr.*, 48:61, 1952.

24. Nelson, M. M., et al. "Effect of 36-hour period of pteroylglutamic acid deficiency on fetal development in the rat." *Proc. Soc. Exp. Biol. Med.*, 92:554, 1956.

25. Asling, C. W. "Congenital skeletal abnormalities in fetal rats resulting from maternal pteroylglutamic acid deficiency during gestation." *Anat. Rec.*, 121:775, 1955; Warkany, J., and Nelson, R. C. "Appearance of skeletal abnormalities in the offspring of rats reared on a deficient diet." *Science*, 92:383, 1940.
See also "Folic acid and pregnancy I." *Nutr. Rev.*, 25:325, 1967; "Folic acid and pregnancy II," 26:5, 1968.

26. Stone, M. L., et al. "Folic acid metabolism in pregnancy." *Am. J. Obstet. Gynecol.*, 99:638, 1967.

27. Grainger, R. B., et al. "Congenital malformations as related to deficiencies of riboflavin and vitamin B$_{12}$, source of protein, calcium to phosphorus ratio and skeletal phosphorus metabolism." *J. Nutr.*, 54:33, 1954.

28. Warkany, J., and Nelson, R. C. "Congenital malformations induced in rats by maternal nutritional deficiency." *J. Nutr.*, 23:321, 1954.

29. In the government report *Hunger, U.S.A.* (Washington, D.C.: New Community Press, 1968), with an introductory by Robert Kennedy, the Medical Board of Inquiry declared, "Medical schools do not train students to recognize malnutrition. Medical schools do not emphasize nutritional problems. Members of the faculty at a number of leading medical universities, including Harvard, Vanderbilt, Columbia, and Tulane have deplored the poor training of medical students to identify the problems of malnutrition that might be underlying the medical problems of poor and nonpoor alike. Concerned professionals have corroborated this evaluation. In practice, they say, this nation's doctors are ill-prepared to identify malnutrition in a patient who walks in the door." (p. 40).

30. Burke, B. S., et al. "The influence of nutrition during pregnancy upon the condition of the infant at birth." *J. Nutr.*, 26:569, 1943; Burke, B. S., et al. "Nutrition studies during pregnancy." *Am. J. Obstet. Gynecol.*, 46:38, 1943.

31. For an excellent account of this, see Taussig, H. B. "The thalidomide syndrome," *Scientific American*, 207:29, 1962.

32. Frank, O., et al. "Metabolic deficiencies in protozoa induced by thalidomide." *Science*, 139:110, 1962. *See also Science News Letter*, 82:22, July 14, 1962; Rauen, H. M., "Are thalidomide and its biological metabolites vitamin antagonists?" *Arzeimittel-Forsch.*, 13:1081, 1963; Friedman, L., et al. "Response of rats to thalidomide as affected by riboflavin or folic acid deficiency." *J. Nutr.*, 85:309, 1965; Riva, G., and Uboldi, L. "Pantothenic acid and coenzyme A concentrations in fetuses and offspring from thalidomide-treated rats." *Atti Accad. Med. Lombarda*, 19:301, 1964; Leck, I. M., and Miller, E. L. M. *Brit. Med. J.*, 1:16, 1962.

33. Holmes, J. O. "Dental caries in the rat, mus norvegicus." *J. Nutr.*, 46:323, 1952. *See also* Williams, R. J., *Biochemical individuality*. New York: Wiley, 1963, pp.

191–193; Shaw, J. H. "A survey of the literature of dental caries." Pub. 225, Nat. Acad. Sci., Nat. Res. Council, Washington, D.C., 1952, pp. 490–494.

34. Maurer, S., and Tsai, L. S. "Vitamin B deficiency and learning ability." *J. Comp. Psychol.*, 11:51, 1930.
See also Maurer, S. "III: The effect of partial depletion of vitamin B (B₁) upon performance in rats." *J. Comp. Psychol.*, 20:309, 1935; Maurer, S. "IV: The effect of early depletion of vitamin B₂ upon performance in rats." *J. Comp. Psychol.*, 20:385, 1935.

35. O'Neill, P. H. "The effect of subsequent maze learning ability of graded amounts of vitamin B₁ in the diet of very young rats." *J. Genet. Psychol.*, 74:85, 1949.

36. Harrell, R. F., et al. "The influence of vitamin supplementation of the diets of pregnant and lactating women on the intelligence of their offspring." *Metabolism,* 5:555, 1956.

37. Coursin, D. B. "Undernutrition and brain function." *Borden's Rev. Nutr. Res.*, 26:1, 1965.
See also Coursin, D. B. *Nutr. Rev.*, 23:65, 1965.

38. Bennett, E. L., et al. "Chemical and anatomical plasticity of brain." *Science,* 146:610, 1964.

39. Stoch, M. B., and Smythe, P. M. "Does undernutrition during infancy inhibit brain growth and subsequent intellectual development?" *Arch. Dis. Childh.*, 38:546, 1963.
See also Ramos-Galvan, R. "Application of newer knowledge of nutrition on physical and mental growth and development." *Am. J. Publ. Health*, 53:1803, 1963; Kugelmass, I. N., et al. "Nutritional improvement of child mentality." *Am. J. Med. Sci.*, 208:631, 1944.

40. Macy. I. G. *Nutrition and chemical growth in Childhood.* Vol. 1. Springfield, Ill.: Thomas, 1942.

CHAPTER 5

Protecting the Hearts We Have

1. Nelson, M. M., et al. "Effect of 36-hour period of pteroylglutamic acid deficiency on fetal development in the rat." *Proc. Soc. Exp. Biol.* 92:554, 1956.

See also Nelson, M. M., et al. "Multiple congenital abnormalities resulting from transitory deficiency of pteroylglutamic acid during gestation in the rat." *J. Nutr.*, 56:349, 1955; Wilson, F. G., and Warkany, J. "Aortic-arch and cardiac anomalies in the offspring of vitamin A-deficient rats." *Am. J. Anat.*, 85:113, 1949; Considering the extreme variability of human hearts called attention to in my book *Biochemical Individuality* (p. 28), it seems likely that many individuals, during fetal development, have encountered mild nutritional deficiencies. Also it is apparent that susceptibility to cardiovascular disorders in later life may be greatly influenced by these anatomical anomalies.

2. Williams, R. J., and Siegel, F. L. " 'Propetology,' A new branch of medical science?" *Am. J. Med.*, 31:325, 1961.

3. Stare, F. J. "How to cut the risk of heart attack." *Redbook*, May 1968.

4. Williams, R. J. *Biochemical individuality*. New York: Wiley, 1956, p. 28

5. Burton, B. T. (Ed.) *The Heinz handbook of nutrition.* New York: McGraw-Hill, 1959, pp. 135–138. The editorial board of this publication consists of Floyd S. Daft, Ph.D.; Grace A. Goldsmith, M.D.; Helen A. Hunscher, Ph.D.; G. Glen King, Ph.D.; W. Henry Sebrell, Jr., M.D.; and Frederick J. Stare, Ph.D., M.D. These are among the most prominent and most respected names in nutrition in the United States. Several of them hold prominent positions carrying tremendous responsibility. This gives the quotation from their book high significance.

6. As aptly stated by Ancel Keys, a leading researcher in this field, "Among adults in the United States, at least, the question is not who has atherosclerosis, but rather who has more and who has less" (Publication 338, National Research Council, 1954). The annual incidence of coronary heart disease is close to 1000 cases for every 100,000 males ages forty-five to sixty-four.

7. For a good description of the composition of arterial lipid deposits and their role in atherosclerosis, see Hinsch, E. F., and Weinhouse, S. "The role of lipids in atherosclerosis." *Physiol. Rev.*, 23:185, 1943.

For descriptions of the gross and microscopic changes

occurring in arterial and aortic tissues in atherosclerosis, see Blumenthal, H. T., et al. "Calcification of the media of the human aorta and its relation to intimal arteriosclerosis, aging and disease." *Am. J. Path.*, 20:665, 1944; Lansing, A. I., et al. "Calcium and elastin in human arteriosclerosis." *J. Gerontol.*, 5:112, 1950; Carlstrom, D. et al. "Studies on the chemical composition of normal and abnormal blood vessel walls. 1: Chemical nature of vascular calcified deposits," *Lab. Invest.*, 2:325, 1952; Duff, G. L., *Arch. Path.*, 20:81, 259, 1935; Duff, G. L. *Arch. Path.* 22:161, 1936; Leary, T. *Arch. Path.*, 32:507, 1941; Aschoff, L. In E. V. Cowdry (Ed.) *Arteriosclerosis.* New York: MacMillan, 1933.

8. A good review of the professional literature covering the effects of dietary fat, carbohydrate (to some extent), and cholesterol on arterial lipid deposits and heart disease, supplying also 350 references, is given in *The Medical Journal of Australia*, 1:309, 1967. While covering considerable data, this review wholly neglects vast areas of relevant data on nutrient deficiencies.

9. Byers, S. "The origins of plasma cholesterol." *Am. J. Clin. Nutr.*, 6:638, 1958; Friedman, M., et al. "Cholesterol metabolism." *Ann. Rev. Biochem.*, 25:613, 1956.

10. Early investigators Antischkow and Ignatowski (*Virchow's Arch.*, 249:73, 1924) found that by feeding rabbits and other laboratory animals diets rich in cholesterol, they were able to induce elevated serum cholesterol values and lesions of the aorta and coronary arteries. C. B. Taylor and colleagues were able to produce the fatal myocardial infarction in the rhesus monkey by long-term feedings of diets rich in butterfat and cholesterol (*Circulation,* 20:975, 1959). Myasnikov and coworkers experimentally induced the fatal heart attack in cholesterol-féd rabbits (*Am. Heart J.*, 61:76, 1961). Other investigators have obtained similar results with pigs, guinea pigs, rats, chickens, pigeons, hypothyroid dogs, and rhesus monkeys. (Katz, L. N., et al. *Nutrition & atherosclerosis,* Philadelphia: Lea & Febiger, 1958; Anitschkow, N., and Chalatow, S. *Centrabl. f. allg. Path. w. path. Anat.*, 24:1, 1913; Wacker, L., and Hueck, W. *Munchen, med. Wchnschr.*, 60:2087, 1913; Bailey, C. H. *Proc. Soc. Exp. Biol. Med.*, 13:60, 1915–1916.) Subsequent relatively unsuccessful attempts were made to raise the serum cholesterol levels of human beings by cholesterol ingestion. (Duff, L. G. *Arch. Path.*, 20:81, 1935, p. 269; Turner, K. B., and Steiner, A. J. *Clin. Invest.*, 18:45, 1939; Steiner, A. and Domanski, B. *Am. J. Med. Sci.*, 201:820, 1941; Keys, A. *Circulation*, 5:115, 1952; Kinsell, L. W., et al. *J. Clin. Endocrin.*, 12:909, 1952; Ahrens, E. H., et al. *J. Clin. Invest.*, 34:918, 1955; Mayer, G. A., et al. *Am. J. Clin. Nutr.*, 2:316, 1954; Heymann, W., and Rack, F. *Am J. Dis. Childh.*, 65:235, 1943.)

In a 1956 report, Ancel Keys and his associates criticize the early dietary cholesterol clinical studies on the grounds that dietary fat was not controlled (*J. Nutr.*, 59:39, 1956). In their own series of studies reported in the article, Keys and coworkers concluded that serum cholesterol levels in humans are "essentially independent of the cholesterol intake over the whole range of natural human diets."

Later carefully controlled studies, however, have taken issue with these early conclusions of Keys and colleagues. Steiner and Howard found that the addition of 3 grams of crystalline cholesterol to a formula diet containing olive oil or corn oil significantly increased the serum cholesterol levels of eight hospitalized patients (*J. A. M. A.*, 181:186, 1962). The carefully controlled experiments of Connor and colleagues (*J. Lab. Clin. Med.*, 57:33, 1961) conclusively demonstrated that under specific conditions, dietary cholesterol does affect serum cholesterol values and is a factor to be considered in the treatment and prevention of atherosclerosis.

11. Eggs, for example, have been condemned by many physicians on the ground of the high cholesterol content of the yolks. Eggs, however, are one of the most perfect foods, rich in vitamins, minerals, and essential amino acids. The "Prudent Diet" used by Joliffe and his colleagues of the Anti-Coronary Club Study, an otherwise excellent, balanced diet, had one major fault in that it reduced the eating of eggs to three per week (Joliffe, N., et al. "The anticoronary club: the first four years." *New York State J. Med.*, 63:69, 1963).

This unwarranted fear of dietary cholesterol apparently ignores research on the effects of egg yolks on atherosclerosis. Animal studies support the position that eggs consumed in large quantities in the diet, other things remaining equal, are not atherogenic. While both the cholesterol *and* lecithin of egg yolks may increase serum cholesterol levels—the actual amount *circulating* in the blood—the cholesterol/phospholipid *ratio* remains normal, and arterial fatty deposits are prevented from forming. (See references 13 and 14 below for data relating the importance of the cholesterol/phospholipid ratio.)

In 1941, Steiner and Domanski reported the elelation of the serum cholesterol levels in both dogs and humans by the daily feeding of egg yolk powder (*Am. J. Med. Sci.*, 201:820, 1941). The addition of 100 grams of egg yolk powder to the daily diet of ten patients for eight weeks raised their serum cholesterol by an average increment of 102 milligram percent. These results were later confirmed by Messinger and coworkers (*Arch. Inter. Med.*, 86:189, 1950).

But is this increase in *circulating* serum cholesterol *necessarily* bad? Asking this question, Steiner and Domanski kept their dogs on this daily diet, high in egg yolks, for fifty-six weeks. The animals were sacrificed, and gross examination of their organs "revealed no structural changes beyond wrinkling of the intima of the arota." The investigators concluded that hypercholesterolemia due to egg yolk feeding over an extended time "did not result in significant arterial lesions."

In experiments with rats, G. Sperling and coworkers found that rats fed long-term high-cholesterol diets in the form of dried whole eggs (10 percent of the diet) suffered no morbidity and no shortening of their life. In fact, those animals whose diets were supplemented daily with eggs had the largest life span (*J. Nutr.*, 55:399, 1955).

The recent and best clinical report on the problem of egg yolk cholesterol in human atherosclerosis is that reported by S. D. Splitter and his associates (*Metabolism*, 17:1129, 1968). These investigators fed large amounts of egg yolk, 50 to 110 grams of egg yolk lipids daily (the yolk of one medium-sized egg contains 5.5 grams of total lipid) to thirteen subjects. Only two subjects showed marked blood cholesterol elevation, while the majority of subjects showed no change in blood plasma levels, despite the fact that they ingested amounts of egg yolk far in excess of the amount ingested by most individuals.

12. Gould and Taylor have reported (*Fed. Proc.*, 9:179, 1950) that the feeding of cholesterol has an inhibitory effect on endogenous cholesterol synthesis of the liver. In a series of experiments with nineteen human subjects covering a two week period. Karinen and coworkers found that the average maximal capacity of the human intestine to absorb cholesterol was of the order of magnitude of the liver's capacity to synthesize cholesterol (*J. App. Physiol.*, 11:143, 1957). This was approximately 2.5 grams per day on a daily 9 gram intake. During this time the investigators observed no significant increase in serum cholesterol of their subjects.

From these data, it is apparent that dietary cholesterol, other things remaining equal, will have no greater effect on plasma cholesterol concentrations in humans than the effect of the quantity produced by the liver itself. Under healthy conditions, the liver synthesizes both cholesterol and phospholipids and maintains them in the plasma in a balanced ratio (Gould, G. *Am. J. Med.*, 11:209, 1951; Ahrens, E. H., and Kunkel, H. G. *J. Exper. Med.*, 90:409, 1949).

Virtually all the tissues of the human body synthesize cholesterol (Byers, S. *Am. J. Clin. Nutr.*, 6:638, 1958). According to the studies of Hellman and his coworkers, this newly synthesized cholesterol appears immediately in the blood plasma (Hellman, L., et al. *J. Clin. Invest.*, 33:142, 1954). However, a great many studies have demonstrated that the major contributor to the plasma cholesterol is the liver (Eckles, N. E., et al. *J. Lab. Clin. Med.*, 46:359, 1955; Tennent, D. et al. *J. Biol. Chem.*, 228:241, 1957; Triedman, M., et al. *Am J. Physiol.*, 164:789, 1951). Generally, the concentrations of cholesterol of the blood appear to be determined largely by the amount synthesized by the liver.

13. Lecithin (phospholipids) has been proven by many studies to play a major role in maintaining the stability and clarity of the blood system (Ahrens, E. H., and Kunkel. H. G. *J. Exper. Med.*, 90:409, 1949; Byers, S. O. *Ab. J. Clin. Nutr.*, 6:638, 1958; *Nutr. Rev.*, 20:220, 1962; Zilversmit, D. B., et al, *Am. J. Clin. Nutr.*, 6:235, 1958; Artom, C. *Am. J. Clin. Nutr.*, 6:221, 1958; Horlick, L. *Circulation*, 10:30, 1956; Aldersberg, D., et al. *J. Nutr.*, 25:255, 1943).

Phospholipids are found in every tissue of the body, and are an important constituent of all tissue cells, including those of the brain and nerves. Because of its emulsifying capacity, lecithin acts to reduce the size of the lipid particles in the blood stream, thus acting to inhibit or improve the atherosclerotic condition (Horlick, 1956; Aldersberg, 1943; *See also* Leathes, J. B. *Lancet*, 1:1019, 1925; Ahrens, E. H., et al. *J. Exper. Med.*, 90:409, 1949).

14. Aldersberg, D., et al. "Electrophoresis and monomolecular layer studies with serum lipoproteins." *Clin. Chem.*, 1:18, 1955.

15. Gould, R. G. "Lipid metabolism and atherosclerosis." *Am. J. Med.*, 11:209, 1951.

16. Morrison. L. M. "Serum cholesterol reduction with lecithin," *Geriatrics*, 13:12, 1958.

17. Morrison, L. M. " The serum phospholipid-cholesterol ratio as a test for coronary atherosclerosis." *J. Lab. Clin. Med.*, 39:550, 1952.

See also Kellner, A., et al. "Modification of experimental atherosclerosis by means of intravenous detergents." *Am. Heart J.*, 38:455, 1949; Ahrens, E. H., and Kunkel, H. G. "The stabilization of serum lipid emulsions by serum phospholipids." *J. Exper. Med.*, 90:409, 1949; Aldersberg, D., and Sobtka, H. "Effect of prolonged lecithin feeding on hypercholesterolemia." *J. Mt. Sinai Hospital*, 9:955, 1943; Downs, W. G., Jr, "Lecithin in experimental atherosclerosis." *Am. J. Med.*, 41:460, 1935; Keston, H. D., and Silbowitz, R. "Experimental atherosclerosis and soyalecithin." *Proc. Soc. Exp. Biol. Med.*, 49:71, 1942; Labecki, T. D. "Effect of lipotropic factors upon serum lipids and vascular disease in man." *Am. J. Clin. Nutr.*, 6:325, 1958.

A. T. Ladd and his associates found that animals will not develop atherosclerosis by excessive feedings of cholesterol provided enough lecithin is also given (*Fed. Proc.*, 8:360, 1949). Ladd and his team concluded, from their rabbit experiments, that increased blood phospholipids "may modify or prevent the development of atherosclerosis."

The earlier experiments of Keston and Silbowitz, above cited, on the effect of soya lecithin on twenty-three atherosclerotic chinchillas bear out the later findings of Ladd and his coworkers. Also, the complementary effects exerted by phospholipids and cholesterol have been demonstrated in the rat and rabbit experiments of Friedman and Byers (*Am. J. Physiol.*, 186:13, 1956; *Proc. Soc. Exp. Biol. Med.*, 94:452, 1957).

18. Mann, G. V., et al. "Experimental atherosclerosis in cebus monkeys." *J. Exper. Med.*, 98:195, 1953. *See also* Mann, C. V., and Andrus, S. B. "Xanthomatosis and atherosclerosis produced by diet in an adult rhesus monkey." *J. Lab. Clin. Med.*, 48:533, 1956.

Mann and his coworkers found that a methionine deficiency in cebus and rhesus monkeys fed high fat, cholesterol diet produced elevated serum cholesterol levels and atherosclerosis. Most importantly, animals that were fed the atherogenic diet supplemented with methionine showed no atherosclerosis or elevated cholesterol levels. The determining variable here is the presence or absence of methionine, not fat or cholesterol. However, when fat or cholesterol were removed from the methionine-deficient diet, serum cholesterol remained normal. Elevated serum cholesterol and atherosclerosis resulted only when methionine deficiency was combined with a high fat and cholesterol diet.

From these data, it is strongly indicated that diets rich in protein, specifically rich in the lipotropic amino acid methionine, will maintain the phospholipid/cholesterol ratio of the blood, and thus prevent the hypercholesterolemic response and atherosclerosis.

From the evidence, it is apparent that atherosclerosis can be produced in animals by reducing endogenous phospholipid production. (See also Aldersberg, D., et al. *Clin. Chem.*, 1:18, 1955.) The role of choline and inositol in endogenous phospholipid production and in the maintenance of normal blood lipid ratios has been shown in animal experiments (Zilversmit, D. B., et al. *Circulation,* 9:581, 1954; Rosenfeld, B., et al. *Canad. J. Biochem. Physiol.*, 35:845, 1957; Ashworth, C. T. *Arch. Path.*, 72:620, 1961).

It has been reported that a choline deficiency impairs cholesterol utilization in the tissues (Ashworth, 1961), the efficient oxidation of fats in energy production (Artom, M. *Am. J. Clin. Nutr.*, 6:221, 1958), and the effective removal and excretion of cholesterol in the feces (Clemet, G., et al. *Arch. Sci. Physiol.*, 11:101, 1957).

In observing that laboratory animals have radically differing degrees of susceptibility to experimental atherosclerosis, Pilgeram suggests that those highly susceptible animals have a "metabolic block" which prevents the efficient synthesis of phosphatidyl choline (Pilgeram, L. O. *Fed. Proc.*, 14:728, 1955).

Perlman and Chaikoff (*J. Biol. Chem.*, 128:735, 1939) pointed out in an early study that lecithin synthesis in the rat is three times as high when both choline and cholesterol are fed as when cholesterol alone is given. Rats readily synthesize lecithin, and this capacity is facilitated by choline or dietary lecithin or cholesterol. For this reason, it is more difficult to produce experimental atherosclerosis in rats by the common means of increasing dietary fat and cholesterol, for the endogenous production of phosphatides efficiently regulates cholesterol and fat metabolism and keeps the lipids of the arteries free-flowing.

W. S. Hartroft and his associates of the Medical Research Department of Toronto University have found that rats on a choline-deficient diet suffered pathological changes of the aorta and coronary arteries morphologically resembling those in man (W. S. Hartroft, et al. "Atheromatous changes in aorta, carotid and coronary arteries of choline-deficient rats." *Proc. Soc. Exp. Biol. Med.*, 81:384, 1952). These pathological changes of the cardiovascular system were not found in the control rats on the same basal diet supplemented with choline. This diet was low in protein and high in hydrogenated vegetable fat.

19. Morrison, L. M., and Gonzales, W. F. "Effect of choline as a lipotropic agent in the treatment of human coronary atherosclerosis." *Proc. Soc. Exp. Biol. Med.*, 73:37, 1950.

20. See Shute, E., et al. *The heart and vitamin E.* London: The Shute Foundation for Medical Research, 1963.

See also Shute, Evan and William, and Vogelsang, A. *Ann. Inter. Med.*, 30:1004, 1948; Shute, E., et al. *Surg. Gyne. Abst.*, 86:1, 1948; Puente-Dominguez and R. Dominguez. *Summary*, 8:1956, 21.

21. Madsen first showed that myocardial scarring was promoted in vitamin E-deficient rats (*J. Nutr.*, 11:471, 1936). Later Mason and Emmels corroborated this early finding while reporting gross cardiac enlargement in autopsied rats (*Anat. Rec.*, 92:33, 1945). After about the tenth to twelfth month of vitamin E deficiency in the rat, these investigators observed the appearance of pigment globules in "cardiac muscle fibers, usually as linear groups located irregularly in the sarcoplasm but sometimes as small clusters at each role of the nucleus resembling 'brown atropy' in man." After a year on an E-deficient diet, definite histological injury to the cardiac muscle was apparent, with the peripheral portion of the ventricles showing the "most marked lesions." Autopsies of rats on a long term E-deficient diet showed gross evidence of cardiac enlargement or dilatation.

A. J. Gatz and O. B. Houchin reported similar findings in the hearts of E-deficient rabbits (*Anat. Rec.*, 97:337, 1946); W. Bragdon confirmed this in similar observations (*Proc. Second Vitamin E Confer.*, Columbia University, N. Y., Jan. 23, 1948).

As early as 1944, in a study of cardiac insufficiency in E-deficient rats, Houchin and Smith concluded, from the evidence of severe myocardial damage. that the sudden death of the E-deficient animals "in an advanced stage of musclar dystrophy is due directly to myocardial failure" (*Am. J. Physiol.*, 141:242, 1944). Other studies corroborated these earlier findings (Martin, E. V., and Faust, F. B. "The heart in avitaminosis E." *Exper. Med. & Surg.*, 5:455, 1947; Butturini, U. "The heart in avitaminosis E." *Gior. di Clin. Med.*, 27:400, 1946).

During this same decade, other researchers reported heart lesions in E-deficient monkeys, while in the macaque species, vascular damage was more predominant (Mason, K. E., and Telford, I. R. "Some manifestations of vitamin E deficiency in the monkey." *Arch. Path.*, 63:363, 1947). Russell Holman's experiments with dogs revealed an association between E-deficiency and arterial lesion (*Proc. Soc. Exp. Biol. Med.*, 66:307, 1947). In twenty-two of twenty-five dogs fed high fat diets (3.0 cubic centimeters/kilograms of cod liver oil daily), Holman found that vitamin E was "equally effective in preventing or retarding the arterial lesions when its administration by mouth was started 0, 1, and 2 days after renal insufficiency was induced."

Cattle fed E-deficient rations were observed to have decreased functional activity of the heart in the terminal stages of E-deficiency with atrophy and scarring of the cardiac muscle fibers (Gullickson, T., and Calverley, C. *Science*, 104:312, 1946). All of these cattle died prematurely, suddenly, apparently of myocardial infarction.

A German physician reported experiments with vitamin

E combined with calcium or magnesium in the treatment of peripheral vascular disease (Osten, W. *Sonder. aus Inter. Zeits. f. Vitaminforsch.*, 26:19, 1955). According to Osten, the majority of his patients were improved or greatly improved. Improvement was due, he noted, not only to the effects on the vascular lesions, but also to the "influence on metabolic and oxidative processes."

South American investigators induced heart attacks in dogs by ligating a branch of the coronary artery. On the day of the infarct, dogs were injected with 10 milligrams of alpha tocopherol daily for a period of one to three months; other dogs with experimentally induced infarct were given no vitamin E. Upon autopsy, the E-treated dogs showed a greater dilation of the vessels in the area of the infarction. Microscopic examination revealed a less dense fibrous structure; the internal aspects of the infarct revealed an abundance of many new capillaries, increased vascularization in the coronary areas, due partly to the dilation of old vessels and partly to the formation of new ones (Puente-Dominguez and Dominguez, R. *Summary*, 8:1956). This experiment lends possible support to Evan Shute's contention that large doses of alpha tocopherol given to victims of myocardial infarction opens up unused blood vessels and thus salvages heart attack victims (See Shute, E. *J. Obstet. & Gyn. Brit. Empire*, 49:482, 1942).

Horn and his associates administered 50 milligrams of vitamin E and 10 milligrams of vitamin A to atherosclerotic rabbits for sixteen days, and found that this combination had some preventive effect "as regards the deposition of lipids in the arterial wall" (*Inter. Con. Geront.*, 1965, p. 353). These researchers ascribe this effect to the antioxidizing capacity of vitamin E involving a protective influence on vitamin A. "In all probability," they propose, "inhibition of autooxidation of unsaturated fatty acids may enhance occasionally the antiatherosclerotic effect of this vitamin combination."

Many researchers have reported the anticlotting effect of alpha tocopherol (Mason, K. E. *Yale J. Biol. Med.*, 14:605, 1942; Ames, S. R. et al. *Inter. Rev. Vit. Res.*, 22:401, 1951). Some physicians have expressed the view that vitamin E's effectiveness and value is greater in this regard than the anticoagulant drugs, and without dangerous side effects (Suffel, P. *Canad. Med. Assoc. J.*, 74:715, 1956).

Alpha tocopherol has been credited with permitting the

heart muscle to use oxygen more effectively. For this reason, it is of special merit for heart patients (De Nicola, P. *Inter. Cong. Vitamin E.,* 1955). Death from a heart attack due to a clot or occlusion is the result of a shutting off of the oxygen supply. In his address to the International Congress on Vitamin E, 1955, Evan Shute reported that much less of the heart tissue is destroyed during an attack if alpha tocopherol has been adequately supplied. and the patient is much more likely to survive the attack.

Both Zierler of Johns Hopkins and Kay of Tulane have reported that alpha tocopherol, under normal conditions, is a natural antithrombin which circulates in the blood of all people, and prevents undue clotting; but it does not interfere with the normal process of blood clotting in the case of a wound (Zierler. M., et al. *Ann. N.Y. Acad Sci.,* 52:180, 1949; Kay, J. H., et al. *Surgery,* 28:124, 1950). In fact, it is said to enhance and shorten the time of healing in burns and wounds.

Shute's interpretation is that vitamin E functions best to conserve oxygen. Houchin and Mattill report that the oxygen need of the cardiac muscle *is* reduced by as much as 43 percent when vitamin E is administered (*J. Biol. Chem.,* 146:309, 313, 1942). This *may* allow the amount of oxygen of the narrowed stream of blood of the coronary artery reaching the heart to be adequate, in many patients, in preventing anoxia, thus preventing angina.

Finally, another important function of vitamin E appears to be its prevention of the formation of permanent and objectionable scar tissue; this function, of course, is important in myocardial infarction (See Steinberg, C. L. *Arch. Surg.,* 63:824, 1951; Ross. J. A. *Brit. Med. J.,* 2:232, 1952).

22. Kopjas, T. "Effect of folic acid on collateral circulation in diffuse chronic arteriosclerosis." *J. Am. Geriac. Soc.,* 14:1187, 1966.

23. Rinehart, J. F., and Greenberg, L. D. "Plasma cholesterol levels of cholesterol fed control and pyridoxine deficient monkeys." *Proc. Soc. Exp. Biol. Med.,* 76:580, 1951.

See also Rinehart, J. F., and Geenberg, L. D. *Am. J. Clin. Nutr.,* 4:320, 1956; Rinehart, J. F., and Greenberg, L. D., *Arch. Path.,* 51:12, 1951; Greenberg, L. D., et al. *Arch. Biochem.,* 21:237, 1949.

Mushett and Emerson (*Fed. Proc.*, 15:526, 1956) have confirmed the findings of Rinehart, Greenberg, and their coworkers in both the monkey and the dog. Norman Olson reported producing hypertension in the rat on a pyridoxine-deficient diet, a disease often found associated with the atherosclerotic syndrome (*Am. J. Clin. Nutr.*, 4:325, 1956). In line with these animal findings, Kheim and Kirk report lower levels of pyridoxine in atherosclerotic arterial tissue in humans in comparison with normal tissue (*Am. J. Clin. Nutr.*, 20:702, 1967). The difference was more pronounced in the human male than in the female.

In the histological examination of pyridoxine-deficient rats, C. D. Cambridge reported heavy lipid infiltrations in the centrilobular region of the livers (*Brit. J. Nutr.*, 10:347, 1956). In their experiments with pyridoxine-deficient cholesterol-fed chicks, H. Dam and his coworkers reported significantly higher cholesterol values for the plasma and aorta of the deficient chicks than in those provided pyridoxine supplement (*Acta Physiol. Scand.*, 44:67, 1958). They were able to demonstrate a relationship between cholesterol metabolism and dietary pyridoxine in chicks. These findings were later substantiated by N. J. Daghir and S. I. Balloun who also found increased cholesterol concentrations in the aorta and serum of pyridoxine-deficient chicks (*Poultry Sci.*, 41:1868, 1962).

Other investigators have reported increased hypercholesterolemia in pyridoxine-deficient rats (Tremolieres, J., et al. *Proc. Inter. Conf. 5th Vienna*, 1958, p. 156; Goswani, A., and Sadhu, D. P. *Nature*, 187:786, 1960; Shah, S., et al. *J. Nutr.*, 72:81, 1960) and also in the pyridoxine-deficient rabbit (Swell, L. et al. *J. Nutr.*, 75:181, 1961).

It has also been reported that the administration of a vitamin B_6 antagonist, deoxypyridoxine, to the diets of chicks and rats results in elevated cholesterol levels (Maggi, V., et al. *Boll. Sci. Ital. Biol. Sper.*, 35:564, 1959; *Nutr. Rev.*, 24:274, 1966); the use of this vitamin antagonist in man increased free cholesterol in red blood cells (*Nutr. Rev.*, 21: 259, 1963).

24. Greenberg, L. D., and Rinehart, J. F. "Xanthurenic acid excretion in pyridoxine deficient rhesus monkeys." *Fed. Proc.*, 7:157, 1948; Greenberg, L. D., and Rinehart, J. F. "Plasma cholesterol levels of cholesterol fed control and pyridoxine deficient monkeys." *Proc. Soc. Exp. Biol. Med.*, 76:580, 1951.

25. Xanthurenic acid has been reported to be excreted in the pyridoxine-deficient rat (Lepkovsky, S., et al. *J. Biol. Chem.*, 149:195, 1943), mouse (Miller., E. C., et al. *J. Biol. Chem.*, 157:551, 1945), dog (Axelrod, H. E., et al. *J. Biol. Chem.*, 160:155, (1945), pig (Cartwright, G. E., et al. *Bull. Johns Hopkins Hosp.*, 75:35, 1944), monkey (Greenberg, L. D., and Rinehart, J. F. *Fed. Proc.*, 7:157, 1948), and man (Greenberg, L. D., et al. *Arch. Biochem.* 21:237, 1949).

26. Sarma, P. S. "Egg-white injury (induced biotin deficiency) in rice-moth larvae (Corcyra Cephalonica St.)." *Indian J. Med. Res.*, 32:149, 1944; Sarma, P. S. "Pyridoxine and tryptophane metabolism in rice moth larvae." *Proc. Soc. Exp. Biol. Med.*, 58:140, 1945.

27. Greenberg, L. D., et al. "Xanthurenic acid excretion in the human subject on a pyridoxine deficient diet." *Arch. Biochem.*, 21:237, 1949.

28. Bessey, O. A., et al. "Vitamin B$_6$ intake and infantile convulsions." *Pediatrics*, 20:33, 1957.

29. For material on "pyridoxine dependency" see Malory, C. J., and Parmelee, A. H. "Convulsions in young infants as a result of pyridoxine (vitamin B$_6$) deficiency." *J. A. M. A.*, 154:405, 1954; Hunt, A. D., et al. "Pyridoxine dependency: report of case of intractable convulsions in infant controlled by pyridoxine." *Pediatrics*, 13:140, 1954; Harris, J. W., and Horrigan, D. D. "Pyridoxine responsive anemia: Prototype and variations on theme." *Vitamins & Hormones*, 22:721, 1964; Rosenberg, L. E. "Inherited aminoacidopathies demonstrating vitamin dependency." *New Eng. J. Med.*, 281,145, 1969.

See also Stokes, J. J., Jr., et al. *Pediatrics*, 13:140, 1954; Waldinger, C. *PostGrad. Med.*, 35:415, 1964; Coursin, D. B. *J.A.M.A.*, 154:406, 1954.

30. Kotake, Y., and Inada, T. "Studies of xanthurenic acid: I. the effect of fatty acid on the excretion of xanthurenic acid, and its relation to pyridoxine." *J. Biochem.* 40:287, 1953.

31. *See also* Kratzer, F. H., and Williams, D. E. "The relation of pyridoxine to the growth of chicks fed rations containing linseed oil meal." *J. Nutr.*, 36:297, 1948.

32. Miller, E. C., and Baumann, C. A. "Relative effect of casein and tryptophan on the health and xanthurenic acid excretion of pyridoxine-deficient mice." *J. Biol. Chem.*, 157:551, 1945; *Ibid.*, 159:173, 1945.

See also Cerecedo, L. R., and Foy, J. R. "Protein intake and pyridoxine deficiency in the rat." *Arch. Biochem.*, 5:207, 1944.

There are seemingly contradictory studies which, on the one hand, demonstrate that diets rich in animal protein protect against atherosclerosis; on the other hand, equally valid reports indicate that low protein diets are protective against atherosclerosis. Some of the data in favor of the high protein diet are: Polcak, J., et al. "The effect of a meat-enriched diet on the development of experimental atherosclerosis in rabbits." *J. Atheroscler. Res.*, 5:174, 1965; Salmon, W. D., and Newberne, P. M. *Arch. Path.*, 73:190, 1962; Brown, H. B., and Lewis, G. L. *Lancet*, 2:488, 1958; Stamler, J., et al. *Circulation Res.*, 6:442, 1958; *Ibid.*, 6:447, 1958; *Ibid.*, 7:866, 1959; Hess, R., and Loustalot P. *J. Atheroscler, Res.*, 3:16, 1963.

Some of the data in favor of the low protein diet are: Olson, R. *Am. J. Clin. Nutr.*, 6:310, 1958; Olson, R. *Fed. Proc.*, 15:877, 1956; Kempner, W. *Am. J. Med.*, 4:545, 1948; Kempner, W. *North Carolina Med. J.*, 8:128, 1947; Lofland, H. B., et al. *Circulation Res.*, 9:919, 1961; Clarkson, T. B., et al. *Circulation Res.*, 11:400, 1962; Enselme, J. *Sem. Hop.*, 34:1599, 1958; Annand, J. C. *J. Atheroscler. Res.*, 3:153, 1963.

To my knowledge no satisfactory explanation has been given to account for these two sets of data. It is my view that these ostensibly contradictory data can be reconciled by the consideration of the relative amounts of pyridoxine, methionine, and tryptophan in the diet as key factors. From the evidence, it seems probable that the diets rich in animal protein—when they *work* in preventing atherosclerosis—are not only rich in the lipotropic factor methionine but are also rich in sources of pyridoxine. Both of these nutrients are protective against atherosclerosis, and probably more than offset the atherosclerosis-producing effect of high tryptophan in animal protein. The diets low in protein (or rich in *vegetable* protein as those used by Olson and Kempner) are also low in tryptophan, and this may be the overriding factor that makes them protective.

When diets rich in animal protein have been found to be

less effective than vegetable protein diets, in all probability it is the imbalanced pyridoxine/tryptophan ratio that is responsible. Much above cited research (reference 23) has clearly demonstrated that diets rich in the amino acid tryptophan (as found in eggs, dairy products, and meat) also require higher amounts of pyridoxine in the diet for effective metabolism. The data have shown that where pyridoxine is deficient (in the presence of a tryptophan-rich diet), the diet is productive of atherosclerosis.

In all probability this would explain the reports of Hodges and coworkers who found that "as soon as vegetable protein replaced animal protein, serum cholesterol levels decreased markedly and remained low regardless of source of carbohydrate (sugar or starch) or level of fat (15 percent to 45 percent of calories)" (*Am. J. Clin. Nutr.,* 20:198, 1967). In their experiments on cholesterol- and fat-fed cockerels, Katz, Stamler, and Pick also noted that a vegetable protein diet was less atherogenic than one rich in casein (*Fed. Proc.,* 16:101, 1957).

The clinical data of Hodges and his colleagues, I believe, highlights the proposition that high or low amounts of fats or carbohydrates in the diet are not atherogenic providing supportive nutrients (specifically pyridoxine) are present. But if pyridoxine is not adequately provided on a heavy tryptophan (high animal protein) load, regardless of the relative amounts of fat or carbohydrate, the diet will be atherogenic.

Thus, it is my suggestion that the important variable, hitherto overlooked in these many protein studies, is *not* the amount or type of protein as such, but the presence or absence of sufficient pyridoxine.

Incidentally, sources of vegetable protein are also often accompanied by carbohydrates of a type that have been found to promote pyridoxine (and other B vitamin) synthesis by the intestinal flora (Grande, F., et al. "Effect of carbohydrates of leguminous seeds, wheat and potatoes on serum cholesterol concentration in man." *J. Nutr.,* 86:313, 1965; *See also* Elvehjem, C. A., et al, *J. Am. Dietet. Assoc.,* 22:959, 1946). Pectin, found in vegetables and fruit, also promote this synthesis (Elvehjem, C. A., et al. *J. Agri. Food Chem.,* 5:754, 1957; Nath, N. *Biochem. J.,* 81:220, 1961).

Finally, the experiments involving high levels of proteins,

such as those of Katz, Stamler, and Pick, supplied either pyridoxine supplements or excellent sources of this vitamin —as found in liver meal, fish meal, soy protein, and yeast.

33. White, A., et al. *Principles of biochemistry.* (4th. ed.) New York: McGraw-Hill, 1968, pp. 495, 1013.

34. In his review of the literature on pyridoxine and fat metabolism, including especially the effect of pyridoxine deficiency on the cardiovascular system, J. F. Mueller concluded that "the major evidence seems to support the proposition that pyridoxine deficiency in animals is more often than not associated with hypercholesterolemia and cholesterolosis of tissues" (*Vitamins & Hormones,* 22:787, 1964). While there is much doubt about what the mechanism might be, Mueller notes that there is much to suggest that "pyridoxine might be exerting an effect on transport of cholesterol, perhaps through its effect on fatty acids."

Regarding human studies of pyridoxine deficiency and fat metabolism, Mueller cites those of his own and his coworker J. M. Iancono (*Am. J. Clin. Nutr.,* 12:358, 1963). In their study of the fat metabolism of seventeen chronically ill subjects before, during, and after induction of B_6 deficiency. Mueller tentatively puts forth the observation that for the first time pyridoxine *has* been implicated in human fat metabolism. "It is particularly important to note," he says, "that the results are consistent with those found by the majority of investigators in animals." While pyridoxine deficiency caused elevated blood cholesterol in his subjects, the mechanism of this action, he notes, is left unexplained.

In this same regard, the studies of D. B. Tower are worth noting (*Am. J. Clin. Nutr.,* 4:329, 1956). Normally, notes Tower, rats convert about 30 percent of dietary carbohydrate into fatty acids when fat is not present in the diet. Pyridoxine-deficient animals were unable to make this conversion. However, when the diet of the pyridoxine-deficient rats was supplemented with fat, there was no impairment in converting this to body fat. In other words, pyridoxine deficiency does not impair the absorption of fat, protein, or carbohydrate, but it does impair the animal's ability to convert dietary carbohydrate or protein into essential body fat. Rinehart and Greenberg,

Mushett and Emerson, in their experiments with pyridoxine-deficient monkeys, also confirm this finding. All the animals showed a considerable loss of body fat on a low fat, pyridoxine-deficient diet. This indicates that pyridoxine does exercise a key control over the conversion of proteins and carbohydrates into fatty acids. Fried and Lardy (*Ann. Rev. Biochem.*, 24:393, 1955) suggest that this defect in converting protein into essential storage fat in the pyridoxine-deficient animal is the result of an impaired amino acid metabolism which deprives the rat or monkey of accessible protein reserve for fat or carbohydrate synthesis.

The early studies of T. W. Birch (*J. Biol. Chem.*, 124:775, 1938) indicated that pyridoxine is involved in unsaturated fat metabolism. The more recent studies of Witten and Holman (*Arch. Biochem.*, 41:266, 1952) confirm this early report. They conclude "That pyridoxine is involved in the synthesis of very highly unsaturated acid from linoleate and linolenate seems clear."

Pyridoxine plus linoleate relieved symptoms of fat deficiency, stimulated growth and fat synthesis, and activated the conversion of linoleate or linolenate to arachidonate and hexaenoic acid. The metabolic products of linolenic or linoleic acid in the presence of pyridoxine stimulates the synthesis of arachidonic and hexaenoic acid in the organism. Moreover, R. W. Engel has found that pyridoxine is essential, together with unsaturated fatty acids, for choline to exert its lipotropic action (*J. Nutr.*, 24:175, 1942). The importance of the lipotropic action of choline in protecting against atherosclerosis on a high fat diet has already been covered in reference notes 18 and 19 above.

L. Swell and his colleagues showed that the level of arachidonic acid in the serum cholesterol ester fraction is lower in species more highly susceptible to atherosclerosis than more resistant species (*Proc. Soc. Exp. Biol. Med.*, 104:325, 1960). In the atherosclerotic-resistant dog and rat, 17 to 50 percent more arachidonic acid was found, respectively, in the cholesterol ester fraction, while in species of lesser resistance—the chicken, rabbit, pig, guinea pig, goose, and man—the low levels of 1.0 to 7.0 percent were found.

Accordingly, these investigators suggested that the

degree of atherosclerosis in different species may be related to their respective *ability to synthesize arachidonic acid*. Since it is known that pyridoxine is a key coenzyme catalyst in this conversion (Witten and Holman. *Arch. Biochem.*, 41:266, 1952), the investigators suggest that a deficiency of this vitamin may be a limiting factor in this conversion, possibly resulting in more severe atherosclerotic lesions.

In support of this hypothesis, the German investigators, H. Kleinsorge and A. Zielke reported that feeding rats linoleic and pyridoxine or arachidonate along with a high cholesterol diet prevented lipid deposition in the aorta (*Therap. Umsch.*, 16:367, 1959).

In their rabbit studies, Swell and his coworkers found a higher saturated and oleic acid content and significantly less linoleic acid in the cholesterol ester fractions of the serum and aorta of atherosclerotic rabbits than in the normal animals (*J. Nutr.*, 75:181, 1961). This is in agreement with their earlier findings in man (*Proc. Soc. Exp. Biol. Med.*, 103:651, 1960; *Ibid.* 105:662, 1960). This lends further support, these authors contend, to the view that a derangement of essential fatty acid metabolism, and of cholesterol ester metabolism in particular may be a most important factor in the etiology of atherosclerosis.

This position of Swell and coworkers is given considerable support by the careful studies of P. T. Kuo and his colleagues (*Am. J. Clin. Nutr.*, 20:116, 1967). Their studies were highly suggestive that hyperlipemic subjects suffered an abnormality in phospholipid and fatty acid metabolism (see reference note 68). While the adipose tissues of normal individuals convert dietary carbohydrate into phospholipids, the tissues of hyperlipemic individuals divert these carbohydrates into the production of free fatty acids which are eventually converted into low density lipoproteins via the liver. It may very well be that pyridoxine deficiency is the limiting factor in this metabolic abnormality.

Russian scientists have reported very low plasma levels of the coenzyme forms of vitamin B_6 in thirty-one of forty-eight atherosclerotic patients with hypercholesterolemia (Gvozdova, L. G., et al. *Voprosy Pitanyia*, 25:40, 1966; *Nutr. Rev.*, 25:116, 1967). The Russian investigators offered no explanation for this low pyridoxine status of their patients. It seems most probable that the subjects may have had an excessively high pyridoxine requirement, or may have subsisted previously on a diet deficient in B_6, or, alternatively, may have been unable to absorb the vitamin at its normal concentration in the diet, and responded only to therapeutic doses (100 milligrams per day).

In brief conclusion, it seems patently clear that there is an interdependence of many nutrients as cocatalytic agents in the metabolism of fat and carbohydrate and in the health of the cardiovascular system, in the production of phospholipids, and finally in the synthesis of arachidonic acid, together with their synergistic functioning. Furthermore, that pyridoxine is a key catalytic agent in this process is also evident.

35. Tappan, D. V., and Elvehjem, C. A. "Observation on the nutrition of rhesus monkeys receiving highly processed rations." *J. Nutr.*, 51:469, 1953; Tappan, D. V., et al. *J. Nutr.*, 51:479, 1953. *See also* Register, U. D., et al. *J. Nutr.*, 40:281, 1950.

36. Tomarelli, R. M., et al. "Biological availability of vitamin B_6 of heated milk." *J. Agri. Food Chem.*, 3:338, 1955; Hodson, A. Z. *J. Agri. Food Chem.*, 4:876, 1956.

37. Hunt, A. D., Jr., et al. "Pyridoxine dependency: report of case of intractable convulsions in infant controlled by pyridoxine." *Pediatrics,* 13:140, 1954; Coursin, D. B. *J. A. M. A.*, 154:406, 1954; Gyorgy, P. *J. Clin. Nutr.*, 2:44, 1954.

38. See particularly H. A. Schroeder's article, "Is atherosclerosis a conditioned pyridoxal deficiency?" *J. Chron. Dis.*, 2:28, 1955.

For the relative values of pyridoxine in canned foods, see Ives, M., et al. "The nutritive value of canned foods. XVII; Pyridoxine, biotin and 'folic acid'." *J. Nutr.*, 31:347, 1946.

Unfortunately, these investigators make no comparisons here between the pyridoxine values of fresh foods as against the canned, but give only the relative values, and do not suggest the amount of loss involved in the canning.

For good, recent data on vitamin and mineral losses resulting from canning and processing, see Schroeder, H. A. "Losses of vitamins and trace minerals resulting from processing and preservation of foods." *Am. J. Clin. Nutr.* (in press).

39. Williams, R. R. *Toward the conquest of beriberi,* Cambridge, Mass.: Harvard. 1961, pp. 176–189.

40. Richards, M. B. "Imbalance of vitamin B factors." *Brit. Med. J.,* 1:433, 1945; Richards, M. B. *Nature,* 158:306, 1946.

41. Tepley, L. J., et al. "Nicotinic acid, pantothenic acid and pyridoxine in wheat and wheat products." *J. Nutr.,* 24:167, 1942.
For a good account of pyridoxine in foods and athero-sclerosis, see especially H. A. Schroeder's article, "Is atherosclerosis a conditioned pyridoxal deficiency?" *J. Chron. Dis.,* 2:28, 1955.

42. Williams, R. J., *Biochemical individuality.* New York: Wiley, 1956, p. 13.

43. The need of pyridoxine in the diet seems to be dependent on many variables, the most important among these being the amount and kind of protein in the diet (whether rich in tryptophan and methionine), the amount and kind of fat, and the amount of cholesterol. In his study of tryptophan and fat metabolism and its relationship to vitamin B_6, Kotake warns us that in the presence of a pyridoxine deficiency, the ingestion of too much fat greatly affects tryptophan and methionine metabolism, leading to the formation of xanthurenic acid (*J. Vitaminology,* 1:73, 1955). "This convinces us," he says, of "the importance of keeping constantly a harmonious combination of fat, protein and vitamin B_6 in food." Bearing this in mind, the remarks of H. B. Lofland and coworkers in their study of the effects of dietary variables on atherosclerosis in animals is worth noting: "Suggestive evidence," they concluded, "was obtained for the concept that the severity of atherosclerosis is influenced by the type of dietary fat, the level of protein, and the presence or absence of cholesterol in the diet, and that biological interactions exist among these dietary variables" (*Circulation Res.,* 11:919, 1961).

From a consideration of the evidence we have reviewed (see reference notes 23, 25, 32, 34), the surest guarantee against the possible pernicious effects of various protein/fat/cholesterol combinations, in whatever proportions is the daily intake of a sufficient amount of pyridoxine.

44. Bersohn, I., and Oelofse, P. J. "Correlation of serum-magnesium and serum cholesterol levels in South African Bantu and European subjects." *Lancet,* 1:1020,

1957; see earlier report, Malkiel-Shapiro, et al. *Med. Proc.*, 2:455, 1956.

45. Vitale, J. J., et al. "Effect of feeding an atherogenic diet on magnesium requirement." *Fed Proc.*, 16:400, 1957; Vitale, J. J., et al. *J. Exper. Med.*, 106:757, 1957; Hellerstein, E. E., et al. *J. Exper. Med.*, 106:767, 1957; Hegsted, D. M., et al. *J. Nutr.*, 58:175, 1956; Colby, R. W., and Frye, C. M. *Am. J., Physiol.*, 166:408, 1951; Tufts, E. V., and Greenberg, D. M. *J. Biol. Chem.*, 122:693, 1937–1938; *Ibid.* 122:715, 1937–1938; Vitale, J. J., et al. *Am. J. Clin. Nutr.*, 7:13, 1959; Bunce, G. E., et al. *J. Nutr.*, 76:17, 23, 1962; Tufts, E. V., and Greenberg, D. M. *J. Biol. Chem.*, 122:715, 1938; Moore, L. A., et al. "Cardiovascular and other lesions in calves fed diets low in magnesium." *Arch. Path.*, 26:820, 1938.

46. Vitale, J. J., et al. "Effect of feeding an atherogenic diet on magnesium requirement." *Fed. Proc.*, 16:400, 1957.

47. Hegsted. D. M., et al. "The effect of low temperature and dietary calcium upon magnesium requirement." *J. Nutr.*, 58:175, 1956; Colby, R. W., and Frye, C. M. *Am. J. Physiol.*, 166:408, 1951; Tufts, E. V., and Greenberg, D. M. *J. Biol. Chem.*, 122:693, 1937–1938; *Ibid.*, 122:715, 1937–1938; Vitale, J. J., et al. *Am. J. Clin. Nutr.*, 7:13, 1959.

48. Seelig, M. S. "The requirement of magnesium by the normal adult." *Am. J. Clin. Nutr.*, 14:342, 1964 (177 references). An excellent review on the magnesium requirements in man.

49. In her review article on the magnesium requirements in man, Dr. Seelig's data show that women are better able to metabolize magnesium than men, and their dietary need is less. She suggests this may be *one* reason why the incidence of heart disease is less among the female population.

The fact that premenopausal young women are highly resistant to atherosclerosis has been the basis of considerable research into the possibility that estrogen hormone production is a factor in this relative immunity. Numerous studies established the fact that the estrogen hormones play a crucial role in the blood lipid ratios, the lipoprotein patterns, and the human female's relative immunity to coronary heart disease (Eilert, M. L. *Metabolism,* 2:137, 1953; Oliver, M. F., et al. *Clin. Sci.,* 12:217, 1953; *Ibid. Am. Heart J.,* 47:348, 1954: Oliver, M. F., et al. *Circulation,* 13:82, 1956).

In a series of experiments on cholesterol-fed chicks, Stamler, Katz, and Pick found that estrogens, when jointly administered, caused an extraordinary increase in phospholipids, and maintained the cholesterol/phospholipid ratio in optimum levels (Stamler. J., and Katz, L. N. *Am. J. Physiol.,* 163:752, 1950; Pick, R., et al. *Circulation,* 6:585, 1952).

We have already noted (see reference notes 11, 12, 13, 17) the primary protective role of keeping the phospholipids (specifically lecithin) high in the circulatory system, and the possible harm of allowing a higher amount of circulating cholesterol. The present evidence of the role of the estrogen hormones in keeping the phospholipids high and their protective value in atherosclerosis and heart disease lends more proof of the proposition that the *ratio* of circulating phospholipids/cholesterol in the blood is all important, and *not* the amount of circulating cholesterol per se.

Estrogens administered to cholesterol-fed cockerels showed a marked reduction in cholesterol with a corresponding increase of phospholipids (Stamler, Katz, *Ibid.* 1950; Pick, et al. *Ibid,* 1952). Histologic studies revealed that the estrogen-treated birds were remarkably free of "lesions in the coronary arterial tree," while the birds without the estrogens disclosed marked "atherogenesis of the aortas." Estrogen administration could actually *reverse* the cholesterol-induced atherosclerotic plaques, even when the diet included continuous cholesterol feedings (Pick, et al. *Ibid.* 1952). Estrogens reversed both lipid and fibroblastic components of the plaques.

In still another experiment, both estrogen and insulin were administered to cholesterol-fed cockerels (Stamler, J., et al. *Ann. New York Acad. Sci.,* 64:596, 1956). Previous studies have shown that insulin feeding to cockerels—that were taken off an atherogenic diet and returned to normal feeding—retarded the usual return of the cholesterol/phospholipid ratio to normal balance. In this experiment, it was found that insulin also prevented the estrogen from counteracting the atherogenic effects of high fat-cholesterol feedings. The cockerels showed the usual signs of coronary lesions and disproportionate cholesterol/phospholipid ratios.

50. Thomas, W. A., and Hartroft, W. S. "Myocardial infarction in rats fed diets containing high fat, cholesterol, thiouracil and sodium cholate." *Circulation,* 19:65, 1959; Taylor, C. B., et al. "Fatal myocardial infarction in rhesus monkeys with diet-induced hyper-cholesterolemia." *Circulation,* 20:975, 1959.

In the above experiments, the investigators found that prolonged feeding of butter and cholesterol to monkeys or butter or lard to rats resulted in hyperlipemia and finally coronary thrombosis and myocardial infarction with lesions similar to those found in human beings. The diets of these animals were regarded as otherwise "normal" in respect to their intake of supplementary vitamins, minerals, and amino acids. Other data, however (see reference note 52 below), demonstrate that when fat and cholesterol (or animal protein) are increased in the diet, certain nutrients (particularly pyridoxine) must be increased above "average" or "normal" requirements.

51. Barboriak, J. J., et al. "Influence of high-fat diets on growth and development of obesity in the albino rat." *J. Nutr.,* 64:241, 1958.

52. Naimi, S., et al. "Cardiovascular lesions, blood lipids, coagulation and fibrinolysis in butter-induced obesity in the rat." *J. Nutr.,* 86:325, 1965.

In this more recent study, Naimi and his colleagues were directly interested in the effects of a high fat butter-induced obesity on the cardiovascular system of seventeen male Wistar albino rats. Butter constituted 65 percent of the total calories, with 20 percent protein (casein) and generous vitamin and mineral supplements equal to if not superior to those used in the above-mentioned Yale study.

Under the conditions of their experiment, these investigators found that a high fat butter diet causing obesity in rats *did not* produce changes in blood cholesterol nor result in cardiovascular lesions, as other data had led them to expect. The authors note, "The absence of such adverse changes, despite the development of gross obesity in these animals, may be significant, since both obesity and animal fats have been considered to be associated with lipemia and vascular lesions. It may be suggested that other dietary factors might have protected the experimental group against such changes. Yet, even if this happens to be the case, it should not detract from the significance of the fact that large amounts of saturated fat and obesity are not necessarily associated with lipemia and vascular lesions."

We are confident that other dietary factors did protect these rats, and that *only in the absence of sufficient supportive nutrients* are obesity and high fat and high cholesterol diets associated with atherosclerosis and heart disease in the human population.

53. Malhotra, S. L. "Serum lipids, dietary factors and ischemic heart disease." *Am. J. Clin. Nutr.*, 20:462,1967.

See also Malhotra, S. L. "Geographical aspects of acute myocardial infarction in India, with special reference to the pattern of diet and eating." *Brit. Heart J.*, 29:777, 1967.

54. Mann, G. V., et al. "Cardiovascular disease in the Masai." *J. Atheroscler. Res.*, 4:289, 1964.

In an extensive review of the various peoples of the earth who have little or no atherosclerosis and are virtually free of heart disease, Lowenstein found that the fat intake ranged from 21 grams per day to as much as 355 grams per day (Lowenstein, F. W. *Am. J. Clin. Nutr.*, 15:175, 1964). In both the Somalis and the Samburus of East Africa, the diet is from 60 to 65 percent fat (animal), and yet they are nearly free from atherosclerosis and heart attacks. While it might be argued that ethnic differences are involved here, population groups of wide ethnic variation have been reported who subsist on high fat, high cholesterol, high caloric diets while remaining virtually free of coronary heart disease.

In the text we have mentioned the report of Mann and his colleagues of the Masai tribe who subsist on a diet excessively high in butter fat (and cholesterol), the fat constituting as much as 60 percent of the total calories consumed, yet are virtually free of cardiovascular disease. Gsell and Mayer report that the semiisolated peoples of the Loetschental valley in the Valaisian Alps of Switzerland habitually eat a diet high in saturated fat and cholesterol, high in calories, but evidence low serum cholesterol values and little cardiovascular disorders (Gsell, D., and Mayer,

J. "Low blood cholesterol associated with high calorie, high saturated fat intake in a Swiss Alpine village population." *Am. J. Clin. Nutr.,* 10:471, 1962).

Stout and his coworkers report that an Italian immigrant colony in Roseta, Pennsylvania, consumes diets much richer in saturated animal fats than other Americans, yet have less than half the incidence of coronary heart disease (*J. A. M. A.,* 188:845, 1964).

In a survey study of 27,000 Kenya East Indians, A. D. Charters and B. P. Arya report (*Lancet,* 1:288, 1960) that the animal fat consumption was relatively high among the Punjabi nonvegetarians and relatively low among the vegetarian Gujeratis, but the percentage of heart disease morbidity "is closely proportional to that of the population." The statistics of their survey, conclude these investigators, suggest that in the case of the East Indian population in Kenya, "the ingestion of animal fats is not an important etiological factor" in heart disease morbidity. Interestingly, besides their low animal fat diet, the Gujerati vegetarians consume foods rich in polyunsaturated oils, as groundnut, cottonseed, and simsim oils, yet were not "protected from coronary occlusion by a high intake of unsaturated fatty acids."

In an epidemiological study of coronary heart disease in a general population of 106,000 Americans conducted over a one year period, W. J. Zukel and his coworkers found the highly provocative fact that farmers showed a much lower incidence of coronary heart disease than males of other groups, in spite of the fact that there were no substantial differences in their mean caloric intake or fat and cholesterol consumption (Zukel, W. J., et al. *Am. J. Pub. Health,* 49:1630, 1959).

In an epidemiological study of two Polynesian island groups, Hunter compared the diet, body build, blood pressure, and serum cholesterol levels of the tradition-following Atiu and Mitiaro with the more Europeanized Rarotongan neighbors (Hunter. J. D. *Fed. Proc.,* 21, Supp. 11:36, 1962). The Atiu-Mitiaro people live on a diet low in calories and protein but rich in highly saturated coconut fat. The Rarotongans are better off economically, more sedentary in their habits, eat more food, but eat comparatively little coconut fat. Hunter found that 25 percent of the Rarotongans (males) suffered from hypertension as compared to only 10 percent of the Atiu-Mitiaro males. While the serum cholesterol levels of the saturated coconut fat-eating Atiu-Mitiaro males were higher (as high as European males), Hunter was unable to discover by electrocardiographic readings any tendency to coronary heart disease.

Finally we turn to the early primitive Eskimo who subsisted almost totally on an excessively high animal fat diet. In an early 1927 issue of the *Journal of the American Medical Association* (May), in an article titled "Health of a Carnivorous Race," Dr. William Thomas reports that of 142 adults between the ages of forty and sixty who were completely examined, he found no unusual signs of vascular or renal morbidity, and all indications were that diseases of the cardiovascular system were not prevalent among these people. This is in agreement with other reports of scientists of the primitive Eskimo (e. g., C. Lieb. *J. A. M. A.*, July, 1926; V. Stefansson, in his book *Cancer: Disease of Civilization*, p. 76; I. M. Rabinowitch, *Canad. Med. Assoc. J.*, 31:487, 1936; W. Price, *Nutrition and Physical Degeneration*. New York: Hoeber, 1939).

It is clear, therefore, that adult males of widely differing ethnic stock can subsist on a high fat, high cholesterol, high caloric diet, and yet remain relatively free of cardiovascular disorders. Even if prevailing views are to the contrary, I think that the evidence points strongly toward the conclusion that the nutritional environment of the body cells—involving minerals, amino acids, and vitamins—is crucial, and that the amount of fat or cholesterol consumed is relatively inconsequential.

55. Antar, M. A., et al. "Changes in retail market food supplies in the United States . . . " *Am. J. Clin. Nutr.*, 14:169, 1964.

56. *Control of Dietary Fats as a Prophylactic Against Coronary Heart Disease: An Interpretative Review*
(Because of the major importance prominent nutritionists accord manipulation of dietary saturated and polyunsaturated fats as a means of reducing serum cholesterol and preventing atherosclerosis, this extensive interpretative review is presented as an important adjunct to what is in the text.)

Numerous studies, both animal and human, have demonstrated that the substitution of unsaturated for saturated fats in the diet reduces blood cholesterol values. The following are some of these studies: Messinger, W. J., et al. *Arch. Inter. Med.*, 86:189, 1950; Bronte-Stewart, B., et al. *Lancet*, 1:521, 1956; Kinsell, L. W., et al. *J. Clin. Nutr.*, 1:224, 1953; Ahrens, E. H., Jr., et al. *Proc. Soc. Exp. Biol. Med.*, 86:872, 1954; Green, J., et al. *Voeding*, 13:556, 1952; Barnes, R. H., et al. *J. Nutr.*, 69:261, 1959; Aftergood, L., et al. *J. Nutr.*, 62:129, 1957; Hauge, *Physiol. Scand.*, 45:19, 1959; *Ibid.* 45:26, 1959; Nath, N. R., et al. *J. Nutr.*, 67:289, 1959; Hegsted, D. M., et al. *J. Nutr.*, 63:273, 1957; *Ibid.* 63:377, 1957; Leveille, G. A., and Fisher, H. *Proc. Soc. Exp. Biol. Med.*, 98:630, 1958.

See also the reviews: Olson, R. E., and Vester, J. W. *Physiol. Rev.*, 40:677, 1960; Portman, O. W. and Stare, F. J. *Physiol. Rev.*, 39:407, 1959.

Within the last decade, many long-term studies have been made to test the hypothesis that an alteration in the ratio of polyunsaturated to saturated fats in the human diet will have favorable consequences in reducing serum cholesterol values, preventing atherosclerosis, and lowering coronary heart mortality. These therapeutic trials have been largely based on the premise that lowering serum cholesterol will alter the course of coronary heart disease.

In their study of the effect of dietary fat and cholesterol on serum cholesterol values in rats, Swell and Flick found higher serum cholesterol concentrations in rats fed a diet rich in soy bean oil than in animals fed stearate (Swell, L., and Flick, D. F. *Am. J. Physiol.*, 174:51, 1953). P. D. Klein (*Arch. Biochem.*, 76:56, 1958), Funch, et al. (*Brit. J. Nutr.*, 41:1, 1960), and N. Nath and his coworkers (*J. Nutr.*, 67:289, 1959) have separately reported observing higher serum cholesterol concentrations in rats fed diets *without cholesterol* when saturated fats were replaced with polyunsaturated fats. This observation concurs with the clinical observations of W. E. Connor and his colleagues (*J. Clin. Invest.*, 43:1691, 1964) and those of B. A. Ericson, et al. (*J. Clin. Invest.*, 43:2017, 1964) who found that when cholesterol is entirely absent from the human diet, the effect on serum cholesterol values produced by feeding different ratios of fatty acids is considerably reduced.

Why may polyunsaturated fatty acids be effective?

It is apparent from an enormous amount of research data that dietary polyunsaturated fatty acids, under certain favorable dietary conditions, will reduce blood lipid values, specifically serum cholesterol; the data suggest, in some cases at least, they may favorably affect the course of coronary heart disease. The mechanism by which polyunsaturated fatty acids act to lower serum cholesterol, however, is not presently satisfactorily understood (Mead, J. F. "Present knowledge of fat," In *Present knowledge in nutrition*. New York: The Nutrition Foundation, 1967, p. 16). However, a number of recent studies are pointing in the direction most likely to answer this question.

Early answers to this question were never satisfactory. H. Sinclair suggested that serum lipid abnormalities are due to a basic deficiency in essential fatty acids. While animal data demonstrated that cholesterol and saturated fat feeding could accelerate essential fatty acid deficiency (Holman, R. T., and Peiffer, J. J. *J. Nutrition,* 70:411, 1960), and while Nath and his colleagues found "definite dermal symptoms of essential fatty acid deficiency" in rats fed cholesterol-containing diets (*J. Nutr.,* 74:389, 1961), these latter investigators also found that polyunsaturated fatty acids other than the "essential" ones were even more effective in lowering serum cholesterol. This was concurred in the experiments of Ahrens and associates (*Lancet,* 1:115, 1959) who found that menhaden oil which is low in essential fatty acids but rich in other polyunsaturated fatty acids is equally effective as corn oil in reducing serum cholesterol in man.

Beveridge and coworkers have attributed the effectiveness of vegetable fats to their sterol components and other unidentified factors (*J. Biochem. Physiol.,* 35:257, 1957). While vegetable sterols, such as sitosterol, may possibly have some effect in lowering serum cholesterol, the data suggest their effect is minimal (Spritz, N. et al. *J. Clin. Invest.* 44:1482, 1965; Malmros, H., and Wigard. G. *Lancet,* 2:1, 1957; Connor, W. E., et al. *J. Clin. Invest.,* 40:894, 1961).

On the other hand, it has been shown that the effectiveness of polyunsaturated fatty acids in lowering serum cholesterol is *not* due to an ability to inhibit cholesterol synthesis (Ardlie, N. G., et al. *Brit. Med. J.,* 1:888, 1966) nor to an effect in accelerating its excretion (Spritz, N., et al. *J. Clin. Invest.,* 44:1482, 1965; Lindstedt, S. et al.

J. Clin. Invest., 44:1754, 1965). From recent animal studies, it is judged that polyunsaturated fatty acids act to remove cholesterol from the plasma and redistribute it to the tissues of the liver and muscle (Bloomfield. D. "Cholesterol metabolism: enhancement of cholesterol absorption and accumulation in safflower oil-fed rats." *J. Lab. Clin. Med.*, 64:613, 1964; Bieberdorf, F. A., and Wilson, J. D. "Studies on the mechanism of action of unsaturated fats on cholesterol metabolism in the rabbit." *J. Clin. Invest.*, 44:1834, 1965). The effect of this transfer of cholesterol to these organs, however, remains to be determined.

In view of the above cited studies of Swell and Flick, Klein, Funch et al., Nath et al., Connor et al., and Ericson et al., who found that in the absence of dietary cholesterol, dietary polyunsaturated fats, when substituted for saturated fats, either slightly raised serum cholesterol or had little effect, it seems probable that polyunsaturated fats in the diet are limited in their effects in cholesterol metabolism, and act chiefly in the metabolism of exogenous cholesterol. (However, the role of dietary and endogenous arachidonic acid is reported to be more extensively associated with arterial health, and apparently plays a greater role than the simple removal of exogenous cholesterol. (See the discussion in reference 34 above.)

Other data show that the favorable effects of polyunsaturated fatty acids are interdependent on other nutrients. Nath et al. found that when the diet rich in polyunsaturated fatty acids was low in protein (10 percent casein) there was an *increase* in cholesterol and total lipids of the liver, but this was not observed when the dietary protein was increased (*J. Nutr.*, 74:389, 1961). Shapiro and Freedman demonstrated that supplementary methionine in diets of cholesterol-fed rats was ineffective in reducing serum cholesterol after 40 days unless polyunsaturated fatty acids were added (*Am. J. Physiol.*, 181:441, 1955). Nath et al., also found that when rats fed diets of 10 percent protein and 4 percent of either corn oil or "wheat gluten lipid" (rich in linoleic acid) the serum cholesterol remained unaffected; when the protein was increased to 25 percent of the diet, serum cholesterol was lowered. From these data, there appears to be an interdependence between amino acid and fatty acid metabolism, and this involves the presence of catalytic coenzymes such as pyridoxine.

The reader will recall from the discussion in reference 34 above that a number of investigators have reported that the susceptibility to atherosclerosis in different species and individuals seems to be measured by their relative ability to synthesize arachidonic acid; this ability involves pyridoxine as the coenzyme catalyst in the conversion of dietary linolenic and linoleic acids into arachidonic acids (Witten and Holman. *Arch. Biochem.*, 41:266, 1952; L. Swell et al. *Proc. Soc. Exp. Biol. Med.*, 104:325, 1960). It was also mentioned that German investigators reported that feeding rats either linoleic and pyridoxine or arachidonate with their high cholesterol diet did prevent deposition of lipids in the aorta. If any dietary unsaturated fatty acid were itself *the* answer to arterial health, arachidonic acid might fill the bill. A broad view of the data, however, indicate that no single nutrient is the answer, but rather the metabolic interdependence of many nutrients.

While therapeutic trials have indicated that an alteration in the ratio of saturated to unsaturated fat in the diet will lower serum cholesterol under certain favorable dietary conditions, definite evidence is lacking that such changes will significantly lower the incidence of coronary heart mortality. On the other hand, much data, cited above and elsewhere in this chapter, has indicated that polyunsaturated fatty acids (1) are limited in their effect in cholesterol metabolism, (2) may actually act adversely (see below), and (3) act interdependently with other nutrients. (Parenthetically, on this last point, in reference note 34 above we mentioned the studies of R. W. Engel who found that both pyridoxine and unsaturated fatty acids are necessary for the B vitamin choline to exert its lipotropic action in the synthesis of lecithin [*J. Nutr.* 24:175, 1942]. The presence of lecithin, you will recall, is vital to arterial health.)

Moreover, some of the data indicate that saturated/unsaturated fat ratios are of little consequence in modifying the course of coronary heart disease (Bierenbaum, M. L., et al. "Modified fat dietary management of the young coronary male: a five-year controlled study." *Circulation*, 31–32, Suppl. II, 3, 1965; Bierenbaum, M. L. et al. *J. A. M. A.*, 202:1119, 1967).

We have also cited numerous reports (see reference note 54) that show conclusively that many peoples on all continents of the earth may eat diets rich in saturated animal fats and low in polyunsaturated fats while remaining virtually free from atherosclerosis and coronary heart disease.

At this point it may be good to review other strong evidence concerning the possible *harmful* effects of increasing dietary polyunsaturated fats and/or of lowering saturated fats or total fats in the diet.

May excess dietary polyunsaturated fats be harmful?

The question persistently arises whether it is always judicious to recommend dietary changes in the saturated/ unsaturated fatty acid ratio without taking into account other nutrient variables. There are a number of important reasons why much deliberation should precede recommendations of changes in the fat content of the diet.

Biochemical variability as a factor. F. Hatch and F. Kendall report (*J. Clin. Invest.*, 31:636, 1952) that in placing forty hospitalized hypertensive patients on low fat diets (below 40 grams per day), serum cholesterol levels dropped in 68 percent, but another 12 percent actually showed a rise in serum cholesterol, while 18 percent developed a blood lipid condition characterized by turbid serum and elevation of free cholesterol and triglycerides. They concluded that a restricted saturated fat diet cannot be *generally* recommended, but is exceedingly variable in its effect on different individuals, This again points up the biochemical individuality of the human nutrition status, and the need for physicians to be continually alert to this factor.

Polyunsaturated fat may induce weight gains. Studies have shown that the addition of polyunsaturated fats to a diet without a reduction of other fats will cause a gradual increase in body weight, a result that may outweigh the cholesterol-lowering advantage of the change (Jolliffe, N. *Metabolism,* 10:497, 1961; Bronte-Stewart, B., et al. *Lancet,* 1:521, 1956).

Vitamin E deficiency may contribute to the deleterious effects of polyunsaturated fats. Polyunsaturated fatty acids, particularly linoleic acid, are, of course, easily oxidized. From numerous studies of poultry, rats, rabbits, cattle, and man, investigators have found that increased ingestion of polyunsaturated fats requires greater amounts of antioxidants in the diet, particularly vitamin E. (See Horwitt, N. K. *Am. J. Clin. Nutr.*, 4:408, 1956; *Ibid.* 8:451, 1960; Hove, E. L., and Harris, P. L. *J. Nutr.*, 33:95, 1947; Dam, H. *Proc. Soc. Exp. Biol. Med.*, 52:285, 1943; Century, B., and Horwitt, M. K. *J. Nutr.*, 72:357, 1960; Filer, L. J., Jr., et al. In *trans. First Conf. Biol. Antioxidants.* New York: Macy, 1946, pp. 67–77; Witting, L. A., and Horwitt, M. K. *J. Nutr.*, 82:19, 1964; Horwitt, N. K., et al. *J. Am. Dietet. Assoc.*, 38:231, 1961; Harris, P. L., and Embree, N. D. *Am. J. Clin. Nutr.*, 13:385, 1963; Hassan, H. et al. *Am J. Clin. Nutr.*, 19:147, 1966; Ritchie, J., et al. *Proc. Soc. Pediat. Res.*, Apr. 1967, p. 107; Blaxter, K. L., et al. *Brit. J. Nutr.*, 7:287, 1953.)

Increasing polyunsaturated fats in the diet appears to augment the amount of vitamin E needed daily (Horwitt, M. K. *Borden's Rev. Nutr. Res.*, 22:1, 1961; Council on Foods and Nutrition, *J. A. M. A.*, 181:411, 1962). Horwitt and his associates found that in man the higher the unsaturated fats in the diet, the lower was the tocopherol in the plasma (*J. Am. Dietet. Assoc.*, 38:231, 1961). Tocopherol requirements, they determined, will vary from 5 milligrams to 30 milligrams or more per day, depending on the amount of polyunsaturated fatty acids in the diet.

Lipid peroxidation may be important with respect to cellular aging. A. L. Tappel has presented evidence that implicates polyunsaturated fatty acids as being the primary source of free peroxy radicals that damage the cellular membranes (endoplasmic reticulum and mitochondria) and accelerate aging (*Nutr. Today*, 2:2, 1967). Tappel points out that if the intake of polyunsaturated fatty acids exceeds the intake of nutrient antioxidants (such as vitamin E and selenium, a trace antioxidant) required for their stability in the body, the condition will be dangerously productive of lipid peroxidation (*Geriatrics*, 23:97, 1968; *Fed. Proc.*, 24:73, 1965). He points out that there are "upper limits to the recommended intake of polyunsaturated lipids."

Ceroid pigment formation may be highly significant. W. S. Hartroft and E. A. Porta describe the morbid condition of ceroid pigment deposition in animal and human tissues (*Am. J. Med. Sci.*, 250:324, 1965). This pigment is classified as a lipochrome, similar to such pigments as found, for instance, in the muscle of experimental nutritional muscular dystrophy. Authorities in this area of research appear to agree that ceroid pigment results from "oxidation and peroxidation of polyunsaturated fats with the formation of long-chain polymers of an insoluble nature" (Hartroft, W. S., and Porta, E. A. "Present Knowledge of Ceroid Pigments," In *Present knowledge in nutrition.* New York: The Nutrition Foundation, 1967; Endicott, K. M. *Arch. Path.,* 37:49, 1944; DeOlivera, J. D. *Ann. N.Y. Acad. Sci.* 52:125, 1949–1950; Dam, H., and Granadox, H. *Science,* 103:327, 1945).

Ceroid pigment formation has been reported in man to be a relatively early and constant condition in atherosclerotic aortas and coronary arteries "as well as in occlusive thrombi found obstructing the latter in cases of fatal myocardial infarction" (Hartroft and Porta, *op cit.*). Hartroft and Porta note that vitamin E and other antioxidants will decrease the formation of ceroid pigment. (*See also* Tappel, A. L. *Arch. Biochem.,* 54:266, 1955.)

They also state, "It is apparent . . . that the nutritional status of the entire organism may play an important role in whether or not ceroid will be deposited in any part of the body. A high intake of polyunsaturated fat or a low intake of vitamin E (and particularly the simultaneous presence of both conditions), will favor its formation, particularly if abnormal deposits of lipid form in liver, muscle, or other organs."

Hartroft and Porta have stated the hypothesis that "the greater the ratio of polyunsaturated to saturated fat at the site of any local accumulation of lipid, and the greater the ratio of oxidative catalysts to tissue antioxidants at the same site, the more abundant will be the formation of ceroid pigment. Such a coexistence of factors will more likely occur in the animal fed large amounts of polyunsaturated fats and low amounts of tocopherols. . . ."

Moreover, ceroid pigment is likely to be "fibrogenic," according to the results of animal experiments. Clots containing polyunsaturated fats showed ceroid pigment deposition in rabbits (Legge, D. A., and Bear, R. A. *Fed. Proc.,* 25:324, 1966; Bear, R. A., et al. *Fed. Proc.,* 25:324, 1966). These clots resisted fibrinolysis to a greater extent than those containing equal amounts of saturated fat. In view of these results, Hartroft and Porta suggest: "If dietary polyunsaturated fat can be similarly incorporated in thrombi formed in man, one might postulate on this basis an increased resistance to thrombolysis with high oral intakes of vegetable fat. The implication in terms of current notions about dietary prophylaxis of myocardial infarction is obvious, but needs more exploration."

Summary. Briefly, we have reviewed data which indicate that, (1) not only may the substitution of polyunsaturated fats for saturated fats decrease serum cholesterol levels, but in a significant number of cases it may actually *increase* serum cholesterol and triglycerides; (2) a high polyunsaturated fatty acid intake may cause a critical shortage of vitamin E in the system unless additional tocopherols are included in the diet; (3) if additional antioxidants (vitamin E, selenium, vitamin C) are not included in a high unsaturated fat diet, it may be dangerously productive of lipid peroxidation and, hence, cellular aging; (4) if additional antioxidants are not provided (specifically alpha tocopherol), a high polyunsaturated fat diet may promote ceroid pigment formation which has been found in atherosclerotic aortas and coronary arteries in man. Moreover, these ceroid pigments (containing polyunsaturated fatty acids) found in occlusive thrombi or clots are *more* resistant to dissolution than those clots containing saturated fat.

If the above indictments are correct, it is suggested that individuals who ingest a large amount of polyunsaturated fats on the notion that it will protect them against atherosclerosis and coronary heart disease may actually be exposing themselves to the disease! It may well be that one of the main reasons why Evan Shute and his colleagues have had such success with mega-alpha tocopherol therapy in a considerable number of coronary cases (see reference notes 20 and 21) is because of our excessive intake of polyunsaturated fats in the last three decades, creating a vitamin E deficiency in numerous members of our population.

The situation, if true, is indeed ironical; current popular proposals to prevent atherosclerosis and coronary heart disease virtually ignore the nutritional balance of cellular environments; consequently, their advocacy of more polyunsaturated fatty acids in the diet may actually be accelerating cardiovascular morbidity in our population, while creating a nutritional vitamin E deficiency.

Is our consumption of antioxidant nutrients keeping step?

To avoid some of the dangers to our health cited by Horwitt, Harris and Embree, Tappel, and Hartroft and Porta, the increased consumption of foods rich in polyunsaturated fats requires an increasing intake of antioxidant nutrients, chiefly alpha tocopherol, though the trace mineral selenium and vitamin C may also be important. While Americans are eating more polyunsaturated fats than they were before 1900, they are also eating foods that provide *less* antioxidants. One good source of vitamin E in the past was the germ of our wheat. This is now largely extracted from our flours. In an intensive study and analysis of common foods purchased in food markets, R. H. Bunnell and his associates determined that the average American diet contains approximately 7.5 milligrams of alpha tocopherol daily (*Am. J. Clin. Nutr.*, 17:1, 1965). This figure, noted the authors, was lower than the 14.9 of Harris and Embree (*Am. J. Clin. Nutr.*, 13:385, 1963) who were estimating the contents of fresh uncooked foods. The data of Bunnell et al. indicated that the processed, frozen, and cooked foods actually eaten in typical American meals supply vitamin E in amounts considerably below the 10 to 30 milligrams recently recommended by the Food and Nutrition Board, a recommendation that was relative to the daily consumption of polyunsaturated fats (*J. A. M. A.*, 181:441, 1962).

Food survey studies have shown that 40 percent of the daily calories of the average American diet is fat, while approximately 17 percent of these are polyunsaturated fats. This high amount of polyunsaturated fats demands increasing amounts of antioxidant nutrients (and pyridoxine) in the diet. From the study of Bunnell et al., it is apparent that Americans on the average are getting less than half the amount of vitamin E recommended by the Food and Nutrition Board. In other words, the typical American diet is rich in polyunsaturated fat and defficient in antioxidant alpha tocopherol. This is exactly the dangerous condition Hartroft and Porta warned will favor the formation of ceroid pigment which they found so often to be an early and constant accompaniment of human atherosclerotic aortas and coronary arteries.

Does a high ingestion of polynusaturated fats increase the need for pyridoxine?

It would be well to also remember that studies have shown (see reference note 34) that pyridoxine is vital in the metabolism of unsaturated fatty acids. From the evidence of his studies on rats, Kotake cautioned us that fatty acids in the diet demand increasing amounts of B_6 (*J. Vitaminology*, 1:73, 1955). Also, Elvehjem and his associates have shown that unsaturated fats act as depressants on endogenous B vitamin synthesis via the intestinal flora, while saturated fats—particularly butterfat—do not.

It is thought-provoking incidentally, that this fact may possibly explain such data as that of the Northern and Southern Indian studies. The Northern Indian group ingest a considerable amount of butterfat and lactic acid products (which promote the intestinal synthesis of B vitamins, including B_6), and their diet contains little unsaturated fats, yet they have exceptionally low cardiovascular morbidity. The Southern Indian group ingest virtually no butterfat or lactic acid products while 44 percent of their small amount of fats were polyunsaturated (in contrast to 2 percent unsaturated fats of the Northern Indians). Yet the mortality due to coronary heart disease was 15 times higher among the low animal fat-high unsaturated fat Southern group (Malhotra, S. L. *J. Assoc. Physic. India*, 14:93, 1966; Malhotra, S. L. *Brit. Heart J.*, 29:777, 1967; Malhotra, S. L. *Am. J. Clin. Nutr.*, 20:462, 1967). It may be that the diets of the Northern Indians are favorable in promoting intestinal synthesis of B vitamins, particularly pyridoxine, which protect against atherosclerosis, and do not create cellular (antioxidant) malnutrition from a too high consumption of polyunsaturated fats. The Southern Indians' diet may act to depress intestinal synthesis while promoting both vitamin E and B_6 deficiencies by a too high consumption of polyunsaturated fats, finally resulting in atherosclerosis. Be that as it may, no other current hypothesis, as far as we know, has been offered in explanation of these (unpopular) data.

Numerous studies have shown that pyridoxine deficiency is often found linked with atherosclerosis (see references 23, 24, 25, 32, and 34). We have noted that an increased intake of unsaturated fats together with a high ingestion of

animal protein (rich in tryptophan), both typical of American diets, make greater demands for B_6 in the diet. Even
aside from this consideration, our diets appear to be actually deficient in this nutrient. The earlier-mentioned study
of Schroeder (*J. Chron. Dis.*, 2:28, 1955) and of Kheim
and Kirk (*Am. J. Clin. Nutr.*, 20:702, 1967) have strongly
indicated that the typical American diet is deficient in
this vital cofactor, and low B_6 levels have been found in
human atherosclerotic tissue.

*Is atherosclerosis a matter of "overnutrition," or a defi-
ciency disease?*

This entire question of the ratio of saturated to polyunsaturated fats in our diet becomes a problem only
because current views hold that saturated fats are "bad,"
and that we are a nation suffering from "overnutrition," an
ill-defined, misleading term. The overconsumption of calories, a common error in our eating, is *not* the equivalent of
an overconsumption of vital nutrients. The real problem of
the American diet, as others have ably pointed out, is not
one of "overnutrition" of fats but one of imbalanced nutrition, with the emphasis on the relative absence of
nutrients needed for efficient metabolism. Essentially, this
indicts not only our choice of foods, but also the inadequacy of many of the processed foods we consume.

Thus, Katz, Stamler, and Pick, in an editorial in the
Journal of the American Medical Association, point out:
"The contemporary American diet . . . places . . . a continuing strain upon the metabolic processes. This diet is
pernicious to the cardiovascular system not only because
of its excess in calories, lipids, and cholesterol . . . It tends
to be quite high in salt and in 'empty' calories, i.e., calories
derived from highly processed refined carbohydrates and
fats . . . foods rich in energy but low in essential nutrients.
Hence, the American diet, despite its high caloric level,
is not infrequently inadequate, relatively or absolutely, in
specific vitamins, essential fatty acids, minerals, and amino
acids" (*J. A. M. A.*, June 9th, 1956).

Unfortunately, this is the strongest indictment in the
professional literature—virtually standing alone—any reputable research team has made of the American diet and
its possible deficiency implications. By their continual sins
of omission, medical educators and researchers tend to
perpetuate these deficiencies in our diet, and aggravate the

prevailing degenerative diseases, with atherosclerosis and coronary heart disease being the most disastrous to the public health.

In his article "Atherosclerosis: Overnutrition or Malnutrition?" (*Am. J. Digest. Dis.*, 22:206, 1955) E. Van Handel also calls our attention to the view that cardiovascular disease is not a problem of overnutrition but a result of a deficiency of nutrients in our civilized, processed foods. We emphatically argee with Van Handel that "the deficiency theory has not yet been consistently tested by the leading scientists, working on the relationship between food and atherosclerosis."

Note might be made, however, that the work of Jolliffe and his colleagues with the Anti-Coronary Club Project was an overall attempt to correct nutritional imbalance (Christakis, G., et al. "The Anti-Coronary Club: a dietary approach to the prevention of coronary heart disease—a seven-year report." *Am. J. Public Health*, 56:299, 1966; Jolliffe, N. et al. *New York State J. Med.*, 63:69, 1963). The long-term, seven-year study of the Anti-Coronary Club was one of the most successful attempts to date to correct coronary heart disease by dietary means. Aside from the fact that the 814 volunteers were required to reduce their intake of animal fat and hydrogenated vegetable fat—replacing them with nutritional foods such as fish, lean meats, whole grains, vegetables, and fruits—another very important rule was that each member, to remain in the Club, had to maintain normal weight and was required to exercise.

In regard to this, Jolliffe asserted that the most important nutritional rule to follow in maintaining normal weight control was the elimination of "empty" calories from the diet, a term coined by him (*Metabolism*, May 1955) to describe foods essentially devoid of "protein, essential minerals, and vitamins." In writing of Jolliffe's work with the Anti-Coronary Club, Arthur Blumenfeld, author of *Heart Attack: Are You a Candidate?* (Introduction by Paul Dudley White) wrote, "The most glaring example is sugar, which Dr. Jolliffe held up as the 'pure' example of 'empty calories.' Other 'empty calorie' foods are (1) highly refined white flour, (2) most saturated fats, and (3) foods made by combining sugar and highly refined flour and saturated fats, such as most commercial baked goods.

"The simple elimination of most of the 'empty calories'

was considered an important step in the Prudent Diet. Cereals, whole grains, and vegetables were to replace the 'empty calories,'" (New York: Eriksson, 1964, p. 193).

It is our view that the nutrition rules followed by the Anti-Coronary Club members were successful not solely because of their adherence to a restricted fat diet, but perhaps mainly because of the improvement in their overall nutrition. In other words, the success of the Anti-Coronary Club Project may not have been due to the restriction of fat consumption per se, but rather to a correction of nutritional imbalance by the elimination of foods containing little or no amino acids, vitamins and minerals (empty calories) and replacing them with foods of high nutritional value. Though the "Prudent Diet," I feel, is subject to further improvements, probably by mineral and vitamin supplementation as insurance, it is a step in the right direction of correcting nutritional imbalance.

In conclusion, from a consideration of these many factors, it is clear to us that the general recommendation of increasing the intake of polyunsaturated fats and reducing saturated fats in the diet is not the kind of advice that can be given indiscriminately. Better advice, it would seem, is to make certain that plenty of other nutrients, notably vitamin E, vitamin C, vitamin B_6, other B vitamins (choline particularly), minerals (magnesium, calcium), and trace minerals together with good sources of protein (rich in methionine) are included in any diet containing adequate amounts of polyunsaturated fats. Chances are, if an individual improves his nutrition in this respect, he will not need to concern himself with the ratio of saturated to unsaturated fats in his diet.

57. Wolbach, S. B., and Howe, P. R. "Intercellular substance in experimental scorbutus." *Arch. Path.*, 1:1, 1926.

58. See the cited material in McCormick, W. J. "Coronary thrombosis: a new concept of mechanism and etiology." *Clin. Med.*, July, 1957, pp. 839–842. See particularly citations M. Lamy, et al., and W. Koch (p. 841).

59. Williams R. J., and Deason, G. "Individuality in Vitamin C needs." *Proc. Nat. Acad. Sci.*, 57:1638, 1967.

60. McCormick, W. J. "Coronary thrombosis: a new

concept of mechanism and etiology." *Clin. Med.*, July 1957, p. 839.

See also Aschoff, L. *Lectures on pathology.* New York: Hoeber-Harper, 1924; Duff, G. L. *Arch. Path.*, 20:81, 1935; Moon, H. G., and Rinehardt, J. F. *Circulation,* 3:481, 1952; Patterson, J. C. *Canad. Med. Assoc. J.*, 44:114, 1941; Willis, G. C. *Report Ann. Meeting and Proc. R. C. P. & S. of Canada,* Oct. 30–31, 1953; Burton, A. C. *Am. J. Physiol.*, 164:319, 1951; Laseque, C., and Legroux, A. *Arch. Gen.*, 2:680, 1871; Findlay, G. M. *J. Path, & Bact.*, 24:446,1921; Lamy, M., et al. *Bull. et mem. Soc. med. d. hop. de Paris,* 445, 1946; Wolbach, S. B. *Am. J. Path.*, 9:689, 1923; Biskind, M. S. *J. Ins. Med.*, 1951.

Since the early findings of Virchow, pathologists have considered that vascular lesions in atherosclerosis depend on alterations of the ground substance of the arterial intima (Duff, G. L. *Arch. Path.*, 20:81, 1936). This is based on the fact that lipids are deposited in this ground substance. Willis demonstrated that an ascorbic acid deficiency in the guinea pig resulted in "arterial lessions morphologically typical of atherosclerosis" (*Canad. Med. Assoc. J.*, 69:17, 1953). Asorbic acid injections into guinea pigs with cholesterol-fed induced atherosclerosis had a marked effect in inhibiting the atherosclerotic condition.

Because of these findings of ascorbic acid deficiency in atherosclerosis, Willis and Fishman conducted clinical studies of human arteries for the ascorbic acid content under varying conditions (Willis, G. C., and Fishman, S. "Ascorbic acid content of human arterial tissue." *Canad. Med. Assoc. J.*, 72:500, 1955). They found that a localized ascorbic acid depletion often existed in segments of arteries afflicted with atherosclerosis. Adjacent arterial segments without lesions had higher ascorbic acid contents, and atherosclerosis was rare in these arteries. Noting that studies have shown that the conversion of acetate into cholesterol in tissues is several times more rapid in tissues depleted of ascorbic acid, these investigators suggest that ascorbic acid deficiency in the arteries may account for the release of glucoprotein noted in the blood of subjects with severe atherosclerosis."

Boris Sokoloff and his associates point out that the enzyme, lipoprotein lipase, is found throughout the body tissues (*J. Am. Geriac. Soc.*, 14:1239, 1966). This enzyme has been determined to be localized in the capillary walls, and D. S. Robinson suggests that it is found at the surface of the capillary endothelial cells (*Rev. Canad. Biol.*, 17:1, 1958). Since lipoprotein lipase is localized in the capillary wall, Sokoloff and his associates hypothesized that ascorbic acid and related factors which are actively engaged in the normal functioning of the capillaries may also be involved in fat metabolism and hence in atherosclerosis. In a series of experiments with rats and rabbits, Sokoloff and his coworkers found that long-term dosages of ascorbic acid given to hypercholesterolemic animals reduced blood lipid levels considerably, including cholesterol and triglycerides, and enhanced the lipoprotein lipase activity. It also reduced the extent and severity of arterial lesions as compared with atherosclerotic control animals.

Vitamin C, in its natural state, is found associated with "flavonoids." There are a number of studies that have shown the flavonoids themselves exert some protective effect against thrombosis and atherosclerosis. Russian researchers in 1959 reported that vitamin C and flavonoid combinations reduced atherosclerosis in cholesterol-fed rabbits (Smolenskii, V. S., et al. *Sb. Nauch. Akad. Nauk. Inst. Biokkim.*, 4:158, 1959). Around the same time, Di Maggio independently reported that the flavonoid quercitin reduced the total quantity of cholesterol held in colloidal suspension in blood plasma *in vitro* (Di Maggio, G. *Inter. Z. Vitaminforsch.*, 29:223, 1959).

In 1963, Robbins and French reported that the rutin flavonoid reduced serum cholesterol in rats, depending on the kind of fat in the diet (*Proc. Assoc. Agri. Workers*, 60:186, 1963). In addition to these reports on the protective effect of the flavonoids against atherosclerosis, T. Neageli and P. Matis asserted, on the basis of clinical studies, that the flavonoids may have a therapeutic value in treating thromboembolism (*Inter. Z. Vitaminforsch.*, 27:324, 1957).

In a recent study, Robbins found that in twenty groups of rats (260 animals) fed either a thrombogenic or atherogenic diet plus various flavonoids (rutin, narigin, hesperidin), eighteen groups showed an average increase in survival time over control rats fed similar regimens without flavonoids (Robbins, R. C. *J. Atheroscler. Res.*, 7:3, 1967). On the basis of his studies, Robbins hypothesizes that flavonoids may act in the manner as certain dextrans of low molecular weight, increasing suspension stability of blood, deaggregating blood cells and improving blood flow.

61. Wintrobe, M. M., et al. "Electrocardiographic changes associated with thiamine deficiency in pigs." *Bull. Johns Hopkins Hosp.*, 73:169, 1943; Ashburn, L. L., and Lowry, J. V. "Development of cardiac lesions in thiamine-deficient rats." *Arch. Path.*, 37:27, 1944; Swank, R. L. et al. "The production and study of cardiac failure in thiamine-deficient dogs." *Am. Heart J.*, 22:154, 1941; Toman, J. E. P. et al. "Origin of cardiac disorders in thiamine-deficient cats." *Proc. Soc. Exp. Biol. Med.*, 58:65, 1945; Waisman, H. A., and McCall, K. B. "A study of thiamine deficiency in the monkey (macaca mulatta)." *Arch. Biochem.*, 4:265, 1944.

Thiamine is vital to the integrity of the myocardial fiber. Animal experiments cited above reveal that thiamine deficiency results in myocardial alterations and severe damage. Sudden death has also been found to be a part of the thiamine deficiency syndrome in swine. On autopsy, microscopic lesions have been described in thiamine-deficient rats, dogs, foxes, and swine.

62. For a good review of the effects of many nutritional deficiencies on the function of the heart and the cardiovascular system in general, see especially Follis's account, "The effects of nutritional deficiency on the heart: a review." *Am. J. Clin. Nutr.*, 4:107, 1956.

In this review, it is shown that a deficiency of potassium, biotin, riboflavin, thiamine, vitamin A, iron—also of many other nutrients—act to produce myocardial anomalies and vascular disorders.

Elsewhere, L. A. Carlson and his coworkers hypothesize that nicotinic acid inhibits the mobilization of free fatty acids from the body's fat tissue, thus reducing the uptake of these fatty acids by the liver which in turn reduces the formation of very low density lipoproteins in the liver (*J. Atheroscler. Res.*, 8:677, 1968). The ultimate effect of niacin would be to reduce the amount of low density lipoproteins in the blood, this lowering the plasma cholesterol.

Parenthetically, we are reminded here of Peter Kuo and his associates' studies of the uptake of carbohydrates (fructose) in the adipose tissues of his "hyperlipemic" subjects (Kuo, P. T., et al. "Dietary carbohydrates in hyperlipemia [hyperglyceridemia]; hepatic and adipose tissue lipogenic activities." *Am. J. Clin. Nutr.*, 20:116, 1967, see especially reference note 68 below). According to Kuo and colleagues, hyperlipemia or atherosclerosis is, in the majority of cases, the product of a malfunctioning phospholipid and fatty acid metabolism. Accordingly, dietary fructose is diverted via the adispose tissue into accelerated mobilization of free fatty acids which are subsequently incorporated into low density lipoproteins via the liver. This does not occur in the adipose tissues of "normolipemics"; in this latter case, dietary carbohydrates are utilized in the synthesis of phospholipids. Could it be, then, that a deficiency of niacin, as the studies of Carlson and coworkers suggest, is one factor at least that prevents this normal phospholipid production in hyperlipemics, and that possibly —because of biochemical individuality—their niacin requirement is much higher than "normolipemics"? At least this is an intriguing possibility that could warrant further study.

In line with the hypothesis of Carlson, et al., J. Merrill and his colleagues report that 0.4 percent of this B vitamin added to the chow of cholesterol-fed rabbits significantly reduced cholesterol deposition in the aorta (*Circulation,* 16:916, 1957). Thus, it appears that dietary niacin can *prevent* cholesterol deposition in the aorta if taken in relatively large amounts along with a nutritionally rich diet. This is in addition, incidentally, to the numerous studies in the last fifteen years that demonstrate that niacin taken in drug proportions has a therapeutic effect in reducing plasma cholesterol in human subjects (Parsons, W., Jr., et al. *Proc. Staff Meet. Mayo Clinic.* 31:377, 1956; Parsons, and Flinn, *Circulation,* 16:499,1957; Ochor, R., and McKenzie, B. *Circulation,* 16:499, 1957).

63. Antar, M. A., et al. "Changes in retail market food supplies in the United States in the last seventy years in relation to the incidence of coronary heart disease with special reference to dietary carbohydrates and essential fatty acids." *Am. J. Clin. Nutr.,* 14:169, 1964.

64. Yudkin, J. "Diet and coronary thrombosis." *Lancet,* 2:155, 1957; *Ibid.* 2:4, 1964.

65. Yudkin, J. "Dietary fat and dietary sugar in relation to ischemic heart-disease and diabetes." *Lancet,* 2:4, 1964.

66. Yudkin, J., and Morland, J. "Sugar intake and myocardial infarction." *Am. J. Clin. Nutr.,* 20:503; 1967.

67. Kaufman, N. A., et al. "Change in the serum lipid levels of hyperlipemic patients following the feeding of starch, sucrose, and glucose." *Am. J. Clin. Nutr.,* 18:261, 1966; Kuo, P. T., and N. N. Huang. *J. Clin, Invest.,* 44:1924, 1965; Antar, M. A. *Fed. Proc.,* 22:327, 1963; Hodges, R. E. *Fed. Proc.,* 22:209, 1963.

For other excellent reports on the subject of sugar and starch consumption and atherosclerosis, see the special symposium issue of the *American Journal of Clinical Nutrition,* 20, 1967.

68. Kuo, P. T., et al., 'Dietary carbohydrates in hyperlipemia (hyperglyceridemia); hepatic and adipose tissue lipogenic activities." *Am. J. Clin. Nutr.,* 20:116, 1967.

In this intensive study, the authors were endeavoring to ascertain the specific mechanism in the body by which sugar-induced hyperlipidemia is produced. They pointed out that the carbohydrate-induced hyperglyceridemia is relatively common and is most often found in association with atherosclerosis. Its chief features are (1) the concentration of low density beta lipoprotein compounds in the serum, compounds with a large cargo of triglyceride, and is directly related to excess sugar intake; (2) elevated blood triglycerides (hyperglyceridemia) occurs when the subject eats his ordinary diet; (3) when the patient is maintained on a high carbohydrate diet, marked fluctuations occur to the serum triglyceride levels, with radical elevations occurring at times of the largest ingestion of sugar.

In their study of eight "hyperlipidemic" patients, Kuo and colleagues found that dietary sugar (sucrose) administered to patients causes blood fats to increase, while starch tends to lower them. They found that individuals who had low blood fat levels were relatively resistant to the effects of sugar, and that 85 to 90 percent of the total calorie intake in sugar was required in these resistant individuals to produce hyperglyceridemia.

In eight hyperlipidemic patients maintained on special feeding periods from three to six weeks, Kuo and his coworkers found that when sugar was substituted for starch three blood lipid values were raised; conversely, when starch replaced sugar, serum lipid levels were lowered toward normal values.

Kuo and his team then undertook an intensive investigation of the possible mechanism(s) involved in the production of high serum cholesterol/triglyceride concentrations in hyperlipidemic individuals. Lipid synthesis from carbohydrate is believed to take place chiefly in the liver. Studies have also suggested that the adipose tissues are involved. Kuo and colleagues studied the respective roles of hepatic and adipose tissues of endogenous lipogenesis from glucose, sucrose, and acetate precursors in six normal and fourteen hyperlipidemic subjects.

From their carefully conducted studies, they ascertained first, and to their surprise, that in both normal and hyperlipidemic subjects, 97.5 to 99.7 percent of all labeled fructose glucose, and acetate carbons are incorporated by the liver into phospholipid, chiefly lecithin. While the liver tissues of the hyperlipemic subjects synthesized fructose and acetate into lipids other than phospholipids more actively than the livers of normal individuals, it did not account for the high blood lipids.

These investigators then found that the adipose tissue of hyperglyceride patients incorporated labeled fructose carbon into lipids seven to eight times higher than the tissue of normal individuals. On the other hand, glucose was incorporated into lipids by the adipose tissues at a much slower rate in both groups. Since starch, by hydrolysis, yields only glucose molecules, these observations of Kuo and his coworkers together with data obtained from fructose, sucrose, and glucose feeding experiments in animals and man (Kuo, P. T. *Trans. Assoc. Am. Physicians,* 78:97, 1965; Macdonald, I. *Am. J. Clin. Nutr.,* 18:369, 1966; Macdonald, I., and Roberts, J. B. *Metab. Clin. Exper.,* 114:991, 1965) partly explain why sucrose causes a rise in blood lipids while starch lowers them.

Moreover, Kuo and colleagues found that the fat tissue of normal subjects converted much of the carbohydrate precursors into water soluble moieties of the lipid molecule, particularly phospholipids, while the tissue of hyperlipemic subjects incorporated major parts of the precursors into fatty acids. Also, the lipolytic or triglyceride breakdown was greatly accelerated from as much as sixteen to forty-five times higher in the adipose tissues of hyperlipidemic fasting patients.

The fat tissues of the hyperlipidemic subjects were highly active in synthesizing lipids from simple sugars and in releasing free fatty acids. The high influx of free fatty acids from fat tissues are transported to the liver, explains Kuo et al.; there they are incorporated into triglyceride and then released into the blood stream as low density lipo-proteins, producing hyperglyceridemia.

Finally, Kuo et al. point out that these data suggest "an abnormality in phospholipid metabolism." Whereas the fat tissues of normal individuals convert most carbohydrate precursors into water-soluble moieties of the phospholipids, the fat tissues of hyperlipemic subjects divert these dietary precursors into accelerated production of free fatty acids, to be eventually incorporated into low density lipoproteins via the liver.

69. Dahl, L. K. "Effects of chronic excess salt feeding; elevation of plasma cholesterol in rats and dogs." *J. Exper. Med.*, Oct. 1960, p. 635.

70. Talbott, G. D., et al. "Effects of excess sodium chloride on blood lipids: a possible factor in coronary heart disease." *Ann. Inter. Med.*, 54: 257, 1961.

These investigators report that excess sodium chloride in the diet depresses serum cholesterol but elevates triglycer-ides. Since many studies of atherosclerosis have revealed high triglyceride concentrations in the blood, the authors suggest that early limitation of salt intake, particularly during youth, might be one means of helping control atherosclerosis.

71. Studies of the female rat (Okey, R., et al. *J. Am. Dietet. Assoc.*, 36:441, 1960) and of the chicken (Cohn, C., et al. *Circulation Res.*, 9:139, 1961) have shown that large meals ingested once or twice a day elevate the serum cholesterol levels and increase the incidence and severity of atherosclerosis.

S. A. Hashim and his coworkers report a drop in serum cholesterol in patients that were taken off the customary three-meal-a-day routine and fed smaller amounts of food six times daily (*Lancet*, 1:1105, 1960). This decrease in serum cholesterol, they noted, was evident regardless of the amount or kind of fat in the diet, though the kind of fat influenced the magnitude of the fall.

Numerous reports have shown that when rats consume food in larger amounts between longer intervals, certain adaptive changes take place, including not only alterations in energy metabolism (Fabry, P., et al. *Brit. J. Nutr.*, 17:295, 1963), but also more rapid absorption of glucose and fat from the intestine, increased glycogen synthesis, and a considerable increase in lipogenesis (Fabry, P., et al. *Adaptation to changed pattern of food intake*. Prague, 1962; Cohn, C. *Ann. N.Y. Acad. Sci.*, 110:395, 1963; *Ibid. Fed. Proc.*, 23:76, 1964; Tepperman, H. M., and Tepperman, J. *Fed. Proc.*, 23:73, 1964). Also, studies on volunteers have shown that there is an inverse relation between meal frequency and blood lipid levels (Cohn, C., *J. Am. Dietet. Assoc.*, 38:433, 1961; *Ibid.* 1964; Guinup, G., et al. *Am. J. Clin. Nutr.*, 13:209, 1963) and a decrease in tolerance to glucose when food is consumed at one large meal (Guinup, G. et al. *Lancet*, 2:165, 1963).

Pursuing this question of meal size and frequency and its possible connection with hypercholesterolemia and glucose tolerance, Fabry and his associates studied a group of 379 men, ages 60 to 64, divided according to frequency of food intake (Fabry, P., et al. *Lancet*, 2:614, 1964). They found that excessive weight gains, increased serum cholesterol, and diminished glucose tolerance were much more frequent among those who ate three meals or less a day than among those who took five or more small "meals." Those men who ate three or four meals with or without snacks showed "intermediate values."

Cohn and his colleagues (*Am. J. Clin. Nutr.*, 11:356, 1962) list three advantages of more frequent feedings: (1) a decrease in the amount of protein needed to maintain nitrogen balance; (2) a resultant increased resistance to metabolic diseases, as obesity, atherosclerosis, and diabetes mellitus; and (3) an "increase in the efficacy of therapy of metabolic" diseases.

While the evidence strongly supports the position that frequent feedings of small "meals" is better for metabolic and cardiovascular health than large meals taken between longer intervals, we are cautioned by Frederick Stare that this does not mean "a free ticket to go ahead and nibble all one wants, but to take the normal caloric intake for a twenty-four hour period and divide it into frequent feedings" (*Am J. Clin. Nutr.*, 11:365–366, 1962).

72. Not only have we intentionally refrained from discussing non-nutritional aspects of coronary heart disease, but we have also avoided going into lengthy discussions of some of the more controversial nutritional data. However, certain of these data do warrant some attention.

Pectin and cholesterol.

Many reports have demonstrated that the polysaccharide pectin, found in many fruits and vegetables, has a cholesterol-lowering effect in man and animals (Fahrenbach, M. J., et al. *Proc. Soc. Exp. Biol. Med.*, 123:321, 1966; Ershoff, B. H., and Wells, A. F. *Proc. Soc. Exp. Biol. Med.*, 110:580, 1962; Fisher, H., et al. *J. Atheroscler. Res.*, 7:381, 1967; Wells, A.F., and Ershoff, B. H. *J. Nutr.*, 74:87, 1961; Keys, A., et al. *Proc. Soc. Exp. Biol. Med.*, 106:555, 1961; Fisher, H., et al. *J. Nutr.*, 86:113, 1965). Riccardi and Fahrenbach reported that guar gum, a mucilaginous polysaccharide from seaweed, was more effective in lowering serum cholesterol than pectin (*Proc. Soc. Exp. Biol. Med.*, 124:749, 1967).

In a series of controlled experiments at the Hastings State Hospital, Keys and his associates tested the effect of fiber, cellulose, and fruit pectin on the possible lowering of serum cholesterol. These investigators found that cellulose showed no significant effect, but there was a consistant cholesterol-lowering effect produced by supplements of pectin.

In their rat experiments, Wells and Ershoff (*J. Nutr.*, 74:87, 1961) found that animals had cholesterol concentrations in the serum and liver which varied inversely with the amount of pectin in the diet. The 2.5 percent level, the 5 percent level, and the 10 percent level progessively depressed the cholesterol levels. In another experiment Wells and Ershoff fed the rats pectin and cholesterol on alternative days, with the same reduction in cholesterol occurring. There was no increase in cholesterol excretion as a result of pectin feeding. The fact that alternate feeding was just as effective suggests that a "physical complex" between cholesterol and pectin or impaired absorption does not account for the noted effects. Nor did pectin's known ability to augment intestinal flora activity appear to account for the effect, for the addition of antibiotics failed to alter the cholesterol-lowering effect of pectin.

While no explanation has been satisfactory to account for pectin's cholesterol-lowering effect (*Nutr. Rev.,* 24:209, 1966), Fisher suggests that "pectin produces a lowering of blood cholesterol only in the presence of dietary cholesterol." (The same has been found true of polyunsaturated fatty acids; see reference note 56 above.) There is not enough evidence to justify the indiscriminate use of pectin as a therapeutic agent for lowering cholesterol levels, but there is good reason to think that eating foods rich in pectin (as apples, other fruits, carrots, etc.) may help offset the deleterious effects of dietary cholesterol.

Seaweed

H. S. Mitchell and her coworkers have reported that feeding kelp in quantities to yield 25 milligrams of iodine per day per rat, "tended to lower the blood cholesterol and to decrease aorta injury" (*Mass. Agr. Expt. Sta. Bull.,* 374:7, 1940). The ash from the same amount of kelp, however, afforded no protection to the aorta. These workers concluded that some factors in kelp other than iodine are essential for the protection of rats against aortic damage associated with increased serum cholesterol. It has already been mentioned just above that Riccardi and Fahrenbach found that the guar gum of seaweed was especially effective in lowering serum cholesterol, more effective than pectin.

Besterman and Evans (*Brit. Med. J.,* 1:310, 1957) report their experiments with extracts of "laminarin sulphate M" from a type of seaweed (Laminaria cloustoni). This seaweed extract was found, upon subcutaneous injection, to increase serum lipid mobility (after a high fat-cholesterol meal) equal to the effect of heparin, and without its anticoagulant action.

Milkfat and processed milk.

That cardiovascular lesions are not induced by the fat of whole milk, but may be caused by the lack of accompanying nutrients in processed milk products gains support from a number of controlled rat experiments. S. Dreizen and his coworkers (*J. Nutr.,* 74:75, 1961) have shown that rats restricted to a diet of nonfat dry cow's milk induced atherosclerosis of the aorta and its major branches, together with a syndrome of accompanying afflictions in 50 percent of the animals.

Other investigators have demonstrated that rats reared on an exclusive whole milk diet supplemented with iron, iodine, manganese, and copper do not develop cardiovascular lesions (Kemmerer, A. R., et al. *Am. J. Physiol.*, 102:319, 1932; McCay, C. M., et al. *J. Gerontol.*, 7:61, 1952). This, incidentally, would be in agreement with those epidemiological studies of the African herdsmen tribes—the Masai, Somalis, and Samburus—who live almost exclusively on a milk-meat diet.

In one other experiment, Dreizen and his colleagues conducted a series of studies with ten groups of rats on different kinds of milk diets (*J. Atheroscler. Res.*, 6:537, 1966). The results of these tests disclosed that rats reared on a diet of dry whole cow's milk (without supplements) developed overt atherosclerosis in 30 percent of the animals, while 40 percent succumbed to vascular lesions on a diet of nonfat dry milk. However, the investitgators found that complete protection was afforded virtually all the animals against cardiovascular complications on diets of (1) reliquified whole milk; (2) dry whole milk supplemented with iron, copper, manganese, and iodine; (3) reliquified whole milk plus the trace elements; and (4) reliquified nonfat dry milk plus 3.6 percent sweet cream and the trace elements. These investigators assert that "a diet of nonfat dry milk, 3.5 percent butter, and the trace minerals gave almost complete protection, slight arteriosclerotic damage being found on histologic examination in only one of the thirty animals." They noted that neither the inception or prevention of atherosclerosis was related to cholesterol levels, nor, for that matter, to calcium or phosphorous levels.

These data suggest that adequate whole milk, including the butterfat, and essential trace minerals actually protect against cardiovascular damage. This, we have noted, concurs with other findings (Lowenstein, 1964; Mann, 1964; Shaper, *Am. Heart J.*, 63:437, 1962) of the African tribes who live on a diet of raw whole cow's and goat's milk, a 60 to 65 percent butterfat diet, yet are virtually free of coronary heart disease. According to Dreizen and his colleagues, not only was the saturated butterfat of whole milk not to blame, but its inclusion in the diet was vital to the health of the cardiovascular system. It was the lack of adequate nutrients in a diet totally *free* of fat that caused medical atherosclerosis and renal damage. Butterfat, itself, appears to protect *against* atherosclerosis! More material on this subject will be presented later.

Are edible oils damaged by heat treatment?

There are a number of reports that the feeding of heated vegetable oils to rabbits promotes atherosclerosis lesions (Nishida, T., et al. *Circulation Res.*, 6:194, 1958; Kritchevsky, D., et al. *J. Am. Oil Chem. Soc.*, 38:74, 1961; Kritchevsky, D., et al. *J. Atheroscler. Res.*, 2:115, 1962; Kritchevsky, D., and Tepper, S. A. *J. Atheroscler. Res.*, 7:647, 1967). Kritchevsky and his colleagues discovered that when an oil was added to a standard ration of cholesterol in a rabbit diet, atherosclerotic lesions were more pronounced than when cholesterol alone was given. They found that this startling result occurred only when oils were first heated to 200 degrees centigrade for a period of fifteen minutes. Heat-treated oils increased the severity of the atherosclerotic lesions.

Nishida and his associates suggested that the effect may be due to oxidation of the essential fatty acids which would reduce their availability; or possibly heat-treated oils may disturb the stability of serum lipoproteins, alter their distribution, and enhance aortic deposition.

In testing their earlier findings, Kritchevsky and co-workers conducted a series of studies with rabbits and found (1) that atherogenesis was increased when dietary cholesterol was suspended in heat-treated oils, (2) that a slight addition of 0.25 percent linoleic, stearic, or free fatty acids increased the atherogenicity of the diet, and (3) that while the serum cholesterol levels were not necessarily increased by the addition of free fatty acids, the aortic deposition of lipids was accelerated.

In their most recent 1967 studies, Kritchevsky and Tepper compared heated and unheated olive and corn oils in their relative atherogenic capacity. For a period of eight weeks, they fed four groups of twelve rabbits diets of pellets supplemented with a 2 percent cholesterol solution either suspended in 6 percent unheated corn or olive oil or

dissolved in these oils while heated to 215 degrees centigrade for twenty minutes before being mixed with the food.

They found that both heated and unheated olive oil and
heated corn oil promoted atherosclerotic lesions, increased
blood cholesterol, triglycerides, and phospholipids in the
three groups of test rabbits, while the unheated corn oil-
cholesterol fed rabbits showed a markedly lower blood
lipid level and a much lesser severe atherogenicity.

What practical meaning do these data have for the
consumer? It strongly indicates to us that, once again, the
mistaken notion of increasing one's daily intake of vegetable oils in line with the current fad of eating lots of
polyunsaturated fats may expose the consumer to even
greater risk of atherosclerosis and coronary heart disease.
The indiscriminate eating of polyunsaturated vegetable oils,
for a number of reasons (see reference note 56 above),
must be strongly condemned. The above data are highly
suggestive that unheated vegetable oils, under the conditions of their experiments, (and with the exception of olive
and coconut oils), are protective against atherosclerosis.
Heated oils—oils that have been subjected to temperatures
of 215 degrees centigrade for fifteen minutes or longer—
are another source of danger to the cardiovascular system.

Commonly available polyunsaturated vegetable oils, unless otherwise specified on the label as "unrefined" or
"cold-pressed," have undergone (1) heat-treated extraction,
(2) bleaching, (3) refinement to neutralize the free fatty
acids, and (4) finally, and most disastrously, deodorization
in which the oils are held above 215 degrees centigrade
for *several hours* (Lachle, F. B. "Are you eating the right
fats?" *Nat. Health Fed. Bull.*, 15:3, 1968; see also "Fats
and fatty oils." *Kirk-Othmer Encyclopedia of Chemical
Technology*, 8:805–6, 1965). This means, according to
the above data, that most commercial "polyunsaturated"
vegetable oils are possibly productive of atherosclerosis and
should be avoided by the consumer.

There are polyunsaturated oils on the market which
have not undergone deodorization and other excessive
heat treatment. Some of these oils may be found in super-
markets, particularly in California; but most consumers
will have to go out of their way to purchase them at
"health food stores," where they will find oils for sale that
specify "unrefined, cold-pressed."

When medical education, physicians, and consumers become more acutely aware of the role of nutrition in cardiovascular health and more discriminating in their food purchases, the food industry will necessarily want to stock a product that will cater to the wants of the buyer. But until the public demands it, it is unlikely that the quality of food products now offered will change appreciably.

Does drinking hard water protect against heart disease?

Several studies have been made that implicate the relative hardness of drinking water as a possible factor in cardiovascular mortality rates (Crawford, T., and Crawford, M. D. *Lancet,* 1:229, 1967; Schroeder, H. A. *J. A. M. A.,* 172:1002, 1960; Biorck, G., et al. *Acta Med. Scand.,* 178:239, 1965).

These data show that the cardiovascular mortality rate is higher in areas with softer drinking water, Crawford and Crawford found more cases of ischemic heart disease in the soft-water Glasgow area than in the hard-water London area, even though these cases did not show more atherosclerosis. The authors question whether the myocardium becomes more sensitive to minor degrees of ischemia in the soft-water area. They also question whether there are causes of myocardial lesions that are distinct from causes of arterial lesions, and whether the hardness of water may have a bearing on this difference.

The place of the hardness of drinking water in mineral metabolism is only incompletely understood. Magnesium, calcium, and trace minerals (see below) may all be of importance. In view of studies cited earlier concerning the balance between magnesium and calcium in relation to coronary heart disease in rats and dogs, perhaps the mineral content of drinking water does influence cardiovascular health.

Does fat (butterfat) protect? How is fat related to mineral metabolism?

Within this same area of research, it is known that various minerals serve as cofactors in enzyme systems essential in the metabolism of lipids, and are therefore indirectly involved in fat and cholesterol metabolism (Dixon, M., and Webb, E. C. *Enzymes.* New York:

Academic, 1958). While a large body of knowledge is accumulating on the physiological role of minerals in the metabolic process, the complex relationship between lipid and mineral metabolism is still only incompletely understood (Speckman, E. W., and Brink, M. F. *J. Am. Dietet. Assoc.*, 51:517, 1967).

Studies have shown that the absorption of calcium and fat are interrelated; the malabsorption of one results in the malabsorption of the other (Bassett, S. H. et al. *J. Clin. Invest.*, 18:101, 1939; Hegsted, D. M. "Calcium, phosphorous and magnesium." In *Modern nutrition in health and disease.* Phila.: Lea and Febiger, 1964; Lutwak, L., et al. *Am. J. Clin. Nutr.*, 14:76, 1964; Harkins, R. W. et al. *J. Nutr.*, 87:85, 1965). Animal studies indicate that the absorption of dietary calcium also requires the presence of sufficient fat (Werner, M., and Lutwak, L., *Fed. Proc.*, 22:553, 1963; Speckmann and Brink, *J. Am. Dietet. Assoc.*, 51:517, 1967), but if fat consumption is excessive, calcium absorption is depressed. Conversely, fat absorption requires the presence of sufficient calcium in the diet, but in the presence of excessive calcium, fat absorption is impeded.

R. Chanda found a negative calcium balance in rats fed a fat-free diet (*Brit. J. Nutr.*, 3:5, 1949). While a positive calcium balance resulted on a fat-supplemented diet, it varied greatly according to the type of fat. Clarified butterfat (ghee) was more effective in calcium and phosphorous balance than fats with high melting points, as hydrogenated vegetable fats. These findings were later substantiated by N. Nicolaysen and his associates (*Physiol. Rev.*, 33:424, 1953).

Cheng and his colleagues found that increasing the amount of calcium and magnesium in the diet decreases digestibility of vegetable fats, particularly those with lauric, myristic, palmitic, and stearic acid components (Cheng, A. L. S., et al. *J. Nutr.*, 37:237, 1949). N. I. Inglis and his coworkers give data which indirectly supports the proposition that butterfat aids in the absorption of calcium (*Proc. Soc. Exp. Biol. Med.*, 124:699, 1967).

In view of these facts that butterfat both permits calcium absorption and also augments the growth of intestinal flora (Elvehjem, C. A. *J. Amer. Dietet. Assoc.*, 22:959, 1946; Elvehjem, C. A. *Arch. Biochem.*, 6:403,

1945), thus aiding in the intestinal synthesis of pyridoxine, and in view of the fact that some vegetable oils (with high palmitic, stearic, myristic, or lauric fatty acids) depress calcium absorption, while fats with high linoleic acid increase pyridoxine requirements also inhibiting intestinal synthesis, it is highly questionable whether the current fad to avoid animal fats will lead to a decrease in coronary heart disease and overall better health.

We wish to call attention again to the studies of S. I. Malhotra (*Brit. Heart J.*, 29:777, 1967); *J. Assoc. Physic. India*, 14:93, 1966; *Am. J. Nutr.*, 20:462, 1967) in which the Northern Udaipur Indians are reported to consume a daily diet rich in milk products and ghee with a fat content comprised of 45 percent of the short-chain fatty acids (Hiditch, T. P. *Brit. J. Nutr.*, 3:347, 1949), while the Southern Madras Indians, with fifteen times more coronary heart disease consumed diets with only 2 percent saturated fats, the greater portion of their fats consisting of the long-chain oleic, linoleic, and palmitic acids. Surveys by the Indian Council of Medical Research (*Sp. Rept. Ser. No. 21*, 1951) showed that the consumption of fats are as much as nineteen times higher among the Northern Indians, yet their coronary heart disease rate was as much as fifteen times lower. The butterfat and fermented milk drinks common to the Northern Indians promote the intestinal flora and presumably the intestinal synthesis of pyridoxine, while the unsaturated fats of the Southern Indians need to be accompanied by more pyridoxine in the diet, depress intestinal flora synthesis, and depress calcium absorption.

Moreover, in the above cited studies of Denizen and his coworkers, we noted that nonfat dry milk produced atherosclerosis in rats, while milk with added butterfat did not. Thus, we must question the wisdom of the current fad of removing the butterfat from milk, or recent proposals to substitute polyunsaturated fats for saturated fats in some ninety-odd types of foods. This includes the recent attempts to alter the lipid ratio of egg yolks (Wells, V. M., and Bronte-Stewart, B. *Brit. Med. J.*, 1:577, 1963). S. D. Splitter and his colleagues found that eggs from hens fed a 30 percent safflower oil diet—having yolks with a linoleic content of 40 percent—had no appreciable effect in altering the cardiovascular health of their subjects (*Metabolism*, 17: 1129, 1968).

Furthermore, Ancel Keys and his colleagues, and other investigators, have shown that the complex carbohydrates of leguminous seeds have a cholesterol-lowering action, though these investigators are unable to explain the mechanism by which this occurs (Grande, F., Anderson, J. T., and Keys, A. *J. Nutr.*, 86:313, 1965; Keys, A., and Keys, M. H. *The benevolent bean.* New York: Doubleday, 1967; Mathur, K. S. *Indian Heart J.*, 16:257, 1964; Luyken, R. et al. *Voeding*, 23:447, 1962). Elvehjem had shown that this type of carbohydrate, in contrast to sucrose, also promotes the growth of intestinal flora. It may possibly be that the intestinal synthesis of pyridoxine is the important factor in protecting against hypercholesterolemia in all of these various studies.

Returning to the more immediate question of butterfat, calcium metabolism, and atherosclerosis, we have found, from above-cited studies, that a sufficient amount of butterfat enhances calcium absorption. Other studies have shown that serum cholesterol levels are elevated by calcium deficiency and are kept at normal levels by adequate calcium in the diet (Fleischman, A. I., et al. *J. Nutr.*, 88:255, 1966; Fleischman, A. I., et al. *J. Nutr.*, 91:151, 1967; Yacowitz, H., et al. *Brit. Med. J.*, 1:1352, 1965; Iacono, J. M., and Ammerman, O. B. *Am. J. Clin. Nutr.*, 18:197, 1966; Vitale, J. J. *Am. J. Clin. Nutr.*, 7:13, 1959).

These studies of Fleischman and his colleagues of the effect of dietary calcium on lipid metabolism in rats suggests that the cholesterol-lowering effect of calcium may be due to an increased excretion of bile acids. In this regard, Speckmann and Brink point out that "calcium may retard increases in cholesterol and other lipids in the blood and exert a protective action against the development of arteriosclerosis" (*J. Am. Dietet. Assoc.*, 51:517, 1967). Yacowitz et al. found that increased calcium in the diets of young men and women did cause a significant reduction in serum cholesterol and triglycerides. With increased calcium ingestion, these was a corresponding increase in bile acid and fat excretion through the feces, further supporting the view that calcium acts to promote bile acid excretion and a more rapid elimination of cholesterol via the feces.

In view of the fact that (1) milk and dairy products

provide 75 percent of the calcium in the American diet (Swanson, P. *Calcium in nutrition.* Chicago: Natl. Dairy Council, 1965), (2) butterfat is vital to adequate calcium absorption, and (3) calcium deficiency may contribute to atherosclerosis, it is suggested that adequate amounts of *whole* milk be recommended.

Do trace minerals play any role in cardiovascular health?

In the studies of Schroeder (*Circulation,* 35:570, 1967) and Schroeder and Balassa (*Am. J. Physiol.,* 209:433, 1965) rats fed cadmium developed hypertension, with increased aortic lipids and cardiac hypertrophy. The inclusion of more calcium in the diet prevented this development. Rats receiving cadmium and soft water (low in calcium) developed hypertension, while those receiving cadmium and hard water (high in calcium) did not. (It must not be forgotten that increases in calcium intake must be balanced with adequate magnesium in the diet. Tufts, E. V., and Green D. M. *J. Biol. Chem.,* 122:693, 1937–38; *Ibid.* 122:715, 1937–38.)

Schroeder also found that chromium deficiency in rats increased aortic lipid deposits. He suggested that an imbalance of cadmium to chromium in the diet may contribute to atherosclerosis. Schroeder also noted that other trace minerals such as manganese, copper, and selenium may play an active part in lipid metabolism and atherosclerosis. Copper, for example, has been shown to be a catalyst in the activation of enzymes in lipid metabolism (Dixon and Webb, *Enzymes,* 1958), and in phospholipid synthesis (Schutte, K. H. *The biology of the trace elements.* Phila.: Lippincott, 1964). Selenium has been reported by Hamilton and Tappel (*J. Nutr.,* 79:493, 1963) and also by Zalkin and coworkers (*Arch. Biochem.,* 91:117, 1960) to have an anti-oxidant property 50 to 500 times as potent as alpha tocopherol, and protects oxidizable lipids from destruction in the cardiovascular system. In this respect, selenium may have a sparing action on vitamin E. (*See also* Levander, O. A. In *Present knowledge of nutrition.* New York: The Nutr. Found., 1967, p. 138.)

Curran and his colleagues report that both vanadium and iron inhibit the synthesis of cholesterol in the livers of animals and man (Curran, G. L., et al. *J. Clin. Invest.,*

38:1251, 1959) and this, in turn, decreases the concentration of cholesterol in the aorta and plasma.

R. H. Follis and his colleagues report cardiac and renal lesions in rats on a potassium-deficient diet (*Am. J. Path.*, 18:29, 1942). In another study, Follis found that the trace mineral rubidium substituted for potassium in rats on a potassium-deficient diet, and protected the animals from myocardial necroses (*Am. J. Physiol.*, 138:246, 1943).

According to the studies of Cannon and his associates, far more extensive myocardial lesions occur when sodium chloride is given to rats on a potassium-deficient diet (*Metabolism,* 2:297, 1953). Death occurs suddenly, and histologic examination reveals extensive necrosis and disintegration of the muscle fibers (French, J. E. *Arch. Path.*, 53:485, 1952). Cannon and his associates question whether the lesions are due to potassium deficiency or sodium toxicity.

Follis notes (*Am. J. Clin. Nutr.*, 4:107, 1956) that states of potassium depletion in man are generally conditioned deficiencies brought about by such changes as severe diarrhea (Darrow, D. C., *J. Pediat.*, 28:515, 1946), Cushing's syndrome (McQuarrie, I., et al. *Endocrinology*, 21:762, 1937), treatment for diabetes (Danowski, T. S., et al. *J. Clin. Invest.*, 28:1, 1949), and in some kinds of chronic nephritis (Brown, M. R., et al. *J. A. M. A.*, 124: 545, 1944). However, morphologic changes in the heart under these conditions are rare, aside from electrocardiographic readings of disturbed myocardial activity (Currens, J. H., and Crawford, J. D. *New England J. Med.*, 243:843, 1950). There is a possibility that potassium deficiency may be, in some cases, a contributing factor in coronary heart disease.

73. Williams, R. J. *Nutrition in a nutshell.* New York: Dolphin Books, 1962.

CHAPTER 6

The Fight Against Obesity

1. Gould, G. M., and Pyle, W. L. *Anomalies and curiosities of medicine.* New York: Julian Press, 1956, p. 403.

2. In addition to reference 1, see also Stunkard's description of obese individuals with a pattern of "eating-without-satiation" (Stunkard, A. J. "Eating patterns and obesity." *Psychiatric Quart.*, 33:284, 1959), found particularly in some brain-damaged individuals.

3. Bruch, Hilde. "Perceptual and conceptual disturbances in anorexia nervosa." *Psychoso. Med.*, 24:187, 1962; Bliss, E. L., and Branch, C. H. *Anorexia nervosa.* New York: Hoeber-Harper, 1960.

4. Adolph, E. F. et al. "Multiple factors in thirst." *Amer. J. Physiol.*, 178:538, 1954; Stellar, E. "The physiology of motivation." *Psychol. Rev.*, 61:5, 1954; Montemurro, D. G., and Stevenson, J. A. F. "The localization of hypothalamic structures in the rat influencing water consumption." *Yale J. Biol. Med.*, 28:396, 1955; Morrison, S. D., and Mayer, J. "'Adipsia and aphagia in rats after lateral subthalamic lesions." *Amer. J Physiol.*, 191:248, 1957; Wyrwicka, W., and Dobrzecka, C. "Relationship between feeding and satiation centers of the hypothalamus." *Science*, 132:805, 1960; Anand, B. K., and Brobeck, J. R. "Hypothalamic control of food intake." *Yale J. Biol. Med.*, 24:123, 1951; Anand, B. K., et al. "Hypothalamic control of food intake in cats and monkeys." *J. Physiol.*, 127:143, 1955.

See also Mayer, J. *Australasian Ann. Med.*, 13:282, 1964, for evidence supporting the hypothesis that food intake is regulated by glucoreceptors in the ventromedial nuclei of the satiety center of the hypothalamus; Mayer, J. *New Engl. J. Med.*, 249:13, 1953.

5. See Teitelbaum, P. "Disturbances in feeding and drinking behavior after hypothalamic lesions." In M. R. Jones (Ed.), *Nebraska Symposium on Motivation.* Lincoln: University of Nebraska Press, 1961, p. 39.

6. Mayer, J. "Some advances in the study of the physiologic basis of obesity." *Metabolism*, 6:435, 1957. *See also* Anand, B. K., and Brobeck, J. R. "Localization of a 'feeding center' in the hypothalamus of the rat." *Proc. Soc. Exp. Biol. Med.*, 77:323, 1951(a); Larrson, S. "On the hypothalamic organization of the nervous mechanism regulating food intake: Part I, hyperphagia from stimulation of the hypothalamus and medulla in sheep and goats." *Acta Physiol. Scandinav.*, 32: Suppl. 115, 1, 1954; Kirschbaum, W. R. "Excessive hunger as a symptom of cerebral origin." *J. Nerv. & Ment. Dis.*, 113:95, 1951; Delgado, J. M. R., and Anand, B. K. "Increase of food intake induced by electrical stimulation of the lateral hypothalamus." *Am. J. Physiol.*, 172:162, 1953; Morgane, P. J. "Medial forebrain bundle and 'feeding centers' of the hypothalamus." *J. Comp. Neurol.*, 117:1, 1961(b).

7. Brooks, C. M., et al. "Experimental production of obesity in the monkey (Macaca mulatta)." *Fed. Proc.*, 1:11, 1942; Heinbecker, P., et al. "Experimental obesity in the dog." *Am. J. Physiol.*, 141:549, 1944; Wheatley, M. D. "The hypothalamus and appetite behavior in cats: a study of the effects of experimental lesions, with anatomical correlations." *Arch. Neurol. & Psychiat.*, 52:296, 1944; Mayer, J., et al. "Hypothalamic obesity in the mouse: production, description and metabolic characteristics." *Am. J. Physiol.*, 182:1, 1955; Hetherington, A. W., and Ranson, S. W. "Hypothalamic lesions and adiposity in the rat." *Anat. Rec.*, 78:149, 1940; Hetherington, A. W., and Ranson, S. W. "The spontaneous activity and food intake of rats with hypothalamic lesions." *Am. J. Physiol.*, 136:609, 1942.

8. Brobeck, J. R. "Mechanism of the development of obesity in animals with hypothalamic lesions." *Physiol. Rev.*, 26:541, 1946; Stevenson, J. A. F. *Recent progress in hormone research*. Vol. 4. New York: Academic, 1949, p. 363.

9. Hoebel, B. G., and Teitelbaum, P. "The effect of prior obesity induced by insulin on the food intake and weight regulation of normal and hypothalamic hyperphagic rats." Unpublished. Cited in Teitelbaum, P., 1961 (reference 5 above).

10. Teitelbaum, P., and Epstein, A. N. "The lateral hypothalamic syndrome: recovery of feeding and drinking after lateral hypothalamic lesions." *Psychol. Rev.*, 69:74, 1962.

11. Brugger, M. "Fresstrieb als hypothalamisches Symptom." *Helvet. Physiol. Acta*, 1:183, 1943; Hess, W. R. *Das zwischenhirn*. Basle, Switzerland: Benno Schwabe, 1949; Delgado, J. M. R., and Anand, B. K. "Increase of food intake induced by electrical stimulation of the lateral hypothalamus." *Am. J. Physiol.*, 172:162, 1953;

Larrson, S. "On the hypothalamic organization of the nervous mechanism regulating food intake: part I, hyperphagia from stimulation of the hypothalamus and medulla in sheep and goats." *Acta Physiol. Scandinav.*, 32, Supp. 115:1, 1954; Brobeck, J. R., et al. "A study of the electrical activity of the hypothalamic feeding mechanism." *J. Physiol.*, 132:358, 1956.

12. Teitelbaum, P. "Ingestion patterns in hyperphagic and normal rats." *J. Comp. Physiol. Psychol.*, 51:135, 1958; Epstein, A. N., and Teitelbaum, P. "Regulation of food intake in the absence of taste, smell, and other oropharyngeal sensations." *J. Comp. Physiol. Psychol.*, 51:135, 1958; Teitelbaum, P. "Random and food-directed activity in hyperphagic and normal rats." *J. Comp. Physiol. Psychol.*, 50:486, 1957; Teitelbaum, P. "Sensory control of hypothalamic hyperphagia." *J. Comp. Physiol.*, 48:156, 1955; Brobeck, J. R. "Neural control of hunger, appetite and satiety." *J. Biol. Med.*, 1957; Brobeck, J. R., et al. "Experimental hypothalamic hyperphagia in the albino rat." *Yale J. Biol. Med.*, 15:831, 1943; Miller, N. E., et al. "Decreased 'hunger' but increased food intake resulting from hypothalamic lesions." *Science*, 112:256, 1950; Graff, H., and Stellar, E. "Hyperphagia, obesity, and finickiness." *J. Comp. Physiol. Psychol.*, 55:418, 1962; Corbit, J. D., and Stellar, E. "Palatability, food intake, and obesity in normal and hyperphagic rats." *J. Comp. Physiol. Psychol.*, 58:63, 1964.

13. Miller, N. E., et al. "Decreased 'hunger' but increased food intake resulting from hypothalamic lesions." *Science*, 112:256, 1950.

14. Miller, N. E., et al. "Decreased 'hunger' but increased food intake resulting from hypothalamic lesions." *Science*, 112:156, 1950; Graff, H., and Stellar, E. "Hyperphagia, obesity, and finickiness." *J. Comp. Physiol. Psychol.*, 55:418, 1962; Corbit, J. D., and Stellar, E. "Palatability, food intake, and obesity in normal and hyperphagic rats." *J. Comp. Physiol. Psychol.*, 58:63, 1964.

15. Teitelbaum, P. "Ingestion patterns in hyperphagic and normal rats." *J. Comp. Physiol. Psychol.*, 51:135, 1958; Epstein, A. N., and Teitelbaum, P. "Regulation of food intake in the absence of taste, smell and other oropharyngeal sensations." *J. Comp. Physiol. Psychol.*,

51:135, 1958; Teitelbaum, P. "Random and food-directed activity in hyperphagic and normal rats." *J. Comp. Physiol. Psychol.*, 50:486, 1957; Teitelbaum, P. "Sensory control of hypothalamic hyperphagia." *J. Comp. Physiol. Psychol.*, 48:156, 1955; Graff, H., and Stellar, E.,"Hyperphagia, obesity, and finickiness." *J. Comp. Physiol. Psychol.*, 55:418, 1962; Corbit, J. D., and Stellar, E. "Palatability, food intake, and obesity in normal and hyperphagic rats." *J. Comp. Physiol. Psychol.*, 58:63, 1964.

16. Stunkard, A. "Obesity and the denial of hunger." *Psychosoc. Med.*, 21:281, 1959; Stunkard, A., and Koch, C. *Arch. Genet. Psychiat.*, 11:74, 1964.

17. Stunkard, A. J., and Wolff, H. G. "Studies on the physiology of hunger: I. the effect of intravenous administration of glucose on gastric hunger contractions in man." *J. Clin. Invest.*, 33:954, 1956; Stunkard, A. J., et al. "The mechanism of satiety: effect of glucagon on gastric hunger contractions in man." *Proc. Soc. Exp. Biol. Med.*, 89:258, 1955; Anliker, J., and Mayer, J. "The resultation of food intake: some experiments relating behavioral, metabolic and morphologic aspects." Cited in J. Mayer, *Metabolism*, 6:435, 1957.

18. Schachter, S. "Obesity and eating; internal and external cues differently affect the eating behavior of obese and normal subjects" *Science,* 161:751, 1968.

See also Schachter, S., et al. "Effects of food deprivation and fear on eating behavior." *J. Per. Soc. Psychol.*, 10:91, 1968; Schachter, S., and Gross, L. "Eating and the manipulation of time." *J. Per. Soc. Psychol.*, 10:98, 1968; Goldman, R., Gaffa, M., and Schachter, S. "Yom Kippur, Air France, dormitary food, and the eating behavior of obese and normal persons." *J. Per. Soc. Psychol.*, 10:117, 1968.

19. Schachter, S., et al. "Effects of food deprivation and fear on eating behavior." *J. Per. Soc. Psychol.*, 10:91, 1968.

20. The parallels in hypothalamic obese rats and some obese humans are especially remarkable in this respect. Clinicians have long lamented that the prognosis for "curing" the overweight individual of his obesity (and high caloric intake) over a long term period is very poor. R. E. Nisbett found that formerly obese individuals who, through dieting or other means, have brought their weight down to

near normal levels, tend to react to external food-associated stimuli in the same hyperreactive way as obese individuals ("Taste, deprivation and weight determinants of
eating behavior." *J. Per. Soc. Psychol.*, 10:197, 1968). In
testing nonobese and obese subjects' responses to differences of taste of ice cream, Nisbett reports "that subjects
with a history of overweight ate more good ice cream and
less bad ice cream than those without such a history. The
interaction is significant at the .02 level. The formerly
overweight individuals thus retain their overresponsiveness
to the external variable of taste, and in general the data
for the normal subjects with a history of overweight more
nearly resembled that of the currently overweight than
that of the normal subjects with no history of overweight."

Nisbett reflects, from the basis of his data and from the
reported clinical evidence of weight-reducing therapy, that
people differ in their orientation to food and eating in
ways which are enduring.

In regard to the same phenomenon in hypothalamic
hyperphagic obese rats, Teitelbaum points out (see reference
note 5 above) that the nature of the derangement is not
that the animals are impelled to overeat per se, but
"that they stop overeating when their weight has reached
a new high plateau." He suggests the defect is one of
weight regulation. Hypothalamic hyperphagic rats, when
forced to reduce to their normal weight by restricted feeding, will again overeat and reach their former obese weight
once they return to ad libitum feeding. Teitelbaum pro-
poses that this specific anomaly of the deranged hypothalamus causes the hyperphagic rat to overeat *in order to get
fat,* and once it has reached a certain high plateau of body
weight, it levels off to normal eating.

Not all obese rats react the same. Teitelbaum and
Hoebel found that rats made obese by overeating through
insulin injections will return to normal eating and normal
weight once the injections are stopped. Teitelbaum pro-
poses that "body weight is somehow detected by an animal
so that its daily food intake is regulated accordingly."

While the normal animal regulates its weight level,
so also does the animal with ventromedial hypothalamic
damage, only the two levels are vastly different. A normal
rat regulates its weight at around 300 grams, while a rat
that has suffered hypothalamic damage does not level off

its food intake until it reaches from 500 to 600 grams. The hypothalamic hyperphagic obese animal must be about twice as heavy as normal before its food intake is curbed.

From these data, it could be hypothesized that human individuals who have become obese through a possible disorder of the hypothalamus, and thus who respond to *external* food-associated stimuli in a similar way as the hypothalamic hyperphagic rat, will find all internally-directed reducing schemes—as appetite dampeners or calorie counting—largely ineffectual. Such obese people apparently, as the hyperphagic rat, are driven to overeat, hyperreact to external stimuli, rapidly gain weight, and reach a plateau of obesity before they level off in their eating.

This hypothesis may help explain, in part at least, such data as that of Johnson, Burke, and Mayer ("Relative importance of inactivity and overeating in the energy balance of obese high school girls." *Am. J. Clin. Nutr.*, 4:37, 1956) in which it was found that the caloric intake of obese high school girls of a Boston suburb was no larger than the intake of nonobese girls of the same height and age. The investigators attribute the obesity to a difference in activity, the obese girls being much less active than the nonobese ones. The question occurs, however, did the obese girls become less active due to their obesity (as hyperphagic rats are known to do), or was their inactivity an antecedent cause of their obesity?

It could be, then, that one type of human obesity, similar perhaps with the derangement of the hypothalamic hyperphagic obese rats, has to do with a weight-regulating malfunction of the hypothalamus. The next important question becomes: How did the hypothalamus become disordered?

The fact that not all forms of human obesity are alike was stressed by Stunkard (see reference note 2 above). Obesity, he concluded, is a symptom having multiple etiologies, a view held also by Mayer who has devoted years of research to the problem (Mayer, J. "Correlation between metabolism and feeding behavior and multiple etiology of obesity." *Bull. N.Y. Acad. Med.*, 33:744, 1957).

In view of the eating orientation of many obese individuals with a seeming compulsion to gain weight, as the hypothalamic hyperphagic rats, and in view of their characteristic hyperreactivity to external food cues and their decreased sensitivity to internal food-relating cues, Nisbett suggests that the most profitable therapeutic approach to weight reduction in the obese would first concern itself with the individual's "response to internal and external cues to eating than with ephemeral reductions in weight."

I would also suggest that attention given to obtaining optimal nutrition may help correct the original disordered hypothalamus, as data given shortly will indicate, and will bring the weight-regulating mechanism to normal functioning.

21. Nisbett, R. E. "Taste, deprivation and weight determinants of eating behavior." *J. Per. & Soc. Psychol.,* 10:107, 1968.

22. Schachter, S. and Gross, L. P., "Manipulated time and eating behavior." *J. Per & Soc. Psychol.,* 10:98, 1968.

23. Hashim, S. A., and Van Itallie, T. B. "Studies in normal and obese subjects with a monitored food-dispensing device." *Ann. N.Y. Acad. Sci.,* 131:654, 1965.

24. Mayer reviews the hereditary and environmental factors in the etiology of obesity in man in an earlier publication (Mayer. J. "Genetic, traumatic and environmental factors in the etiology of obesity." *Physiol. Rev.,* 33:472, 1953).

The genetic etiology of obesity is very clear in some strains of mice, and ways leading to its possible correction have been studied by Mayer and others: Silides, D. J., and Mayer, J. "Effect of hormonal and dietary treatment on lipogenesis from acetate in hereditarily obese-hyperglycemic mice."*Experientia,* 12:66, 1956; Mayer, J., et al. "Exercise, food intake and body weight in normal rats and genetically obese adult mice." *Amer. J. Physiol.,* 177:544, 1954; Shull, K. H., Ashmore, J., and Mayer, J. "Hexokinase, glucose-6-phosphatase and phosphorylase levels in hereditarily obese-hyperglycemic mice." *Arch. Biochem. Biophys.,* 62:210, 1956; Wrenshall, B. A., Clarke, D. W., and Mayer, J. "Effects of pituitary growth hormone on the insulin and HGF extractable from the pancreas of the obese-hyperglycemic mouse." *Nature,* 177:1235, 1956.

See also Bielschowsky, M., and Bielschowsky, F. "The New Zealand strain of obese mice: their response to stilbestrol and to insulin." *Aust. J. Exp. Biol. and Med. Sci.,* 34:181, 1956.

In regard to heredity as an etiological factor in human obesity, Mayer has these salient comments: "It has been repeatedly shown that obesity runs in families, with genetic as well as environmental factors involved. Studies in the United States have shown that less than 10 percent of the children of parents of normal weight are obese, but that the proportion rises to 50 percent if one parent is obese and to 80 percent if both parents are obese. Studies of identical and fraternal twins have shown that food habits are not the main factor. Instead of denying the facts of heredity it would be more intelligent and effective to use them to detect other overweight persons and, more important, to try to prevent the development of obesity in susceptible children. Obesity is most malignant when the onset is early" (Mayer, J. "Correlation between metabolism and feeding behavior and multiple etiology of obesity." *Bull. N.Y. Acad. Med.,* 33:744, 1957).

25. See Sarkisov, S. A. *The structure and functions of the brain.* Bloomington: Indiana University Press, 1966, p. 214; see also Lashley, K. S. *Psychol. Rev.,* 54:333, 1947.

26. Ingle, D. J., "A simple means of producing obesity in the rat." *Proc. Soc. Exp. Biol. Med.,* 72:604, 1949.

27. Williams, R. J., et al. "Individuality as exhibited by inbred animals: its implications for human behavior." *Proc. Nat. Acad. Sci.,* 48:1461, 1962.

Barnes and his coworkers also made note of the wide range of variation in energy potential of individual rats (*Am. J. Physiol.,* 207:1242, 1964). These investigators reported that they eliminated some rats from their swimming tests before they undertook their study because these animals had a virtual inexhaustible ability to swim without becoming fatigued. "Some rats," they commented, "will be unable to continue swimming after a few minutes while others may go on for hours." In a similar kind of study, Levitt and Webb (*J. Pharm. Sci.,* 53:1125, 1964), in testing the effects of aspartic acid salts on exhaustion time of walking rats, reported removing three animals from their revolving wheel after 136 hours as they seemed to be "interminable walkers," and were inadequate for the purposes of the study. In his studies on rats' responses to stress, C. P. Richter (*Psychosomatic Med.*, 19:191, 1957) remarks that in using the endurance swim test, his experiments were initally thwarted by the extreme variability in individual rats. Some rats, he reported, swim no longer than five to ten minutes after immersion; others "apparently no more healthy," he said, swam for as long as eighty-one hours!

28. Yudkin, J. "The practical treatment of obesity." *Proc. Roy. Soc. Med.*, 58:200, 1965.

Numerous investigators have held the view that food intake is regulated by energy demands; the amount of energy required in exercise and heat production is matched by the amount of energy gained from food. The assumption is that as physical activity increases or decreases, caloric intake correspondingly rises or falls. While this holds true within what Mayer and his coworkers call a "normal activity range," it will not hold true below that range in what is termed the "sedentary zone," a zone of relative inactivity or inertia (Mayer, J., et al. "Relation between caloric intake, body weight, and physical work: studies in an industrial male population in West Bengal." *Am. Clin. Nutr.*, 4:169, 1956). Further decreases in activity do not show corresponding decreases in caloric intake but, on the contrary, cause increased eating, resulting in obesity. Investigators have found this to hold true for both animals (Ingle, D. J. *Proc. Soc. Exp. Biol. Med.*, 72:604, 1949; Mayer, J., et al. "Exercise, food intake and body weight in normal rats and genetically obese adult mice." *Am. J. Physiol.*, 177:544, 1954; Mayer, J. "Decreased activity and energy balance in the hereditary obesity-diabetes syndrome of mice." *Science*, 177:504, 1953) and man (Mayer, J., et al. *Am. J. Clin. Nutr.*, 4:169, 1956; see also Mayer, J. "Genetic, traumatic and environmental factors in the etiology of obesity." *Physiol. Rev.*, 33:472, 1953; Mayer, J. "The physiological basis of obesity and leanness." Parts I and II. *Nutr. Abst. Rev.*, 25:597, 871, 1955).

It may seem, prima facie, confusing that the mechanism that regulates food intake which responds so appropriately to variations in energy output would function inappropriately below a certain zone of activity. In reflecting on this problem, Mayer and his colleagues suggest that an inactive life is an abnormal state in both animals and man, and during the course of evolution no provision has been made for periods of relative inertia.

The question of losing weight, for obese people, is not, then, simply a matter of increasing energy expenditure. For if this were the case only, then an energy output increase, as some investigators argue, would act merely to increase food intake. The real problem is that below a certain range of "normal activity" the regulatory energy intake-output appestat no longer functions appropriately, and an increased sedentary living pattern causes an increased food intake.

Greene ("Clinical study of the etiology of obesity." *Ann. Inst. Med.*, 12:1794, 1939) reported, for instance, that in the study of the etiology of obesity in 200 overweight individuals, their increase in weight could be traced to a sudden change to a more sedentary life style. In a study of obesity in childhood, H. Bruch found that physical inactivity was closely linked with overweight ("Obesity in childhood: IV. Energy expenditure of obese children." *Am. J. Dis. Child.*, 60:1082, 1940). Johnson, Burke, and Mayer found that while the caloric intake of obese high school girls was no greater than that of normal weight girls of comparable age and height, their physical activity was significantly less ("Relative importance of inactivity and overeating in the energy balance of obese high school girls." *Am. J. Clin. Nutr.*, 4:37, 1956).

Mayer and his colleagues, then, express the view that our increasing dependence on mechanization as part of our urban life style "may be pushing an ever greater fraction of the population into the 'sedentary' range" and this may be "a major factor in the increased incidence of obesity" (Mayer, J., et al. *Am. J. Clin. Nutr.*, 4:169, 1956).

29. Mayer, J., and Marshall, N. B. "Specificity of goldthioglucose for ventromedial hypothalamic lesions and obesity." *Nature*, 178:1399, 1956; Liebelt, R. A., and Perry, J. H. "Hypothalamic lesions associated with goldthioglucose-induced obesity." *Proc. Soc. Exp. Biol. Med.*, 95:774, 1957; Marshall, N. B., and Mayer, J. "Energy balance in goldthioglucose obesity." *Am. J. Physiol.*, 178:271, 1954; Waxler, S. H., and Brecher, G. "Obesity and food requirement in albino mice following administration of goldthioglucose." *Am. J. Physiol.*, 162:428, 1950; Mar-

shall, N.B., et al. "Hypothalamic lesions in goldthioglu-cose-injected mice." *Proc. Soc. Exp. Biol. Med.*, 90:240, 1955.

30. Williams, R. J. *You are extraordinary*. New York: Random House, 1967, p. 61.

31. Ingle, D. J. *Endocrinology*, 39:43, 1946; Cohn, C., and Joseph, D. "Changes in body composition attendant on force feeding." *Am. J. Physiol.*, 196:965, 1959; Feldhan, S. E., et al. *Am. J. Physiol.*, 191:259, 1957; Levin, L. *Am. J. Physiol.*, 141:143, 1944; Cohn, C., et al. *Metabolism*, 6:381, 1957; Cohn, C., et al. *Am. J. Physiol.*, 180:503, 1955.

Ingle and other above-cited investigators have demonstrated that "force feeding" or forcing rats to eat via stomach tube or to consume their food in one or two hours during a twenty-four-hour period will definitely result in obesity. But more importantly, these investigators have shown that the timing of food ingestion plays a major role in "the economy of calorie disposition" (Cohn, C., and Joseph, D. *Am. J. Physiol.*, 196:965, 1959).

On the basis of the water, fat, and protein constituents of control and force-fed animals, Cohn and Joseph found that the carcasses of force-fed rats contained 23.6 percent fat and 17.7 percent protein, while the tissue of the pair-fed control rats with free access to food contained only 7.8 percent fat and a high 22.4 percent protein. Cohn and Joseph point out emphatically that while two animals (or human individuals) may weigh the same on the scales, one may contain a large amount of fat tissue with a corresponding lesser amount of protein tissue, while the other animal may be the opposite. These differences may be due solely to the way the two animals ingest their food.

Keys and Brozek ("Overweight versus obesity and the evaluation of calorie needs." *Metabolism*, 6:425, 1957) and Mayer (*Physiol. Rev.*, 33:472, 1953) remind us that it is misleading to suppose that obesity can be determined by weight measurement alone. Since the body is composed of salts, protein, fat, and water, all of them may vary proportionally in different individuals.

The disproportionate increase in adipose tissue that is attendant on force feeding, Cohn and Joseph term "non-obese obesity."

In regard to this same matter, Van Putten and his colleagues ("Influence of hypothalamic lesions producing hyperphagia, and of feeding regimens on carcass composition in the rat." *Metabolism,* 4:68, 1955) have reported that hypothalamic hyperphagic rats when pair-fed with unoperated control animals, showed a disproportionate increase in body fat tissue and less water and nitrogen. What was of particular importance, however, was their discovery that when the hyperphagic rats and controls were offered their daily ration all at one time, the hyperphagic rats ingested their ration at a single feeding, while the unoperated control rats ate various portions of it during the entire twenty-four-hour period. (Both groups of animals were given the same amount of food to eat.) On the basis of this single difference of rate of ingestion, Van Putten and coworkers found that the differences in body fat of the controls and operated hyperphagic animals was considerable. When the food was divided into two portions and given to both groups of animals (operated and control) at two feedings during the twenty-four-hour period, the body fat differences were much less marked.

How much fat an individual's body will contain, relative to protein and water, may well depend on how much he eats how often.

32. Hollifield, G., and Parson, W. "Metabolic adaptations to a 'stuff and starve' feeding program. II: Obesity and the persistence of adaptive changes in adipose tissue and liver occurring in rats limited to a short daily feeding period." *J. Clin. Invest.,* 41:250, 1962.

33. Cohn, C., and Joseph, D. "Effect of meal eating compared to nibbling upon atherosclerosis in chickens." *Circulation Res.,* 9:139, 1961.

34. McAllister, F. F., et al. "Accelerating effect of muscular exercise in experimental atherosclerosis." *Arch. Surg.,* 80:54, 1960.

35. Rakes, A. H., et al. "Some effects of feeding frequency in the utilization of isocaloric diets in young and adult sheep." *J. Nutr.,* 75:86, 1961.

36. Cox, G. E., et al. "Atherosclerosis in Rhesus monkeys." *Arch. Path.,* 66:32, 1958; Gopalan, C., et al. "Effect of the mode of feeding of fats on the serum cholesterol

levels and plasma fibrinolytic activity of monkeys." *Am. J. Clin. Nutr.*, 10:322, 1962.

37. Studies have shown that alterations in lipid metabolism occur in rats limited to a one hour feeding period each day. Rats that have been trained to ingest their food in a single brief feeding show accelerated hepatic lipogenesis with increased fat deposition (Tepperman, J. et al. "The effects of hypothalamic hyperphagia and of alterations in feeding habits on the metabolism of the albino rat." *Yale J. Biol. Med.*, 15:855, 1943; Dickerson, V. C., et al. "The role of liver in the synthesis of fatty acids from carbohydrate." *Yale J. Biol. Med.*, 15:875, 1943).

Tepperman and Tepperman reported ("Effects of antecedent food intake pattern on hepatic lipogenesis." *Am. J. Physiol.*, 193:55, 1958) that the liver slices of one-meal-a-day rats showed increased incorporation of acetate and glucose precursors associated with accelerated hexose monophosphate shunt enzyme activity; while Hollifield and Parson found ("Metabolic adaptations to a 'stuff and starve' feeding program. I: studies of adipose tissue and liver glycogen in rats limited to a short daily feeding period." *J. Clin. Invest.*, 41:245, 1962) that the adipose tissue of one-meal-a-day rats showed an increased incorporation of acetate precursors into lipids, also associated with accelerated enzyme activity. These changes are greatly accelerated in animals adapted to the one-meal-a-day regime.

Hollifield and Parsons (see reference note 32) have suggested that while the satiety centers of the hypothalamus of normal rats fed ad libitum are highly sensitive to optimum food-quantity intake, taken in many nibblings over a long period, rats forced to adapt to a single feeding period may suffer a breakdown in the sensitivity of these hypothalamic satiety centers. This decrease in sensitivity, they suggest, thus permits the rat to adapt to his restricted regime, and gorge himself on large quantities of food in a brief period. "The present observation on body weight of rats limited this way," they remark, "suggests that this (hypothalamic) control is 'damped' to a degree that obesity results."

Moreover, the observations of rats returned to ad libitum feeding after being restricted for seven days to a two-hour feeding period daily, shows that these metabolic alterations of adipose and liver tissue tend to persist, and that the desensitized hypothalamic satiety centers do not recover normal control for some time.

Interestingly, there is also good evidence that while gorging may desensitize the hypothalamic satiety centers, fasting may aid in their recovery (Hollifield, G., and Parson, W. "Studies of the satiety response in mice." *J. Clin. Invest.*, 36:1638, 1957; Finger, F. W. "The effect of food deprivation and subsequent satiation upon general activity in the rat." *J. Comp. Physiol. Psychol.*, 44:557, 1951). Rats subjected to a one-meal-a-day regime for a week, then fasted for three days, showed a lowered incorporation of acetate precursors into lipids via the adipose tissues, while the free fatty acid levels were high, suggesting, the authors note, that the metabolic alteration of these animals had reverted to that evinced in normal animals fed an ad libitum diet. But the liver glycogen of these animals was still higher than control rats that had fasted after having been fed ad libitum for seven days, suggesting that the metabolic alterations were not fully reversed in the gorged rats.

Since it is common for obese human individuals to ingest large amounts of food in one or two meals daily (Stunkard, A. J., et al. "The night-eating syndrome: pattern of food intake among certain obese patients." *Am. J. Med.*, 19:78, 1955) Hollifield and Parson suggest that it may be possible that such one-meal-a-day gorgers suffer a metabolic alteration quite similar to that found in the restricted rat. "Once adapted to this eating pattern," they remark, "it is possible that the metabolic adaptation of adipose tissue and liver, or the hypothalamic feeding centers, or both, would tend to perpetuate it. These adaptations would make it difficult for obese patients to limit themselves to small spaced feeding generally used in weight reduction diets."

38. Gwinup, G., et al. "Effect of nibbling versus gorging on serum lipids in man." *Am. J. Clin. Nutr.*, 13:209, 1963.

39. Stillman, I. M., and Baker, S. S. *The doctor's quick inches off diet*. New York: Prentice-Hall, 1969.

40. Teitelbaum, P., and Stellar, E. "Recovery from the failure to eat produced by hypothalamic lesions." *Science*, 120:894, 1954.

41. Agnew, L. R., and Mayer, J. "Mechanism of

Anorexia in vitamin-deficient hyperphagic animals." *Nature,* 177:1235, 1956.

42. Plummer, W. A. "Body weight in spontaneous myxedema." *Tr. Am. A. Study Goiter,* p. 8, 1940; Williams, R. H. "Relation of obesity to the function of the thyroid gland." *J. Clin. Endocrin.,* 8:257, 1948; Cleghorn, R. A. "The interplay between endocrine and psychological dysfunction." In E. Wittkower and R. Cleghorn (Eds.) *Recent developments in psychosomatic medicine.* Philadelphia: Lippincott, 1954; Robinson, A. M., and Norton, J. M. "Estimation of corticosteroid-like substances in human urine." *Endocrinology,* 7:321, 1950.

43. Freyburgh, R. H. "A study of the value of insulin in undernutrition." *Am. J. Med. Sci.,* 190:28, 1955; Grossman, M. I., et al. "The effect of insulin on food intake after vagotomy and sympathectomy." *Am. J. Physiol.,* 149:100, 1947; MacKay, E. M., and Cullaway, J. W. *Proc. Soc. Exp. Biol. Med.,* 36:406, 1937.

44. Stunkard, A. J., Van Itallie, T. B., and Reis, B. B. "The mechanism of satiety: effect of glucagon on gastric hunger contractions in man." *Proc. Soc. Exp. Biol. Med.,* 89:258, 1955.

45. Bruch, H. "Psychiatric aspects of obesity." *Metabolism,* 6:461, 1957; Mendelson, M. "Psychological aspects of obesity." *Inter. J. Psychiat.,* 2:599, 1966; Hamburger, W. W. "Psychological aspects of obesity." *Bull. N.Y. Acad. Sci.,* 33:771, 1957; Kaplan, H. I., and Kaplan, H. S. "The psychosomatic concept of obesity." *J. Nerv. & Ment. Dis.,* 125:181, 1957.

46. We will also recall that obese individuals, on the whole, are oriented to external food associated cues and much less influenced by their internal physiological condition. In view of this consideration, Stanley Schachter appropriately notes, "The use of anorexigenic drugs such as amphetamine or of bulk-producing, nonnutritive substances such as methyl cellulose is based on the premise that such agents dampen the intensity of the physiological symptoms of food deprivation. Probably they do, but these symptoms appear to have little to do with whether or not a fat person eats" ("Obesity and eating." *Science,* 161:751, 1968).

47. Williams, R. J. *Biochemical individuality.* New York: Wiley, 1956, pp. 48–49.

48. Kinsell, L. W. "Some thoughts regarding obesity." Editorial, *Am. J. Clin. Nutr.*, 2:350, 1954.

49. For data on hereditary obesity in mice, see Mayer, J. "The physiologic basis of obesity and leanness." *Nutr. Abst. & Rev.*, Part I, 25:597, 1955; Part II, 25:871, 1955; Alonzo, L. G., and Maren, T. H. "Effect of food restriction on body composition of hereditary obese mice." *Am. J. Physiol.*, 183:284, 1955; Kriss, M., et al. "The specific dynamic effects of protein, fat and carbohydrate as determined with the albino rat at different planes of nutrition." *J. Nutr.*, 8:503, 1949; Mayer, J., and Yanonni, C. Z. "Increased intestinal absorption of glucose in three forms of obesity in the mouse." *Am. J. Physiol.*, 185:49, 1956.

50. Williams, R. J. *Biochemical individuality*. New York: Wiley, 1956, chapter V.

51. Marks, H. H. "Relationship of body weight to mortality and morbidity." *Metabolism*, 6:417, 1957; Martin, L. "Effect of weight reduction on normal and raised blood pressures in obesity." *Lancet*, 2:1051, 1952; Keys, A. "Obesity and degenerative heart disease." *Am J. Pub. Health*, 44:864, 1954; Keys, A. "Obesity and heart disease," *J. Chronic Dis.*, 1:456, 1955; Lew. E. A. "Insurance mortality investigations of physical impairments." *Am. J. Publ. Health*, 44:641, 1954. Karam, J. H., et al. "Excessive insulin response to glucose in obese subjects as measured by immunochemical assay." *Diabetes*, 12:197, 1963; Ishmael, W. K. "Atherosclerotic vascular disease in familial gout, diabetes and obesity." *Med. Times*, 94:157, 1966.

According to Ishmael, the disease cluster of diabetes, atherosclerosis, gout, and obesity are causally connected to sucrose-induced hypertriglyceridemia. In Ishmael's words, "The association between impaired carbohydrate metabolism and atherosclerosis, and between dietary carbohydrate (sucrose) and hypertriglyceridemia, and the increased triglyceride concentration accompanying hyperuricemia, are consistent with the hypothesis that the genetically associated diseases of gout, diabetes, atherosclerosis, and obesity are causally related to carbohydrate (sucrose) induced or aggravated hypertriglyceridemia."

A higher consumption of empty calorie carbohydrate foods heavily sweetened with white sugar is, no doubt, a major causative factor in this disease cluster of obesity, diabetes, and atherosclerosis (Cohen, A. M. "Effect of dietary carbohydrate on the glucose tolerance curve in the normal and the carbohydrate-induced hyperlipemic subject." *Am. J. Clin. Nutr.*, 20:126, 1967; Kuo, P. T., et al. "Dietary carbohydrates in hyperlipemia (hyperglyceridemia): hepatic and adipose tissue lipogenic activities." *Am. J. Clin. Nutr.*, 20:116, 1967; Cheraskin, E., et al. *Diet and disease*. Emmaus, Pennsylvania: Rodale Books, 1968, chapter 7).

52. Bruch, H. "Psychiatric aspects of obesity." *Metabolism,* 6:461, 1957.

CHAPTER 7

Prevention of Dental Disease

1. Bodecker, C. F. "Pathology of dental caries," In *Survey of the literature of dental caries.* National Academy of Sciences, National Research Council, Publication 225, Washington, D.C., 1952, p. 203.

2. Toverud, K. U., and Toverud, G. "Studies of the mineral metabolism during pregnancy and lactation and its special bearing on the disposition to rickets and dental caries." *Norsk Mag. Laegevidenskap.*, 91:53, 286, 1930; Toverud, K. U., and Toverud, G. "Studies on the mineral metabolism during pregnancy and lactation and its bearing on the disposition to rickets and dental caries." *Acta Paediat.*, 12: Suppl. II, 1931, p. 116.

3. Toverud, G. "The influence of pregnancy on teeth." *Dent. Cosmos*, 69:1213, 1927; Toverud, G. "Svangerskapets indflydelse pa tandene." *Norsk Magas. f. Lagevitensk.*, 88: 169, 1927.

4. Sognnaes, R. B. "A possible role of food putrification in the etiology of dental caries." *Science,* 106:447, 1947; Sognnaes, R. B. "Experimental rat caries: I. Production of rat caries in the presence of all known nutritional essentials and in the absence of coarse food particles and the impact of mastication." *J. Nutr.*, 36:1, 1948.

5. Shaw, J. H. "Effects of dietary composition on tooth decay in the albino rat." *J. Nutr.*, 41:13, 1950.

6. Stuart, H. C. "Findings on examinations of newborn infants and infants during the neonatal period which appear to have a relationship to the diets of their mothers during pregnancy." *Fed. Proc.*, 4:271, 1945.

7. Strusser, H., and Dwyer, H. S. "A contribution to our knowledge of dental caries." *Weekly Bull. Dept. Health,* New York City, 21:49, 1932.

8. Berk, H. "Some factors concerned with the incidence of dental caries in children: multiple pregnancy and nutrition during prenatal, postnatal and childhood periods." *J. Am. Dent. Assoc.*, 30:1749, 1943.

9. Cox, G. J. "Experimental dental caries in animals." In *Survey of the Literature of Dental Caries,* National Academy of Sciences, National Research Council, Publication 225, Washington, D.C., 1952, p. 108.

10. Hunt, H. R., et al. "Inheritance of susceptibility to caries in rats." *J. Dent. Res.*, 23:205, 1944; Hunt. H. R., et al. "Inheritance of susceptibility to caries in albino rats (Mus Norvegicus)," *J. Dent. Res.*, 23:385, 1944. B. S. Hollingshead also notes how the application of genetic principles in the inbreeding of strains of rats modifies their susceptibility or resistance to dental caries. He reports that rats have been bred that "develop caries in thirty-five days; another strain on the same diet shows resistance for over five hundred days" (B. S. Hollingshead, Director, *The Survey of Dentistry,* American Council on Education, Washington, D. C., 1961, p. 425).

11. Holmes, J. O. "Dental caries in the rat, Mus Norvegicus." *J. Nutr.*, 46:323, 1952.

12. Steggerda, F. R., and Mitchell, H. M. "Variability in the calcium metabolism and calcium requirements of adult human subjects." *J. Nutr.*, 31:407, 1946.

13. Greenberg, L. D. "Arteriosclerotic, dental, and hepatic lesions in pyridoxine-deficient monkeys." *Vitamins and Hormones,* 22:677, 1964; Strean, L. P., et al. *N.Y. State Dent. J.*, 24:133, 1958; Strean, L. P., et al. *N.Y. State Dent. J.*, 22:325, 1956; Hillman, R. W., et al. *Am. J. Clin. Nutr.*, 10:512, 1962; Jenkins, G. N. In R. F. Sognnaes (Ed.) *Chemistry of food and saliva in relation to caries.* Springfield, Ill.: Thomas, 1962, pp. 126–163.

According to Jenkins (1962) and Strean (*N.Y. State*

Dental J., 23:85, 1957) vitamin B_6 is relatively high in molasses and cane juice, and is a possible protective agent that is removed in the refining of cane sugar. In agreement with this view, G. E. Boxer and associates report (*J. Nutr.*, 63:623, 1957) that Cuban children who chew on raw sugar cane exhibit fewer dental caries and have higher blood concentrations of B_6 than a comparable group of Cuban children in New York City. According to a Swedish investigator (A. Stralfors, *Arch. Oral Biol.*, vol. II, 1966) raw sugar contains nutritive elements that actually protect against dental caries. Aside from higher amounts of calcium and phosphorus, one of the elements is most probably vitamin B_6.

14. Strean, L. P., et al. *N. Y. State Dent. J.*, 24:133, 1958.

15. Cox, G. J. "Fluorine and dental caries." In *Survey of the Literature of Dental Caries,* National Academy of Sciences, National Research Council, Publication 225, Washington, D. C., 1952, p. 325.

16. See especially Schweigert, B. S., et al. "Dental caries in the cotton rat: III. effect of different dietary carbohydrates on the incidence and extent of dental caries." *J. Nutr.*, 29:405, 1945.

See also McCay, C. M., and Eaton, E. M. "The quality of the diet and the consumption of sucrose solutions." *J. Nutr.*, 34:351, 1947.

17. Shaw, J. H. "Nutrition and Dental Caries." In *Survey of the Literature of Dental Caries.* National Academy of Sciences, National Research Council, Publication 225, Washington, D.C., 1952, pp. 430–447.

CHAPTER 8

The Nutritional Approach to Arthritis and Related Disorders

1. Kaufman, W. *The common form of joint dysfunction: its incidence and treatment.* Brattleboro, Vermont: Hildreth, 1949.

See also Algostino, Lorenzo D'. "The vascular or erythremic effect of nicotinic acid upon various portions of the body of men in health and various diseases." *Acta Vitaminol.*, 1:130, 1947.

2. Barton-Wright, E. C., and Elliott, W. A. "The pantothenic acid metabolism of rheumatoid arthritis." *Lancet,* Oct. 26, 1963, p. 862.

See also Nelson, M. M., et al. "Changes in endochondral ossification of the bibia accompanying acute pantothenic acid deficiency in young rats." *Proc. Soc. Exp. Biol. Med.,* 73:31, 1950.

3. Strandberg, O. "Anemia in rheumatoid arthritis." *Acta Med. Scand.,* Suppl., 454:153, 1966; Raymond, F. D., et al. "Iron metabolism in rheumatoid arthritis." *Arthritis Rheumatism,* 8:233, 1965; Brodanova, M., et al. "Serum iron and copper and total serum binding capacity for iron in relation to the activity of progressive polyarthritis." *Casopis Lekaru Ceskych.,* 103:1242, 1964; Gough, K. R., et al. "Folic-acid deficiency in rheumatoid arthritis." *Brit. Med. J.,* 1:212, 1964; Deller, D. J., et al. "Folic-acid deficiency in rheumatoid arthritis: relation of levels of serum folic-acid activity to treatment with phenylbutazone." *Brit. Med. J.,* 1:765, 1966.

4. Stephens, Charles, A. L., et al. "The use of folic acid in the treatment of anemia of rheumatoid arthritis: a preliminary report." *Ann. Inter. Med.,* 27:420, 1947.

5. Sobota, S., and Bialecki, M. "Riboflavine in the blood of rheumatoid arthritis patients." *Proc. European Rheumatol. Cong. 4th. Istanbul 1959,* pp.739–743 (Published 1964).

See also Kalliomaki, J. L., et al. "Urinary excretion of thiamine, riboflavine, nicotinic acid, and pantothenic acid in patients with rheumatoid arthritis." *Acta Med. Scand.,* 166:275, 1960.

6. Benedek, T. "Preeminent role of vitamin A metabolism in rheumatoid arthritis, peripheral and spinal, and in psoriasis." *Acta Rheumatol. Scand.,* 4:178, 1958.

7. Bett, I. M. "Urinary tryptophan metabolites in rheumatoid arthritis and some other diseases." *Ann. Rheum. Dis.,* 25:556, 1966; Spiera, H. "Excretion of typtophan metabolites in rheumatoid arthritis." *Arthritis Rheumat.,* 9:318, 1966.

See also Dispensa, E., et al. "Changes in the metabolism

of tryptophan in subjects with rheumatoid arthritis." *Reumatismo*, 16:276, 1964; Carcassi, A., et al. "Elimination of xanthurenic acid in subjects with rheumatoid arthritis after a loading test with L-tryptophan." *Reumatismo*, 16:246, 1964.

8. Ellis, John M. *The doctor who looked at hands.* New York: ARC Books, 1966.

See also Gerocarni, B., and Caldarera, C. "Synergism between cortisone and vitamin B_6." *Acta Vitaminol.*, 9:261, 1955.

From earlier cited literature in Chapter 5, we recall that the higher the intake of fat in the diet, the greater the requirement of B_6. If vitamin B_6 deficiency is a possible factor in some cases of arthritis, it would follow that high fat diets, without a corresponding increase in B_6 intake, may aggravate this condition. One report supports this thesis: Silberberg, R., and Silberberg, M. "Effect of a high-fat diet in the development of arthrosis deformans in castrated mice," *Schweiz. Z. Allgem. Pathol. u. Bakteriol.*, 22:447, 1959.

9. Shideler, R. W. *Individual differences in mineral metabolism.* (Doctorate dissertation, University of Texas at Austin) June 1956.

10. Williams, R. J. *Biochemical individuality.* New York: Wiley, 1956, pp. 136–137; Steggerda, F. R., and Mitchell, H. M. *J. Nutr.*, 31:407, 1946.

11. Williams, R. J. *Biochemical individuality,* New York: Wiley, 1956, p. 64.

12. Kuzell, W. C. "Diseases of bones and joints." *Ann. Rev. Med.*, 2:367, 1951. See especially pp. 373, 374.

13. Maynard. L. A., et al. "Dietary mineral interrelations as a cause of soft tissue calcification in guinea pigs." *J. Nutr.*, 64:85, 1958; MacIntyre, I., and Davidsson, D. "The production of secondary potassium depletion, sodium retention, nephrocalcinosis and hypercalcaemia by magnesium deficiency." *Biochem. J.*, 70:456, 1958.

14. Smith, S. E., et al. "The wrist stiffness syndrome in guinea pigs." *J. Nutr.*, 38:87, 1949.

See also Wulzen, R., and Bahrs, A. M. "Effects of milk diets on guinea pigs." *Am. J. Physiol. Proc.*, 133:500, 1941.

15. Coburn, A. F., et al. "Effect of egg yolk in diets on anaphylatic arthritis (passive Arthus phenomenon) in the guinea pig." *J. Exper. Med.*, 100:425, 1954.

16. Brown, W. D. *Individual patterns in normal humans: organic blood constituents.* (Doctorate dissertation, University of Texas at Austin) 1955.

17. Greenwood, J., Jr. "Optimum vitamin C intake as a factor in the preservation of disc integrity." *Med. Ann. Dist. Columbia,* 33:274, 1964.

18. Williams, R. J., and Deason, G. "Individuality in vitamin C needs." *Proc. Nat. Acad. Sci.,* 57:1638, 1967.

19. For other data on the role of vitamin C in the prevention and treatment of arthritic diseases, see: Houssay, A. B., et al. "Ascorbic acid concentrations in different periods of experimental arthritis in rats." *Acta Physiol. Latino Am.,* 16:43, 1966; Ballabio, B. C., and Sala, G. "Research on arthritis treatment." *Lancet,* 258:644, 1950; Gallini, R., and Grego, B. "Chorionic gonadotropin and ascorbic acid in experimental arthritis of the rat." *Sperimentale,* 101:169, 1951.

CHAPTER 9

How Can We Delay Old Age?

1. Castro, Josue de. *The geography of hunger.* Boston: Little, Brown, 1952. Foreword by Lord Boyd-Orr.

2. Slonaker, J. R. "The effect of different per cents of protein in the diet: IV. reproduction." *Amer. J. Physiol.,* 97:322, 1931; Slonaker, J. R. "The effect of different per cents of protein in the diet: V. the offspring." *Amer. J. Physiol.,* 97:573, 1931; Slonaker, J. R. "The effect of different per cents of protein in the diet in successive generations." *Amer. J. Physiol.,* 123:526, 1938.

3. A demonstration of this proposition is patently disclosed in Boris Sokoloff and his coworkers' investigation of the relationship between fat metabolism, lipoprotein lipase enzyme activity, the presence of ascorbic acid in the environment of the capillary cells, atherosclerosis and aging

(Sokoloff, B., et al. "Aging, atherosclerosis and ascorbic acid metabolism." *J. Am. Geriatrics Soc.*, 14:1239, 1966).

In one part of their study, Sokoloff et al. divided 234 "normal" noncardiac subjects into four age groups, and discovered that with increasing age, there were increasing deviations in the subjects' blood fat metabolism. "Particularly striking," note the authors, "was the fact that in the 75 to 80 age subgroup" (consisting of 64 subjects) "8 subjects showed normal values for lipoprotein lipase and triglycerides.

"The findings indicate: (1) the increased frequency of abnormalities in blood fat metabolism with aging beginning with the 35 to 40 age group, and (2) that abnormalities in fat metabolism factors are not necessarily present in advanced age, since completely normal values were observed in 8 patients of the 76–80 age group. These data lend support to our postulate that disturbances in fat metabolism are not an unavoidable attribute of aging, but are related to certain metabolic changes which may be prevented or corrected, e.g., by ascorbic acid therapy."

Thus, the metabolic symptoms of old age are not necesssarily "inevitable," as it is popularly believed, but can be avoided (or delayed) by judicious attention to maintaining an optimum nutritional environment for the body's cells, as is demonstrated here with ascorbic acid and the capillary cells.

In regard to this, these investigators found that in a group of sixty elderly patients with pronounced hypercholesteremia and/or cardiac diseases, fifty showed a "definite and often marked improvement," with lipoprotein lipase enzyme activity increasing by 100 percent, and the dangerously high triglyceride blood levels declining by 50 to 70 percent after mega-ascorbic acid therapy. This remarkable improvement occurred with the enhancement of only *one* factor in the nutritional chain of life—ascorbic acid. In our earlier chapter on heart disease, we found equally remarkable improvements when other single nutrients were employed therapeutically—e.g., pyridoxine (B_6), methionine, choline, folic acid, magnesium, vitamin E. We also found that when fat-fed mice were given high nutritional supplements and excellent protein, they did not succumb to cardiovascular abnormalities, even though they became tremendously overweight due to the high fat content of their diet (65 to 80 percent of the total calories). Attention to excellent nutrition, giving the body's cells all they need, prevents atherosclerosis and lengthens the life span.

4. Bjorksten, J. "The crosslinkage theory of aging." *J. Am. Geriatrics Soc.*, 16:408, 1968; Verzar, F. "The aging of collagen." *Scientific American*, 208:110, 1963; Verzar, F. "Aging of connective tissue." *Gior. di Gerontol.*, 12:915, 1964; Sinex, F. M. "Cross-linkage and aging." *Adv. Gerontol. Res.*, 1:173, 1964; Tappel, A. L. "Lipids linked to aging process." *Med. World News,* Aug. 14, 1964, p. 115.

5. Boenig, H. V. "Free radicals and health: indicators for a unifying concept." *J. Amer. Geriat. Soc.*, 14:1211, 1966; Harman, D. "Free radical theory of aging: effect of free radical reaction inhibitors on the mortality rate of male LAF mice." *J. Gerontology*, 23:476, 1968.

6. Carpenter, D. G., and Loynd, J. A. "An integrated theory of aging." *J. Am. Geriatrics Soc.*, 16:1307, 1968.

7. McCay. C. M., et al. "Growth, aging, chronic diseases, and life span in rats." *Arch. Biochem.*, 2:469, 1943.
See also McCay, C. M. "Effect of restricted feeding upon aging and chronic diseases in rats and dogs." *Am. J. Pub. Health*, 37:521, 1947; McCay, C. M. "Diet and aging." *Vitamins and Hormones*, 7:147, 1949; Carlson, A. J., and Hoelzel, F. "Apparent prolongation of the life span of rats by intermittent fasting." *J. Nutr.*, 31:363, 1946.
These investigators found that rats fasted one day in two and one day in three increased the life span of littermate males about 20 percent and littermate females 15 percent. Both the male and female rat that lived longest among the 137 rats (1057 and 1073 days, respectively) were rats fasted one day in two. The authors note that no drastic growth retardation was caused by the intermittent fasting, and the development of mammary tumors was retarded in relationship to the proportion of fasting.

8. Pelton, R. B., and Williams, R. J. "Effect of pantothenic acid on longevity of mice." *Soc. Exp. Biol. Med.*, 99:632, 1958.

9. Sokoloff, B., et al. "Aging, atherosclerosis and ascorbic acid metabolism." *J. Am. Geriatrics Soc.*, 14:1239, 1966.

10. Rafsky, H. H., and Newman, B. "Vitamin C: studies in the aged." *Am. J. Med. Sci.*, 201:749, 1941.

11. Tappel, A. L. "Will antioxidant nutrients slow aging processes?" *Geriatrics*, Oct. 1968, p. 97; Curtis, H. J. "Radiation and aging." *Soc. Exp. Biol.*, Symposia, 21:51, 1967.

12. Weglicki, W. B., et al. "Accumulation of lipofuscin-like pigment in the rat adrenal gland as a function of vitamin E deficiency." *J. Gerontology*, 23:469, 1968.

See also Weglicki, W. B., et al. *Nature*, 221:185, 1968.

CHAPTER 10

Environmental Control of Mental Disease

1. Lashley, K. S. "Structural variation in the nervous system in relation to behavior." *Psychological Reviews*, 54:333, 1947.

2. Quoted by Alvarez, W. C. *Practical leads to puzzling diagnoses.* Philadelphia: Lippincott, 1958, p. 18.

3. Freud, S. Quoted in Jastrow. *The house that Freud built.* New York: Greenberg, 1932, p. 293.

4. Freud, S. *An outline of psycholanalysis.* New York: Norton, 1949.

5. Freud, S. Quoted by Sackler, M. D., et al. In "Recent advances in psychobiology and their impact on general practice." *Inter. Record of Med.*, 170:551, 1957.

6. Spies, T. D., et al. "The mental symptoms of pellagra: their relief with nicotinic acid." *Am. J. Med. Sci.*, 196:461, 1938.

7. See Cleckley, H. M., et al. "Nicotinic acid in the treatment of atypical psychotic states associated with malnutrition." *J. A. M. A.*, 112:2107, 1939; Sydenstricker, V. P., and Cleckley, H. M. *Am. J. Psychiat.*, 99:83, 1941.

Corn as a staple and nearly exclusive item of diet is deficient for humans in two conspicuous ways: It is low in the vitamin niacinamide, and corn protein is low in the amino acid tryptophane which can be transformed chemically into niacinamide, especially if there is not a lack of vitamin B_6. (This is an unusual case; no other amino acid can be transformed into a vitamin.) With this double barrelled weakness, the diet of pellagrins in the southern states were so bad that even the brain, protected as it is, was often affected. It is worth noting that dementia does not always occur in pellagra cases. In some cases the individuals may die of pellagra, and yet their brains are maintained sufficiently well so that they do not exhibit insanity.

8. As we have noted earlier, pellagra, a disease resulting from nicotinic acid deficiency, does produce mental disorders which are correctable by the administration of nicotinic acid (see reference note 6 above). See also, for further data, Spies, T. D., et al. *South. Med. J.*, 31:483, 1938; Spies, T. D., et al. *J. A. M. A.*, 111:584, 1938; Matthews, R. S. "Pellagra and nicotinic acid." *J. A. M. A.*, 111:1148, 1938; Sydenstricker, V. P., et al. "The treatment of pellagra with nicotinic acid." *South. Med., J.*, 31: 1155, 1938.

Many recent studies have indicated that in a large percentage of nonpellagrin patients suffering from mental disease, niacin deficiency is clearly evident. When this deficiency is corrected through the administration of massive doses of niacinamide, the mental symptoms are also altered in the positive direction. (For data, see Sydenstricker, V. P., and Cleckley, H. M. "The effect of nicotinic acid in stupor, lethargy and various other psychiatric disorders." *Am. J. Psychiat.*, 98:83, 1941; Hoffer, A. "The effect of nicotinic acid on the frequency and duration of rehospitalization of schizophrenic patients: a controlled comparison study." *Inter. J. Neuropsychiat.*, May–June 1966, p. 234; Hoffer, A., and Osmond, H., et al. "Treatment of schizophrenia with nicotinic acid and nicotinamide." *J. Clin. Exper. Psychopatho.*, 18:132, 1957; Hoffer, A. "Treatment of schizophrenia with nicotinic acid: a ten year follow-up." *Acta Psychiat. Scand.*, 40:171, 1964; Hoffer A., and Osmond, H. *How to live with schizophrenia.* New York: Universal, 1966).

9. Pauling, L., "Orthomolecular psychiatry." *Science*, Apr. 19, 1968, pp. 265–271.

10. Thomas, A. M., and Freedman, B. *Trans. Roy. Soc. Trop. Med. Hyg.*, 40:399, 1947.

11. See particularly Lubin, R., et al. "Studies of pan-

tothenic acid metabolism." *Am. J. Clin. Nutr.*, 4:420, 1956; Bean, W. B., et al. *J. Clin. Invest.*, 34:1073, 1955.

12. Ralli, E. P., and Dumm, M. E. "Relation of pantothenic acid to adrenal cortical function." *Vitamins & Hormones,* 11:135, 1953.

13. Stein, S. I. "Some observations on pyridoxine and L-tryptophan in a neuropsychiatric medicinal regimen." *Ann. N.Y. Acad. Sci.*, 166:210, 1969.

14. Heeley, A. F., and Roberts, G. E. "A study of tryptophan metabolism in psychotic children." *Develop. Med. Child Neurol.*, 8:708, 1966.

For further data on B_6 deficiency, tryptophan metabolism and mental disease, see: Benassi, C. A., and Allegri, G. "Tryptophan metabolism in special pairs of twins." *Clinica Chimica Acta*, 9:101, 1964; Price, J. M., et al. "Tryptophan metabolism in porphyria, schizophrenia, and a variety of neurologic and psychiatric diseases." *Neurology*, 9:456, 1959; O'Brien, D., and Jensen, C. B. "Pyridoxine dependency in two mentally retarded subjects." *Clin. Sci.*, 24:179, 1963; Coursin, D. B. "Convulsive seizures in infants with pyridoxine-deficient diet." *J. A. M. A.*, 154:406, 1954; Coursin, D. B. "Relationship of nutrition to central nervous system development and function." *Nutr. Soc. Symposium,* Jan.–Feb. 1967, p. 134; Sloane, H. N., Jr., and Chow, B. F. "Vitamin B_6 deficiency and the initial acquisition of behavior." *J. Nutr.*, 83:379, 1964; Jun-Bi Tu, and Zellweger, H. "Blood-serotonin deficiency in Down's Syndrome." *Lancet*, Oct. 9, 1965, p. 715.

In the treatment of children with severe mental disorders, Bernard Rimland and his colleagues of the Institute for Child Behavior Research (San Diego, California) have reported that high dosage levels of certain vitamins, including pyridoxine, have had remarkable results.

15. Wiener, J. S., and Hope, J. M. "Cerebral manifestations of vitamin B_{12} deficiency." *J. A. M. A.*, 170:1038, 1959; Bowman, K. M. "Psychoses with pernicious anemia." *Am. J. Psychiat.*, 92:371, 1935; Shulman, R. "Vitamin B_{12} deficiency and psychiatric illness." *Brit. J. Psychiat.*, 113:252, 1967; Edwin, E., et al. "Vitamin B_{12} hypovitaminosis in mental diseases." *Acta Med. Scand.*, 177:689, 1965; Strachan, R. W., and Henderson, J. G.

"Psychiatric syndromes due to avitaminosis B_{12} with normal blood and marrow." *Quart. J. Med.*, 34:303, 1965; Fraser, T. N. "Cerebral manifestations of Addisonian pernicious anemia." *Lancet*, Aug. 27, 1960, p. 458; Henderson, J. G., et al. "The antigastric-antibody test as a screening procedure for vitamin B_{12} deficiency in psychiatric practice." *Lancet*, Oct. 15, 1966, p. 7468; Hansen, T., et al. "Vitamin-B_{12} deficiency in psychiatry." *Lancet*, Oct. 29, 1966, p. 965.

16. Sydenstricker, V. P., et al., "The 'egg-white injury' in man and its cure with a biotin concentrate." *J. A. M. A.*, 118:1199, 1942.

17. Shulman, R. "A survey of vitamin B_{12} deficiency in an elderly psychiatric population." *Brit. J. Psychiat.*, 113: 241, 1967.

18. Hunter, R., Jones, M., et al. "Serum B_{12} and folate concentrations in mental patients." *Brit. J. Psychiat.*, 113: 1291, 1967.

19. Hurdle, A. D. F., and Williams, T. C. P. "Folic-acid deficiency in elderly patients admitted to hospital." *Brit. Med. J.*, 2:202, 1966.

20. *See also* Reynolds, E. H. "Epilepsy and schizophrenia." *Lancet*, Feb. 24, 1968, p. 398; Carney, M. W. P. "Serum folate values in 423 psychiatric patients." *Brit. Med. J.*, 4:512, 1967; Reynolds, E. H. "Mental effects of anticonvulsants, and folic acid metabolism." *Brain*, 91, Pt. 2:11, 1968; Murphy, F., et al. "Screening of psychiatric patients for hypovitaminosis B_{12}." *Brit. Med. J.*, 3:559, 1969; Wells, D. G., and Casey, H. J. "Lactobacillus casei C. S. F. Folate Activity." *Brit. Med. J.*, 3:834, 1967; Kallstrom, B., and Nylof, R. "Vitamin-B_{12} and folic acid in psychiatric disorders." *Acta Psychiat. Scand.*, 45:137, 1969; Strachan, R. W., and Henderson, J. G. "Dementia and folate deficiency." *Quart. J. Med.*, 36:189, 1967.

21. See, for example, Kallstrom's and Nylof's above cited work (1969). According to the authors, "Association between deficiency states and psychiatric symptoms cannot be evaluated from our material. All patients with abnormal values were given therapeutic doses of vitamin B_{12} and folic acid together with ordinary psychiatric treatment. All patients improved. We had no control group" (author's italics).

Ross and his colleagues report improvement in three cases of psychotic patients treated with folic acid (Ross, J. F., et al. *Blood,* 3:68, 1948). Hall and Watkins have noted improvement of paraesthesiae after folic acid therapy in eight of ten patients with pernicious anaemia (Hall, B. E., and Watkins, C. H. *J. Lab. Clin. Med.,* 32:622, 1947). Other investigators have reported benefits from folic acid therapy (Doan, C. A. *Am. J. Med. Sci.,* 212:257, 1946; Wagley, P. F. *New Eng. J. Med.,* 238:11, 1948).

22. Lucksch, F. "Vitamin C and schizophrenia." *Wien. klin. Wochenschr.,* 53:1009, 1940.

23. VanderKamp, H. "A biochemical abnormality in schizophrenia involving ascorbic acid." *Inter. J. Neuropsychiatry,* 2:204, 1966.

24. Milner, G. "Ascorbic acid in chronic psychiatric patients: a controlled trial." *Brit. J. Psychiat.,* 109:294, 1963.

See also Herjanic, M., and Moss-Herjanic, B. L. "Ascorbic acid test in psychiatric patients." *J. Schizo.,* 1:257, 1967; Milner, G. "Malnutrition and mental disease." *Brit. Med. J.,* 1:191, 1962; Briggs, M. H. "Possible relations of ascorbic acid, ceruloplasmin and toxic aromatic metabolites in schizophrenia." *New Zealand Med. J.,* Apr. 1962, p. 229; Briggs, M. H., et al. "A comparison of the metabolism of ascorbic acid in schizophrenia, pregnancy and in normal subjects." *New Z. Med. J.,* 61:555, 1962.

Since 1952, Hoffer and Osmond have reported using massive doses of both niacin and ascorbic acid on mentally ill patients, particularly schizophrenics, with excellent results. Bernard Rimland of the Institute for Child Behavior Research has also communicated that excellent results have been obtained with mega-vitamin ascorbic acid therapy with severely mentally disordered children (personal communication).

25. Burton, B. T. *The Heinz handbook of nutrition.* New York: McGraw-Hill, 1959, p. 124.

26. Jacobs, J. K., and Merritt, C. R. "Magnesium deficiency in hyperparathyroidism." *Ann. Surg.,* 163:260, 1966.

27. Personal communication. Data relating the amino acids to brain development and mental health are found in the following articles: Cravioto, J., and Robles, B.

"Evolution of adaptive and motor behavior during rehabilitation from kwashiorkor." *Am. J. Orthopsychiat.*, 35:449, 1965; Barnes, R. H. "Experimental animal approaches to the study of early malnutrition and mental development." *Fed. Proc.*, 26:144, 1967; Hin, P. S., et al. "Serum free amino acids in children with protein-calorie deficiency." *Am. J. Clin. Nutr.*, 20:1295, 1967; Rajalakshmi, R., et al. "Effect of dietary protein content on visual discrimination learning and brain biochemistry in the albino rat." *J. Neurochem.*, 12:261, 1965 (see reference note 28 below for further studies).

28. Clark, H. E., et al. "The effect of certain factors on nitrogen retention and lysine requirements of adult human subjects." *J. Nutr.*, 72:87, 1960.

See also Clark, H. E., et al. "Amino acid requirements of men and women. II: Relation of lysine requirement to sex, body size, basal caloric expenditure, and creatinine excretion." *J. Nutr.*, 71:229, 1960.

29. Scrimshaw, N. S. "Malnutrition, learning and behavior." *Am. J. Clin. Nutr.*, 20:493, 1967; Cravioto, J. "Appraisal of the effect of nutrition on biochemical maturation." *Am. J. Clin. Nutr.*, 11:484, 1962; Cravioto, J., et al. "Nutrition, growth and neurointegrative development: an experimental and ecologic study." *Pediatrics*, 38, Supp. 319, 1966; Caldwell, D. F., and Churchill, J. A. "Learning ability in the progeny of rats administered a protein-deficient diet during the second half of gestation." *Neurology*, 17:95, 1967.

30. See the review Woolley, D. W. "The nutritional significance of inositol." *J. Nutr.*, 28:305, 1944.

31. Cohen, M. E., and White, P. D. "Life situations, emotions and neurocirculatory asthenia (Anxiety neurosis, neurasthenia, effort syndrome)." In *Proceedings of the association for research in nervous and mental diseases, Vol. XXIX: Life stress and bodily disease*. Baltimore: Williams & Wilkins, 1950.

32. Pitts, F. N., Jr., and McClure, J. N., Jr. "Lactate metabolism in anxiety neurosis." *New Eng. J. Med.*, 227:1329, 1967; Granville-Grossman, K. L., and Turner, P. *Lancet*, 1:788, 1966.

33. Pitts, F. N., Jr. "The biochemistry of anxiety." *Scientific American*, Feb. 1969, p. 69.

34. Kumudavalli, I., and Swami, K. S. "Interaction between ascorbic acid and fatigue substance of amphibian muscles." *Indian J. Exp. Biol.*, 2:120, 1964; Khan, L. A., and Swami, S. K. "Ascorbic acid in muscular fatigue." *Current Science*, 1:17, 1967; Khan, L. A., and Swami, K. S., "Fatigue effect of lactic acid on gastrocnemius muscle of rat in relation to ascorbic acid." *Indian J. Exp. Biol.*, 4:101, 1966; Sievers, J. "Effect of ascorbic acid on muscle function." *Arch. ges. Physiol. (Pflugers).*, 242:725, 1939; Basu, N. M., and Ray, G. K. "The effect of vitamin C on the incidence of fatigue in human muscles." *Ind. Jour. Med. Res.*, 28:419, 1940; Basu, N. M., and Biswas, P. "The influence of ascorbic acid on contractions and the incidence of fatigue of different types of muscles." *Ind. Jour. Med. Res.*, 28:405, 1940; Crandon, J. H., et al. "Experimental human scurvy." *New Eng. J. Med.*, 223:353, 1940.

See also Horvath, S. M., and Tebbe, D. "Phosphorus compounds in the gastrocnemius muscles of scorbutic guinea pigs." *J. Bio. Chem.*, 165:657, 1946.

35. In an excellent study of the biochemical effects of isolation in amphetamine-injected white mice, Mast and Heimstra found that animals that had been isolated prior to drug treatment showed a higher mortality rate than control mice (Mast, T. M., and Heimstra, N. W. "Prior social experience and amphetamine toxicity in mice." *Psychol. Rep.*, 11:809, 1962).

For other studies of biochemical and behavioral changes accompanying sensory isolation, see: Carpenter, P. B. "The effect of sensory deprivation on behavior in the white rat." *Dissert. Abst.*, Feb., 20:3396, 1960; Mendelson, J., et al. "Catechol amine excretion and behavior during sensory deprivation." *Arch. Gen. Psychiat.* 2:147, 1960; Quiroga, C., and Angel, M. "Physiological observations of human behavior in isolated groups in the Polar area." *Acta Neuropsiquiot. Argent.*, 6:359, 1960 (the investigators interpreted the subjects' reactions in terms of cortical exhaustion; one case of schizophrenic breakdown was reported); Rosenzweig, M. R., et al. "Variation in environmental complexity and brain measures." *J. Comp. Physiol. Psychol.*, 55:1092, 1962; Jencks, B. "Influence of the environment in preparing an animal to meet stress: effects of isolation and of multiple stress." *Dissert. Absts.*, 24 (1):382, 1963.

36. Freud, S. *A general introduction to psychoanalysis.* New York: Liveright, 1920.

37. Wortis, J. *Fragments of an analysis with Freud.* New York: Simon and Shuster, 1954.

CHAPTER 11

The Battle Against Alcoholism

1. Terhune, W. B. "How to drink and stay sober." *Harper's Bazaar,* March 1965.

2. Cohen, G., and Collins, M. "Alkaloids from catecholamines in adrenal tissue: possible role in alcoholism." *Science,* 167:1749, 1970.

3. Roach, M. K., and Williams, R. J. "Impaired and inadequate glucose metabolism in the brain as an underlying cause of alcoholism—and hypothesis." *Proc. Nat. Acad. Sci.,* 56:566, 1966.

4. Moskow, H. A., et al. "Alcohol, sludge, and hypoxic areas of nervous system, liver and heart." *Microvascular Research,* 1:174, 1968.

5. Moskow, H. A., et al. "Alcohol, sludge, and hypoxic areas of nervous system, liver and heart." *Microvascular Res.,* 1:174, 1968; Courville, C. B. "Effects of alcohol on the nervous system of man." (2nd ed.) Los Angeles, Calif.: San Lucas Press, 1966.

6. Lieber, C. S., and Rubin, E. "Alcoholic fatty liver." *New Eng. J. Med.,* 280:705, 1969.

7. Trulson, M. F., Fleming, R., and Stare, F. J. "Vitamin medication in alcoholism." *J. A. M. A.,* 155:114, 1954.

8. Some of these are reported in: Williams, R. J. *Nutrition and alcoholism.* Norman: University of Oklahoma Press, 1951; Williams, R. J. *Alcoholism: the nutritional approach.* Austin: University of Texas Press, 1959.

9. Rogers, L. L., Pelton, R. B., and Williams, R. J. "Voluntary alcohol consumption by rats following administration of glutamine," *J. Biol. Chem.,* 214:503, 1955.

10. Shive, W. "Glutamine as a general metabolic agent

protecting against alcohol poisoning." In *Biochemical and nutritional aspects of alcoholism.* Symposium, University of Texas, Austin, Texas, 1965; pp. 17–25.

See also Rogers, L. L., and Pelton, R. B. *Quart. J. Studies Alcohol,* 18:581, 1957; Trunnell, J. B., and Wheeler, J. I. Paper presented at the Southwest Regional Meeting of the American Chemical Society, Houston, Dec. 1955; Rogers, L. L., et al. *J. Biol. Chem.,* 214:503, 1955; Rogers, L. L., et al. *J. Biol. Chem.,* 220:321, 1956; Mardones, J., *Inter. Rev. Neurobiol.* C. C. Pfeiffer and J. R. Smythies (Eds.) New York: Academic Press, 1960, p. 41.

11. Erex Health Products, 1000 Washington Ave., St. Louis, Miss. 63101.

12. Jones, J. E., et al. "Magnesium balance studies in chronic alcoholism." *Ann. New York Acad. Sci.,* 162:934, 1969; Smith, W. O., and Hammarsten, J. F. "Serum magnesium in clinical disorders." *South. Med. J.,* 51:1116, 1958; Smith, W. O., et al. "The clinical expression of magnesium deficiency." *J. A. M. A.,* 174:77, 1960; Martin, H. E., et al. "Electrolyte disturbance in acute alcoholism with particular reference to magnesium." *Am. J. Clin. Nutr.,* 7:191, 1959; Martin, H. E., and Bauer, F. K. "Magnesium studies in the cirrhotic and alcoholic." *Proc. Roy. Soc. Med.,* 55:912, 1962; Suter, C., and Klingman, W. O. "Neurologic manifestations of magnesium depletion states." *Neurology,* 5:691, 1955; Sullivan, J. F., et al. "Magnesium metabolism in alcoholism." *Am. J. Clin. Nutr.,* 13:297, 1963; Heaton, F. W., et al. "Hypomagnesemia in chronic alcoholism." *Lancet,* 2:802, 1962; Fankushen, D., et al. "The significance of hypomagnesemia in alcoholic patients." *Amer. J. Med.,* 37:802, 1964.

13. Jones, J. E., et al. "Magnesium balance studies in chronic alcoholism." *Ann. New York Acad. Sci.,* 162:934, 1969.

14. Mendelson, J. H., et al. "Effects of alcohol ingestion and withdrawal on magnesium states of alcoholics: Clinical and experimental findings." *Ann. New York Acad. Sci.,* 162:918, 1969; Martin, H. E., and Bauer, F. K. "Magnesium 28 studies in the cirrhotic and alcoholic." *Proc. Roy. Soc. Med.,* 55:912, 1962; McCollister, R. J., et al. "Magnesium balance studies in chronic alcoholism." *J.*

Lab. Clin. Med., 55:98, 1960; Mendelson, J. H. (Ed.) "Experimentally induced chronic intoxication and withdrawal in alcoholics." *Quart. J. Studies Alco.*, Suppl. No. 2, 1964.

15. Pitts, F. N., Jr. "The biochemistry of anxiety." *Scientific American*, Feb. 1969, p. 69.

16. "Nutricol Forte." From Vitamin-Quota, 880 Broadway at 19 St., New York, N.Y. 10003, or 1125 Crenshaw Blvd., Los Angeles, Calif. 90019. "Basic Nutritional Supp." known as No. 127 is obtainable from Walgreen Drug Stores or by writing their office at 4260 Peterson Ave., Chicago, Illinois 60646.

"Nutrins" from General Nutrition Corp., 418 Wood St., Pittsburgh, Penn. 15222.

17. Some of the author's writings in relation to this subject are cited below: Williams, R. J. "The etiology of alcoholism: a working hypothesis involving the interplay of hereditary and environmental factors." *Quart. J. Stud. Alcohol.*, 7:567, 1947; Williams, R. J., et al. "Individual metabolic patterns, alcoholism, genetotrophic diseases." *Proc. Natl. Acad. Sci.*, 35:265, 1949; Williams, R. J., et al. "Biochemical individuality. III: Genetotrophic factors in the etiology of alcoholism." *Arch. Biochem.*, 23:275, 1949; Williams, R. J., et al. "Genetotrophic diseases: alcoholism." *Texas Rpts. Biol. Med.*, 8:238, 1950; Beerstecher, E., et al. "Biochemical individuality. V: Explorations with respect to the metabolic patterns of compulsive drinkers." *Arch. Biochem.*, 29:27, 1950; Williams, R. J., et al. "Metabolic peculiarities in normal young men as revealed by repeated blood analyses." *Proc. Natl. Acad. Sci.*, 41:615, 1955; Williams, R. J. "The genetotrophic approach to alcoholism." Origins of Resistance to Toxic Agents, Proceedings of Symposium held in Washington, D. C., March 25–27, 1954. New York: Academic Press, 1955. No reprints; Williams, R. J. "Identifying and treating potential alcoholics." *J. Criminal Law, Criminology and Police Science*, 49:218, 1958.

18. Williams, R. J., et al. "Identification of blood characteristics common to alcoholic males." *Proc. Nat. Acad. Sci.*, 44:216, 1958.
See also Pelton, R. B., et al. "Metabolic characteristics

of alcoholics: I. Response to glucose stress." *Quart. Jour. Stud. Alco.*, 20:28, 1959.

CHAPTER 12

How Is the Cancer Problem Related?

1. Pollack, M. A., Taylor, A., and Williams, R. J. "B vitamins in human, rat and mouse neoplasms." In *Studies on the vitamin content of tissues II*, pp. 56–71, Texas University Publication No. 4237, 1942; Taylor, A., Pollack, M. A., and Sortomme, C. L. "Effect of B vitamins in the diet on tumor transplants." Ibid., pp. 72–80; Isbell, E. R., Mitchell, H. K., Taylor, A., and Williams, R. J. "A preliminary study of B vitamins in cell nuclei." Ibid., pp. 81–83.

2. Greenstein, J. P. *Biochemistry of cancer.* Chapter VIII, "Chemistry of Tumors." New York: Academic, 1947, pp. 175–309.

3. Burchenal, J. H., et al. "The effects of the folic acid antagonists and 2,6-Diaminopurine on neoplastic disease." *Cancer*, 4:549, 1951. This contains a bibliography of about twenty articles dealing with folic acid antagonists.

4. White, F. R., and White, J. "Effect of diethylstilbestrol on mammary tumor formation in strain C3H mice fed a low cystine diet." *J. Natl. Cancer Inst.*, 4:413, 1944; White, J., and Andervont, H. B. "Effect of a diet relatively low in cystine on the production of spontaneous mammary-gland tumors in strain C3H female mice." *J. Natl. Cancer Inst.*, 3:449, 1943; White, J., White, F. R., and Mider, G. B. "Effect of diets deficient in certain amino acids on the induction of leukemia in dba mice." *J. Natl. Cancer Inst.*, 7:199, 1946.

5. Engel, R. W., et al. "Carcinogenic effects associated with diets deficient in choline and related nutrients." *Ann. N.Y. Acad. Sci.*, 49:49, 1947.

6. Strong, L. C. *Biological aspects of cancer and aging.* Chapter 6, "The effect of liver extracts on spontaneous tumors in mice." New York: Pergamon, 1968, pp. 107–133.

7. Visscher, M. B., et al. "The influence of caloric restriction upon the incidence of spontaneous mammary carcinoma in mice." *Surgery,* 11:48, 1942.

8. Sugiura, K., and Rhoads, C. P. "Experimental liver cancer in rats and its inhibition by rice-bran extract, yeast and yeast extract." *Cancer Res.,* 1:3, 1941.

9. Antopol, W. and Unna, K. "The effect of riboflavin on the liver changes produced in rats by p-Dimethylaminoazobenzene." *Cancer Res.,* 2:694, 1942.

10. Sugiura, K. "Effect of feeding dried milk on production of liver cancer by p-Dimethylaminoazobenzene." *Proc. Soc. Exp. Biol. Med.,* 57:231, 1944; Sugiura, K. "On the relation of diets to the development, prevention and treatment of cancer, with special reference to cancer of the stomach and liver." *J. Nutr.,* 44:345, 1951; Miller, E. C., et al. "Certain effects of dietary pyridoxine and casein on the carcinogenicity of p-Dimethylaminoazobenzene." *Cancer Res.,* 5:713, 1945; Harris, P. N. "The effect of diet containing dried egg albumin upon p-Dimethylaminoazobenzene carcinogenesis." *Cancer Res.,* 7:178, 1947.

11. Ligeti, C. H. "Effect of fresh milk on the production of hepatic tumors in rats by dimethylaminoazobenzene." *Cancer Res.,* 6:563, 1946; Sugiura, K. "Effect of feeding dried milk on production of liver cancer by p-Dimethylaminoazobenzene." *Proc. Soc. Exp. Biol. Med.,* 57:231, 1944.

12. Kensler, C. J., et al. "Partial protection of rats by riboflavin with casein against liver cancer caused by dimethylaminoazobenzene." *Science,* 93:308, 1941.

13. Sugiura, K., and Rhoads, C. P. "Experimental liver cancer in rats and its inhibition by rice-bran extract, yeast and yeast extract." *Cancer Res.,* 1:3, 1941.

14. McCormick, W. J. "Cancer: the preconditioning factor in pathogenesis." *Arch. Pediat.,* 71:313, 1954.

15. Robertson, W. V. B., et al. "Changes in a transplanted fibrosarcoma associated with ascorbic acid deficiency." *J. Natl. Cancer Inst.,* 10:53, 1949.

16. Johnson, J. E., et al. "Relationship of vitamin A and oral leukoplakia." *Arch. Dermatology,* 88:607, 1963.

17. Costa, G., and Weathers, A. P. "Cancer and the nutrition of the host." *Am. J. Dietet. Assoc.,* 44:15, 1964.

CHAPTER 13

Food Fads

1. Huang, Shi-Shung, and Bayless, T. M. "Milk and lactose intolerance in healthy orientals." *Science*, 160:83, 1968; Bayless, T. M., and Rosensweig, N. S. "Incidence and implications of lactase deficiency and milk intolerance in white and negro populations." *Johns Hopkins Med. J.*, 121:54, 1967; Newcomer, A. D., and McGill, D. B. "Disaccharidase activity in the small intestine: prevalence of lactase deficiency in 100 healthy subjects." *Gastroenterology*, 53:381, 1967 (in this study, the investigators found that of 100 healthy Caucasian volunteers with no history of milk intolerance, eight of them showed lactose intolerance); Bayless, T. M., and others. "Absence of milk antibodies in milk intolerance in adults." *J. A. M. A.*, 201:128, 1967; Huang, Shi-Shung, and Bayless, T. M. "Lactose intolerance in healthy children." *New Eng. J. Med.*, 286:1283, 1967; Bayless, T. M., and Rosensweig, N. S. "A racial difference in incidence of lactase deficiency." *J. A. M. A.*, 197:138, 1966; Davis, A. E., and Bolin, T. "Lactose intolerance in Asians." *Nature*, 216:1244, 1967; Duncan, D. L. "The physiological effects of lactose." *Nutr. Abst. & Rev.*, 25:309, 1955; McGillivray, W. A. "Lactose intolerance." *Nature*, 219:615, 1968; Newcomber, A. D., and McGill, D. B. "Incidence of lactase deficiency in ulcerative colitis." *Gastroenterology*, 53:890, 1967; Medical Staff Conference, "Lactose intolerance." *Calif. Med.*, 107:350, 1967.

2. Williams, R. J., et al. *Biochemical Institute Studies IV* "Individual metabolic patterns and human disease: an exploratory study utilizing predominantly paper chromatographic methods." University of Texas Publication 5109, May 1951.

3. Rissel, E., and Wewalka, F. *Klin. Wochschr.*, 30:1065, 1069, 1952.

4. Newcomer, A. D., and McGill, D. B. "Disaccharidase activity in the small intestine: prevalance of lactase deficiency in 100 healthy subjects." *Gastroenterology*, 53:881, 1967.

5. For references on this, and a brief coverage, see: Williams, R. J., *Biochemical individuality*. New York: Wiley, 1956. p. 74.

For some individual references, see: Meister, A., and Greenstein, J. P. *J. Natl. Cancer Inst.*, 8:169, 1948; Albritton, E. C. (Ed.) *Standard values in blood*. Philadelphia: Saunders, 1952; Wolff, R., et al. *Science*, 109:612, 1949; Fishman, W. H., et al. *J. Clin. Invest.*, 30:685, 1951; Berkman, E. N. *Pediatriva*, 5:31, 1951; Fishman, W. H. *Ann. N. Y. Acad. Sci.*, 54:548, 1951; Cohen, S. L., and Bittner, J. J. *Cancer Res.*, 11:723, 1951.

6. Levine, R. A., et al. "Prolonged gluten administration in normal subjects." *New Eng. J. Med.*, 274:1109, 1966.

The results of this investigation by Levine and coworkers patently demonstrates the biochemical individuality of intestinal enzyme systems relative to the digestion of gluten, and contradicts the prevailing faddist notion that *all* cereal products containing gluten (e.g., wheat, rye, oats) are ipso facto harmful to the human system. Levine and his colleagues found that in subjects with sufficient ("normal") intestinal-enzyme systems, "excessive and prolonged dietary supplementation with either gluten, gliadin, egg whites or dextrose failed to induce a sprue-like syndrome in normal subjects . . . . Certain antigens in wheat gluten may elicit circulating precipitins in patients with nontropical sprue and a variety of gastrointestinal diseases, but rarely do so in healthy subjects."

For further demonstration of the biochemical individuality of gluten sensitivity (and also milk protein sensitivity) see: Kivel, R. M., et al. *New Eng. J. Med.*, 271:769, 1964; Taylor, K. B., et al. *Gastroenterology*, 46:99, 1964; Heiner, D. C., et al. *J. A. M. A.*, 189:563, 1964; Heiner, D. C., et al. "Precipitins to antigens of wheat and cow's milk in celiac disease." *J. Pediat.*, 61:813, 1962.

It is indeed unfortunate that many thousands of misinformed people are currently being led astray by a widely circulated idea that all (nutritionally-rich) milk and cereal products are ipso facto harmful for human consumption. When *nutrition* and the *human element* (biochemical individuality) in health and disease receive the recognition that is their due in medical colleges, such easily circulated faddist misinformation will cease to be tolerated by an informed public.

7. Visakorpi, J. K., and Immonen, P. "Intolerance to cow's milk and wheat gluten in the primary malabsorption syndrome in infancy." *Acta Pediatrica Scandinavica,* 56: 49, 1967.

For further excellent data on this subject see: Ross, J. R. "Gluten enteropathy and skeletal disease." *Med. Times,* 96:759, 1968; Beckwith, A. C., and Heiner, D. C. "An immunological study of wheat gluten proteins and derivatives." *Arch. Bio. Biophy.,* 117:239, 1966; Gryboski, J. D., et al. "Gluten intolerance following cow's milk sensitivity: two cases with coproantibodies to milk and wheat proteins." *Ann. Allergy,* 26:33, 1968; Bronstein, H. D., et al. "Enzymatic digestion of gliadin: the effect of the resultant peptides in adult celiac disease." *Clin. Chim. Acta,* 14:141, 1966; Ross, J. R., and Nugent, F. W. "Malabsorption syndrome." *Med. Clin. North America,* 44:495, 1960; Ross, J. R., and Nugent, F. W. "Gluten-induced enteropathy." *Med. Clin. North America,* 47:417, 1963; Binder, H. J., et al. "Gluten and the small intestine in rheumatoid arthritis." *J. A. M. A.* 195:169, 1966; Schenk, E. A., and Samloff, I. M. "Clinical and morphologic changes following gluten administration to patients with treated celiac disease." *Am. J. Path.,* 52: 579, 1968.

8. Nikiforoff, C. C. "Soil organic matter and soil humus." Yearbook of Agriculture, 1938. *Soils and men,* U.S. Department of Agriculture, Washington, D.C., *See also* Pfeiffer, E. E. "Balanced nutrition of soils and plants." *Nat. Food & Farm.,* 4, #2, May 1957; Asenjo, C. F., *Am. J. Clin. Nutr.,* 11:368, 1962.

9. Schopfer, W. H. *Plants and vitamins.* See especially Part I. Waltham, Mass.: Chronica Botanica, 1943.

10. Voisin, A. *Soil, grass and cancer.* New York: Philosophical Library, 1959, p. 6.

11. *Ibid.* p. 9.

12. Underwood, E. J. *Trace elements in human and animal nutrition* (2nd ed.) New York: Academic Press. 1962.

13. Voisin, A. *Op. Cit.,* p. 15.

CHAPTER 14

What the Food Industries Can Do

1. Williams, R. R. *Toward the conquest of beriberi.* Cambridge, Mass.: Harvard University Press, 1966.

2. To each pound of "enriched" flour was added: pyridoxine, 2 milligrams; pantothenate, 4.5 milligrams; cobalamine, 2.2 micrograms; vitamin A, 2160 units; vitamin E, 20 milligrams; folic acid, 0.5 milligrams; L. lysine, 0.5 milligrams; calcium, 300 milligrams; phosphate, 713 milligrams; magnesium (oxide), 150 milligrams; manganese (sulfate), 20 milligrams; copper (sulfate, 4 milligrams.

As the experiment progressed, supplementation with vitamin D was also included. Under the conditions of our experiment this seemed to make no substantial difference. We look upon the particular formulation used as primarily illustrative. Undoubtedly, the nutritional value could have been increased further by adding more lysine, but under present conditions this would have increased the cost materially.

3. Williams, R. J. "Should the science-based food industry be expected to advance?" Paper presented to Natl. Acad. of Sci., Oct. 21, 1970; to be published as a chapter in *Orthomolecular Psychiatry,* David R. Hawkins and Linus Pauling, Eds. San Francisco: Freedman (in press).

4. Horn, M. J., et al. "The distribution of amino acids in wheat and certain wheat products." *Cereal Chem.,* 33:18, 1956.

See also Orr, M. L., and Watt, B. K. *Amino acid content of foods. Home Eco. Res. Rep.* No. 4, Superintendent of Documents, U.S. Government Printing Office, Washington, D.C., 1966; Csonka, F. A. "Amino acids in staple foods. I: Wheat (*Triticum vulgare*)." *Jour. Biol. Chem.,* 118:147, 1937; Albanese, A. A. (Ed.) *Protein and amino acid nutrition.* New York: Academic, 1959, p. 18.

5. Wilcke, H. L. *Proceedings Amino Acid Conference.* MIT, Sept. 1969. In preparation.

Wilcke found that the lowest cost solution to the problem of completing the amino acid requirements in wheat protein was by adding pure lysine. Since it can now be purchased at $1.00 per pound, this was more economical than adding either animal or soy protein. For an excellent coverage of the procedure and need of fortifying wheat protein, see Altschul, A. M. "Amino acid fortification of foods." *Third Inter. Cong. Food Sci. & Tech.*, SOS 70, Aug. 9–14, 1970.

6. Flink, E. B. "Magnesium deficiency syndrome in man." *J. A. M. A.*, 160:1406, 1956; Vallee, B. L., et al. "The magnesium deficiency tetany syndrome in man." *New Eng. J. Med.*, 262:155, 1960; Tambascia, J. J. "Magnesium deficiency tetany syndrome in man." *J. Med. Soc. N.Y.*, 59:530, 1962; Shils, M. E. "Experimental human magnesium depletion: I. Clinical observations and blood chemistry alterations." *Am. J. Clin. Nutr.*, 15:133, 1964.

7. *Recommended dietary allowances*, 1968. (7th revised ed.) "A report of the Food and Nutrition Board, National Research Council." National Acad. Sci., Washington, D.C., 1968.

8. Czerniejewski, C. P., et al. "The minerals of wheat, flour and bread." *Cereal Chem.*, 41:65, 1964.
Also, in his article on the need of the trace metal chromium in human nutrition, Schroeder accounts for part of the chromium deficiency in the tissues of Americans (based on a comparison with other peoples) as due to its removal in food processing, particularly in the refining of wheat. See Schroeder, H. A. "The role of chromium in mammalian nutrition." *Am. J. Clin. Nutr.*, 21:230, 1968.

9. The data demonstrating this statement is extensive and is covered in the chapter on mental disease. One good study of this problem is found in Giok, L. T., Roxe, C. S., and Gyorgy, P. "Influence of early malnutrition on some aspects of the health of school-age children." *Am. J. Clin. Nutr.*, 20:1280, 1967.

10. "Food additives." Editorial, *Lancet*, Aug. 16, 1969, p. 361.

11. Turner, J. S. (Project director) *The chemical feast*. The Ralph Nader Study Group Report on Food Protection, and the Food and Drug Administration, New York: Grossman, 1970.

12. *Eat to live.* Chicago, Ill.: Wheat Flour Institute, 1970.

CHAPTER 15

New Developments in Basic Medicine

1. Kensler, C. J., et al. "Partial protection of rats by riboflavin with casein against liver cancer caused by dimethylaminoazobenzene." *Science,* 93:308, 1941.

2. Williams, R. J. *Biochemical individuality.* Chapter V. "Individual Enzymic Patterns" and Chapter VIII. "Pharmacological Manifestations." New York: Wiley, 1963.

3. Trulson, M. F., Fleming, R., and Stare. F. J. "Vitamin medication in alcoholism." *J. A. M. A.,* 155:114, 1954.

4. Downes, J. "An experiment in the control of tuberculosis among negroes." In *Nutrition in relation to health and disease.* New York: Milbank Memorial Fund. 1950, pp. 188–220.

5. Getz, H. R. "The effect of nutrient supplements on the course of tuberculosis." In *Nutrition in relation to health and disease.* New York: Milbank Memorial Fund. 1950, pp. 221–229.

6. See particularly *Nutr. Rev.,* 20:245, 1962. See also Sydenstricker, V. P., et al. *Proc. Soc. Exp. Biol. Med.,* 64:59, 1947.

7. Daughaday, W. H., et al. "The synthesis of inositol in the immature rat and chick embryo." *J. Biol. Chem.,* 212:869, 1955.

8. Eagle, H., et al. "Myo-inositol as an essential growth factor for normal and malignant human cells in the tissue culture." *J. Biol. Chem.,* 226:191, 1957.

9. The rationale behind the use of these cellular nutrients involves recognizing the importance of individual metabolic patterns. Pioneer work on this subject was reported in the University of Texas Publication 5109 (1951). This publication is presently out of print but was furnished to a large number of libraries. Some background material is given in *A Short History of the Clayton Foundation Biochemical Institute* by R. J. Williams. This publication is available gratis.

10. Schneider, H. A. "Ecological ectocrines in experimental epidemiology." *Science*, 158: 597, 1967.

11. Harper, A. E., et al. "Some effects of excessive intakes of indispensable amino acids." *Proc. Soc. Exp. Biol. Med.*, 121:695, 1966; Sanahuja, J. C., et al. "Decrease in appetite and biochemical changes in amino acid imbalance in the rat." *J. Nutr.*, 86:424, 1965; "The toxic effect of methionine." *Nutrition Rev.*, 23:202, 1965; "Amino acid imbalance." *Nutrition Rev.*, 18:113, 1960; 18:144, 1960.

12. "Excessive vitamin intakes." *Dairy Council Digest*, Vol. 33, No. 1, January–February, 1962.

13. The existence of individual imbalances is suggested by the work on individual metabolic patterns (see reference 9) and by other studies: Ripperton, L. A. "A study of urinary excretion patterns of diabetic individuals." (Doctoral dissertation, University of Texas) Austin, Texas, 1953; Bloch, E. "I: The effect of dietary supplementation upon the growth and reproduction of individual mice of three strains fed an adequate diet." (Doctoral dissertation, University of Texas) Austin, Texas, 1953; Brown, W. D. "Individual patterns in normal humans: organic blood constituents." (Doctoral dissertation, University of Texas) Austin, Texas, 1955; Shideler, R. W. "Individual differences in mineral metabolism." (Doctoral dissertion, University of Texas) Austin, Texas, 1956; Hakkinen, H. M. "A study of some metabolic patterns in alcoholic and schizophrenic individuals." (Doctoral dissertation, University of Texas) Austin, Texas, 1957; Doebbler, G. F. "Biochemical individuality: urinary sulfur patterns." (Doctoral dissertation, University of Texas) Austin, Texas, 1957; Siegel, F. L. "Individuality in baby chicks as related to their responses to alcohol." (Doctoral dissertation, University of Texas) Austin, Texas, 1960; Williams, R. J., and Pelton, R. B. "Individuality in nutrition: effects of vitamin A-deficient and other deficient diets on experimental animals." *Proc. Nat. Acad. Sci.*, 55:126, 1966; Williams, R. J. "The genetotrophic approach to metabolic diseases." In *Exploratory concepts in muscular dystrophy and related disorders*, Amsterdam, The Netherlands: Excerpta Medica

Foundation, 1967, 103–111: Williams, R. J., and Deason, G. "Individuality in vitamin C needs." *Proc. Nat. Acad. Sci.*, 57:1638, 1967; Gutierrez, R. M. "Gas chromatographic determination of urinary 17-ketosteroids in postoperative breast cancer subjects." (Doctoral dissertation, University of Texas) Austin, Texas, 1967; Williams, R. J. "Normal Young Men." *Persp. Biol. Med.*, 1:97, 1957; Williams, R. J., et al. "Individuality as exhibited by inbred animals: its implications for human behavior." *Proc. Nat. Acad. Sci.*, 48:1461, 1962.

14. Personal communication. Clinton H. Howard, President, American Biomedical Corp., Dallas, Texas.

15. Ripperton, L. A. "A study of urinary excretion patterns of diabetic individuals." (Doctoral dissertation, University of Texas) Austin, Texas, 1953.

16. Williams, R. J., and Siegel, F. L. " 'Propetology,' A new branch of medical science?" *Amer. J. Med.*, 31:325, 1961.

APPENDIX I:

The Nutrient Value of Selected Foods

The three-page table that follows was largely prepared by my colleague Charles W. Bode, to whom I am indebted for the permission to use it here.

The table in its present form is derived from many sources and is far more comprehensive with respect to the foods listed than those published previously. By comparison, the usual "food tables" that one sees are inadequate to the point of misrepresentation. In fact, a layman would have extreme difficulty in obtaining from any readily-available source more than about half of all the quantities appearing in the table. These difficult-to-obtain figures are shown in italics.

But equally significant are the things that do not appear on the table. The many blank spaces do not necessarily mean that a given nutrient is absent from a particular food. They simply mean that we do not yet know what figures to put in the spaces—i.e., that an analysis has never been made or, if it has, either has not been reported or has not been located. This is a striking illustration of how incomplete our knowledge of the nutritive content of many common foods really is.

Finally, there is a vitally important factor that would be missing from the table, even if all the blanks were filled in. Any individual who wished to make optimum use of the chart would have to know his own specific and unique nutritional requirements. And that, of course, is something that modern medical science should be able to—but in fact cannot—tell him.

HOW TO USE THE TABLE

1. Across the top of the table are listed 20 foods. Most of them are common; two—wheat germ and brewer's yeast—are uncommon but are occasionally consumed because of their special nutritional value. Roman numerals beneath each listed food indicate to which of the four basic "food groups" that food belongs.

2. On the extreme left-hand column are listed most of the nutrients we have so far identified. The first 38 are those shown on "The Nutritional Chain of Life" illustration on page 46.

3. The second column from the left indicates the unit of measurement (grams, milligrams, micrograms, or international units) used to indicate the amount of a nutrient to be found in 100 grams (about 1/4 pound) of a given food.

4. Symbols used in the table:

> : more than, but on the order of

< : less than, but on the order of

(number in parentheses): approximately

(n.d.) or (0): insignificant amount or probably none

5. Some equivalents:

   1 gm = 1000 mgms = 1,000,000 mcgs

  25 gms = about 1 cup corn flakes, slice bread, etc.

100 gms = about 1 small orange, 1/4 head of lettuce, etc.

250 gms = about 1 cup milk, 1/2 pound beef, etc.

Nutrient	Units	"Enriched" White Bread I	"Enriched" Corn Flakes I	"Enriched" Puffed Rice I	Cottage Cheese II
Iodide	mgms		(.002–.007)	(.003)	
Cobalt	mgms	0.0022	(.0002)	(.0006)	
Selenium	mgms			0.002	
Molybdenum	mgms	0.032	0.184		
Fluoride	mgms				
Copper	mgms	0.23	(.06–.08)	(.06–.19)	
Chromium	mgms	0.003	0.004		
Manganese	mgms	0.059	(.15)	(1.08)	
Zinc	mgms	0.97	(1.82)	(1.5)	
Iron	mgms	2.5	1.4	1.8	0.4
Magnesium	mgms	22.0	16.0	13–28	
Calcium	mgms	84.0	17.0	20.0	90.0
Phosphorous	mgms	97.0	45.0	92.0	175.0
Potassium	mgms	105.0	120.0	100.0	72.0
Sodium	mgms	507.0	1005.0	2.0	290.0
Linoleic acid	gms	Trace	(1)		Trace
Choline	gms		(.06)		
Lysine	gms	0.225	0.154	0.056	1.428
Methionine	gms	0.14	0.135		0.469
Phenylalanine	gms	0.465	0.354	0.286	1.099
Leucine	gms	0.668	1.047		1.826
Valine	gms	0.435	0.386		1.472
Isoleucine	gms	0.429	0.306		0.989
Threonine	gms	0.282	0.275		0.794
Tryptophan	gms	0.091	0.052	0.046	0.179
Ascorbic Acid (Vitamin C)	mgms	Trace	(0)	(0)	(0)
Niacin	mgms	2.4	2.1	4.4	0.1
Vitamin E (α)	mgms	<.23	(.84)	(<.23)	
Pantothenate	mgms	0.43	0.185	0.378	0.22
Vitamin A	i.u.	Trace	(0)	(0)	10.0
Pyridoxine (Vitamin B_{12})	mgms	0.04	0.065	0.075	0.04
Riboflavin (Vitamin B_2)	mgms	0.21	0.08	0.04	0.28
Thiamine (Vitamin B_1)	mgms	0.25	0.43	0.44	0.03
Folic Acid	mgms	0.015	0.0055	0.0076	0.0293
Vitamin K	mgms				
Biotin	mgms	0.0011	(.0066)	0.0013	
Vitamin D	i.u.				
Cobalamine	mcgs	Trace	0	0	1.0
Miscellaneous Information					
Inositol	mgms	51.0	(51)	19.0	
Cholesterol	mgms				15.0
Fat	gms	3.2	0.4	0.4	0.3
Protein	gms	8.7	7.9	6.0	17.0
Carbohydrates	gms	50.5	85.3	89.5	2.7
Water	% of	35.6	3.8	3.7	79.0
Calories		270.0	386.0	399.0	86.0

Nutrient	Units	American Cheddar Cheese II	Whole Milk (Cow) II	Fresh Lettuce III	Fresh Tomatoes III
Iodide	mgms		0.021	0.004	.001-.003
Cobalt	mgms		0.006	.005-.023	0.009
Selenium	mgms				
Molybdenum	mgms		0.02		
Fluoride	mgms		0.016		
Copper	mgms		0.019	.04-.15	.06-.11
Chromium	mgms		0.001		
Manganese	mgms		0.019	.5-1.08	0.14
Zinc	mgms		0.35	.18-.47	0.24
Iron	mgms	1.0	Trace	2.0	0.5
Magnesium	mgms	45.0	13.0	11.0	14.0
Calcium	mgms	750.0	118.0	35.0	13.0
Phosphorous	mgms	478.0	93.0	26.0	27.0
Potassium	mgms	82.0	144.0	264.0	244.0
Sodium	mgms	700.0	50.0	9.0	3.0
Linoleic acid	gms	1.0	Trace		
Choline	gms	0.0453	0.015		
Lysine	gms	1.834	0.272	0.07	0.042
Methionine	gms	0.65	0.086	0.004	0.007
Phenylalanine	gms	1.34	0.17		0.016
Leucine	gms	2.437	0.344		0.014
Valine	gms	1.794	0.24		0.022
Isoleucine	gms	1.685	0.223		0.029
Threonine	gms	0.929	0.161		0.033
Tryptophan	gms	0.341	0.049	0.012	0.009
Ascorbic Acid (Vitamin C)	mgms	(0)	1.0	8.0	23.0
Niacin	mgms	0.1	0.1	0.3	0.7
Viatmin E (α)	mgms	1.0	0.1	0.29	0.27
Pantothenate	mgms	0.5	0.34	0.2	0.33
Vitamin A	i.u.	1310.0	140.0	970.0	900.0
Pyridoxine (Vitamin B_{12})	mgms	0.08	0.04	0.055	0.1
Riboflavin (Vitamin B_2)	mgms	0.46	0.17	0.06	0.04
Thiamine (Vitamin B_1)	mgms	0.03	0.03	0.06	0.06
Folic Acid	mgms	0.015	0.0006	0.021	0.0037
Vitamin K	mgms		0.008		
Biotin	mgms	0.0033	0.0047	0.0031	0.004
Vitamin D	i.u.				
Cobalamine	mcgs	1.0	0.40	0	0
Miscellaneous Information					
Inositol	mgms	23.3	13.0	51.0	46.0
Cholesterol	mgms	100.0	11.0		
Fat	gms	32.2	3.5	0.2	0.2
Protein	gms	25.0	3.5	1.2	1.1
Carbohydrates	gms	2.1	4.9	2.5	4.7
Water	% of	37.0	87.4	95.1	93.5
Calories		398.0	65.0	14.0	22.0

Nutrient	Units	Fresh Oranges III	Fresh Carrots III	Raw Potatoes III	Whole Chicken Eggs IV
Iodide	mgms		0.002		0.012
Cobalt	mgms			0.01	0.01
Selenium	mgms			n.d.	
Molybdenum	mgms			0.003	0.049
Fluoride	mgms				0.06
Copper	mgms	.07–.31	0.34		0.17
Chromium	mgms			0	0.016
Manganese	mgms	0.03	.06–.25		0.04
Zinc	mgms	0.17	0.11	0.868	1.3
Iron	mgms	0.4	0.7	0.6	2.1
Magnesium	mgms	11.0	23.0	22.0	9.0
Calcium	mgms	41.0	37.0	7.0	54.0
Phosphorous	mgms	20.0	36.0	53.0	210.0
Potassium	mgms	200.0	341.0	407.0	149.0
Sodium	mgms	1.0	47.0	3.0	111.0
Linoleic acid	gms				2.2
Choline	gms	0.012	0.013	0.029	0.532
Lysine	gms	0.024	0.052	0.107	0.87
Methionine	gms	0.003	0.01	0.025	0.422
Phenylalanine	gms		0.042	0.088	0.691
Leucine	gms		0.065	0.1	1.09
Valine	gms		0.056	0.107	1.05
Isoleucine	gms		0.046	0.088	0.896
Threonine	gms		0.043	0.079	0.704
Tryptophan	gms	0.003	0.01	0.021	0.243
Ascorbic Acid (Vitamin C)	mgms	50.0	8.0	20.0	0
Niacin	mgms	0.4	0.6	1.5	0.1
Vitamin E (α)	mgms	0.23	0.45		2.0
Pantothenate	mgms	0.25	0.28	0.4	2.7
Vitamin A	i.u.	200.0	11,000.0	Trace	1140.0
Pyridoxine (Vitamin B12)	mgms	0.06	0.15	0.22	0.25
Riboflavin (Vitamin B2)	mgms	0.04	0.05	0.04	0.29
Thiamine (Vitamin B1)	mgms	0.1	0.06	0.1	0.1
Folic Acid	mgms	0.00216	0.008	0.0068	0.0094
Vitamin K	mgms				
Biotin	mgms	0.00033	0.0025		0.0225
Vitamin D	i.u.				
Cobalamine	mcgs	0	0		0.282
Miscellaneous Information					
Inositol	mgms	120.0	48.0	29.0	33.0
Cholesterol	mgms				550.0
Fat	gms	0.2	0.2	0.1	12.8
Protein	gms	1.0	1.1	2.1	11.5
Carbohydrates	gms	12.2	88.2	17.1	0.7
Water	% of	86.0	9.7	79.8	74.0
Calories		49.0	42.0	76.0	162.0

Nutrient	Units	Medium Quality Beef IV	Pork IV	Lamb Chops IV	Oysters IV
Iodide	mgms				
Cobalt	mgms	0.052	0.017	0.02	0.016
Selenium	mgms	0.028	<.052	0.03	0.049
Molybdenum	mgms	0.007	0.368	0.5	(.01)
Fluoride	mgms				
Copper	mgms	0.09	0.39	0.713	13.7
Chromium	mgms	0.009	0.01	0.012	0.009
Manganese	mgms	0.005	0.034	0.034	0.006
Zinc	mgms	5.66	1.89	5.33	148.7
Iron	mgms	2.6	1.5	1.3	5.5
Magnesium	mgms	21.0	20.9	24.9	15.4
Calcium	mgms	10.0	6.0	10.0	94.0
Phosphorous	mgms	155.0	103.0	151.0	143.0
Potassium	mgms	300.0	285.0	295.0	121.0
Sodium	mgms	65.0	70.0	75.0	73.0
Linoleic acid	gms	Trace-1	5.0	Trace	
Choline	gms	0.068	0.077	0.084	
Lysine	gms	1.45	0.804	1.384	
Methionine	gms	0.41	0.245	0.41	
Phenylalanine	gms	0.76	0.386	0.695	
Leucine	gms	1.35	0.721	1.324	
Valine	gms	1.0	0.51	0.843	
Isoleucine	gms	0.86	0.503	0.886	
Threonine	gms	0.735	0.455	0.782	
Tryptophan	gms	0.193	0.127	0.222	
Ascorbic Acid (Vitamin C)	mgms	0	(0)		30.0
Niacin	mgms	4.2	2.7	4.9	2.5
Vitamin E (α)	mgms	0.47	0.63	0.62	
Pantothenate	mgms	0.47	0.5	0.59	0.49
Vitamin A	i.u.	45.0	(0)		310.0
Pyridoxine (Vitamin B_{12})	mgms	0.33	0.46	0.33	0.037
Riboflavin (Vitamin B_2)	mgms	0.15	0.12	0.21	0.18
Thiamine (Vitamin B_1)	mgms	0.08	0.5	0.15	0.14
Folic Acid	mgms	0.009	0.0024	0.0033	0.0113
Vitamin K	mgms				
Biotin	mgms	0.0026	0.0052	0.0059	0.0087
Vitamin D	i.u.				
Cobalamine	mcgs	1.42			
Miscellaneous Information					
Inositol	mgms	11.5	45.0	58.0	44.0
Cholesterol	mgms	70.0	70.0	70.0	>200.0
Fat	gms	23.0	52.0	22.6	1.8
Protein	gms	23.0	10.2	16.8	8.4
Carbohydrates	gms	0	0	0	3.4
Water	% of	54.0	37.3	59.3	84.6
Calories		260.0	513.0	276.0	66.0

Nutrient	Units	Peanuts	Beef Liver	Brewer's Yeast	Wheat Germ
		IV			
Iodide	mgms				
Cobalt	mgms	(.026)	<.016		0.0017
Selenium	mgms	0.037	0.018		0.11
Molybdenum	mgms	(.1)	0.197		0.067
Fluoride	mgms				
Copper	mgms	0.783	1.1	1.779	0.74
Chromium	mgms	(.035)			0.007
Manganese	mgms	0.691	0.016		13.74
Zinc	mgms	3.24	3.923	8.379	10.08
Iron	mgms	2.1	6.5	17.3	9.4
Magnesium	mgms	175.0	20.3	231.0	336.0
Calcium	mgms	74.0	8.0	210.0	72.0
Phosphorous	mgms	401.0	352.0	1753.0	1118.0
Potassium	mgms	674.0	281.0	1894.0	827.0
Sodium	mgms	418.0	136.0	121.0	3.0
Linoleic acid	gms	14.0	Trace		5.0
Choline	gms	0.162	0.56	0.24	0.46
Lysine	gms	1.099	1.475	3.3	1.534
Methionine	gms	0.271	0.463	0.836	0.404
Phenylalanine	gms	1.557	0.993	1.902	0.908
Leucine	gms	1.872	1.819	3.226	1.708
Valine	gms	1.532	1.239	2.723	1.364
Isoleucine	gms	1.266	1.031	2.398	1.177
Threonine	gms	0.828	0.936	2.353	1.343
Tryptophan	gms	0.34	0.296	0.71	0.265
Ascorbic Acid (Vitamin C)	mgms	0	31.0	Trace	(0)
Niacin	mgms	17.2	13.6	37.9	4.2
Vitamin E (α)	mgms	4.6	1.4	0	12.5
Pantothenate	mgms	2.13	7.7	12.0	3.3
Vitamin A	i.u.		43,900.0	Trace	(0)
Pyridoxine (Vitamin B12)	mgms	0.3	0.84	2.5	0.918
Riboflavin (Vitamin B2)	mgms	0.13	3.26	4.28	0.68
Thiamine (Vitamin B1)	mgms	0.32	0.25	15.61	2.01
Folic Acid	mgms	0.0566	0.293	2.2	0.305
Vitamin K	mgms				
Biotin	mgms	0.034	0.1	0.2	(.016)
Vitamin D	i.u.				
Cobalamine	mcgs		80.0	0	
Miscellaneous Information					
Inositol	mgms	180.0	51.0		770.0
Cholesterol	mgms		300.0		
Fat	gms	49.3	3.8	1.0	10.9
Protein	gms	26.0	19.9	38.8	26.6
Carbohydrates	gms	18.8	5.3	38.4	46.7
Water	% of	1.6	69.7	5.0	11.5
Calories		585.0	140.0	283.0	363.0

APPENDIX II:

A Vitamin Supplement

Formulated below is a nutritional supplement which constitutes, for the general public, a far better package of insurance than most commonly used formulations. For practical reasons the items are placed in two groups, the vitamins and the minerals.

Vitamins		Minerals[a]	
Vitamin A	10,000 units	Calcium	300.0 mg.
Vitamin D	500 units	Phosphate	250.0 mg.
Ascorbic Acid	100 mg.	Magnesium	100.0 mg.
Thiamine	2 mg.	Cobalt	0.1 mg.
Riboflavin	2 mg.	Copper	1.0 mg.
Pyridoxine	3 mg.	Iodine	0.1 mg.
Niacinamide	20 mg.	Iron	10.0 mg.
Pantothenate	20 mg.	Manganese	1.0 mg.
Vitamin B_{12}	5 mcg.	Molybdenum	0.2 mg.
Tocopherols		Zinc	5.0 mg.
(Vitamin E)	5 mg.		
Inositol[b]	100 mg.		
Choline	100 mg.		

NOTES: 1 gram = 1/28 oz.
1 milligram (mg.) = 1/1000 of a gram
1 microgram (mcg.) = 1/1,000,000 of a gram

ᵃ Some of the items and the proportions indicated may require adjustment due in part to possible restrictions which are under consideration by the Food and Drug Administration.

ᵇ Many nutritionists will assert justifiably that this item has not proven to be a nutritional essential. It is included, however, on a somewhat different basis. In my judgment, partly on the basis of unpublished findings with which I am acquainted, its inclusion is wise even though it may be argued that the chance of its being helpful is relatively low.

Other chemical items that deserve some consideration as nutritional supplements (at least in special cases) include: (1) folic acid; (2) rutin and related glucosides which have been recommended (on the basis of unsatisfactory evidence) for capillary weakness and prevention of hemorrhage; (3) glutamine (in gram quantities) for help in the prevention of stomach ulcers, alcoholism, and epileptic seizures; (4) asparagin and/or salts of aspartic acid (in gram quantities) for possible benefit in increasing stamina, etc.; (5) lysine (in gram quantities) which markedly supplements the value of many vegetable proteins; (6) lipoic acid, one of the newer vitamin-like substances to be discovered; (7) lecithin which furnishes phosphate and choline and may have other advantages; (8) the "intrinsic factor" which with B_{12} protects against pernicious anemia. This is not an exhaustive list, since additional amino acids and other physiologically important substances may have some value in particular instances. The use of unfamiliar supplements—those which are not now used —may be around the corner.*

It is obviously impossible to formulate a supplement which is best for everyone under all circumstances. The amounts of each nutrient in the supplement proposed above were determined on the basis of the available answers (with respect to each nutrient) to the following questions: How much is in our bodies? How

* From NUTRITION IN A NUTSHELL by Roger J. Williams. Copyright © 1962 by Roger J. Williams. Reproduced by permission of Doubleday & Company, Inc.

much do we get when we eat good food? How much appears to be needed? How widely variable are human needs? How effectively is it utilized? Is the nutrient easily destroyed in processing? Is it readily produced by intestinal bacteria? Can excess amounts be harmful?

For special reasons and conditions the amounts of some of the nutrients are inadequate. For example, to follow Linus Pauling's suggestion about the use of vitamin C to prevent and cure the common cold, much larger amounts of vitamin C are required. Those who are properly concerned about atherosclerosis and heart disease will want to increase their intake of vitamin B_6, vitamin E, magnesium, etc. Megavitamin therapy involves much larger amounts of several nutrients, e.g., niacinamide, pyridoxine, pantothenic acid, vitamin E, etc. These larger amounts do not belong in a supplement for general use.

Below is a partial list of sources (arranged alphabetically) of good commerical supplements for general use which are similar to those formulated in *Nutrition in a Nutshell*. This formula was and is, of course, for free public use. I have no financial interest in any of the concerns mentioned below or in others in the same business.

1. General Nutrition Corporation
   418 Wood Street
   Pittsburgh, Pennsylvania
   (Under the name of "Nutrins")

2. Vitamin-Quota
   880 Broadway   or   1125 Crenshaw Blvd.
   New York, New York   Los Angeles, California
   (Under the name of "Nutricol")

3. Walgreen Drug Stores
   4260 Peterson Avenue
   Chicago, Illinois
   (Under the name of Basic Nutritional Supp. No. 127)

Index

How's Your Health?

Bantam publishes a line of informative books, written by top experts to help you toward a healthier and happier life.

Bantam Book Catalog

It lists over a thousand money-saving best-sellers originally priced from $3.75 to $15.00 —bestsellers that are yours now for as little as 50¢ to $2.95!

The catalog gives you a great opportunity to build your own private library at huge savings!

So don't delay any longer—send us your name and address and 10¢ (to help defray postage and handling costs).